RITUAL
PASSAGE
SACRED
JOURNEY

Smithsonian Series in Ethnographic Inquiry

William L. Merrill and Ivan Karp, Series Editors

Ethnography as fieldwork, analysis, and literary form is the distinguishing feature of modern anthropology. Guided by the assumption that anthropological theory and ethnography are inextricably linked, this series is devoted to exploring the ethnographic enterprise.

RITUAL
PASSAGE
SACRED
JOURNEY

The Process and Organization
of Religious Movement

Richard P. Werbner

Smithsonian Institution Press, Washington
and
Manchester University Press, Manchester

Library of Congress
Cataloging-in-Publication Data
Werbner, Richard P.
Ritual passage, sacred journey:
The form, process and organization of religious
movement /
Richard P. Werbner
(Smithsonian Series in Ethnographic Inquiry)
p.   cm
Bibliography: p.
Includes index.
ISBN 0-7190-1929-X (Manchester University
Press)
1. Regional religious cults.
Anthropological perspectives.
I. Title
ISBN 0-87474-976-X (Smithsonian)
1. Rites and ceremonies.
2. Change–Religious aspects.
I. Title
BL600.W47 1989   88-29298
299'.6–dc19

British Library Cataloging-in-Publication data is
available.

2 4 6 5 3 1
90 92 94 93 91 89

Editors, Johnson & Vranas Associates
Production Editor, Craig A. Reynolds
Designer, Linda McKnight

CONTENTS

Transformational Analysis of Possession . . . Possession and
Strategic Action . . . The Case of the Homecoming Worker . . .
Possession and the Changing Domestic Domain . . . Conclusion

For Ben and Donna

INTRODUCTION

This book is about religious movement as a ritual passage and a sacred journey. The ritual passage, the main subject in the first half of the book, is a process of symbolic action focused upon the body. By means of the body, performers of the ritual passage find and resituate themselves in cosmological space. By means of the body, also, performers personify who they are, and what they intend to become in relation to the forces around them. Sometimes the body is simply their own; sometimes, it is that of some other as well, such as a domestic or wild animal, whose parts may be broken down and recombined. There is variation in the presentation of the person, from direct disclosure, presenting the true selves of the performers and others around them, to impersonation, perhaps through grotesque disguise (for an overview of such variation in public occasions see Handelman, in press). Much depends upon the felt qualities that concern performers in their symbolic action. According to such qualities, of themselves or of the other, they bring about physical embodiments, and they change these over the ritual passage as a whole, from phase to phase, or even from one kind of moment to another. The relation to themselves or to the other varies, and so too does the embodiment and its personification.

The second half of the book is devoted to the kind of sacred journey that has both a special focus and a distinct basis of its own. It is the sacred journey focused upon a sacred center, to and from which the journey takes place, and based upon sacred exchange across community and other boundaries. Sacred exchange, like all social exchange, involves the giving and receiving of valued goods. It is distinctive of sacred exchange, however, that the giving and receiving of substances, such as bits of the earth, is a means of renegotiating the distance to the invisible world and thus the moral condition, even the vitality, of a person or a community. In other words, what are transferred in sacred exchange are qualities of life.

The differences in sacred exchange depend on the persons involved, on the substances used to engender the qualities, and on the direction traveled. It is important that this direction may be either towards or away from the community or sacred center, either centripetal or centrifugal. It is important also that the primary focus is a sacred center of the immediate or the wider universe. In other words, the sacred center is a focus of the cosmos, either of the *microcosm,* which is the exclusive cosmos of particular gods and their creatures, or of the *macrocosm,* which is the inclusive cosmos of the God of everyone, boundless, all-embracing, and complete.

For convenience of exposition, I start by analyzing the *processual* forms of the ritual passage and move to the *organizational* forms around the sacred journey. In practice, the link between ritual passage and sacred journey is an integral one. Thus, discussing the ritual passage of demonic possession requires an understanding of sacred journeys home or to the hamlets of close relatives; it demands as well a full account of the crossing back and forth between the domains of the domestic, and the wild and alien. Similarly, examining the processual form of masquerade during an annual return to a festival center leads on to the organizational contradictions in dual organization and, recursively, back from the latter to the former. Hence it is more a matter of emphasis than a sharp break in analysis that divides the halves of the book, or the treatment from chapter to chapter. Throughout I am concerned with the primary focus, the body or the sacred center, with the crossing of boundaries, and with sacred and other social exchange.

In my approach I bring together formal techniques derived from structuralism, particularly from Lévi-Strauss and de Huesch, and methods of situational and regional analysis developed by members of the Manchester School (for an overview see Werbner 1984). No less important than the form, I would argue, is the symbolic content and the felt quality of experience. Hence my approach also builds upon the semiotics of Pierce, the dialogics of Bakhtin, and the phenomenology of Eliade and others.

My ethnography is comparative. It comes primarily from southern and western Africa and the Lowlands of New Guinea, although I also discuss examples from Sri Lanka, North Africa, and South America. I write about Kalanga and Northern Tswapong on the basis of repeated fieldwork in southern Africa since 1960. My account of southern African churches springs, in part, from that fieldwork as well, although I rely mainly on the rich literature for my evidence. My choice of ethnography has also been influenced by its importance for wider debates. Concerning West Africa, for example, the personal security cults of the Tallensi and Ashanti of Ghana have been much discussed. So too has there been a wealth of studies about historical transformation in the wider political economy of Ghana and even about the changing predicaments of strangers within that political economy. But because previously each of these–the cults, the historical transformation, and the predicaments of strangers–was discussed separately, the systematic relations between them were disregarded. My account brings them together within a single transformational perspective. Similarly, the ethnography of the *ida* festival of Umeda in New Guinea has been at the heart of a considerable debate about secret knowledge, order, and disorder in Melanesian religion (see the reviews in Wagner 1984; Werbner n.d.; Juillerat n.d.). One tendency in the debate was to dismiss coding as an artefact of the ethnographer's attempt to apply structuralist techniques. However, the outstanding need, which my contribution meets, is for a substantial reanalysis of the ethnography along with a full assessment of the adequacy of the ethnographer's use of structuralist techniques. My own use of structuralist techniques can thus be appreciated in relation to my critique of an alternative usage.

As a consequence of my ethnography's being comparative, my argument and the evidence for it can be better controlled. The reader can check the cases where I am the source of the facts, the interpretation, and the analytic framework, against the cases where certain facts have already been known within alternative interpretations and constructs.

A further consequence is that my argument progresses through a continuum, first of processual forms and second of organizational forms. At one extreme is the processual form of ritual which, while methodical, is nevertheless remade in a somewhat *ad hoc* fashion on each occasion. This form is tied to discovery, as a preliminary to other ritual, and the presentation of the person is a disclosure of hidden actualities, not a grotesque representation. The presentation is somewhat of an allegory. It presents personal agency, including that of the dead, through other creatures, such as animals, who epitomize the true characteristics of persons. In such allegoric action, the other embodies or stands for oneself and those around one.

My first example of processual forms is Northern Tswapong wisdom divination viewed as reflexive, symbolic discourse. I begin with it in Chapter 1. Northern Tswapong use bits of other living creatures, their locomotive parts, to present persons as they really are, to reveal their actual motives in everyday life, and to convey their true character. The disclosure of the hidden, of an otherwise unknowable personal microcosm, is the main objective of Northern Tswapong wisdom divination. This ritual is intended to enable the people to see who and what actually moves for or against a person. The quest, which is for purposes of taking further action, is to obtain extraordinary knowledge of personal agency, including that of the dead. I show how, on different occasions, there is a variable play of the visual and the verbal in the disparate moments of Northern Tswapong seances.

I begin with wisdom divination, in part because it is often a necessary step on the way to other kinds of ritual for the performers themselves. It foreshadows other ritual passages yet to come. Of even more importance, given the current anthropological scepticism about intellectualizing or decoding during ritual (see Sperber 1975), starting with wisdom divination allows me to correct the failure, in recent years, to consider divination as reflexive ritual (for outstanding exceptions see Fortes 1966; Turner 1975).

Divination is the ritual of rituals. It opens our understanding of the people's *own* interpretive process, for in a sense divination is ritual that, to a great extent, operates on a reflective meta-level. It is a ritual in which the people themselves give interpretations of their symbols, icons, and indices (for the distinction see Chapter 1). We shall see that they do not merely respond to their signifying practices unreflectively, as people often insist they do when harried by the "meaning-seeking" anthropologist. But if divination, with its prescribed procedures designed to overcome baffling complexity, is an intellectualist's dream, and thus something of a repressed nightmare for certain symbolic anthropologists, divination is no less ritual. I want to stress that it is ritual not merely because divination is symbolic action, but also because it is action in which people are moved by what they feel to be their experience of the occult. And divination, no less than other ritual, has its disparate moments as well as its capacity to play on different levels at once, as I argue elsewhere (Werbner 1973).

The next processual form, which I consider in Chapter 2, is more regular and less variable from occasion to occasion. It is dominated by grotesque representation, whereby one ceases to be oneself, rather than by allegoric presentation, in which the other epitomizes the everyday person. The ritual passage is in four phases of Kalanga demonic possession, from disorder to order, and includes rites for playful burlesque, satire, and joking. The intent is for Kalanga women to bring about purification and healing from affliction. The Kalanga women impersonate lions; or rather, from their own viewpoint, Lions become them, temporarily displacing their own personalities. The Lions are tricksters, or clownlike figures, who invade the domestic domain from beyond a community's moral universe. Otherness, the alien and the wild, including the otherness of commodity relations, is represented and transformed through their symbolic action.

Following the argument from the domestic to the public domain leads me in Chapter 3 to Kalanga sacrifice, a processual form that also has four main phases. However, these do not include interludes for fun and burlesque which, being playfully improvised afresh on each occasion, are said not to belong to the ritual. The ritual precludes impersonation. Instead, agency is personified according to actual status, living or dead, elder or junior, and so forth. In this form, the other as life belonging to oneself, a domestic animal and thus *of* oneself, is broken down into elementary parts. Once combined with other elements, shared as gifts, and remade as a different whole, the other of oneself serves *for* oneself. Through the other one's own renewed wholeness, the composure of one's being is embodied. The ritual passage still has the intent of moving away from affliction, but it is through Kalanga sacrifice of cattle in the public domain rather than through Kalanga demonic possession.

Finally, regarding a domain that extends through social exchange between communities, I end the first half of the book in Chapter 4 with the processual form of the festival of *ida* in the New Guinea Lowlands village of Umeda. The ritual passage is an annual return from the everyday world to the place for the beginning of time. The form is tripartite, after the classic model of Van Gennep. In this ritual passage one impersonates oneself in a grotesque mask. Every man caricatures through masquerade on the outside the man he is becoming on the inside. The characterization embodies personal, kinship, and cosmic identities within a totality, the many men and the oneness of man. Reconstruction of classifications and categories through play, along with an invasion by figures from beyond a community's moral universe, are typical of this and other ritual passages that move through grotesque performance. During the festival, the liminal phase, dominated by the playful masquerade of men, is the most elaborate. Its rites take up most of the festival at the sacred center of the village. I account for the dialectical sequencing of these rites as a rebirth of the person, of the community, and of the whole cosmos.

The second half of the book takes up the continuum in the organizational forms associated with the sacred journey. At one extreme are annual and seasonal movements in cults or festivals of the microcosm. The most contained and relatively homogeneous are those in which, around the sacred center of a microcosm, spatially close yet socially distant persons of diverse identities are brought together to be identified with each other.

My example in Chapter 5, which completes the interpretation of Umeda's *ida* festival, is the form in the nearby trips of New Guinea Lowlands dual organization. The Umeda villagers' annual return as a sacred journey is an ascension from the bush lowlands to their ridge-top hamlets. They produce in the bush lowlands for most of the year. Their ridge-top hamlets are their festival centers for the "high" time when women and other valuables are exchanged and luxuries freely are consumed. In organizing their festival centers, their journeys, and their exchanges, the villagers make wide use of binary principles. My analysis highlights certain social predicaments in relation to organizational contradictions; Umeda symbolic management compounds what it appears to resolve.

This analysis leads me to a critique of the literature on dual organization in what Maybury-Lewis calls dialectical societies (1979). In contrast to Maybury-Lewis, I demonstrate the usefulness of Lévi-Strauss' classic distinction between diametric and concentric dualism. But the conventional notion of dual organization, so obsessed with surface manifestations such as moieties, is obviously stultifying. Hence that notion is discarded in favor of a dynamic view of what I call an axial system. The system is binary, and has variable axes and coordinates. It applies to the arrangement of social exchange in ranked spheres. I show how the villagers' sacred journey as an annual return between bush and village represents an oscillation between alternative stages of the axial system.

In Chapter 6, I turn to historical change in the more heterogeneous forms associated with long-distance pilgrimage. I account for the waxing and waning of West African personal security cults, which are cults of the microcosm yet extend over vast distances between culturally unrelated peoples, including labor migrants and their employers, former slaves and former slave-raiders. These West African cults are addressed to highly particularistic spirits, not the God of everyone found in the cults of the macrocosm. Conventional labels, such as witch-finding movements or anti-witchcraft cults, put the emphasis wrongly and are somewhat misleading. Instead, I call them personal security cults, and stress the following characteristics: the cult members are a security circle for each other; mutually harmless, they are bound together by a covenant and an ethic; they are purified and under the same powerful protection of a shrine or spirit; and strangers from outside a community or aliens in culture are included in the security circle along with their hosts, the non-strangers at home.

At the other extreme from these sacred journeys of the microcosm are the organizational forms around a macrocosmic sacred center. My example in Chapter 7 is from the cult that among Kalanga is addressed to God Above, Mwali. The Mwali cult has ritually protected its own sacred journeys across numerous scattered communities and the peace and welfare of their land and people. In its lasting viability, documented for well over a century, the Mwali cult has, through its oracles, voiced a conservative opposition to the spread of capitalist commodity relations and to political oppression under colonialism and, more recently, under post- or neo-colonialism (see also Ranger 1985). In my account I explain how, around sacred centers and across local, tribal, national, and quite marked cultural frontiers, this hierarchical cult has continued, even through major crises, to organize long-distance sacred journeys, sacred exchange, and a redistributive system of gifts to God.

Finally, in the last chapter, I turn to the sacred journeys and religious movements that southern African labor migrants establish in new Churches of the Spirit. As homecomers (see Schutz 1945), the labor migrants introduce Biblical religious images and organizational forms that comprehend the fact that home and much that it implies can no longer be taken for granted, since it is now in some senses alien. The large-scale polyethnic churches develop a range of Christian alternatives, to all of which conversion is through immersion of the whole body during river baptism. In one, a kind of reincorporation takes place. At home together, the homecomers along with their relatives and neighbors make up circles of the purified. They form congregations within and across their communities. They organize pilgrimages on the Passover to their own Mount Moriah as a fixed center for the Kingdom of God on Earth, or on the Pentecost to temporary encampments. Home appears in the church's locational imagery as an inner space rescued from peripherality through religious recentering. From church to church the recentering varies, and it may or may not be ambiguous in certain respects. Alternatively, through another kind of religious image and organizational form, the homecomers and others are incorporated in congregations that form total communities, as it were, societies within society. Home here appears dislocated and decentered as an outer space. Each alternative can and does lead to the foundation of large-scale, polyethnic churches, and these spread in a characteristic way, outward from home.

In southern Africa, as in so many other parts of the world, religious pluralism is cumulative. New religious movements do not simply rise and fall; nor do they always make indigenous cults disappear. Instead, they are often carried forward alongside established religious bodies, including indigenous cults as well as churches, with which they compete. But this makes relative stability in locational imagery and in organizational form all the more problematic, and in need of explanation no less than the apparent religious innovations that so appeal to the Western social scientist's fascination with things modern and novel. In Chapters 7 and 8, I regard the indigenous and the new religion in turn and in relation to each other. I demonstrate that, allowing for surface differences, the continuity between them is basic, both in the semantic structure of their locational imagery and in their organizational form.

The kind of religious movement I discuss in Chapter 5, at the beginning of the second half of this book, is repetitive. Within a limited context, it calls for little attention either to histories of change or to religious pluralism. In Chapter 6 and thereafter, however, both are a major concern. I examine the change, over time, in the aims or consequences of the sacred journey. I also consider the cumulative emergence of a plurality of kinds of sacred journey from one period to another. Here my approach is, above all, a response to the need for regional analysis of religious change, and I carry a stage further the arguments I had introduced in my early discussion of regional cults (1977a).

The regional cult in my usage, I must stress immediately, is a central place concept. The regional cult's central places are its shrines. Around them are flows of people, goods, services, and ideas that are focused, mapped, and oriented by religious concerns. The shrines may be in towns and villages, by crossroads, or even in the wild, well away from human habitation. People or their representatives come from various communities, in groups or individually, as supplicants, pilgrims, sacrificers, or adepts. Such traffic, as the people themselves see it, is quite unlike any other, even when it flows along public routes in general use. The regional cult has a topography of its own. This is not a mere reflection of other features of cultural landscapes, for it is marked apart on cultural or mental maps by the placement of ritual activities. In brief, central places are stressed in the regional cult concept because a basic concern is the focus and orientation of cult participants' journeying, along with social exchange from center to periphery, or from one kind of central place to another. Moreover, given the analytic importance of central places, it becomes critical to understand how cult regions and their centers wax and wane in relation to regions focused in other ways—specifically, in relation to political, economic, or ecological regions and their capitals, market-places, or other centers.

In my view, a regional cult characteristically has a locally uneven resolution of opposite tendencies, toward exclusiveness on the one hand, and inclusiveness on the other. Together, the tendencies make for a mixture, often highly unstable, of the specific and highly parochial along with the transcultural and more universal. One tendency may prevail more than another, temporarily, and in one part or set of relations within a regional cult; the mixture may vary considerably across the whole of the cult. In one cult's regions, there may be great ethnic heterogeneity, in another the greatest cultural differences may be between some people in towns and others in the countryside, but no regional cult is simply homogeneous. That is why I have suggested that regional cults are cults of the middle range—more far-reaching than any parochial cult of the little community, yet less inclusive in belief and membership than any world religion in its most universal form.

But why in Africa and, indeed, elsewhere have regional cults been so rarely studied? Part of the answer is that regional cults have too easily gone unrecognized, or so much attention has been paid to a fraction of the cult, sometimes for good reasons, given the nature of the main research interests, that the rest, and thus the cult as a whole, has been given little or no notice.

It is useful, for the sake of clarity, and because I draw on Fortes' ethnography of Tallensi for part of my argument, to see the contrast between my concept of a region around a central place and Fortes' concept of a "socio-geographic region" (1945:16, 213ff). The socio-geographic region is a localized area where interconnection is comparatively greater within a wider field of social relations. It can be recognized analytically by the characteristics of close-knittedness of relations, or "maximum confluence," and by spatial continuity. It is a concept of a zonal kind, useful where almost any boundary is indefinite and where relations gradually diminish in intensity or importance.

For my purposes, the most important question is about the concept's force in the study of religious movement. How, for example, did the Tallensi's External Boghar cult fit into the socio-geographic region? As an entirety, it did not. Only the heartland of the cult, surrounding the Tong Hills in the northern interior of Ghana was a roughly contiguous area among the Talis, the Mamprusi, the Bulisi, the Woolisi, the Gorisi, and even some of the Mossi subtribes (Fortes 1945:252). At the time of Fortes' early fieldwork, the shrines and adherents of the cult's hinterland were scattered from the interior toward the coast to the south. Moreover, this southern hinterland was not only ethnically diverse, indeed far more so than the northern heartland, but also highly stratified. The southern hinterland included, as Fortes himself carefully recorded, "rich and poor, farmers, traders, chiefs, commoners, literate and illiterate, pagans and Christians" (1945:243). Clearly, at best, the concept of the socio-geographic region could be used to cope with no more than a fraction of such a cult; the spatial discontinuity and heterogeneity in culture, economic organization, and social structure were too great. At worst, only the cult's heartland was taken to be worthy of analysis, except as a symptom of what Fortes called modern disequilibrium (1945:250ff). Indeed, the fact that it *was* a heartland in quite critical respects had largely to be disregarded, so divorced did it seem from its hinterland (see Worsley 1956).

These difficulties can be avoided by using the concept of a "cult region." A cult region has to be recognized and analyzed according to the full extension of activities from a shrine. Only thus can the area of greatest concentration of activities be located within the total focusing of relations around a cult's primary central place.

One of my aims in the second half of the book is to show how a general framework of regional analysis makes sense of the changing pattern and organization of various flows—of people, goods, services, and ideas—in relation to the location of "central places," for the mere crossing of boundaries is a somewhat gross beginning for analysis. In the literature, there are far too many totally unlike religious movements that cause people to go from their own to politically separate, strange, or culturally alien communities. Therefore a much narrower range of phenomena has to be considered, and I start with central places.

In applying regional analysis to religious movements within a wider, changing social field, I first pursue my discussion of cults of the microcosm, moving from the smaller scale, more homogeneous cult in New Guinea to West African cults of the microcosm, including the External Boghar cult of the Tallensi. This paves the way, in subsequent chapters, for accounts of religious movements of the macrocosm in southern Africa. There are various movements of the macrocosm, including world religions, in the West African social field. However, they are linked to predicaments and aspects of the wider field that I do not attempt to cover in my treatment of West African cults.

I am aware that to speak of religious movement as ritual passage and as sacred journey is to resort to metaphor. In my view, however, metaphor is indispensable to both the outsider's understanding, and the insider's practice, of religious movement. In this respect, I agree with Fernandez' basic view. Commenting upon our own metaphoric usage in speaking of religious movement, Fernandez writes:

No doubt the movement metaphor has a primordial quality—it is lodged in the restlessness and irritability of primary experience—the experience we all have of being inappropriately situated and needing to make a movement so as to more appropriately situate ourselves in real space. (1979:38; see also 1984)

A friendly critic of my use of structuralist techniques has objected that these techniques oversystematize ritual as if it were intellectually coherent. The objection is, further, that in tending to overintellectualize the logic of form, the structuralist techniques underplay the disjointedness of ritual. Hence their use diverts attention away from the importance in ritual of what Fernandez calls "the more inchoate experiences of social life from our primary experiences with self and a limited number of others" (1982:8ff; see also 1979, 1984).

Among Kalanga, for example, one such inchoate experience is the condition of turbulence, unrest, and lack of composure. I argue that Kalanga seek to transcend this condition in sacrifice; their objective is metaphorized as cool. Here the question is whether my approach, using structuralist or formal techniques, is compatible with a metaphoric approach such as Fernandez'. Stressing the inchoate, Fernandez illuminates ritual sequencing as a successive rephrasing of core metaphors, including organizing metaphors, the extension of the body image into secondary structures and institutions (Fernandez 1984:132).

These are important objections. My full response to them is sustained throughout this book, perhaps most prominently in the first half. I show that formal analysis enhances our cross-cultural understanding; that my approach is built upon close attention to the people's own metaphors, such as the metaphor of "cool," *pola,* among Kalanga, or the metaphor of "growing soft," *tadv,* among Umeda of New Guinea; and that a totalizing tendency is actualized in ritual, rather than being a mere artefact of my analytic framework (on the totalizing tendency in ritual, see Tambiah 1985:1ff).

There are obvious differences between an unmixed metaphoric approach, such as Fernandez', and my own, which is more influenced by semiology as well as semiotics. Nevertheless, an important continuity is the concern with the higher order organization of ritual, in Fernandez' case with the systematics of metaphoric transformation, in my case with an even higher order, the dynamics of the terms that are constitutive of the metaphors.

Symbolic anthropology will always have its atomists, preoccupied with the nature of the symbol as symbol. No doubt, also, the study of symbols as the elementary building blocks of ritual, which Victor Turner brilliantly advanced, is far from being exhausted (on Turner's contribution within the Manchester School, see Werbner 1984). But increasingly, anthropologists are turning their attention from the building blocks to the moving moments and phases of ritual (see Handelman 1981, and in press; Kapferer 1983; Maddock 1985; Smith 1978; Wagner 1986; P. Werbner 1986; Devisch 1988; see also the seminal contribution of Stanner 1959). The aim is a better understanding of the systematics of performance through a progression of *actual* events.

The analysis of the processual form in whole sequences of ritual is a study to which Turner also made a major contribution, though one perhaps too heavily concentrated upon the classic form of the three-phase *rites de passage*. As anthropologists we have become so accustomed to that tripartite form that we follow Van Gennep's interest in the threshold, and in liminality, and make a fetish out of boundary-crossing. In this fixation, we respect the boundary but not the extension of the religious imagination around a primary focus such as the body (see Devisch 1985b, Fernandez 1982) or the sacred center (see Werbner 1977b). Again, Turner's contribution, in imaginatively attending to the body as primary focus, is exceptional. That said, I must add immediately that my approach, though partly derived from semiotics and semiology, is not purely formal. With Tambiah I would reject the "extreme semiotic school that supposes that form can be tackled apart from the presentation of contents and the interpretation of symbolism" (1985:143).

With a growing theoretical interest in the higher organization of ritual comes the paradox of the frame and the actual sequencing of ritual. According to the way that people frame their ritual, they tend to exclude usual moments upon which, in performance, the actual sequencing depends, and without which a celebration is incomplete. The paradox is that the more we confine our study within the ritual frame, the less we learn of the ritual sequencing. Should the anthropologist who analyzes ritual ignore the usual non-ritual moments because the people apparently disattend, or show that they regard such usual moments as not part of the ritual proper? Can the anthropologist take the emic view and yet get right what it is that drives a ritual forward from moment to moment?

In an attempt at dissolving this paradox for certain purposes of analysis, I privilege the ritual sequencing over the ritual frame. This enables me in Chapter 3, on Kalanga sacrifice, to bring further into perspective what Douglas (1968:366) calls anti-rites, namely, moments that negate or break down what the rites build up. The anti-rites of sacrifice are playfully improvised interludes that, while usual, nevertheless do not belong within the ritual as it is culturally framed. These anti-rites make fun at the expense of elders. What the anti-rites suspend is that authorized reality of everday life, gerontocracy, that the rest of the sacrificial ritual reinforces. Kalanga demonic possession also has interludes of satire, joking, and fun, but these playfully improvised interludes, primarily ridiculing the bestial carnality of relatives, are ritually framed, obligatory rites. Within the ritual they reinstate the kind of social reality that is consonant with everyday life. The differences between the ritually unframed and the ritually framed interludes are explained in my comparison of the ritual sequencing in demonic possession and sacrifice. But the point I want to make by way of introduction is that each kind of interlude makes its own contribution toward driving the ritual forward. Hence both have to be regarded closely, as indeed they are in my study of processual form.

Every ritual is composed of *disparate* moments. The disparity presents an entire bundle of problems that we can here only begin to explore. Among these are the problems of how the sequencing is driven forward from one disparate moment to another, how the sense of progression is sustained, and how the ritual becomes a totality, not merely the sum of its parts. In my view, furthermore, ritual is typically performed using different styles, and we have to explain how and when they are used in turn. In Chapter 2, contrary to Bloch (1977; and for a somewhat revised view, 1986), I show that ritual cannot be reduced to a single style, such as one that is highly formalized, ahistoric, or free of improvisation, a style that obliterates the idiosyncratic, the personal, and the life historic. Kalanga demonic possession is characterized by stylistic shifts between formalization in the main phases of the ritual and improvisation in its interludes. Similar stylistic shifts are practiced in sacrifice, but as I show more fully in Chapter 3, on sacrifice, there is a difference in the intended purposes and thus in the implications of these shifts.

My comparison of these ritual passages and sacred journeys is predicated upon a number of propositions that I substantiate in the course of my argument. First, the ritual passage has a totalizing tendency; it is, or tends toward becoming, a whole. Second, sequencing of the ritual passage is clearly defined. Third, with the possible exception of preliminary ritual such as divination, the structure of the sequencing, that is, the number and the interrelation of the phases, is determined by elementary coordinates.

Given these propositions, I find it useful to conceptualize the *key idea* of ritual. The key idea is itself a system of coordinates for structuring a process. Its coordinates are the successive terms for what is resituated during ritual. It thus locates both the qualities or states of being, such as corporeality, and the persons or agencies associated with them, defined, for example, by gender or age.

These terms may be a simple dyadic opposition. The familiar tripartite form of Van Gennep is constituted by terms in a simple dyadic opposition, which the ritual process mediates. An instance of this simple opposition is found in the tripartite festival that has the masquerade as its liminal phase. The terms are a dyadic opposition between the identity of the many bodies of men and the one body of man. The liminal phase, in turn, has its own terms, the masquerade itself being a series of rites.

Alternatively, the key idea may have several terms in a more complex opposition. In Kalanga cattle sacrifice, for example, where there is an unfolding hierarchy of divinity and successive generations, the terms form a serial triad: (1) "divinity" in divinities of the dead, (2) "elderhood" in elders, and (3) "juniority" in juniors. The processual form of the ritual, whether it is the classic tripartite form of the festival, or the quadripartite form of demonic possession and sacrifice, or even some other form, depends upon the key idea and its combination of terms. This is because the terms are the coordinates for the sequencing of phases.

An example of coordinated sequencing, which I discuss in Chapters 2 and 3, is illustrated by Figure 1. The figure shows a four-phase ritual that has a serial triad as its key idea, the phases being the successive combinations of the terms. This is a type that is characterized by contrastive oscillation from phase to phase, each phase being in conjunction as well as in disjunction with the preceding and succeeding phases (for a view of this dialectic as "obviation," see Wagner 1986).

It might be argued that thinking of ritual in terms of a Cartesian system of coordinates tells us more about Western thinking and "a characteristic intellectual strategy of Westerners" (Fernandez 1979:39) than it does about non-Western ritual (see Fernandez' critique of his own past use of a Cartesian coordinate scheme, 1979:40ff). Fernandez makes the point that the Cartesian scheme provides its own "intellectual quality space." Yet one of our aims in studying the ritual passage is to understand certain cultural constructions. I refer to the constructions that people themselves put on their experience of movement through various kinds of space, marked by different qualities. The question is whether the key idea enhances such an understanding or subverts it.

My answer is clearly that the coordinate system enhances our understanding. I would argue further that Fernandez' own account of Bwiti is even more illuminating if its coordinates are appreciated and a key idea is recognized (see Fernandez 1982, 1984; and for my response to Fernandez' account see Werbner 1985).

Fernandez has given a schematic representation of the systematics of metaphoric transformation in Bwiti ritual (1984:134). In his summary of its overall basic transformation, the "suffering devitalized individual is incorporated into [the] worshipping body of Bwiti which is incorporated into [the] spiritual body of Bwiti as *banzie* [angel]." I would merely suggest that Bwiti's key idea is constituted by states or

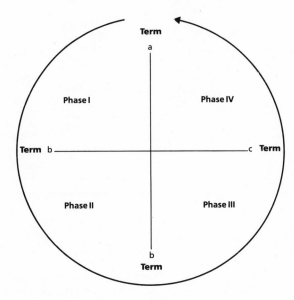

Figure 1. Progression in a Four-Phase Ritual.

qualities of the body and agencies of gender. Bwiti's key idea concerns the agency in gender as it is understood to be sinful or sinless, according to a certain kind of cultural logic.

I am tempted to go even further in dialogue with Fernandez' views. At core, I would say that ritual such as Bwiti is moving because it is a seamless whole. The power of the ritual passage comes from its coordination no less than from its encompassing and, indeed, transcending the inchoate. In the ritual passage, the inchoate is physically embodied, given form, and overpowered.

RITUAL
PASSAGE

～～～～～～～～

CHAPTER I

TSWAPONG WISDOM
DIVINATION

Making the Hidden Seen

INTRODUCTION

Divination is the ritual with which to begin reflecting about ritual.
Its seances start the reconstruction of social reality that other rituals
complete. In divination, people seek to obtain their bearings, and to
prepare for the symbolic relocation of the person in other, later, ritual.
As a preliminary approach to the occult, divination is, in many parts
of the world, preeminently a ritual of orientation and disclosure. It
creates and is created by the sense of discovery; for that reason it is
typically exploratory or variable, and remade for each occasion,
whereas other rituals, tied to foreknowledge of the desired outcome,
unfold in fixed or coordinated sequences that rely on constant terms.
What comes to be known during divination, often through dramatic
modes of searching and finding, is the hidden significance of events in
everyday life. Divination is meant to reveal occult realities through
extraordinary powers of communication; it thus has to be seen and felt
to be extraordinary. In many of the moments in divination, little or
nothing need actually be said. Instead, a silent language of objects is
used for the presentation from the occult of felt realities, for interpretation, and for reflection. Or, if words are at all spoken, they are cryptic,
highly allusive, and perhaps in a special language or in archaic verse.
Almost never are they unambiguous. The imagery used is paradoxical

and puzzling; it is evocative on different levels of meaning at once (see Werbner 1973). At other moments, however, interpretation becomes more explicit, verging on direct statement. Divination takes form as discourse through disparate moments.

Let me introduce my own account of divination as the preliminary discourse of ritual somewhat after the fashion of a diviner. I want to give an example that the missionary Henri Junod records in his classic ethnography of the Tsonga (1913:512). A diviner consulted his divining ensemble of bones and smaller numbers of shells and stones—sixty-two pieces in all—and came to tell Junod this good news:

Be happy my missionary, you will have new tenants who will increase the value of your farm! They prepare their load now. . . . They will come before the tilling season begins. If they do not come I will give you an ox!

The time passed; no one arrived; and Junod says that he went to his old friend, the diviner, to ask for the promised ox. The laugh the diviner gave instead was good-natured, and he said, "Look! I will show you how the bones have told me lies."

With all the skill that an accomplished chess player would have in reconstructing the board and shape of a game through an elaborate series of moves, the diviner placed the sixty-two lots of his ensemble. Once again, they were as they had fallen during his consultation months earlier. He reconstructed an entire microcosm, and it was dualistic. The lots were exhibited clustered in two halves, indicating opposing categories of people. In the upper half was the scene among the would-be visitors; in the lower half, the scene among the would-be hosts.

The diviner interpreted the lots as signs through contrasts. He gave the significance of each piece for the others, and each half for its alternative. The whole was a bounded, structured order in miniature. All of it was coherently and quite circumstantially accounted for by the diviner, with signs, visible to the eye, of person, space, and time of the year. The half that was said to show the procession of strangers was elaborated with matters and characteristics auspicious for the hosts. And so too was the scene among the hosts elaborated with regard to their counterparts.

It was an impressive piece of social analysis and artful conceptualization. Junod first exclaimed, "Wonderful!" and then went on to challenge the diviner, "Only they did not come!"

In response the diviner said, "Never mind." But the missionary continued, "Then the bones have deceived you!"

Not at all! [was the reply] If it is not this year, it will be next year. Moreover, we diviners do not fear to be told that our bones lie. When, later on, our prophecies are fulfilled, then people wonder! They are convinced. And, after all, if the Word (*bula* "the revelation,") [the divining message] lies, it is not our fault.—How is that?—We do not put our ideas into them; we merely interpret them; it is they who speak!—Then they have a power in themselves? [asked Junod]— No, the power is in the chest of the diviner. (Junod 1927:515)

How a diviner is expected to get that power of interpretation is important for the understood nature of the communication in divination; and I say more about that in due course. So far we have seen that a Tsonga diviner may go to great lengths to locate the person within an environment while representing, with iconic and indexical signs, a social mosaic in miniature. The fine spatio–temporal location is an accomplishment of interpretation that a Tsonga diviner makes patent in the face of his awareness of latent ambiguity. In the lots there are indications, but these are regarded as being relative, subject to interpretation and reinterpretation, and not absolute: "If not this year, then next." The Word of divination, if "revelation," is truth-on-balance.

Such Tsonga divination is, in my terms, "microdramatic." That is, it exhibits, in the fine scenes of easily handled lots, a series of encounters between significantly opposed agents, such as friends and foes, prey and predators, the humane and the inhumane, the social and the anti-social, creatures of the day or night, of the domestic or the wild. But Junod's example is a diviner's reconstruction long after the events of a seance. How, from one moment to the next in actual seances, are the microdramatics used for orientation in specific, personal predicaments?

That is a question I want to answer later at some length. Nevertheless, if we regard the spoken along with the silent language of objects, other issues have to be addresed. We have to understand the microdramatics that exhibit the visual, along with what I call the *poetics of divination*. By the poetics of divination I mean the interpretation of the use of cryptic, condensed, and highly ambiguous language, such as in archaic, authoritative verse. What is the interplay between microdramatics and poetics over the course of a seance? How do the people themselves see that? And how are we to interpret reflexively in a way that takes into account the people's own interpretive activity?

All of these are central questions. I pursue them in this chapter through my account of one of the modes of wisdom divination that utilizes lots, which in 1972–73 (fifteen months) and 1978 (two months) I studied among Northern Tswapong of Botswana (for descriptions

*Figure 2. Divining for a Brother's Ill Grandson. A Tswapong diviner points out
to a mother the indications for her infant's recovery from troubled bowels. On the
ground below him, and next to the patient, the client sits with her right leg folded
and her left outstretched. The Hyena (1) is "tired," the Leopard (2) and the Lion
(3) are "going out." But unlike these Enemies of the Night, the Boars (4), as the
Doctors, are "standing up." The bowels "bite and bite" according to the "Biter,"
Selumi, the cast shown by the four sand-tortoise shells of the Kgalagadi. People
crowding around, indicated on the ivory tablets of the Elephant (5) by
Mferephere, "Commotion," are also involved in the invoking of ancestral wrath.*

of similar modes among Tswana, see Schapera 1953:64; Schapera n.d.;
De Jager and Seboni 1964:504–11). The questions raise a problem about
the nature of recent accounts of divination in southern Africa that I
must consider first, before presenting my own ethnography.

DIVINATION AS NEGLECTED RITUAL

Among all the rituals performed in southern Africa, none are so widespread, so commonplace, and yet, in the recent literature, so neglected
as those of divination, especially divination with lots. Almost no attention has been paid, in recent studies, to the enduring importance of
enigmatic divining verse. Yet some of it, which the people themselves

regard as archaic, authoritative, and profoundly revelatory, has remained markedly stable or varied only gradually in form over vast areas of southern Africa (Bartels 1903; Junod 1925; Giesekke 1930; Eiselen 1932; Laydevant 1933; Schapera n.d.; Schapera 1953:64; De Jager and Seboni 1964:504–11). The neglected problem is how, through very different periods of history, archaic verse has continued to be a powerfully effective means for getting one's bearings on disparate personal predicaments. Similarly, there are relatively few articles about southern African divination as ritual, and those that are extant have a more limited scope than articles about divination in other parts of Africa (for a sub-Saharan comparison, cf. Devisch 1985a). There is no recent book on southern Africa that regards divination as a prime concern in its own right, with the notable exception of Turner's *Revelation and Divination in Ndembu Ritual* (1975). However, richly insightful and suggestive as it is, even this book owes most to diviners' self-accounts of basket divination, given apart from seances. Turner himself saw no basket divination in practice and, unlike most of Turner's other studies, here his own observation did not inspire this account.

With rare exceptions (Fernandez 1967; Werbner 1973; Jules-Rosette 1978), divination has become trivialized and marginalized in southern African studies. One reason is that the dominant interest has focused on the outcomes rather than the performance and practice of divination. Divination has been regarded as a transitional phase for selective decision-making within a process of social control or politics and, for that reason, of interest only insofar as it contributes to the wider process. The emphasis has been on what Gluckman described as the "solemn and ritually controlled jockeying" by interested parties for a suitably biased interpretation of misfortune (1965:230).

As a consequence, careful account has been taken of the people's intent to achieve disclosure, to know the hidden, and to sort out alternatives through an authoritative and, in some senses, extraordinary as well as objective procedure. But divination as performance with its own signifying practice has been largely ignored; and by signifying practice I mean not merely the system of signs with an associated grid of categories but the usual patterns of discourse, their actual sequencing over space and time, and their more or less stylized representations of events.

The need is to appreciate that divination is distinctively reflexive as ritual; it is the orientation ritual in which people getting their bearings reflect upon their options in ritual and in everyday life. Divination ritual has to construct implicit and explicit realities of its own, linked to, but not the same as, the realities of everyday life and other ritual. All of this is to raise problems of cognition and communication as well as the social construction of reality. These problems are ones that in my view are already being explored in fresh ways with the quickening of theoretical interest in studies of divination elsewhere in Africa (Devisch 1978a, b; Jackson 1978; Zeusse, 1979; Parkin 1982, 1985; Mendonsa 1982; Shaw 1985; Peek, forthcoming).

In this chapter, I want to look at divination as discourse and as a process of orientation in the light of Pierce's threefold distinction between icon, index, and symbol. For my understanding of this I rely heavily upon Burks (1948; see also Singer 1980). An important point is that a sign can be, in turn or simultaneously, an icon, an index, and a symbol (for a comparative discussion, see Ruel 1987). Hence we may speak of an iconic or non-iconic index, an indexical or non-indexical symbol, and so forth. As put by Burks, the distinction is according to the ways that a sign represents its object to its interpretant (in effect, the interpreter's consciousness). These ways are respectively (1) symbolic, (2) indexical, or (3) iconic for a sign: "(1) by being associated with its object by a conventional rule; (2) by being in an existential relation with its object (as in the case of the act of pointing); (3) by exhibiting its object (as in the case of the diagram)" (Burks 1948:674). One difficulty with Burks' version of the distinction is that it leaves out grounds of resemblance from the definition of an icon. Hence, although Burks criticizes Pierce for inconsistency about this, for my purposes I find it more useful to follow Pierce and also say that an icon is similar to its object. It does not merely exhibit or exemplify it.

MICRODRAMATICS, REVELATION, AND ANALYSIS

Although plain speech is never enough for the orientation through divination towards the implicit and the explicit, the invisible and the visible, the occult and the patent, all divination is not microdramatic (Werbner 1973). As Gluckman long ago pointed out, there is a continuum in the representational dimensions of divination (1965:229). At one extreme is the paucity of visual signs, with the embodiment of a single binary discrimination, for example, in the Azande poison oracle. At another extreme the representation is "a resumé of a whole social order," to use Junod's phrase, with each lot being used for the ambivalences and the multiple aspects, positive and negative, of social persons and institutions. In Gluckman's view, the range in representation is linked to a difference in the interpretive process. At the extreme of visual paucity, interpretation is sustained through a methodical, step-by-step selection whereas at the extreme of elaborate representation, the diviner has to work toward the reading of a pattern as a whole. A similar configurational argument could be made for the client having to reach a holistic reading in situations, as among Sisala, where both the client and the diviner put nothing in words during the indication of elaborate lots (Mendonsa 1982:122–25).

On the basis of such comparison, however, it might be thought that all divination falls simply into the ritual mode that Turner calls "analytical" by contrast to the mode of "revelation." Ndembu divination is analytical, in Turner's view, because its symbols "are used to discriminate between items that have become confused and obscure" (1975:232). It is a methodical search for the definition and resolution of a problem. It is taxonomic, and its logic is dualistic, proceeding through a sequence of binary oppositions. In the mode of revelation, which characterizes Ndembu ritual apart from divination, there is "the exposure to view in a ritual setting, and by means of symbolic actions and vehicles, of all that cannot be verbally stated and classified" (Turner 1975:15).

One difficulty that results from equating all divination with the analytical mode of ritual is raised by Devisch. Devisch takes account of the way that universal human paradoxes are embodied or possibly resolved in the symbolic forms of a Yaka diviner's possession trance and initiation:

Yaka divination realises, in contrast to Ndembu divination, what Turner interprets as being the revelatory function of the cosmogonic Chihamba rite which "asserts the fundamental power and health of society and nature grasped integrally." (Devisch 1978b:43, citing Turner 1975:16)

Clearly, divination too has moments of revelation through verbal and non-verbal communication, through paradox, incongruity, and the evocative synthesis of quite disparate meanings.

I would go further and argue that, instead of different modes of ritual, what we need to appreciate are different momentary emphases and how they are managed in the course of a single ritual. This problem is especially important in wisdom divination, which is poetic as well as microdramatic. The authoritative verse a wisdom diviner recites in praise of the lots is archaic; it is typically cryptic and paradoxical, with highly condensed imagery that is evocative on different levels of meaning at once. Tension is characteristic between what is exhibited visually and what is said in verse; each plays back upon the other. Here the challenge in studying divination is to account for the different moments, for shifts that, in the course of a consultation, move between the analytical and the synthetical, between a logic of discrimination and a unifying insight, and between critical examination and evocative revelation.

Turning now to the ethnography of Tswapong wisdom divination, I want first to provide some essential background about the people themselves and their ways of modeling the universe. Within east-central Botswana, Northern Tswapong live in relatively small, nucleated villages and speak Tswana although they claim origins in the northern Transvaal, among Pedi- and Sotho- speakers. They share with the latter a similar oracle cult of the ancestors. They have a mixed economy of subsistence agriculture and stock-keeping, combined with labor migration, primarily during a man's youth and mainly to the South African mines.

Patrilineal, and with a high regard for gerontocratic authority, the Northern Tswapong preference is for marriage with close relatives, especially cross-cousins. In practice, they also tend to marry within a range of fairly nearby villages, so that most people live surrounded by a circle of kin and affines, intermixed with few unrelated neighbors. Consequently, there is a characteristic overlapping of categories; kin are both affines and neighbors. In common with patterns observed among other Tswana and Sotho (cf. Hammond-Tooke 1981:112–39), this overlapping of categories is a matter of some importance as it affects Northern Tswapong conceptions of pollution and ritual concerned with social boundaries.

As Northern Tswapong conceive of their home universe (kwa gae), political and religious authority are combined at the center. The head of the whole community is the head of the ancestral cult of the microcosm, and thus the priest of the land. The sacred center is within the village; there is no higher order sacred center in an outside community, or otherwise external to the village. The plan of nucleated settlement is focused on the village headman. His family group's ward, the ward being the primary unit of village administration, is at the center, with matrilateral kin in a ward on the western side and strangers on the eastern. This accords with a location of seniors to the west and juniors to the east, in harmony with the flow of the main river from its source in the west. Village homesteads are oriented relative to the orientation of the head's homestead. Huts face inwards, but in various cardinal directions. Except for the orientation to the center, there is no spatial order; order is fixed according to a cardinal geographic axis. There is no cardinal location of categoric or domain oppositions, such as for outsiders vs. insiders, or for the public vs. the domestic (for a contrast, see Chapters 2 and 3 on Kalanga orientation).

The end of the agricultural season is the time for the annual winter return from outlying settlements to the village center. People are expected to come from homesteads near their fields and from cattle posts, although they do not, in fact, always make the return. In the village center, before the beginning of the new year, the community protects itself and its boundaries against the outside. Movement in and out of the community is stopped, and time is arrested. To cross the boundaries then is to incur the ancestors' wrath.

A seance is only held after it is mandated by wisdom divination. In the still of the night, sounds of the founding ancestors' voices echo once again. In a seance with the community head and priest, the ancestors' oracular dialogue is about unwelcome change, and about what is required for the restoration of communal welfare and good order (Werbner 1977). No stranger may approach the sacred space from which the sounds of their voices reverberate. Only initiated members of the community are admitted, and they are exclusively men of the founding ancestors' stock. They are marked apart as insiders by their secret knowledge of the cult and its oracular means of communication; they drum through the night to perform the ritual on behalf of the community as a whole or particular sufferers in its midst.

Unlike rituals discussed in Chapters 2 and 7, no ritual is performed that uses a go-between for sacred exchange across boundaries, between communities or between domains. Nor is there any healing ritual addressed to extra-kin-group divinities. The only ritual addressed to the God of the macrocosm is Christian church ritual, which is not communal, and which is held by the Christians themselves to be incompatible with the ritual in the community's cult of the microcosm.

The danger of movement across boundaries is publicly stressed in this Northern Tswapong way of modeling the home universe. It is a danger that is also tied to the control of reproduction. In its original genesis, pollution is taken to arise when a women, attempting to conceal a miscarriage, a still-birth, or an abortion, does not go through the cleansing ritual needed after delivery. Through contagion comes the spread of pollution. Anyone in contact, however casually, with the polluted woman or her dirt, or who even has stepped along a path she has used, is liable to get the pollution and pass it on. The woman originally to blame need not be known, and usually is not known or named. It is enough for her to be some vague outsider for a villager to get the pollution unwittingly, on a journey away from home. In the case of such pollution, blame for affliction is allocated outwards, upon some generalized other, a person or persons at large, beyond the community.

Coming from within the community, occult attack is attributed in divination to sorcery *(boloi)* or ancestral wrath *(kgaba)*. In sorcery the evil feared is blamed upon a relative or neighbor, someone known but almost never accused directly. Rarely, if ever, does a sorcery accusation take the form of an open or public confrontation between accuser and accused, such as at divination. Contact is avoided, or kept to a minimum. Such accusation, if indirect, does imply conscious intent to do evil, the sorcerer's deliberate use of material substances or a familiar to harm the afflicted. The recognized motive is an excess of greed or sexual desire among lovers or spouses, or envy of the goods and prosperity of a neighbor or nearby relative.

The specific person held responsible for invoking ancestral wrath is always a close senior relative of the afflicted, someone who has what can be considered a just grievance. The grievance is against a named junior relative, not usually the afflicted, who has neglected some moral obligation, or failed to be generous in sharing various goods and cattle; the afflicted victim of ancestral wrath is ordinarily quite innocent. The invoker utters no curse; he or she takes no unambiguous public action asserting authority before the affliction, but he or she later is considered to have grieved in his or her heart, uncontrollably or perhaps even unwittingly. This aggrieved person is invariably someone who was absent from the congregation divining about the affliction, so that the notion of ancestral wrath is used by diviners and members of their congregations to avow obligations to others, rather than to assert their own authority over dependents, as for example among Lugbara (Middleton 1960).

Contact between the aggrieved and the afflicted is avoided by ritual that appeases the ancestral wrath, lest more of a harmful condition—the redness of the aggrieved's heart—be transferred to the afflicted. The aggrieved, who makes no declaration or display of amity, is also absent from the ritual. Instead, family members present blow water beneficially charged by the whiteness of their hearts; they urge the recently dead, who are specifically named as wrathful, to let the living heal from the affliction.

Just as the wider community renews itself as a closed whole in ancestral ritual, so too does its component part, the family or family group. Wives do not remain in-marrying outsiders—set apart in ritual from the kin—on the basis of a categoric opposition between them and us. Given the preference for marriage with kin, kinship is assumed in marriage. Hence the inclusion of women related by marriage to the afflicted among the relatives who blow water; and hence the ritual closure of the family or family group as a whole, apart from the invoker of wrath.

It can be seen that in this way of modeling the universe there are two concentric schemes: a sociocentric scheme of order around the head of the community and an egocentric scheme of disorder around the afflicted. The one that diviners use as an explanatory scheme is egocentric. Diviners recognize and take account of a great variety of symptoms, dangers, and troubles concerning their clients, but they make the great variety intelligible, in moral terms, by reference to that simple, egocentric scheme of pollution, sorcery, and ancestral wrath.

The diviners' egocentric scheme is built upon a progression in ego's moral horizons and in personal responsibility for occult attack. This is shown in Figure 3. On the outermost horizon are persons at large, who are polluters operating by contagion even beyond the community and without regard for ego. On the first horizon within ego's community are specific neighbors and relatives, including family members, who, in their malicious practice of sorcery, are evilly motivated toward ego. Next are close senior kin with just grievances toward ego's kin, or even ego, but without malice. Finally comes ego, incorporated in health, along with healers of ego's family in their conscious goodwill.

This egocentric scheme is constituted, I would argue, by two axes that have their appropriate polarities. On the one hand, there is the axis of morality along which the good and blameless are opposed to the evil and blameful; on the other hand, there is the axis of intent, marked by the deliberate and controlled in opposition to the unwitting and uncontrolled. These axes of morality and intent for the egocentric horizons are shown in Figure 4.

DIVINATION, DANGER, AND THE VISION OF THE VICTIM

Northern Tswapong usually divine when they are concerned about some danger that they regard in terms of moral disorder. The danger may be an affliction that they already suffer, or that they have reason to fear they may suffer. I use the term affliction broadly, since they are concerned about various troubles, including illness, personal loss, or public deprivation, such as may occur when rain fails. Sometimes, also, the danger may be a potential threat to a new and uncertain venture, such as a proposed marriage or even a trip for further divination.

Bound to this concern with affliction and danger is a certain vision of the human predicament. Caring about their own vulnerability,

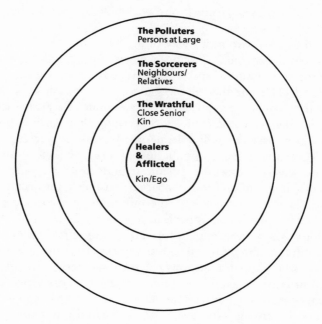

Figure 3. Ego's Horizons in Divination.

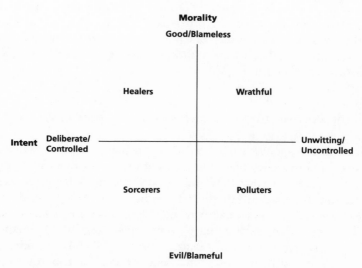

Figure 4. Axes of Morality and Intent.

Northern Tswapong envision the subject of divination as a person who is the victim of envy, greed, or careless egoism, the victim's own and that of others. The world is divided in two, with an opposition between enemies and allies. It is striking that the opposition is made sharply and so importantly in divination among people who share overlapping categories of kin, affines, and neighbors. The opposition is a widespread feature of wisdom divination among others with overlapping categories, such as Sotho and Tswana, whereas it is absent or extremely rare among exogamous people, such as Kalanga and other Shona, who make a sharp divide in everyday life between kin and affines, between us and them. The relation between the overlapping categories in everyday life and the binary opposition of categories in divination is not fortuitous. I am tempted to suggest that it is a function of wisdom divination as a process of orientation, which is not compatible with overlapping categories, and thus it is not to be explained merely by reference to a requirement that everyday life imposes upon divination. In Northern Tswapong divination what the person as victim needs for personal orientation is (1) knowledge in the form of a plan of the ongoing duel between the opposed sides and, (2) a prescription, to provide a plan for effective and powerful counteraction, often in the form of further ritual following divination.

Underlying Assumptions

The Northern Tswapong vision of the victim is predicated upon certain assumptions that the practice of divination embodies and sustains. Perhaps most basic is an assumption about the shortcomings of the human senses. From this starting point, divination is used to begin the search for knowledge of the hidden and, in some respects, for a truer reality. What is directly known to the human senses is ordinarily no more than the external reality, and thus the techniques and procedures of divination are needed to externalize the internal reality in order to make this truer reality accessible. At the very start of a consultation, a diviner usually addresses his lots:

Yes, we are divining for this person. Let us see, tell us. It is said you have eyes to see, you who wash in the pools.

Such eyes are represented as the eyes of enhanced sight, of real perception, which sees the invisible truth beyond what is ordinarily visible. Throughout a divination, a diviner often says that the lots "grasp" or apprehend, which implies that they reach to otherwise inaccessible perception.

A second assumption is that, in order to know each other truly and beyond appearances, human beings need knowledge from other creatures. Only in divination is this assumption fully developed. People are called by totemic names, and comparison is often made to animals in everyday discourse—a man living year-round in a homestead away from the village center is a "jackal"—but wild animality, lionness for example, is not ritually represented, as it is elsewhere in Botswana, such as among Kalanga (see Chapters 2 and 7). In the past, male initiation may have been an occasion for instruction about, and dramatic representation of, animality, as it was among Transvaal Sotho (see Roberts 1916; Hammond-Tooke 1981). Presently, in ritual other than in divination, the use of animal metaphor is minimal, whereas its extensive use gives divination distinct realities that are authoritatively its own.

Along with these assumptions about the shortcomings of the human senses and the need for alternative sources of knowledge from other creatures, a linked assumption is made about physical and moral space. According to this further assumption an existential relation holds between the physical and the moral; events of order and disorder in physical space conform to conditions in moral space. For example, the straying of a man's cattle conforms to the moral condition of his kin being at cross-purposes with each other. In terms of signs in divination, this assumption is the basis for the indexical interpretation of microdramatic events. As Junod put it, "There are signifying and signified objects: the fate of the signifying object will be the fate of the signified" (1927:521). The signs, or signifying objects, are taken to be the indices of conditions in the signified. Thus for Northern Tswapong one indexical sign of being at cross-purposes is the cross. As an icon, it also exhibits that condition. Northern Tswapong call this shape *sefapano*, the abstract noun from the verb *sefapana*, "to pass or cross one another." (See Figure 9, page 45.)

What is not assumed, of course, is that true understanding of icons and indices is possible without achieving the power of interpretation. On the contrary, it is recognized that to gain that power a diviner has to be set apart from other men in his knowledge, in his experience, and in his capacity for speech. Eating a cock, burnt black when roasted with herbs, initially distinguishes the diviner from other men. Among other things, this gives him a knowledge of blackness and bitterness which other men do not have, and it makes him fit to be a mediator in communication about the person as victim.

To put together an elaborate ensemble, the diviner is expected to accumulate personal wisdom from varied experiences of life. This cumulative personal wisdom is objectified in the lots he adds to the ensemble from time to time, such as the bone of a lion whose attack he survived or a shell he stumbled upon during an arduous journey. The occasion for such an addition may be unusual success in the hunt, a narrow escape from death, a surprising find while treating someone or while being treated or initiated. Each of these occasions points to something and, in the light of that, the chosen lot is also later understood to be pointing as an index. The piece for a lot may be a gift from his teacher or from some trusted relative or friend or even something bought from an alien diviner in a distant place. But with each piece goes a bit of his personal history. His lots are thus evocative memorials of the more than ordinary knowledge he gains in the course of becoming and being a diviner, and in the course of surviving the dangers of life, such as in the hunt, in traveling to distant places, and in overcoming the loss of close kin.

I must emphasize that each such lot is not merely a symbol in the restricted sense of a vehicle for the conventional association of meaning. For the diviner himself at least, and through him for the client also, the lot is a means for the embodiment of, and thus the recall and reflection about, personal perceptions from the diviner's own life history. The discourse of divination resonates with experience, with echoes of the passions and suffering of a lifetime.

To get his special capacity for speech and communication, the diviner has to undergo a further ritual. Widespread in southern Africa, this ritual takes a quite simple form, which involves a dual operation, initially on the diviner's lots and then on the diviner himself. It is recognized that there is a separation between the diviner as a man, and the parts of other creatures and things with which he seeks to communicate. To bridge that separation, a diaphragm is used. The various parts are contained within the diaphragm and roasted together, covered by hot embers. They are thus ritually transformed into lots for divination, being brought into a metonymic relation with the container of an animal's breath, the essential for speech. The diviner eats the cooked diaphragm which again is bitter and unpleasant. As I understand it, the logic is that by consuming the diaphragm, the diviner incorporates it in himself; he makes it his own, and thus comes to contain within himself the capacity to speak with the diaphragm of the icons as well as his own diaphragm.

Along with direct and immediate contact between otherwise separate things, knowledge of internal states is taken to be an essential prerequisite for divination. It has to be achieved anew at each seance. Each time a diviner consults his ensemble, he communicates his own internal condition and renews his contact with his ensemble by blowing into its bag, and then tapping his chest. He is also reminded of his experience of bitterness by chewing a herb that is bitter, though not a hallucinogen. Similarly, a mediatory relationship with the client is established through immediate contact—the client, too, blows into the bag. In some cases a client unable to attend the divination due to affliction may have a personal object, such as a garment or pillow, put on the ground in his or her place, and during the divination the consulter and the diviner, in turn, repeatedly bring the lots into contact with the personal object instead of the patient.

Just as the diviner has to undergo a ritual transformation for the sake of extraordinary communication, so too must the client be suspended from his or her ordinary condition. During the consultation the diviner faces his client and sits on a stool, as befits an elder or a man of authority. Below him sits the client, level with the lots on the ground, barefoot, and with the left leg outstretched and the right leg folded under it. This posture confounds the conventions for age and gender, the basic categories of the person. In public it is respectable for a woman to sit on the ground stretching out both her legs; a man ought to sit on a stool or cross-legged on the ground. The posture in divination is an in-between and leveling one. It thus locates the client symbolically in a liminal condition in relation to his or her normal self, and in a condition of dependency as well as inferiority in relation to the authoritative diviner.

Tablets and Dice: Signs and Signifying Practice

Given these assumptions, we can now consider the use of signs as icons, indices, and symbols in relation to the poetics and microdramatics of divination. For the sake of clarity, I begin with a description of each kind of sign and then examine the signifying practice to which it is put in actual seances. The lots are of two kinds: thin, rectangular, two-faced tablets, and dice that have as many as four faces (see Figures 7 and 8). There are four tablets in a set, representing persons by age and sex. The dice represent various categories of person and are not a fixed number. Collectively, the lots are called *ditaolo*. *Ditaolo* are instructions, directions, or resolutions. The word belongs to the same family as law, *molao,* and it is derived from the verb *laola,* "to command, govern, or regulate" (Brown 1967:147). Hence it associates divination with activity that is ordered, authoritative, and prescriptive.

The difference between the two kinds of lots is a major one in semantic terms. It comprises not merely the nature of the sign vehicle but also the way the lots are used for egocentric explanation and for poetic or microdramatic interpretation. This can be seen, first, for the egocentric explanatory scheme about affliction. Only the tablets,

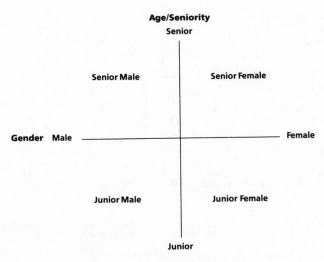

Figure 5. Coordinates of Primary Categories of Tablets.

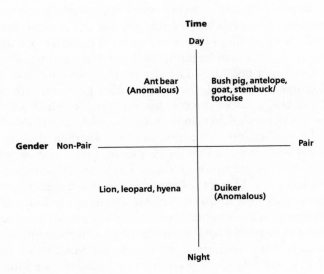

Figure 6. Categories of Dice.

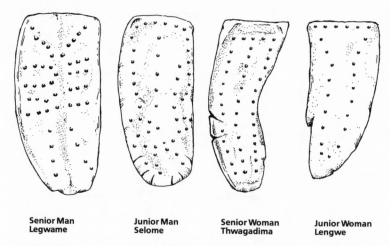

Senior Man
Legwame   **Junior Man**   **Senior Woman**   **Junior Woman**
Selome   **Thwagadima**   **Lengwe**

Figure 7. Tlhabana: Primary Categories of Tablets.

known simply as *tlhabana,* "brown-speckled," after their burnt markings, are used for the whole of this scheme (I comment below on
color and the symbolics of light and dark). The tablets are the more
ambiguous lots and may be interpreted as referring, alternatively, to
wrath, sorcery, or pollution. The dice are more specialized and some,
as for example the leopard, the lion, or other predators, are taken to
convey something about sorcery, but *not* about wrath or pollution.

For the poetics of divination, only the more ambiguous lots are
used. The four tablets in combination are interpreted as symbols.
Traditional verse is recited by the diviner in their praise according to
their selective falling, blank or marked side up, in sixteen possible
combinations. The diviner thus conveys complex images in ways that
are allusive, paradoxical, and somewhat unstable. The four tablets are
also interpreted as icons in that they exhibit features of age or seniority
and gender. The resemblance represents each icon individually as one
of the four primary categories of person: Senior Man, Senior Woman,
Junior Man, Junior Woman. As shown on Figure 5, two binary axes
constitute the categoric discriminations that are involved.

Every combination of the lots has a standard name, usually associated with a plant. The diviner recites the name along with the verse or
separately. The plant itself may be used in treatment or its qualities
may be indicative of the needed prescription. For the primary personal
categories the name epitomizes an appropriate relationship or condition

along with its healing. For example, when all four tablets fall with the marked side up, it is *Mpherefere,* "Commotion, Tumult, Confusion, Riot"; *pherefere* is a shrub with red berries, whose roots are used for healing pain, and, by extension of the term, *pherefere* is "pepper, red and hot."

The tablets are thus a means by which quite different things can be brought together or played off against each other: the visual exhibition of primary personal relationships, such as between Senior Man and Senior Woman; their metaphoric epitomization; their healing; or their verbal representation in the enigmatic imagery of archaic verse.

It is usual for an ensemble to have paired sets of tablets, each from a creature associated with longevity. The more senior is called the Elephant and is made of ivory. The more junior is often made from sand-tortoise shell, and is called the *Kgalagadi,* after the distant Kalahari semi-desert that is its favorite habitat, and the source, some diviners say, of lots and healing knowledge, obtained from Kgalagadi or Bushmen.

Northern Tswapong compare the paired sets of tablets to young and old oxen that are yoked together to give the strength of one, and the wiser, more experienced guidance of the other. Pointing to each set in turn, a diviner told me, "These could speak deceptively, with confusion and treacherously. But if these do say something that is aside from the path, those contradict them." Thus as Northern Tswapong themselves describe it, their logic in divining involves a cross-check.

We might say that this description, given its stress on objectivity, is a rationalization. Indeed, it could be argued that because the tablets are doubled in paired sets there is greater ambiguity, thereby allowing the diviner more flexibility and leeway in his interpretations. That argument misses an important point however, namely, the subjective appreciation by Northern Tswapong themselves of the way that divination proceeds through the reconciling of disparate alternatives. The people themselves are aware that the interpretive process is a resolution of apparent contradictions.

THE FRAME OF PROCEDURE

I discuss below the different moments that are constructed through the microdramatics and the poetics of performance, moments that are framed by a formalized method of search. Here I want to consider this method in order to contextualize my account of actual seances. A highly regular procedure establishes a formal frame within which a process of collusion can take place by means of an informal unacknowledged interaction between the diviner and his congregation.

Interpreting and Eliminating the Lots

To start the procedure, a diviner shakes out the contents of his bag and lets all his icons fall freely to the ground. For most people the initial impression is quite confusing. They are confronted by something like a maze. Sometimes, even other diviners are bewildered at first by the scrambled array of lots strewn on the ground. The lots have to be made recognizable and distinguishable, particularly because a few are roughly similar. In the course of his interpretation of the first fall from the bag, the diviner usually points out each lot by name, even if he does not comment upon them all. This establishes the lots as signs to be intelligible to the client also. After the fall from the bag, it is the client's turn to gather together all the lots, shake them up in both hands, and let them fall smartly on the ground. This second fall, the initial one from the bag, and a third one in a concluding series from the diviner's hands, are the only ones in which all the lots of the whole ensemble are used.

Lots are eliminated according to a simple and highly regular method. Each is said to be "overcome" or "tired" when removed, according to its position. Thus gradually through a series of falls, the diviner instructs his client to take up fewer and fewer lots, until virtually all are eliminated, and then the diviner himself takes over for the conclusion of the seance. I use the following notation for the tablets that face up: M = Old Man, W = Old Woman, B = Young Man, and G = Young Woman. The ball known as *Morarwana,* "Inner Circle," with the Old Man face down and the other lots up, is thus: W B G.

To signify agreement by the lots to the immediate conclusion, both sets of tablets, as it were in unison, are expected to fall as (M W G) *Moraro.* The literal translation is "the Great Circle;" it is also "the Great Moot," according to the seating at such a moot, and the contrast is to *Morarwana,* "the Inner Circle" and "Little Moot." Producing this confirmation usually has to be, and is done, by a sleight-of-hand, with the diviner stacking the tablets in his hand and causing them to fall as required. At no other time in a seance is such a physical trick used. My impression is that it usually is regarded, at least by the diviner, as a matter of form, since the lots have already spoken according to their free fall from the bag and their unstacked fall from the patient's hand.

Poetics in a Seance

Paradoxes, ambiguities, and suspended meanings are systematic properties of the tablets used in conjunction with poetic discourse in a seance. An example is useful to make this point concretely. When all four tablets of a set fall with their marked face down, the diviner may recite a verse for the appearance of darkness. The fall is called *Motha-kola,* "extraction." At the core of the verse's imagery of darkness is the evergreen shrub named *lethakola,* the "extractor." The shrub is a means for the transformation of matter out of place into matter in place. Associated with human dirt, it is used for brooms, and for scraping feces from the anus. Its red fruits may be eaten by humans, but it is thought of as the favorite food of their predatory enemy, the hyena.

The imagery of the verse conveys a state of panic, a running about wildly without knowing where to stop. It also conveys knowing the place of survival. Thus there is a tension between incompatible things conceived together, between matter out of place and matter permanently in place, between internal disorder, attack, pain, confusion, and devastation and, by contrast, release, escape, and everlasting regeneration. To quote the verse at some length:

It is *mothakola,* the extraction of rattling wildly in the heap of hot embers.
Rescue the extractor, the evergreen from burning.
There are no men at home.
Catch hold of them with the herbs of the horn.
It burns to ash.
It burns flailing me to give out bullets.
The riverside reed scoffs at the reeds beyond the river, saying "When the wildfire scorches, where will you go?"
The highlander says, "When the river floods, where will you go?"
"Only stubble remains, and yet I sprout. I am the reed."

I draw on a seance held by Rra Mafaya as an illustration of how meanings suspended in the poetics may be invoked and then placed in a context that bears on an immediate personal predicament. Rra Mafaya, an elder in his early seventies and the powerful head of a large family, is the diviner to whom we are most indebted for our understanding of Tswapong divination. Rra Mafaya welcomed us to live in his home, which we did for most of our Tswapong fieldwork. He made me a trusted pupil and advised me about how to live at peace with my wife. He took so great an interest in my study that he often woke me in the early hours of the morning in order to be certain I would be ready to record his seances. A fuller portrait of him must await a future study.

The following seance is one of more than two hundred that I tape-recorded, about half of which are Rra Mafaya's. I am grateful to my assistant, Ontlogetse Mafoko, for his great patience in transcribing the tapes in Tswana and for helping me to translate the texts, after my consultations with Rra Mafaya and other diviners.

In this seance the client, who came alone for the consultation, was a labor migrant unable to keep any job and visibly suffering from depression; he and the diviner were strangers. At *Mothakola,* the first fall from the bag, the diviner, Rra Mafaya, reduced the ambiguity of the imagery by saying,

They grasp your darkness of face. It is dark even while you go about as you do. You do not see anything [you want], and even if you go to work, you do not get anything. . . . I do not know whether you stepped on this blackness [i.e., whether a trap was prepared on the path through sorcery]. It seems as if a black medicine has been put there, but that I do not know yet. . . . Anyway they have just started. We will hear from the later ones how they will come and speak. . . . This very one who works on you . . . has killed your forehead [i.e., ruined your fortune] so that we can say she has grasped your head. It says that while you go along your mind *[mowa]* gets black and depressed. Then your mind seems to be waking up again, and even your eyes get dark, and they seem to be popping out and changing for the worse. So this person must have touched you on the head. But if this *Mothakola* does not grasp the illness that you once suffered . . . then that may mean this person goes to you at night, according to *Mothakola.* It grasps the night, it grasps the chyme of something. (16th June 1973)

Once having invoked the verse's suspended meanings, the diviner has to contextualize them to convey a definite sense and reference. But given the fact that the fall is the first from the bag, a somewhat open, tentative interpretation is acceptable, and the diviner speaks as one who is probing alternatives rather than confirming a diagnosis, as he does at the end of the divination.

Underlying this interpretation is a cultural logic for the color dynamics of affliction. Although I cannot spell that out fully here, a very brief comment is essential. According to this logic, one dynamic contrast is between light and dark. Light is the bare state of well-being, of moving and being actively alive; dark, the state of being overcome by illness, immobilized. More fundamentally, the light–dark contrast is associated with the very opposition between life and death. It is this opposition that is dominant in the formal semantic structure of the dice, and in the calling of the dice *tlhabana,* "brown-speckled." In other words, what the dice are meant to convey, above all, is revelation about life in relation to death. Calling the dice *tlhabana* puts the cultural stress on life and yet has the suggestion in the speckling of its opposite, the possible presence of death.

With this contrast implicitly understood, the diviner concentrates his client's attention on a simple material quality of the lots: their visible lack of "color," and thus their darkness, when the markings are downwards. At one with that darkness, he suggests, is the state of mind of the afflicted, the cause and occasion for that state, as well as the means for remedying it. The patient may have been fed something black, such as chyme or half-digested matter from a slaughtered animal, a thing of death and darkness. This may have been used to subvert his condition from light to dark. But so too can the subversion be reversed, through a further operation with the darkness of a slaughtered animal. The patient's subjective condition is redefined as an inversion of physical matter within his person, and thus the promise of treatment comes along with the representation of the affliction as objective and external.

In a consultation such as this, having invoked the tension in part or the whole of the verse, the diviner usually goes on to reduce the complexity of the imagery while he resolves the paradoxes by the use of somewhat plainer speech. Moreover, he may also have recourse to the commanding simplifications of gesture. For example, when a diviner talks of a client's depression, he may use an appropriate gesture to relate it to the dangerous condition of a relationship. In such a gesture for depression, the diviner curls one hand and clasps it in the palm of the other. The gesture is called *gothatagana,* "laying one on top of the other," or alternatively, *disalebagana,* "not facing one another." It is one of a set of three gestures, whereby both hands are used by diviners to exhibit the dangerous state of a relationship. In the second gesture, the danger is getting stuck together with something or someone that clings beyond reason. The hands are held palm to palm, and this is called *gotswaragana,* "holding on to one another." Finally, being separated, cleaved asunder *(aroganya),* is the danger in the third gesture, and the hands are spread apart sideways. These gestures simplify the meanings elaborated in the verse and concretely match an affliction to a dangerous relationship.

Microdramatics, Body Icons, and Indices

To pursue the interpretive process further, we need to consider the other lots and the microdramatics of divination. The dice are called *bola.* The verb from which the term is derived, also *bola,* means "to speak, or to reveal a secret" (see above on Junod's translation of *bula* as "revelation"). The dice are interpreted to be revealers of secrets

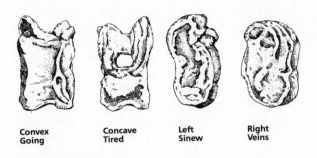

Convex   **Concave**   **Left**   **Right**
Going   **Tired**   **Sinew**   **Veins**

(after Junod 1925: 52)

Figure 8. Categories of Dice.

according to indication and the direct visual resemblances they bear to what they signify. In other words, the dice are indices and icons. Their visual presentation of immediately knowable action is what diviners often urge clients to recognize: "Look at them, you are also a watcher."

Each of the dice is a body icon, with a head (the narrower part) and foot (the opposite, wider end), front (convex, like a belly) and back (concave, like a back) (see Figure 8). When the front falls down the die is said to be "going" and "marching;" with the back down, the die is said to be overcome and "tired." Except for the ant bear, the "doctors" among the dice also have right and left sides. The right side is called "veins," and it is taken to indicate the flow into the veins, decongestion, and release (for example, release from wrath); the left is called "sinew," and stands for congestion, and constraint (again, for example, by wrath). Thus the bloated belly of a patient is indicated by the rounded surface of a bush pig's bone on the left side towards the patient. Similarly, the ant bear's third surface indicates digging for medicines or for a grave.

In some positions, there are exceptions to the dice being exclusively iconic and indexical. The boar dice, called "doctors," are praised in verse, according to two positions. With their concave side down, in the position known as *Kgaranyane,* when they "rest on their backs," a verse typically used is:

I am known to *Kukunyane* [the name for the alternative position, convex side down].
I am known to the child of the one who sleeps lying on the back.

The child of one who sleeps lying on the back waves a mane.

It says, "Unhang that which is hung up."

It says, "The dogs tire at their necks. A civet cat is a great bird.

Come along and let us put colors on each other."

With the left side down, in a position termed Sinew, *Mosifi,* the diviner recites:

You must roast a boar cunningly.

Watch the boar lest it attack you and you remain with injury. It says,

"A shoe is found by one who is strong."

"He who is not strong does not find it."

The main reference from the dice is to motion, direction, location, and certain states of the body as aspects of the person. Time is imputed by pointing to the cardinal location of the dice in relation to the sun and the cardinal points, or by reference to the habits of the creature from which the lot comes. The diviner may also draw attention to other bearings for inference, such as the lot's disposition or place with regard to other lots, its orientation, either relative to the client or the diviner himself, and its location with reference to people's homes and the rest of the social environment. Elsewhere, in an account of Kalanga divination, I noted what I have called the superabundance of under-standing, and the excessive richness of personal knowledge that has to be controlled in divination among intimates (Werbner 1973). In discussing Tswapong divination, I would go further, as there is a more striking superabundance of *signification.* By that I mean that what each lot can indicate visually and non-verbally is always much in excess of what a diviner or a client considers relevant or worthy of notice in a particular instance. The interpretive art is in selecting that which is cogent both for the diviner and the client as well as for the rest of the congregation present.

To create a set of dice, diviners rely on their classification of creatures. Different kinds of knowledge are linked in this classification to unlike habits of attack and defense. The most powerful knowledge comes from a creature that is no respecter of time or space. This is the ant bear which, though zoologically a nocturnal animal, is classified by Northern Tswapong diviners as an animal that goes about day and night. The ant bear burrows under human homes; it goes everywhere, across the divide between the wild and the domestic. Appropriately enough, because it brings together disparate kinds of knowledge, the ant-bear's lot is called the god, *modimo*, or "father." Its importance is stressed as the most powerful indicator of danger in divination. Any or all of the following may also be chosen for the dice: the phalanx of a lion, tortoise scales, snail shells, or the ankle bones of a bush pig, goat, antelope, duiker, or baboon.

It is helpful to illustrate from an actual ensemble. The one I know best is that of my teacher, Rra Mafaya. Rra Mafaya's dice are divided between predators or enemies, primarily creatures of the night, and doctors or allies, primarily of the day. All the doctors, except one, are in sexual pairs; conversely, all the enemies are asexual individuals, except for one pair. In detail, the doctors are the four pairs of bush pig, antelope, goat, and stembuck with a tortoise for its mate along with the ant bear as the one asexual individual. The enemies are the following three asexual individuals: lion, leopard, hyena, and the one sexual pair of duiker. The oppositions are shown in Figure 6.

The apparent anomalies within the classification are significant for the logic of interpretation. They represent deceptive appearance and the transitiveness from one category to its opposite according to a creature's characteristic habits. In a sense, they are the quintessence of ambivalence. Thus the duiker can be taken to be an enemy disguised as a friend, or a friend who betrays one to an enemy. The duiker is sexual and has a mate, since it is a herbivore and as such would belong to the creatures of the day; but it is among the scavengers and predators as a creature that goes by stealth at night. Similarly, the ant bear is asexual, since it is a predator-like creature that goes by stealth in the night and eats bones as well as termites and ants; but it is among the doctors as a friend-like creature that digs on behalf of others. Digging up roots, as exemplified by the wild pig, is the habit, above all, that characterizes a doctor. The integration of the ensemble as a whole is reflected in the fact that an ant bear and a duiker are also opposites as anomalies, the former being the most senior of seniors, i.e., of the doctors, and the latter the most junior of juniors, i.e., of the predators.

Having given this description of Rra Mafaya's dice, let me illustrate his microdramatic use of them in an actual seance. This illuminates, also, how the sign as index and icon serves as a means for the dichotomous yet holistic interpretation of social life in the form of an ongoing duel. The following is an extract from a consultation in which the client came alone from a nearby village.

At the first fall from the bag, Rra Mafaya focused upon the client's evident grief and anxiety. His suffering was not ordinary illness, but "suffering of the mind," and an inability to cope since things "slip through his fingers," Rra Mafaya told him. During succeeding falls in response to Rra Mafaya's ambiguous verse and more direct suggestions

Figure 9. The Cross of Contradiction, Sefapano, in a Tswapong Divination.
A diviner brings leaves suffering from the drought into contact with the lots in order
to reveal the moral disorder causing a cosmic disturbance, a halt in the regular rains
upon which life depends. The cross the diviner has drawn in the sand, at the
right, *next to the leaves, corresponds to the spatial form of intersecting lots.*
It represents as an icon contradiction, conflict, being at odds.

about the nature of the affliction, the client confessed, in an emotional
outburst, that nothing seemed to go right for him following a quarrel
with his father. The quarrel was about the desertion of his wife and
his refusal to let his father sell his cattle. After the client's outburst, Rra
Mafaya pointed to the ant-bear or god, which was headed toward
various predators and away from the client, and said,

The god is now going away in anger. This god should not go away in anger,
it should stay just here. For if it were in-between, we would know that he
would get better, for the god would be stressing the village. But instead there
is the god stressing your mind. Indeed, your father—and you should listen
carefully to me—when you dream about him, you see him facing away from
you. . . . His facing away is ignoring you, caused by these people. This one

is an enemy, a woman [duiker] and this one, a hyena, and this one a leopard
. . . (16th July 1973)

This microdramatic interpretation highlighted a visual representation
of hostilities as a complete whole. Within this whole, the duiker represented the client's wife setting the client's father against him and leaving
him at the mercy of the sorcerers, the hyena and the leopard, who
surround the god, his father. The interpretation was built upon various
oppositions: a person's village versus his mind or willful ego; the allies
versus the enemies; facing away as rejection versus facing towards as
acceptance. Throughout this part of the consultation the stress was on
visual indication, and there was little echo of the earlier emphasis on
paradox or the suspended meanings and elaborated metaphor of the
verse.

The Progression of a Seànce

The successful seance has continuity, and it becomes a whole greater
than its disparate moments. But how does a diviner create a sense of
progression? How does he bring the disparate moments together or
make them seem continuous, eventually linked in significance? Part of
his art is his command of the questioning, or rather the request put to
the lots, since it is not in the form of a question but more like an if–
then proposition of the kind so well-known from Azande (e.g., if x is
so, poison oracle kill the fowl) (Evans-Pritchard 1937). The request is
to be told or allowed to see in response to an assertion, which must be
confirmed, rejected, or qualified. The diviner tells the client the words
to use in making each request.

The following examples that are drawn from the complete series
put by the lone client in the immediate case above illustrate this:

Yes, I am divining for myself to see; I go with an aggrieved heart. I try to run
a business, but it fails, even though I do not lack money. I also do not see my
wife. Let me hear what the fault is.

Yes, I will get people to heal me. Yes, let me see how I will get on if I am
healed!

Yes, I will get better. Yes, I will do well. Yes, I will get people to heal me.

Yes, I have to be treated by Rra Mafaya himself.

In this series the requests were brief, highly compressed, even vague in contrast to the diviner's interpretation of the lots' responses. After the first address, the request to hear or see was implied so that its conditional nature as an if–then proposition was understood without being explicitly said.

The following, from a consultation by an unsuccessful hunter, is an example of more explicitly conditional address:

Yes, I am divining for this gun here to see what eats it. If it is from here at home, you must tell. It is said you have eyes to see. Tell what it is eaten by. If it is in the home, you must tell.

It is obvious that such requests, if necessary, are not sufficient for purposes of creating a sense of progression toward greater understanding. The diviner has to command much more than his client's mode of address to the lots if he is to bring the seance's disparate moments together significantly and with decisive authority. Here a case showing the course of a seance from moment to moment is essential to illuminate the diviner's efforts toward organized synthesis in the interpretive process. This case is again from Rra Mafaya's practice.

The seance was held in great privacy in Rra Mafaya's homestead next to his fields. Only the client, his son, the patient, the diviner, and the ethnographer were present. The patient, a labor migrant in his early twenties, at most, came with his father from a village about two or three hours[1] bicycle ride away from Rra Mafaya's homestead. Immediately before the seance, the client and Rra Mafaya had a very brief conversation about the purpose of the visit, which I was unable to hear. Rra Mafaya had some prior knowledge of the client's affairs. The client had consulted Rra Mafaya in the past. I infer that Rra Mafaya gained the impression that the client had come with a strong view about the patient's troubles and the immediate need for protective treatment. After the divination the client told me that he had come wanting his son to be treated, "He is at work, and when a man goes without anything, without anything to hold himself with, it doesn't go well for him." His son had been unstable at work; he had been wasting away his earnings, "playing about," as Rra Mafaya said during the divination.

Once the patient was seated with his right leg folded and his left outstretched, Rra Mafaya took a bite of his bitter herb, rubbed his bag, touched the youth with it, rubbed the bag once more, then let the lots fall freely from the bag while addressing them:

We are divining for this boy here. Let us see, let us see what the fault is, let us see what is bothering him. For it is said that you have eyes to see, you, the washer in pools.

Rra Mafaya followed a simple order, when he interpreted the initial significance of the lots. The order was the orthodox ranking in importance, from the senior set of tablets (the Elephant ivories) to the junior set (the Tortoise), and then to the dice, especially the doctors. In this way he directed the seance initially from the poetics in verse and metaphor, as appropriate for each set of tablets in turn, to the microdramatics in the presentation of the dice.

Rra Mafaya began by announcing the name of the first fall and then praising it in verse:

It comes [W B G] *Morarwana*, "Inner Circle" [a diminutive of circle which is used for an intimates' moot, also the name for a small, creeping vine]. It says, "A thing of Inner Circle is not far. It is like the skin shedding of a *pika* snake. You, heart, return to your dwelling place. He who sought his own has found it. Hee, hee, are the little laughters."

This imagery oriented the seance toward the personal predicament of intimacy at home. It was toward something of one's own and someone close, of one's own kind, who clings around one and yet sheds one or has to be shed like the snake's skin. The orientation, if clearly focused in social space (home), was ambiguous. The ominous laughter was auspicious *or* inauspicious. And it was as if the ambiguity had already been resolved. Rra Mafaya's first remark after the verse recognized his client's intent, his apparent decisiveness about the troubles:

Man, you know it. Maybe you have even been looking yourself [that is, divining before coming to this seance and thus being one who "sought his own" and "found it"].

It was as if Rra Mafaya did not have to put into words what it was all about, because it was already known to the man himself. Their activity in the seance was thus that of confirmation, more than anything else.

To make sure the client and patient could see for themselves that the reading of the tablets was right, Rra Mafaya then pointed out each of them by name and according to whether they were "going" or not. Next, continuing with the Tortoise set, he announced:

They come [B] *Selomi*, "Biter." Biter grasps a person of the night. And it is a sorcerer who is in the home according to Inner Circle [again reciting the earlier verse].

The second set of tablets qualified the first, in Rra Mafaya's inter-pretation. Given the orientation toward *space* and home in the first imagery, the second disclosed *time* and the danger of the night from the aggression of the Biter. The initial ambiguity in the poetics was resolved through further verse; and the client's suspicion about inaus-piciousness was confirmed. There was an occult attack, and it was by means of sorcery.

At this point, Rra Mafaya pursued this confirmation by focusing everyone's attention upon iconic and indexical aspects of certain dice. He began with the boars as doctors:

Now, with this boy of yours, it is dark for him. You see them, they make darkness. As he is, sometimes his eyes would seem to be getting dark, and then they would return to sight. It is as if the person gets dark and then his mind too gets choked in there. Again and again. As you see this one and this one and this one [pointing to three boars], they are saying the same words just as they follow one another in order, *rulagana.*

The dice, he stressed, were face down, thus icons of darkness, and they were indicating a file, "following one another in order," *rulagana.* The indexical aspect was the lining up, the visual indication of unanim-ity among the doctors. The iconic was the embodiment of the subject of their unanimity, as someone forced to face down with loss of sight. There were, of course, other allies, besides the boars, such as the antelope and the stembuck, and they were a disorderly bunch, a fact to be recognized and dealt with later. In this way, having unfolded the orientation in space (home) and time (the night) with its danger (sorcery), Rra Mafaya disclosed the condition of the person as the subject himself in darkness of mind.

For corroboration of the location of sorcery, Rra Mafaya pointed out a possibility that did not occur in the tablets, namely an excluded fall, (B G) *Morupi,* "Tramper":

But now he is being worked against [by sorcery] at home, right at home. Tramper [B G] is the one for which we would say that this person is being worked upon away from home, in the bush.

Earlier, the interpretation of the tablets, from Inner Circle to Biter, was grounded in presence. Here, the appeal to reasoning by absence gave further support to the recognized orientation toward home. Hav-

ing (B) *Selomi,* Biter, alone and not in combination with (G), as in
Tramper, meant a nearby, home location for the sorcery.

To go further, and be more specific, with symptoms appropriate
for a mode of attack with sorcery, Rra Mafaya turned once more from
the tablets to the dice. This time the indices were other pairs of allies,
the antelope and the stembuck. After he named and indicated each, he
got both the client and the patient to look closely at the dice bunching
together around the Young Man of the Tortoise set:

This one then pushes these. It says, "You go on." Now this one sends back,
and the other one sends back, too. It means that he [the patient] once vomited,
and that he had eaten some meat according to this lot which is a stembuck.

Having established and confirmed the location and the nature of
the occult attack, Rra Mafaya specified the mode of sorcery and its
immediate symptoms, poisoned meat and vomiting. He found his
evidence, which was indexical and iconic, in the bunched spatial pattern
of dice that, as allies, are critically associated with the patient's welfare.
If we consider his earlier and present remarks on allies (boars first, then
stembuck and antelope), we see that he explained both *order (rulagana,*
the following on of the boars) and *disorder* (the bunching of the stembuck and antelope) as evidence in support of his interpretation.

With this specific conclusion, he completed his opening interpretation for the free fall from the bag and directed the patient how to throw
the lots.

Divine with them, taking off one shoe [from the right foot, the right leg being
the outstretched one]. We don't kill anyone [that is, don't be fearful]. Hold
them with both hands. You have to hold them like this, my child, and blow
on them like this, "Whew." Say, "Yes, I am divining for myself to find out
what bothers me."

The patient repeated his words: "Yes, I am divining for myself to
see what is bothering me."

Rra Mafaya directed further: "Throw them down. Right, right,
you have thrown them well."

This time Rra Mafaya began with the dice before the tablets,
moving in his interpretation from the indexical to the symbolic, from
the microdramatics to the poetics, and thus reversing his opening
method for the initial free fall. He commented upon the allies, the god
and the boar, first. Here, as throughout the seance, the patient spoke
only when instructed what to say; otherwise his response was nonver-

bal. After questions, the patient and the diviner exchanged knowing looks, which the diviner took for assent.

You see the god [ant-bear] don't you? There is the god somewhat aside. Here is the boar; it comes *kgaranyane* [on its back]. Now these lots are hard. You see, these are all dishes, which means that while he is sitting down his mind gets dark, just as you see them doing this [lying on their backs, as though unconscious].

This confirmed the earlier interpretation of darkness in the patient's mind, and Rra Mafaya continued:

To your face I say, your eyes get dark. Isn't it so? Your mind gets black? Sometimes, it would seem like starting up and then it would go black and seem to be starting up again. Now you see these boars fleeing and staying on the other side, while they are *kgaranyane* [on their backs], and they say . . . [here reciting the praise for *kgaranyane*, as given above]. They are the doctors who are like that.

Next Rra Mafaya pointed to the most powerful of the allies, the god:

The god [ant bear] is that one over there that goes by the edge of the village [its location signifies avoiding the inner area of the others]. It is his grandfather who ought to have been here and through whom he would get up when he was in difficulty.

According to Rra Mafaya's interpretation of the microdramatics, the dice exhibited the scene in which the patient was helpless victim. The helplessness was due to the withdrawal, from a proper place at the center of the home, of his dead grandfather's protection. The god was the dead grandfather. This interpretation explained the effectiveness of the sorcery; it was due to a lack of protection from the dead that ought to have been immediately surrounding the living.

Rra Mafaya completed his reading of this fall with his verse and commentary, regarding the tablets in reverse order, from the junior Tortoise to the senior Elephant. He pointed first to the Old Woman of the Tortoise:

Now, as you see, those of the Tortoise come [W] *Thwagadima*, "Bursting Flash" [a metaphor for lightning, a sunray, a spray of blood]. This is the Old Woman [W], *Pubagadi*.

He recited the praise poetry:

They are *Thwagadima,* child of the disperser of *koma* [the life secret taught at initiation], of the east. But that of the east is all right; it is better, for the patient basks in the sun's rays in the way that you see it facing.

Instead of death, facing the setting sun, Rra Mafaya found the meaning to be life, facing the rising sun. But he carried his more auspicious evaluation no further. Instead, he interrupted himself suddenly, and turned from the verse to the metaphor for the fall, *Thwagadima.* With an exclamation about a further attack by sorcery, he went back to confirming his initial interpretation. Once again, he echoed his initial theme of home and the nearby, reiterating his plain statement of the meaning of the first ambiguous verse.

Aha, so he was once sprayed with blood, this child! And if he wasn't sprayed with blood, he must have been burnt with lightning, according to this [W] Bursting Flash. It is just as they said [in the first fall from the bag, and he here repeated part of the verse for Inner Circle], "A thing of Inner Circle is not far, it is like the little sheddings of *pika* snake skin." That means it [the source of the trouble] is near, in the home. It does not pursue him from the bush.

At this point, Rra Mafaya pointed to the senior, Elephant, tablets and, somewhat more fully than earlier, recited the appropriate verse in their praises.

You see these that come [M B G]? They say, "Carver of the father's sister's hoe handle." They say, "Carve it long." They say, "The father's sister is a reckless plower, even beyond the river she plows."

This outcome was problematic. It could be taken to identify the agent of the occult attack, in as much as the location, the nature, the mode, and the precondition (withdrawal of ancestral protection) of the occult attack had already been seen. Here Rra Mafaya had to address the sensitive issue to which he had been leading: who was the sorcerer? His answer put into words the sense he, his client, and his patient all had of something troublesome and dangerous:

These are falls we do not know [cannot quite understand], because these make people to be at odds with each other *[lothanya].* Yes, for if it were *medimo* [divinities, ancestral wrath], we could say it was due to his father's sister. But this is sorcery, according to [B] Biter [the first fall]. Now that is why we cannot say it is due to the father's sister, for even the doctors fear and flee that.

Even you yourself, you fear her, this woman they speak of. Yes, you point at her with a finger and you say, "This one is not here" [she is not what she seems to be, and not right]. You say so, and these doctor lots say so too, that she is a treacherous person, yes, the very one that you point at and say, "Actually, this one is not here." When they say this, they mean a person who kills other people.

This outcome of the Elephant tablets required him, if he was to sustain the earlier interpretation of sorcery, to reason against an alternative possibility. Was the patient's affliction caused, after all, by *medimo,* by divinities of the dead, and by ancestral wrath? Against that, Rra Mafaya recalled earlier evidence from other tablets, and then pointed once more to the indication of important dice. The connection to the first fall of the Tortoise tablets from the bag, (B) Biter, was his first evidence. His second was the fear of treachery indicated in the dice by the apparent flight of the allies, the doctors.

Still pointing to the doctors, Rra Mafaya went on to spell out the significance for the patient of the way the doctors were lying.

As for this child [the patient], even at home in the village, [sorcery] traps have been set for him, for they are like this. Little pits have been dug and dug in the yard, even in the gateway of the yard, these little pits. Now, when he sees them his heart is not glad. Yes, when he merely glances at them, his heart gets broken.

The indications of sorcery were taken to be cumulative and overwhelming. But a final confirmation was needed. Having voiced the suspicion of the father's sister along with the doubts about it, Rra Mafaya directed the patient to put the suspicion to a test, with a question as a hypothesis for the lots. The patient was to throw for the last time:

What will we do then, man? Well, take them, have them [the lots]. Such a young child having sorcery worked against him as if he were an elder! Do this: "Whew [blow]," and say, "Yes, it is the father's sister who works on me. Let me see whether she is the one who works on me, my father's sister."

The patient threw for the second time and repeated these words after Rra Mafaya. Rra Mafaya's method for this last fall was the same as for the first free fall, proceeding from the tablets to the doctors among the dice, from poetics to microdramatics. He remarked:

You throw them in a manly way. I like a boy who does that. Now about this woman, she also has a dead husband. They say, "You woman, when dishing out you do dish out, but you spoil by many talks. You spoil by talking." It says, "Scratching out and scratching out, of the talks. She did not take them from the ground, she took them from her mother."

The praise Rra Mafaya recited first was for the one new outcome in the tablets, (G), *Lethake* (Reed). It is also known as *Lengwane* (Small Tongue or Uvula), and it is associated with a clicking sound of complaint. The other outcome, (B) Biter, he recalled immediately, was the same as the one from the bag, upon which he grounded the sorcery accusation from the start. In his brief comment, he stressed, "That is a widow," and turned immediately to the other tablets: "They are still beating on the same (B) Biter of the bag (the outcome in the free fall)."

Next Rra Mafaya indicated the doctors' dice, named, and then praised them in the verse for Sinew, *Mosifi* (see above, in the section "Microdramatics, Body Icons, and Indices," where I give the verse for the left side of the doctors' dice). Then he called attention to the doctors' being in disarray.

You see, it is only *diphapaŋnya,* [having things at cross purposes, having things in different directions]. Now you are made to be coming in trials *[meleko,* "ordeals"] wherever you go. These are hard words which call for people to sit down and talk about them.

This led Rra Mafaya to a final homily for the patient's benefit and an unanswered question about the motive for sorcery:

A man should work hard when he goes to work, and not play about. But the way I understand you to tell it, it is merely playing about [the patient was unable to stay for long at any job, and did not earn or save well]. These are hard words. The person who works on him does not have a husband, and is a widow. But I do not know why she is killing your child. Yet they come, [G] Reed, which says, "Mother of reeds." They say, "You woman, dishing out you do dish out."

This was the last throw by the patient, and it brought the main part of the consultation to an end. Rra Mafaya did not attempt to resolve all the issues or concerns that had been raised. It was enough, for immediate purposes of protective treatment, to have identified the location of an agent and mode of sorcery, without trying to find out a motive. What remained was for Rra Mafaya to end the seance with a confirming throw of his own, using all the lots as in the beginning.

While stacking the lots with rapid expertise, Rra Mafaya put the final request, threw the lots, and gave his conclusion:

Yes, let us see. We are no longer to say, "Who is she?" for I have seen that it is this enemy of the night. She is the one who works on this person [repeating for emphasis]. It says, "Yes." Both of them say so. They are [M W G] Great Circle.

Again to make certain his client and patient could see the pattern for themselves, he indicated the lots by name and by movement—by their coming and going in relation to each other—first the tablets, next the dice, and then in turn, the doctors, the lion, the hyena, and the leopard. Rra Mafaya continued:

If he is to be treated, I would say that he has to be treated over there [in the direction pointed to by the Old Man of the senior tablets], according to the *Moremogolo* [Old Man] and this one. And these people's huts—I mean the very people who work on this child—are in that direction [east] when you point to them.

After removing the tablets, he threw the dice until each in turn reached the position of the rest, and he concluded:

We have seen he has to be treated to become all right. We have seen through this Sinew which says, "You must roast a boar cleverly." It comes *Kgaranyane*. It is this woman who works on this child.

Rra Mafaya collected all the lots, put them and then his bitter herb into the bag, closed and tied it, and asked for his fee. This ended the seance insofar as that was focused around the lots. It did not end the meeting of client, patient, and doctor, however.

Although it takes me somewhat beyond my main interest in personal orientation and the dynamics of divination, I want, primarily for the sake of a better ethnographic record, to report the rest of the occasion very briefly. This highlights, among other things, how far the seance was regarded as a step leading to the use of magic and ritual for wealth and success in business.

The patient's father, who had remained silent during the seance, now agreed with Rra Mafaya, "Truly, sir, it is just as you report, 'When you come for things, you seem to be coming for trials.' Yes, that is so." He went on to ask the amount of Rra Mafaya's fee, after explaining that he would have liked to leave his son for longer treatment, had his son not needed to return to work in town.

There was something improper, Rra Mafaya felt, about the question of the fee, as if Rra Mafaya would take advantage and raise it from the amount charged for a past seance for the client. Rra Mafaya stood on his professional dignity in reply, and then asked about the treatment:

I divine in only one way, and I do not change my fee. I am not a crook. But what is the matter that that person works sorcery so much and so often? Now, what do you want done about him [the patient], sir?

The client answered, "I want to give him good fortune [ditshego fatso]." He wanted the boy's body treated.

In carrying out the body treatment with various substances and a lit candle, Rra Mafaya chanted:

A cow with a calf, a goat with a kid, a person with a child, five pounds, twenty pounds, a hundred pounds. He will get it, and laugh and laugh. Each and everyone will laugh and laugh with him, seeing him at work. I will give him this.

After the body treatment (especially around the ankle, knee, and neck joints, as well as a cross from the forehead to the rest of the head) and the payment of his fee for divining (two and a half shillings), plus a preliminary fee for opening his medicines (two and a half pounds, actually five rand), Rra Mafaya told the client that with the treatment:

. . . your son should live and grow old while you are still alive to see him. This only makes wealth, business [papadi]. You must advise him, "When you have collected things, you should bring them here, my son. You must not merely consume."

The full fee for the treatment was payable in the future, he explained, when the youth was pleased and successful, and then too a goat could be used:

He will have to meet with its blood, its chyme, and the tip of its heart to prevent these sorcerers. That is all right now. You will see that you will say, "When I took my child to that old man he helped him."

THE DISCOURSE OF THE SEANCE IN REVIEW

A review of the seance as discourse illuminates its main course. Throughout the seance, the collusion of the client and the patient with the diviner was largely nonverbal. The diviner put interpretations into words, indicated the visual exhibitions of the lots, and directed the patient what to say himself. Under the diviner's direction most of the lots, especially the enemies of the night, such as the lion, leopard, and hyena, were disregarded. The greatest attention was paid to the doctors, and thus the doctor–patient relationship; the seance was a preliminary to ritual treatment by the diviner as doctor.

The diviner began with the poetics of verse for the sake of locating the social space and time of affliction. He used the symbolic in metaphor and verse to open core themes about home and one's own, and about sorcery and the occult attack of the night, which he later developed repeatedly throughout the seance. The first and free fall from the bag, Inner Circle on the senior tablets, was the one to which he gave the greatest weight for the location of his patient's personal predicament. It is important to recognize that the core theme here, like virtually all the others in this diviner's practice, was standard for its tablet outcome from seance to seance. This was usual in other diviners' practice as well.

I observed more than a dozen of Rra Mafaya's seances that had Inner Circle as an outcome and, because of this outcome, something about intimates and intimacy was consistently in the foreground of his interpretation. What this diviner varied from seance to seance was the evaluation of the theme, and not its content. His choice was between good and bad, between auspicious and inauspicious, and between the laughter of thankful rejoicing, when "turtles are crying in the water, for rain is due to arrive," and the laughter of "a clever person with white teeth that kill while laughing." Here the evaluation he understood, and later made plain, was negative and adverse; the laughter was the laughter of cunning by which an intimate who is actually an enemy dissembles love or friendship when appearing to laugh with you.

When it came to confirming the significance of the other tablets in the first fall, showing Biter, he reasoned from the negative to the positive, from the absence of Tramper to the presence of Biter. He used the selective method of proof from exclusion. In this method of interpretation, a hypothesis about actual occurrence is put, and confirmed, by highly selective allusion to one among the many excluded outcomes (on the use of such hypothetical and excluded outcomes in diviners' reasoning, see Werbner 1973).

The diviner was concerned, from the very start, with finding confirmation of a suspicion that he felt the patient already knew to be true. Linked to that was his concern with establishing the continuity of significance. Both of these concerns were evident in his orderly, sequential method of constructing the interpretation, from disclosing the spatial and temporal location of the occult attack, to declaring, in turn, its nature, its mode, its immediate symptoms and, finally, its personal agent.

Once the diviner turned from the poetics to the microdramatics, he made plain the exhibition of an an image of *rulagana,* "following in order," i.e., "being organized together." This he did by pointing out how certain dice, the doctors among the allies, that had fallen somewhat in single file, indicated *rulagana,* "following in order." But rather than ignoring disorder, he later recognized it and explained it as an aspect of the patient's predicament. A later presentation of disorder in the scene among the allies, including the doctors with the god, was thus a proof, rather than a contradiction of his interpretation. The god and the boar were said to be those who should protect the patient, that is his dead grandfather (or any ancestor) and his doctors respectively. Yet, bunched up and overturned, they were so disposed that they could not, or would not, help him. Here the diviner challenged the patient to recognize the concrete representation of the unstable states of the patient's own mind.

Viewed as a whole, the course of the diviner's interpretation was first from poetics to microdramatics, then for the patient's own first throw, the reverse and, finally, in the patient's last throw, back to the start, from poetics to microdramatics. It was also a course according to a hierarchy of authority, starting with the most authoritative lots at the top and moving downward, and then the reverse, and finally again back to the first move, from the top downward. The course of interpretation, like the procedure for excluding dice, was thus highly methodical and authoritative, yet selective, idiosyncratic, and made for the occasion.

CONCLUSION

In Northern Tswapong wisdom divination, lots as the moving parts of friendly or hostile creatures are seen and said to be subjects, not mere objects. What they are expected to disclose, above all, are the hidden characteristics of subjects, their true intent as friends or enemies, their unacknowledged motives, their real force, and power in practice. Each fall of the lots exhibits a microdramatic scene of friends and enemies. It is up to the diviner in his wisdom to get people to see the scene selectively, with regard for a certain foreground or disregard for a particular background. The diviner also is the one to create the poetics of wisdom divination by drawing upon a repertoire of verse and metaphor for each fall.

A double transformation usually takes place, both in knowledge and in experience. On the one hand, the seance moves as a search toward the definition of a plan of, and for, action. On the other hand, the seance also involves a change in the client's or patient's initial impressions that the elaborateness of the lots presents a somewhat baffling complexity. Formally, this impression yields to an impression of simplicity and then intelligible complexity. The use of the lots for nonverbal communication gives a direct knowledge of complexity, of a type that is concretely embodied in the moving parts of other creatures and, thus, manifested as something external to the subjects themselves. The *overcoming* of complexity in their own subjectivity is exhibited and experienced. It is typical of wisdom divination that, apart from the play of imagery or words in puns, it comes without anti-rites (Douglas 1968), pranks, jokes, or play. Hence, there is a recognition of an orderly transformation in experience, the sense of finding a way methodically through some maze, that helps to underwrite the authority of wisdom divination in the face of the intuitive and irregular actualities of the interpretive process.

Pierce's distinction between the symbolic, the iconic, and the indexical enables us to appreciate wisdom divination as ritual performance with its own signifying practice. Wisdom divination is informed by binary oppositions, dichotomous discriminations, and taxonomic classifications. It is, nevertheless, a cultural means for specific, highly contextualized, personal perception, and not merely a means for the conventional recognition of life situations. The interpretations that diviners reach with their clients bring together the archaic and the contemporary, the microdramatic and the poetic, the everyday and the extraordinary. Thus our account of the discourse in wisdom divination illuminates the progression from moment to moment in the people's quest for powerful knowledge of the hidden realities in their lives.

ACKNOWLEDGMENT

I wish to thank the University of Manchester and the Economic and Social Studies Research Council (formerly SSRC) for leave and research funds, which enabled me to study Northern Tswapong. I am grateful also to the Northern Tswapong diviners and their clients from

GoMoremi and its surrounding villages who kindly allowed me to make tape recordings and photographs of their consultations.

At the invitation of the Catholic University of Leuven, I first wrote this chapter as a public lecture; and I am grateful to colleagues at the Catholic University, especially Rene Devisch, for their helpful comments.

CHAPTER 2

KALANGA
DEMONIC POSSESSION

The Cultural Reconstruction
of a Domestic Domain

INTRODUCTION

In ritual for purification and healing, the movement from disorder to order requires boundary crossing. This is often accomplished by figures from beyond a community's moral universe who are tricksters or clownlike. They may be wild, obscene, and sexually licentious; they often are transvestite, and somehow the epitome of an authority alternative to that paramount within the community. Nevertheless, the figures do not merely dramatize disorder. In ritual performance, as go-betweens come from afar, they are agents of change, of purification, and healing. They serve as a means for directing sacred exchange across the community's moral universe. They expel evil, manifested as disease or other affliction, away from the community, toward their own place outside it; and in place of evil, they bring good within the community.

Their boundary crossing, while powerful, is dangerous, and these trickster figures are sometimes violent or out of control, and physically attack people around them. At the same time, the figures or their performers are, in some senses, victims and objects of ridicule and indignity. The performers themselves are characteristically not men in the prime of life, nor are they esteemed, prestigious, or dominant. Commonly, they are the afflicted, the poor, minors, or women. It is characteristic also that for their services they demand symbolic gifts, which are lavished upon them with generosity, the lavish giving in itself constituting merit and good within the community. Through their performance, ordeals are created, the passing of which gives members of the community around the wild or alien figures a sense of having moved toward a higher plane of existence. Here, the unclean is the purifier; the transgressor of moral norms, the agent of moral renewal; the victim, the victimizer; the predator, the agent of sacrifice. In brief, this is one of those archetypal configurations of ritual practice in which the antitheses of everyday life are transcended.

A brief example is helpful. At the turn of this century, in the midst of accounts of numerous other Great Feast masquerades of Moroccan Arabs, Westermark recorded this ritual:

A man . . . dresses himself up in six bloody skins of sacrificed sheep. . . . He is called . . . "the lion with sheepskins." He is generally a person who suffers from some illness, since he is supposed to be cured by the holiness of the bloody skins. Two other men disguise themselves as women, covering up their faces with the exception of their eyes; they are . . . the wives of [the lion]. . . . The [lion] beats with the skins on his arms everybody who comes within his reach; there is *baraka,* "holiness," in this beating, and hence sick people are anxious to approach him. He likewise beats the tents so as to give them also the benefit of his *baraka.* His two wives dance and cry out *"kra', kra',"* in order to induce the inhabitants of the tents to give them a foot *[kra']* of their sheep; and they get what they want, there being merit in such a gift. The [lion] also dances, imitating the roaring of a real lion, and behaves most indecently before the public, pretending to have sexual intercourse with his wives; while the accompanying bachelors from time to time discharge volleys of gunpowder. . . . Before the morning [they] have a feast on the food given them. On the second day after supper one of the bachelors is dressed up as a Jew. . . . Two other bachelors make a camel. . . . The Jew leads the camel by a rope tied round its neck, and thus they walk, like the party on the evening before, from tent to tent in their own and neigbouring villages, accompanied by unmarried men and boys, the Jew asking for fodder for his camel and the people giving him eggs. He is addressed as the . . . "chief of the strips of dried meat." [(1926) 1968:136–37]

Westermark goes on to describe the successive evening tours the Jew makes with other steeds, first a "little she-mule," then a "leopard," ending with several tugs of war in which the sexes are opposed.

The archetypal configuration, which this example illustrates, is most familiar and best described for carnivals or festivals. It is somewhat less well understood for rituals of purification and healing in domestic life, the rituals that are my main concern in this chapter.

Below, in Chapter 4, I return to the subject of transcendence in public festivals, where I look at masquerade in a New Guinea Lowlands festival. First, I want to prepare the way for that by bringing into focus dimensions of domestic ritual practice that ritual is often said to obliterate, namely the idiosyncratic, the personal, and the life historic.

POSSESSION RITUAL
AND THE RECONSTRUCTION OF SOCIAL REALITY

This present chapter is about the reconstruction of social reality during Kalanga demonic possession ritual. In the course of the ritual, boundaries between domains, such as that between the domestic and the alien and wild, are crossed by possessed women, for the sake of purification and healing, both of the women themselves and their patients. The possessed Kalanga women, while mediating between domains, also act as mediators in interpersonal relations. They give their ritual services for intimates who want benevolence and trust among themselves renewed. Kalanga perform the demonic possession ritual in their rural homes, never in town, and it is only certain women, specially associated with home and domestic life, who can be possessed.

My ethnography comes from my long-term and repeated study of Kalanga living in eastern Botswana and western Zimbabwe. I began my study in the course of fifteen months' fieldwork in the low-veld of western Zimbabwe during 1960–61, and continued the fieldwork in the high-veld of eastern Botswana for the following periods: 1964–65, fifteen months; 1969, three months; 1974, one month; 1977–78, two months; 1985, three weeks. I also met some Kalanga briefly during my research among Tswapong in the middle-veld of the Central District of Botswana in 1972–73 (fifteen months) and 1978 (two months). In my initial fieldwork in Zimbabwe my assistant was, first, Saul Gwakuba Ndlovu, and later, Timon Mongwa. Since then, they have encouraged me with their lasting friendship, and I am most grateful to them and the many Kalanga who helped me so generously during my research.

I put my argument forward in several stages. The introduction presents a context for ritual performance in certain activities and social spaces of domestic life. It is a historical context, in which, I suggest, the use of demonic ritual in response to recognized danger in the import of alien things, in commodity relations, and in labor migration is culturally creative. This suggestion leads me to consider the link Kalanga make between the image of the demonic and the nature of trade and exchange. It also raises questions about the definition of domains, about the domestic in relation to the public, and about the alien and wild.

In trying to answer these questions, I find I have to discuss methodological and theoretical difficulties in the making of my account. This is a reflexive stage in my argument. It enables me to show how dual mediation—mediation both of domains and of interpersonal relations—influences the selection of elite women for the possessed. The next stage is a phase-by-phase description, with texts and performers' commentaries on songs and dances, followed by a holistic, transformational analysis of the entire ritual. Here I give the basic terms of what I call the key idea of the ritual. In this transformational analysis I pay close attention to the shifts between the main phases and the interludes, between the use of substances and the use of words, song, and dance, and between the formalized and the improvised, the ahistoric and the historic. My aim is a better appreciation of the effectiveness of ritual. I argue that a view of strategic action is essential, and I substantiate my own view with an actual case—that of a woman at home from labor migration who both sponsors demonic possession and makes a sorcery accusation. Finally, I account for a change against the recruitment of young women to be the possessed.

Many Kalanga, especially young men but some women also, spend long periods in distant places, working as labor migrants away from home. Labor migration in some form or another has been a fact of Kalanga life since the late nineteenth century. Yet it is at home in the countryside that Kalanga have largely continued to try to produce most of the subsistence for their families. They do so under conditions dominated by considerable risk of drought. They rely upon a mixed economy of agriculture and stock-keeping, primarily of cattle and goats.

Kalanga Homesteads and Social Spaces

Kalanga live in clusters of homesteads alongside their fields and pastures within densely settled neighborhoods. Their settlements are scattered throughout the numerous, narrow river valleys of the high-veld (concerning Kalanga neighborhoods, see Werbner 1975, 1982b). Apart from newly established administrative headquarters, Kalanga do not live in centralized or nucleated villages, as among Tswana elsewhere in Botswana (see Chapter 1).

Each Kalanga homestead is a bounded social space. It is usually fenced. It is also ritually demarcated, sometimes with magically treated pegs for protection. Its social boundaries are always acknowledged by outsiders who, in the etiquette of entry and exit, announce, "*Ndapi-*

nda," "I am passing," before coming in, and *"Musale,"* "You remain," upon leaving. Yet, ideally, the homestead is not self-contained. A woman should come to her husband's homestead in marriage. Marriage is virilocal between and never within homesteads. The expressed prescription is against marriage with known relatives, whether of the person's own clan or patrilineal group or of any one matrilaterally linked to oneself.

Kalanga homesteads have a regular layout, marked by conventional social contours. Opposed along an east–west axis are domestic and public domains. (The north–south axis is for a senior to junior house opposition, right and left of the head of the homestead who is himself located in the middle.) The usual space for distinctive activities associated with the public domain is in the front, to the west; the space for activities associated with the domestic domain is in the rear, to the east. At one extreme, within the domain of public space, are the pens for domestic animals (where men may urinate). This is the space allocated for major resources that can be used for long-term investment and for exchange relations such as bridewealth transactions. At the other extreme, in the east, within the space reserved for the domestic domain, the layout is granaries, at the very back of the homestead, and then kitchens, in front of the granaries. The resources stored here may also be used for exchange, but they are not primarily for long-term investment. This is, above all, a space for distribution and consumption. The granaries are not regarded as a place to store grain for sale, except if processed in the form of beer; grain for sale preferably comes from the field, directly after an abundant harvest, and is not stored. In this representation, the distribution and consumption of the domestic domain are in opposition to sale and commodity relations. Also to the east, immediately behind the domestic space, is the direction for waste and "dirt" (women may urinate behind the granaries). It is here that ash and rubbish ought to be thrown, and beyond that is the area where one is expected to defecate.

From this spatial arrangement, it can be seen that an ideological inequality between domains is realized as a taken-for-granted feature of existence in the home setting of everyday life. This superiority of the public over the domestic, and their relation to the wild and the alien, is illustrated by the following directional scheme, from front to back:

FRONT ————————————————— BACK
Public ———————— Domestic ——————— Wild and alien
Investment ———————— Subsistence ——————— Waste
Distribution

Demonic possession begins with a contrary movement, from back to front. It is from the east, where demons dwell, to the west, toward the direction of the divinities of the dead. The movement oscillates, in successive rites, until the demons are returned back eastward from where they came. In no rite, however, does the demonic ritual reach the front of the homestead, the location of the pens for domestic herds. The herds and the Lions, being prey and predator, are of course antithetical. Overcoming danger is thus a transfer backwards. Symbolically it is getting the Lion to put "dirt" where, in the intrinsic order of things, "dirt" belongs, behind and outside. Such movement has an ideological force, of course, in favor of the public domain. The danger to the domestic domain, to subsistence and virtuous sharing, is not represented as coming from the public domain, or from investment. Instead, it is imaged as coming from waste and commodity relations, from beyond and behind both domains, and more immediately, from beyond and behind the domestic domain.

The "Go-Between" and Sacred Exchange

The possessed woman (a "host," in my terms) is a ritual vehicle for making beneficial change in the conditions of divinities and people. She is a ritual vehicle of a distinct kind, however. As an active consumer not only of food but also of alien trade luxuries, such as beads and blankets, she is a "go-between in sacred exchange." The go-between in sacred exchange moves between domains and realms as a whole living being. In the host's case, she moves between the domestic and the alien and wild domains, and the realms of the human and the divine. The things to be exchanged are taken on the body from the space of one domain to that of another. The go-between carries them in and around her own body.

A host is spoken of as *shumba*, "Lion." I must stress that she is a Lion with a distinctive guise. The host wears a mane *(ngala,* "crown") of white and black trade beads around her forehead. The cover around her body is a strikingly designed mantle of printed, store-bought cloth, red and black (or blue) on a white background. Sometimes it is screen-printed with geometric patterns and, usually, with lions or cocks and a surrounding design.

The ritual's core image of Lion, of the wild and the alien, the powerfully dangerous, is thus created with imported trade goods. The Lion represents a vision, an embodiment of consciousness, that contests the matter-of-fact and taken-for-granted character of commodity relations. The imagery is empowered by the conjunction of both a threat to domestic life and also its counteraction.

Figure 10. Kalanga Hosts of Mazenge *Demons. Wrapped in a red, white, and blue printed shawl, one host, now deceased, wears the beaded frills as a crown or Lion's mane around her head. On her daughter's shawls are the lion motif and the words "The British Lion."*

The imported trade beads and the mantle that a host wears characterize her as a focus of social exchange. The mantle is a trade cloth, called a *kangol*. It is worn by women as a special adornment, an imported luxury like the beads, throughout a wide area extending to East Africa. I would speculate that the ritual of demonic possession in its current form was associated with eighteenth- or nineteenth-century trade.

I tentatively propose that the ritual of demonic possession arose when Kalanga defended their domestic domain by using anti-mercantilist imagery to contest mercantilist capitalism. In the ritual, Kalanga gave expression to their consciousness of a threat from without. Their ritual defense of a domestic domain, and thus the cultural force of demonic possession, has taken on renewed importance in the context of widespread labor migration and industrial capitalism, for it continues to create a vision of the disorder and the alien danger in commodity relations.

The overcoming of danger to the domestic domain is aptly imaged by imported luxury goods, once they become objects of sacred exchange. As trade goods, they objectify involvement in commodity relations that threaten the provisioning of food and the production upon which the domestic domain is based. But as gifts removed from commodity relations, and given in return for ritual services, they are a counteraction against that threat, for they are a symbolic earnest of commitment in and to domestic life. Sacred exchange converts the commodities into gifts within a "good-faith economy" (Bourdieu 1977), and thus the ritual process works upon the imported danger and makes it domesticated.

Of course, sacred exchange is a process in history. During Kalanga demonic possession, the sacred exchange is completed through the giving of commodities. Trade beads and trade cloths are imported, wrapped around a possessed woman's body, and given the significance of lionness. But these gifts costuming the possessed in the ritual guise of the bull-lion embody alienness and wildness in a way that is neither static nor timeless. It is an image of the dangerous transgression of a world inside by the outside, in a context that is historically specific, recognizably so in the people's own eyes, and not merely in mine.

Such sacred exchange is important, because it is an active remaking of history. In the case of Kalanga demonic possession, where sacred exchange converts commodities into gifts, the process advances what may be called decommoditization. It is the reverse of what is usually described under the rubric of commoditization and, in Marxist metaphors, as the "penetration of capitalism." Sacred exchange is thus a process by which people remake history in an image of their own. The conversion in sacred exchange is not simply a ritual resistance to the penetration of capitalism. Rather, it is an active remaking of history in which a good-faith economy (Bourdieu 1977) or, more loosely, in Gregory's terms, a "gift economy" (1982) is powerfully extended against forces that threaten to undermine that economy, both morally and materially.

The issue is a general one, and I want to stress its wider importance. Anthropologists with a theoretical interest in the economic dimensions of contemporary transformations are increasingly concerned with decommoditization as a tendency to extend rather than collapse a gift economy (A. Strathern 1979; Gregory 1982; Long 1986).

But decommoditization has yet to be fully appreciated in its semantic dimensions as a process of "semantic conversion." By semantic conversion I mean a process of recreating significance. The commodities turned into gifts cease to be seen as mere things; they are perceived to carry significance for relations between persons and, indeed in some sense, to energize personal relations. It is the social significance of goods that is reworked and revalued by semantic conversion. In my argument, semantic conversion is one of the processes by which people actively protect what they prefer to be the felt qualities of their personal relations, particularly in the domestic domain.

THE KALANGA IMAGE OF THE WILD AND ANIMAL ORDER

The domestic domain that Kalanga defend in possession ritual is centered on women and, as such, it is a domain that men know they cannot and do not fully control. Within it, the authority of women is associated with powerful danger. The danger is an invasion of "dirt" and "rubbish," which belong in the wild and alien; and the means of overcoming that disorder is embodied in women themselves. Possessed, they act playfully and with comic burlesque to bring into the disordered domestic domain the powerful dominator of the wild and alien, the Bull-Lion. Once having used his power for the purpose of healing themselves and their patients, they return the Lion back from where he came. With him should go the affliction troubling them.

It is as though disorder in the domestic domain is order in the wild. But more is done in the ritual, for the sake of a healing restoration of order, than the mere relocation of disorder—the restoration is not simply a removal from the domestic of what belongs in the alien and wild, or a shift of "dirt" as matter-out-of-place to where it properly is in place. Instead, the domestic domain is empowered, for the sake of healing, by the very dominance of the wild; and something from the wild and alien, concretized in ritual goods and substances, remains encompassed within the restored domestic domain.

In performance, women as "healers of the homestead," *nganga (ye nzi,* sing.) or hosts, are figures of gerontocratic authority with occult powers; they become the Bull-Lions, "the Chiefs."[1] *Mazenge,* the alien yet hereditary demons of the wild, possess them. Sometimes, close kinswomen perform together as a band of hosts, organized by seniority.[2] Their patients, like most of their congregation, are their close kin, whether men, women, or children. Minor ills and aches, pains during pregnancy, childlessness, and even loss of employment as a labor migrant are all afflictions that they treat. Their healing is for no exclusive category of physical complaint. Their treatment is primarily not for symptoms, but is, above all, for moral and symbolic conditions, the most important among which are those of pollution and guilty indebtedness for neglect of divinities. (The "demons," *mazenge,* although *not* divinities of the dead, are nevertheless divinities, *midzimu;* on guilty indebtedness in Kalanga cattle sacrifice, see Chapter 3).

As a Bull-Lion, each host is addressed respectfully as "Grandfather" and "Preyer on Meat" *(pondha nyama).* This guise, if wild and male, is also symbolic of gerontocratic authority, the Bull-Lion being supreme and senior, the chief among its kind.[3] For a woman, becoming a Lion is to become wild even in the very scent she gives off. *(Meya,* "soul," is air, smell, or breath.) At initiation her whole body is enveloped in the penetrating musk of a polecat.

During possession, the orientation of her spatial movement toward the wild is east to west and gender-specific, along the main ritual axis of location. At night the host's demon is invoked by name to possess her from the east, from behind. Possessed, and ceasing to be herself, she "falls a Lion" *(wa shumba).* By the end of the ritual, having gone back and forth, between the innermost space of the homestead to the west and the outside to the east, she eventually returns from the east and the wild to become her everyday self, a woman, once more.

The healing movement from disorder to order embodied by demonic ritual has to be understood in the light of Kalanga conceptions of cosmic order. To grasp that we must first unfold what the concept of *laula* means. In Shona, Hannan (1959:257) translates it as "[to] pick out, select (one from many, kind from kind) . . . separate." *Laula* in the form of an abstract noun is *nlao,* "law, commandment, or regulation." Of its multiple meanings, so important for comparisons of law (see the cognate term in Tswana, Schapera 1938:35–36; in Lozi, Gluckman 1955:164), I am concerned only with those that are conceptualized in the ritual.

It is through other creatures, animals and birds, rather than humankind, that *laula* is primarily imaged during demonic possession. Carnivores such as the lion and leopard, termed *zwibanda,* are animals that "pick out and separate." They rule by ravishing and preying on others. They are associated with chiefship, as is *nlao* in its many senses (outside the ritual, a chief is known proverbially as a "snake who can bite his own children"). All these predators are included in demonic ritual along with other ravishers and threats to human subsistence, such as the wild herbivore, the baboon; the intemperate guzzler, the ostrich; and that other pest and danger to crops, the turtle dove.

A second regulator, whose aspects of rule are paired to those of the lion, is recognized in the cult. The complement to the untamed

*Figure 11. Winnowing Grain.
Demonic songs, with verse about
giving the bran without the chaff,
allude to this and other domestic
acts of processing the staple
grains.*

carnivore is the tamed fowl, the cock. The cock announces the time of
day, especially the new day. Its crowing at dawn, when there is hunger
and the children of the household must be fed, is the aspect that cult
chants *(zvihila)* make most explicit:

> It cried.
> It cried, vainly, the cock of my child.
> It cried, "*kokorigori*."
> You remain with this child of mine.
> You give her chaff.
> The chaff without the bran.

The cock rules the ritual temporally, for before the cock crows the
Lions' dancing of the night must cease. The host, when leading a solo,
regulates the rhythm (also spoken of as *laula*) by rattling a gourd that
is symbolic of the chief's or elder's staff.

To understand the demonic itself, we must turn to the condensed
epithets of *mazenge*. Their meanings are expanded in the acts, images,

and metaphors of the ritual. The epithets convey remoteness and contrariness, and the paradoxical purpose of the demons. From a distant grassland near plentiful water, where they eat their prey without want, the demons come in order to deceive or mock *(tsetse)* "cramping, oppression, pinching." The epithets are:

Crushers of Flesh	*Pondha Nyama*
They of the Great River	*Baka Gwizi Lukulu*
They prey at the	
Great Umbrella Thorn Tree	*Banodja ku Mpumbu*
Of snatching	
without shortcoming	*Ya hweze usinga pelevule*
They came from far, far	*Bakadha kule, kule*
They should mock cramping	*Baka tsetse mana.*

The ritual includes a developed but unresolved ambiguity. The use of an infinitive—*mana*, "to cramp" or "oppress,"—in the last epithet allows it to mean that they should mock vice, but also that they should deceive to be vicious, they are tricksters.

In afflicting people, the demons are not bound to act according to specific rules or ethics, for they are capricious. Their demonic order represents disproportion, rapacity, and chaos for mankind. It is in their nature to act according to *lunya,* "peevishness, spite, and antipathy to children" (Hannan 1959:548). They are attracted to "dirt" and pollution. A derangement of domestic morality is imaged in their viciousness and contrariness. For this reason, among others, a woman, while possessed, may sing of herself as "carrying an evil" *(senga mbimbi).* During her dances, her chants are complaints about suffering from neglect, from old age, from the meanness of relatives, from their mocking, backbiting, and ingratitude.

The demonic host is a "Lionized" person and, as such, a predator in pursuit of other animals. Even from afar, a lion knows the internal condition of prey by the scent of dung. The "dirt" of prey attracts the lion. So too the host, as Lion, must reveal and treat that which cannot be seen, but is known from the "dirt" *(shamwa)* and "rubbish" *(malala)* in which it is hidden.

The host's treatment is physical, and achieved by the use of herbs that have occult powers. It is also moral, comprising statements and symbolic actions about the underlying conditions for affliction. The host's role is at once powerful and authoritative. While possessed, she digs up certain needed herbs. To have an impact on the demons, these herbs cannot otherwise be effectively obtained. She is expected to feel, and to show that she feels, overcome by awe; in enacting human vices, she enacts the virtues of wild animals. Selfishness and rapacity are, above all, the attributes that she enacts—human vices that cheat and dispossess close relatives of what should be theirs.

Many human vices cause *mazenge* demons to send afflictions: denying relatives the share that they are to "eat" (for example, bride-wealth or slaughter at a feast); failing to feed relatives; not giving them their due from one's earnings; favoring some kin at the expense of others; or stealing a kinsman's wife through adultery. In brief, human vice consists of exacting the lion's share for oneself. In the host's performance such sins are counteracted physically as well as symbolically.

The host is referred to, during possession, as *dombo*, "the go-between,"[5] a sense of the term that is more common in Shona than in Kalanga. The host is the elder who, as go-between, mediates with her own kin on behalf of her affines in their further marital negotiations. In this role the *dombo* is a go-between that has interests on both sides and is expected to have both sets of interests at heart. As a *dombo* associated with the east, and therefore with waste and pollution, the host is expected to speak an eastern language, preferably Venda, and the host usually does use various Venda and Shona words.[6] Kalanga say about Venda, who have a cognate language and culture, that "they are born of us." In their perpetual relationship, Venda are regarded as sister's children of Kalanga, and thus are linked to them through women. The relationship that women mediate in demonic ritual is seen as one established by women themselves. As a cognate society to the east and thus symbolically in-between the domestic and the alien and the wild, the part of mediator is apt for Venda.

In her role as host, a woman loses her own personality temporarily, after a momentary coma. Having become other than herself, she acts in a representative capacity, not a personal one.[7] Her acts are attributed to the demon "come from far, far." His soul, the wind *(pehpo)* and air (breath, smell, *meya*), "arrives" *(svika)* to her, then "goes beyond" and "returns backwards" from where it came.

The host's personal freedom from responsibility is maintained. Although she intercedes and finds a vice or fault, the intervention is the demon's. Moreover, a denial should be a young or junior host's first reply when the innermost congregation tell her that they have called the Lion to appease her afflicting demon. They say,

We called you ourselves. We report suffering to you. We divined and we caught you. It is you who is about to be aroused in [to rise up for] wrath *[munomusila midzimu*, or *munomusila kaba*, *"kaba"* being a term borrowed from Tswana]. That is truly why we are calling you.[8]

To which, one reply is,

It [the wrath] is not mine. It is of those Bachembere [other Kalanga of Shona origin] and of the old [bawumbe, a Shona word], and of great mother.[9]

The demon is an extra-group divinity, in contrast to the divinity of the dead from one's own group; and this externality is a further aspect of the externalization of responsibility for the host's mediation between kin and affines.

ON THE CONSTRUCTION OF MY OWN ACCOUNT

I am aware of two difficulties that have affected the way I construct my account, and I must mention these briefly to enable the reader to evaluate my argument. The first arises because I must make explicit a conceptual framework that, in Kalanga culture, remains implicit. The difficulty is basic in that I have to interpret the understandings of the possessed women themselves. Yet secretiveness and reticence, along with a need to prove and keep confidentiality, are prescribed in the very nature of my study.

For the sake of healing, possessed women have to transgress a culturally defined boundary between the domestic and the wild. In carrying away pollution, "dirt," and "rubbish," they have to act with licensed vulgarity; their performance, which calls for the use of such powerful yet dangerous substances as blood and feces, is bestial in their own eyes as well as in everybody else's. Their own everyday personalities have to be protected from the dangerous implications of their ritual acts. Hence the split is radical between a woman's everyday personality and her demonic role. Even to mention her demonic role to her, when she is not possessed, is to curse a woman. In the case of demonic possession, only during the events can the intended meaning of the events be sought, on a basis of trust, from the main actors in them.

A second difficulty arises because of certain received yet misleading views in the anthropological literature (for a critical review see Yanagisako 1979; and also La Fontaine 1981). It might be argued that virtually everywhere, perhaps apart from hunter-gatherer societies, some distinction between public and domestic domains is made by the people themselves and that virtually everywhere the distinctions have had gender-specific associations (see Ortner 1974; Rosaldo 1974; Yeatman 1984). In saying that, few would doubt that various types of sociality are associated with the public domain. Yet the other side of the distinction, the domestic domain, has seemed less in need of a spectrum of typifications. It has been taken for granted that the domestic domain is universally anchored around mothering, and around facts of procreation, childrearing, or socialization within a family. That, as Yanagisako rightly argues (1979:189, and compare La Fontaine 1981:340), is a mistaken assumption.

The division of the domestic from the public domain is a matter of cultural definition. It has to be considered empirically (Strathern 1980; MacCormack 1980), instance by instance. Only upon that basis can we say with precision which type of sociality is associated with a specific domestic domain. The question of the people's own conceptualization of the distinction becomes all the more critical, moreover, when it comes to our understanding of their actualization of it in ritual. Therefore, I would go even further, and argue that, in any particular society, what the domestic domain is held to be may vary from one ritual to the next and, even in the same ritual, from one historical period to another.

DEMONIC POSSESSION AND THE KEY ROLE OF WOMEN

I begin with a preliminary approximation to establish the basis for my account of the moral dynamics of demonic possession, its counteracting of disorder for the sake of healing. This approximation covers, at least for demonic possession, certain enduring features of the domestic domain. The less enduring features are discussed below, in the light of a certain long-term trend. In my earlier writing about demonic possession (Werbner 1964, 1970, 1971a, 1972), I did not appreciate that trend; but after my most recent observations (1985) in the twenty-five year period of my study, I now consider that throughout the period the trend has been important, and increasingly so.

The Domestic Domain

As it is represented in demonic possession, the domestic domain is anchored not in procreation and rearing but in food provisioning by women. It is anchored in activities such as their routine hoeing or weeding, their winnowing and stamping of grain, and their preparation of porridge. The performance of possession ritual is itself tied to the agricultural cycle. Apart from unanticipated occasions of affliction, there should be, though in practice there rarely are, three annual performances: at the beginning of the year, before first hoeing or plowing, at the first "biting" of new fruits, such as melons, and at first stamping of the new maize. Insofar as there is a single basis in the ritual for the cultural construction of the domestic domain, that basis is production, not reproduction or procreation.

The ritually specific definition of production, and thus the distinctly demonic construction of the domestic domain, must be emphasized. At all the performances that I attended there was no reference to the provision of shelter, nor to a sphere of a woman's household chores, such as smearing dung and mud on floors,[10] plastering mud walls, binding grass for thatch,[11] collecting firewood,[12] or fetching water.[13] These are all important acts; most are necessary in ritual at a land shrine of God Above (see below Chapter 7) or a kin shrine of the divinities of the dead. Through exclusion of these acts, nuclear significance is stamped only upon subsistence and the virtuous sharing of sustenance; these are primary in the relationships mediated through the demonic cult. Their nuclear significance, rendered in the cult's cryptic and occult idiom, is grasped as axiomatic and ultimately beyond understanding.

Dual Mediation and Selected Women

Given the culturally specific conceptualization of the domestic domain and the danger to it within a hierarchy of domains, we must ask a simple question: How are we to account for the fact that it is women and, more specifically, *certain* women who are possessed?

This question is often asked in the literature on possession (for reviews of major debates, see Werbner 1964, 1972; P. Wilson 1967; Lewis 1971; Saunders 1977; van Binsbergen 1979; Kapferer 1983). Some of the discussion is about modes of possession highly sensitive to fashion; their ephemeral symbolic forms come and go in waves of style that are extremely responsive to the people's current readings of change in their everyday lives (Harris 1959; van Binsbergen 1981; Colson 1984). But it is also well-known that there are more stabilized modes, like *mazenge* demonic possession, in which considerable symbolic viability has been sustained with the same forms over at least four generations, perhaps for more than a century (for early reports of what are now seen to be lasting, present features of *mazenge* demonic possession, see O'Neill 1907; Garbutt 1909). Nevertheless, in this discussion what has been little explored is precisely what is most important for answering our question—the mediatory roles of women.

In my view, different kinds of mediation need to be distinguished. One kind is mediation between domains, such as that between the wild or alien and the domestic. As I show in detail later, such mediation is achieved primarily through symbolic forms and substances. The second type of mediation occurs between relatives of different households or homesteads; it is this interpersonal mediation that affects the management of reciprocity and communication within a kinship network, and that depends on the possibility of negotiated relations over goods and services. In demonic possession, both domain mediation and interpersonal mediation are involved. We can thus rephrase our original question with this duality in mind: When dual mediation is involved, how can we account for the fact that demonic possession focuses on women and certain women in particular?

The question is best approached as a whole after its parts are considered in this order: (1) the domain mediation, (2) the interpersonal mediation, and (3) the selection of women. The ideological representation is that the higher and lower domains of social order, respectively the public and the domestic, are internal, whereas the domain of social disorder, the wild and alien, is external. The perceived dangers to the domains of social order are culturally defined around subsistence and rightful conjugal relations, specifically, rapacious appetite and bestial carnality. In no sense, however, is it construed as a danger represented as arising from the givens of a woman's physiology, or of the natural in any other sense. Kalanga are not preoccupied with the danger of pollution from menstruation or from parturition, although a rite of passage, uniting both new father and new mother, is prescribed before the new parents resume sexual relations. According to the ideological representation of the divide between the domestic and the wild or alien, such danger of pollution (as well as the power and means to counteract the danger) comes from the inferior to the superior domain, from the external to the internal.

Women are central in constituting the domestic domain, yet through their movement they relate it to something beyond itself. Women go from the internal to the external, moving as out-marrying daughters and sisters; they also come from the external to the internal, moving as in-marrying wives. When women are sought as domain mediators, it is to counteract a danger conceived as coming from the external to the internal. Therefore they are sought for domain mediation because of their movement counter to that of the danger, not as wives but as kinswomen who go from the internal to the external, from the superiors (the wife-givers) to the inferiors (the wife-receivers). Furthermore, their authorized healing is as sacred go-betweens in a relation with sister's children, the Venda-speaking demons of the wild and alien.

On the basis of this understanding of the domain mediation of women as kin instead of wives, we can now examine their interpersonal mediation regarding negotiated relations over goods and services within a kinship network. Among Kalanga, the domestic domain is not confined to production and consumption, nor is the public sphere of exchange reserved for men and for the domain they dominate; instead, exchange beyond the household is a feature of the domestic domain. Consequently, the domestic domain we are discussing differs from the domestic domain clearly found in some New Guinea societies (Strathern 1972:160).

In ritual, as apart from it, women make transactions, in their own right, over highly valued goods and services. Therefore, not being confined to the household, the domestic domain has an interfamilial aspect. Similarly, women may be able, or at least in the past, were able, to build on the bonding among themselves, to form small groups across households—bands of initiated kinswomen, for ritual purposes. In addition, a woman who is a host is turned to for treatment by uninitiated kinswomen and kinsmen from very different households. The woman's status, which she inherits from one kinswoman[14] and into which she is initiated by another,[15] is the one that she derives solely from her relations with other women (see Rosaldo 1974:29). Accordingly, sociality of the negotiable type is associated with the domestic domain, in contrast to non-negotiable sociality, which is associated with the public domain.

The distinction needs to be spelled out further. Non-negotiable sociality is defined by rights and duties in a way that tends to preclude people from looking to each other for expedient or makeshift cooperation in production or casual sharing of resources. Expectations are rather narrowly restricted. Goodwill is often assumed to be dubious, rather than a usual premise of interaction. One example is in the usual relations between agnates (men classed as "fathers," "brothers," and "sons"). They have a right and a duty to speak for one another, for instance, in a legal dispute. When a patrimony passes as major wealth from father to son, agnates also have jural claims on the heir. When residing in the countryside, they rarely give or lend each other primary assets, and it is also rare for them, as heads of independent hamlets or homesteads, to be very close neighbors. Relations between them are characterized by avoidance for many purposes, because the various personal transactions that normally arise out of neighborliness are ordinarily incompatible with their jural relations.

The negotiable type of sociality is characterized by giving and sharing on a personal basis, by casual transactions, and by a flow of valued services and productive goods. This type builds on strong moral expectations of generosity and personal concern. These expectations are sustained by, and to some extent even arise from, the continuing flow of reciprocity, and the many short-term investments people make in each other. Below, it will be demonstrated that such sociality is one necessary condition for the interpersonal mediation by women during demonic possession.

Every woman must marry out, usually virilocally. Consanguineous kin are barred from marriage. It is expected that a married woman may have dual loyalties, maintaining, as it were, one foot in her marital home and the other in her natal home, and that these loyalties may develop over time, as she goes back and forth between her relatives. Her interpersonal mediatory role among Kalanga, as elsewhere, is not precluded by her jural status as a legal dependent of a man. Being a man's legal dependent entitles a woman to rights. These, like a woman's interests, vary from one society to another and, within a single society, from one status or phase in a woman's life to the next. A woman need not be barred, because she is the legal dependent of one man, from having a cluster of rights and interests in other men and their goods. Indeed, her interpersonal mediatory role may be great precisely because it is only through her that such a cluster may be combined with the different rights and interests of a legal ward. Thus among Kalanga a woman is not simply involved in various actual or potential inheritances, since she may inherit as a wife, a daughter, and in some circumstances, as a sister. Even more, she canalizes a flow of property in the form of bridewealth, gifts, and loans as well as inheritance. At stake in a woman's rights and interests are those of her male guardian, who may prevent her from alienating her property, in some circumstances at least. His rights and interests, however, are not the only ones at stake—indeed, in some respects, those of others compete with his.

The Power of Elite Women

Demonic possession has tended to thrive where such competing interests and rights have been associated with wealth and public prominence. Hosts have usually been elite women. At the time of my census in 1964–65, covering four adjacent wards, only a minority of the women were hosts, slightly less than 20 percent of the adult women. Of these hosts, more than 80 percent were the immediate, familial kin of men of high status who owned the wards' wells, which were then, apart from cattle, the greatest single assets of a permanent kind. In different kin groups, the number of hosts varies, and in some groups there are none. To an important extent, their presence has depended on a group's standing in terms of wealth, size, public authority, and influence (for a discussion of kin groups, multiple-marriage chains, and competition for land and status, see R. Werbner 1975, 1982a).

The power of women as hosts is not the power of the weak. Nor is it a blackmail by otherwise passive inferiors or nascent suffragettes, as has been suggested for various cults of possession (Lewis 1971). A host mediates and makes her demands as a relative, and she may make these demands on behalf of the demons during possession only at a relative's home. No principal in the demonic ritual—no convener (the head of a homestead), sponsor, patient, host, or demon invoker—makes demands indiscriminately against a category, such as males or females. Demands are always made in respect of specific relationships between kin. A host's unwillingness to accept any offering, any token of responsibility and mutual goodwill, is a sanction she may apply against her kin; such is the leverage she exerts. She may withhold her ritual services entirely, or delay giving them, when she is grieved or feels mistreated by her relatives. In turn, kin seek ritual services from a host whom they trust, at a place where they expect that there is benevolence toward them. They avoid a host or convener whose sorcery they fear.

The role of demonic go-between, *dombo,* is tied to a certain context of negotiation. A woman can expect goods and services from her male patrilineal relatives that a man neither expects nor gets. It therefore follows that when a woman sponsors a demonic ritual she is not bound to avoid the same places that a man would; the relationships are different for her. She may be a sponsor at her father's brother's homestead, for example.

Nevertheless, the basic context of ritual mediation is constant, whether the sponsor is a man or a woman, for it is always a context characterized by negotiable sociality. The ritual mediation does not occur between persons whose mutual interests are regulated solely (or primarily) by jural rights and duties. Instead, the participants are persons who can and do turn to each other for a variety of personal and economic services and for gifts of productive resources, such as land and livestock. There can be no demonic possession where there are no rights of kinship. But where relationships are reduced to rights and little else, demonic possession is irrelevant.

If demonic ritual involved merely domain mediation, possession could be universal among women. Every kinswoman could be a suitable focus for the ritual, given the fact that every kinswoman potentially can control a domestic domain, and that exogamy, and the movement from the internal to the external are universals. But interpersonal mediation is not a matter of universals; it requires that a specific kind of person be the mediator if the role is to be powerful and authoritative. In particular, the interpersonal mediation of demonic possession calls for a person who can be effective (1) because she is important, indeed nodal, in the negotiable relations of intimacy and trust within a kinship network and (2) because that network is in itself important for a flow of goods and services. In ways surpassing other women, elite women can and do serve as foci for strategic action in the management of intimacy and trust within kinship relations. I suggest that, because elite women, more than others, are able to fulfill both of the roles of dual mediator, it is elite women, primarily, who are the possessed, and thereby empowered to heal by ritually restoring order within the domestic domain. In other words, I posit a connection between possession, centrality within the domestic domain, movement between domains, and nodality within a kinship network.

THE TRANSFORMATIONAL ANALYSIS OF POSSESSION

At this point, in order to sustain my argument through a transformational analysis of the whole ritual, I describe the usual sequence of the rites and then examine the sequence in more abstract and comparative terms.

Phases and Interludes

The ritual usually lasts four days, and includes interludes of singing and dancing between each phase of the rites. When the moon is almost full, the ritual begins with *(a)* the invocation of possession; and before the moon wanes, it ends with *(d)* the revocation of possession. In between come *(b)* purification in sacred exchange and *(c)* redemption in sacred exchange. The possession rites *(a,d),* which reverse each other, frame rites *(b,c)* that also reverse each other, but within the contrasting symbolic mode of sacred exchange. From phase to phase there is a switching between alternatives, and a progression across the ritual from one extreme to another. The logic is contrastive and reflexive. In the next chapter I show that demonic possession and cattle sacrifice are alternative manifestations of the same cultural logic. In due course, I demonstrate the transformational capability of that cultural logic, when I clarify the underlying terms and the interrelation between the key ideas of demonic possession and cattle sacrifice.

Even at one of the seasonal performances, the occasion for the ritual is the perilous condition of someone who can be regarded in some sense as a "child" at the ritual venue. The peril lies in the risk of a demonic attack brought on capriciously or by someone's fault, not necessarily the fault of the afflicted. The attraction of demons toward a child, which is the problem to be treated, is represented at the start of the ritual. On the first night, to begin the invocation of possession, a young girl overturns a stamping block, preferably the host's own, behind the granaries. This marks the reversal of domestic order. Acting as a messenger on behalf of responsible adults (a usual errand of children), the young girl climbs on top of the stamping block. While she faces east, she invokes the demons by name to come toward her; using a common idiom for summoning someone, she calls out, "Come over here. You are summoned to Kalangaland (Bukalanga) over here; I crown [gadza, "install"] _____ [host's name]." In response, the host rushes out, usually from a kitchen, and runs back behind the homestead's granaries, where she collapses into a brief coma. Her costume, taken from the granary where it is ordinarily kept secret and hidden from her sight, is put around her while she is on the ground. There she lies until covered by another woman. Fully adorned, the host rises and struts majestically on all fours, being a Lion, into the kitchen and into the presence of the awaiting congregation, who never see her in the act of becoming possessed. Hers is a metamorphosis that is understood to be wondrous.

This reversal of order is itself reversed on the final night, during the revocation of possession. Late in the night, the demons, as embodied in the hosts, chase children. This time, rather than calling the demons to themselves as irresponsible messengers, the children act on their own behalf. They flee and escape the pursuing demons. Afterwards, while everyone else sleeps, the hosts retire to a kitchen hut. Very secretively, not to be observed by anyone else, they go east behind the granary to remove and hide their costumes, before the cock crows. The demons are then said to "pass beyond" (pinda mbeli) and "return back" (bwilila shule) east from where they came.

The rites in between begin at dawn, after the first evening's interlude of song and dance. Clapping hands respectfully and greeting each demon with deference as "Grandfather," the ritual's sponsor and other responsible relatives (both men and women) gift the demons with imported ornaments (the printed shawls and colored beads) for their hosts to wear around themselves. The affliction is reported to the demons, and the hosts reply in cryptic whispers about the blame for it. Then the demons are exhorted to heal and take the affliction outside and away into the bush. The demons' hosts do so, when they "go outside" (the polite euphemism for defecating), after having been fed on a coarse and ill-combined potpourri which makes their feces distinctive. It is a mess said to be suitable for a creature that eats here, there, and everywhere, such as a porcupine. Removing pollution from the homestead, they are expected to transgress the path between the domestic and the wild by defecating upon it. Coming back to the homestead from the wild, they bring with them the herbs they have dug up for the patient. This movement in sacred exchange is shown below:

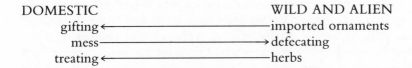

DOMESTIC

    gifting ←————————————imported ornaments
    mess————————————→ defecating
    treating ←————————————herbs

WILD AND ALIEN

The hosts perform another exchange of internal and external, which further amends the condition of the demons and the afflicted. By "going outside" and defecating, they made an internal condition of dirt external. Next, in the kitchen, they drink water with their herbs and spray it over the afflicted. In this way, they introduce from outside a fresh internal condition, in turn in themselves, in the afflicted, and in the homestead as a whole. Instead of the former condition of dirt, the fresh one is "cool," *tonodzwa,* a condition of rest, composure, and freedom from pollution. This condition is much desired, and one of great importance for divinity in Kalanga cosmology. It calls for a full discussion, which I give in Chapter 4.

The spraying to "cool" and to purify is done on the second evening, after the hosts have rested in the daytime. (Hosts should dance and sing tirelessly during the night; they should only sit down to drink beer, but never to sleep until the cock crows.) Later, following an interlude of song and dance, before they do sleep briefly in the daytime, they complete the purification rite, when alone, by smearing themselves all over their bodies with a white ointment; its smell is recognized to be like polecat musk. Whitened in this way, the wild is "bare" and free of pollution. We may say, therefore, that in this initial rite of sacred exchange, the wild and alien, as it is embodied in the possessed women, is put to rest free of pollution. Although still wild, it is in a sense temporarily domesticated.

The next day, the rite of redemption is held. At dawn, when the sun is low and red, the hosts and their kin ladle white beer from a red pot of fired clay still unblackened by soot from cooking. They pour beer to the east, in the bush, behind a towering tree that bears fruit or pods (a marulla or winter thorn) and never to the west, in the tree's shadows. This is in contrast to the libation before a cattle sacrifice for the divinities of the dead on the father's side. Prior to a sacrifice, the libation is poured to the west from a black pot (the color of the divinities of the dead) and within the homestead at the front, in the shadows, by posts of hardwood from a tree which, though fruitless, may flow with ant-honey.

After the libation in the east, a goat is sacrificed (by the Lions). The prescribed method is strangulation by the hosts themselves, in great privacy in the bush behind the granaries. There they drink of the victim's blood. It is a sacrificial method which well becomes Lions: they are predators and the victim is their prey. The victim is a substitute, offered instead of the afflicted, who is being redeemed by the sacrifice. All the close relatives who live in the homestead, apart from the hosts themselves, share in the liver, when it is roasted, and later in the meat, when it is boiled. Unlike the case in cattle sacrifice, no elaborate discriminations are made in the distribution of the meat or liver, nor is there any metaphorization of procreation or bodily nurture, such as the provision of the loins to a father and the breast to a mother. Instead, the relatives' undifferentiated sharing reincorporates them as one.

In the evening, after the hosts have had their daytime rest, the rite of redemption is continued within the kitchen. The hosts breathe in an incense made from chyme, which they burn at the hearth in a shard that lacks any part of the pot's lip. Later, well before dawn but toward the end of the interlude, the ritual's sponsor or a responsible elder takes the victim's collected bones very secretively outside to leave them in a termite mound, where the termites can eat them. This takes them beyond the reach of domestic creatures, especially dogs.

The chyme offering marks a beginning to the end of the meal, whether in demonic ritual, or for the divinities of the dead. Aside from this similarity, the contrast between the rituals is striking. We may say that a shrine for the divinities of the dead (shumba wulu, "Great Lion") is an anti-hearth. It is in the shape of a hearth, with its three stones. It is also, like a hearth, never to be stepped over or walked across, but always walked around (counter-clockwise, in shrine ritual), but it is a place for offering food and meals, without fire.[16] The food, which is offered in a whole pot with a lip, is for beings within the same moral community, including the divinities of the dead, whereas the lipless shard used in demonic ritual is for excluded beings who belong elsewhere, the demons. For the divinities of the dead, blood and chyme are poured; both are released freely in the wind (because the divinities are themselves wind). For the demons, however, Lions as go-betweens seize and contain the blood and chyme; they internalize both within themselves and therefore carry both away to where the demons belong. The act is redemptive in that the life of a domestic animal is taken instead of the life of the afflicted. Thus, if in the purification rites the alien and wild are domesticated, we may say that in the redemption rite the domestic is alienated.

The Terms of Ritual Progression

Viewed as a whole, the ritual's progression can now be seen summarily and then in more abstract terms: Given the condition of a "child" in danger from the attraction of demons to faults, dirt, and pollution, the ritual opens with a child who, as an irresponsible agent, attracts the demons. Next, responsible adults enter into sacred exchange with the demons as Lions, on the demons' own terms, with the giving of alien adornments for the outside of the body, and food for the inside, as a confounded mess, acquired from here and there. In return, the demons as Lions displace dirt by despoiling the way to the outside, then cool and cleanse their own and the afflicted's condition. During the third phase, the demons as Lions seize alternative prey, the sacrificial victim instead of the afflicted; and the responsible adults reincorporate their relatives as one body, sharing the same flesh. The sacrificial bones, kept from domestic creatures, are brought by a responsible adult to be gnawed away by termites. They are not offered to the demons. There is no bond of bone between people and demons, and none is sought. Such a bone offering is only made to the divinities of the dead with whom the past bond of bone, and thus the substance of kinship, is renewed. Finally, no longer attracting demons, children are free to escape them, a flight that occasions the return of demons from where they came.

From this summary it is evident that the basic terms of the ritual are these: responsible adults in responsible adulthood; irresponsible children in irresponsible childhood; demons in the demonic. The key idea of the ritual is the idea of the demonic as it is dangerous to generations of kin in ascending order from children to adults. The progression of the ritual is toward a beneficial relation in which adults redemptively prove their responsibility so that demons are no longer attracted to children; *lunya,* "antipathy toward children" or, in a word, anti-parentage, is the very nature of demons.

Figure 12 shows the terms and the progression of the ritual through the combination of terms, according to a counter-clockwise movement. What is problematic in the ritual is the conjunction between demons and children in terms of anti-parentage. Hence the movement leads to a distancing of demons from children.

In the next chapter, I present a comparison of the terms and the key idea of demonic ritual with those of cattle sacrifice. That comparison illuminates the significance of movement in each ritual, and it also enables us to appreciate further the transformational capability of the underlying cultural logic.

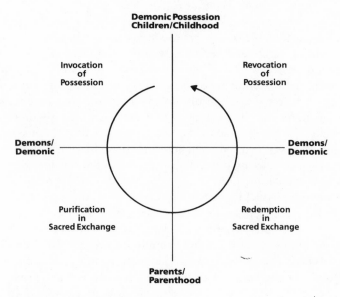

Figure 12. *Progression in Demonic Possession.*

The Personal Meaning of Demonic Interludes

During demonic interludes a negative image is presented, to convey disorder and anti-social "regulation." It is rejected, and recognized for what it is not. In part, the presentation consists of satirical song and burlesque and includes innuendos of illicit sexuality, the absurdities of which are exposed through laughter. Plaintive laments, expressed as bestial carnality, form another aspect of the presentation; they tell of the excessive appetite and rapacity of relatives. But, such carnality, too, is rejected in a counter-affirmation by the congregation.

The rapacity of the lion and his preying on the herds of domesticated animals is satirically mimed during possession, as an aspect of regulation and law *(laula)*. During the first interlude of one performance, the hosts began lionlike rumbling, *mwe, mwe* (another one, another one), about a member of their band who was present but not joining them in possession. Two of the hosts got down on all fours. The younger and junior then danced after the reluctant woman, who played her part by retreating about the hut and avoiding the Lion after her, all in step to the rhythm. The senior host sang, "You are separating *[laula];* you are finishing off the cattle in the pen." The chorus responded to her solo, "Tell about the pen to the leopard." The chase and the dance quickened. Abruptly, it ended, amidst much laughter. The junior host leaped up, landed from behind on the retreating woman, and mounted her as she fell down, unharmed. "Meat [flesh] has been taken," was the glad cry of the chorus.

In the chase, the congregation presented their image of relationships between themselves and an absent kinsman, an elder who had succeeded to his father's position. Much of the meaning of their cry, its joy, and the special significance of the whole act cannot be understood apart from their circumstances and personal relationships. This calls for detailed commentary, but for the sake of my main argument, an abbreviated account must suffice.

These relationships are illustrated by Figure 13, in which I refer to the members of the congregation alphabetically:

A–the elder's wife, who played the part of the reluctant object of the chase; B–the pursuing host, the elder's sister, who came especially for the performance from outside the vicinity to the hamlet of F, another brother; C–the sponsor, who was the mother of the patient, a daughter of the elder, and also the wife of a cousin of the host (E); D–the afflicted patient, a granddaughter of the elder; E–a host whose services were required, the wife of the elder's brother; F–the convener of the ritual, the elder's younger brother; G–the senior host at the performance, the mother of the elder (and of B and F), who was living at the venue of the ritual with her younger son (F); H–the elder's senior wife, who had separated from him and whom he no longer supported; I–this wife's sister; J–a relative (herself a host) who lived with H and I; K, L, and M–adolescent and younger children of the convener, living at the venue of the ritual.

There was trust, mutual goodwill, and even fondness between the host (E) and the sponsor of the ritual (C), the patient's mother. Others in the congregation bore grudges against each other and the sponsor's parents. Thus, those who came with the patient (A, the elder's wife and C, their daughter) confronted a congregation that had cause for complaint against the elder and his wife. As the convener told me, their father had left little; their mother had been rich in cattle and goats. The elder was entitled to inherit the major share of their father's property along with his father's name and position. A share from each parent was also due each of the daughters. But the convener, (F) as the youngest son, should have received most of the property of their mother (G) (who was old and feeble and, sadly, died not long after the ritual). The convener and his wife, the host (E), complained to me that the elder had denied him and his sisters their rightful shares, taking all

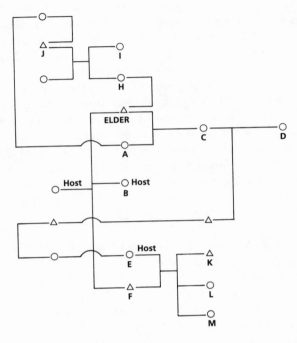

Figure 13. A First Interlude's Congregation.

the mother's property, claiming it as the father's, then devouring it for the benefit of his own immediate family. The elder avoided his mother, though he often drank beer with her neighbors.

The elder's wife (A) had to join in the satire and submit to the mockery for the sake of the patient and the sponsor, respectively her granddaughter (D) and her daughter (C). Her ordeal, being mounted by another Lion in a sexually suggestive way, was a comic reversal, with the pursuer pursued by demonic retribution. For the pursued had herself come to her husband's "pen" and been a party "to separating out" her senior co-wife; she now "ruled the pen" alone, despite being a junior wife.[17] In the chase *(nlao)*, the law of the Lion, was imposed upon her; and she passed through an ordeal that had the significance of an occult attack yet with the sexual playfulness of something to be laughed away in joking shared with the rest of the congregation. Through the chase as a ritual ordeal, her fault and a debt over property were both reconstructed as matters for ritual healing, in the image of the demonic.

During an interlude at another performance, a host mimed a man as if he were a boy cleaning a loinskin; the lewd innuendo occasioned peals of laughter and was enjoyed by all. The host began her take-off by holding a gourd round the bowl and pointing its long curved neck (I could not help seeing it as phallic) at other women:

Soloist [in high-pitched boy's voice]: "My loinskin, my loinskin."
Soloist [in second voice]: "I am going to give you my loinskin."
Chorus: "Mine has been bitten by a dog."
Soloist [in second voice]: "You were cleaning it to bring it where?"
Soloist: "To you, woman."
Soloist [own voice]: "Ah, little man."

At this the soloist turned the gourd round by the neck, holding it like a hoe, and danced about miming a woman at the early weeding *(shakula)* of a garden. In other performances, the focal prop of the act was an elder's staff.

Members of the congregation who watched the woman's performance with the gourd drew my attention to the culmination of the act, where regular production—*shakula,* the early weeding—was featured. They did not comment explicitly on any sexual innuendo in the take-off. In the idiom of the cult, however, adultery, incest, and their consequences are usually implied by allusions to the loin covering, commonly by baring or "cleaning" it (an act of occult significance that suggests cleansing from the wrath of the demons). Children are warned, Kalanga say, to fear and respect the loincovering of their fathers by avoiding adultery and incest. In dramatizing this, women do not play-act at being men to express some deprivation or envy of masculinity; instead, they ridicule carnality. Their act is satire, and it is enlivened by much laughter, for they enjoy the ridiculousness of both men and women who are tempted to transgress carnally.

The woman's act with a gourd is a comic take-off. It proceeds through the caricaturing of a man in the guise of a boy, and a woman in the guise of a man. That juxtaposition plays upon the absurdities in their appearances and realities. The comic moment culminates in the exposure of the disguise. No less a matter for burlesque and laughter is the undisguised reality that follows. Herself once again, the woman assumes the agricultural task to which she devotes herself, day after day, in a routine of rising, long before the cock crows, to prepare a meal for her household, and then to rush to catch the dew on the garden before the dawn breaks, and the ground grows hard. The comedy is that, in such mundane tasks as well, she is a "lion," although a "lion" of everyday labor.

An Ironic Vision of Reality

Such sexual playfulness and comic moments are a feature, as much as any other, of *laula* and the construction of order in the ritual. They make fun of a usual division of labor by gender. This involves shared work as well as interdependence. It is not as if the job of weeding were the affair solely of women. A great share of the burden is borne by men, specifically that minority who are home from labor migration at any time. The task is shared by helping parties of adults or boys and girls. The parties bear the brunt of the work, leaving tedious maintenance for women. When women boast of their roles, as they sometimes do, in a jesting fashion, a favorite theme is the irregularity of much of a man's work. Baka Nyaka, a neighbor of mine, bragged to me, "We women, ah, we work all year long. Men only work when it is a matter of cutting and clearing, in summer or in winter, to cut beams for hamlets. Ah, but our work goes on everyday." Thus, in the interludes of domestic ritual, women play and display where they rule like the cock, regulating time, through the daily and continuous devotion to a task. "Preen yourself, preen yourself," runs a song of the hosts, and they do, with a heightened consciousness of the absurd in the everyday.

Plaintive Laments and the Personal Order in Dialogue

An ironic vision informs the ritual and, indeed, is informed by it, for it is not that the mockery or humor is directed solely against others. Above all, the hosts represent themselves as being the butts of ridicule. In their plaintive chants, hosts often sing of their sorrows as if they have been neglected, mocked, and despised, rather than favored or pampered, as they actually are by the gifting of the congregation. A host's son remarked, when trying to make me understand a song, that it is as if there is a dialogue going on between the hosts and others present. To the host's question, "Why do you hate the Lion?" the others reply, "How can we hate you, Grandfather?" It is as if a host is compelled to challenge the congregation of relatives and put their sympathies to the test. In turn, the relatives have to respond by denying hostility, while they affirm amity and other ideals in their relationships. The ordeal requires them all "to bring their hearts together."

The commentary given me reflects the consciousness people have that the dialogic ordeal in such ritual interludes is transformative. People are aware of undergoing a ritual test in this distinct division of labor; a main subject's challenge, in the form of mockery or being mocked at, is put forth for the sake of a healing response in the congregation's counter-affirmation. In representing herself as a butt of ridicule, a host does her relatives the ritual service of giving them the opportunity to disavow what they should not but often *do* feel, and prove that their true feelings are what they should be.

This transformative ordeal in dialogue can be best seen from the song that an old host, Badlanje (Glutton), sang during the ritual and then commented on to me. I quote her song in full, because it expresses with much evocative power themes that are typical in many *mazenge* songs:

Leave that I speak,

Leave that I speak.

Leave, I say I have hoed.

I am done now we are taking.

Tomorrow they will find you, too.

For there is no one without *mazenge*[18]

Oh, you sing it haltingly.

Ah, this song you sing it poorly, oh chiefs.

Tomorrow, if I should be here

Tomorrow, I am going.

I am being laughed at by those who have them[19] too.

Oh, you sing it sluggishly.

My mother is in love with a diviner,[20] chiefs.

My voice grows hoarse.

Leave, I sing the mouth alone.

Yes, the chest sang long ago.

Who is that over there?

Yes, he is like one with maize-meal paste.

The bull-lion fears others in the hut.[21]

Oh, my voice is rough.

Let us act fervently, lads.

When they came to me, they said I had drunk beer,

But there was no beer, oh chiefs.

My voice shakes roughly.

My days when I danced it!

Oh, respond, you grandmothers, you grow dull.

That one over there, who is it, oh chiefs?

The day when I danced it!

Jump and we be two, oh chiefs.

My voice quakes, there is no one without *mazenge*.

The world is *mazenge* all over.

One who stamps is stamping for hers, oh chiefs.

Leave, I sing the mouth, oh the year.

My old age is shit.

Jumping as if we be two!

There is no one without *mazenge*.

The world is *mazenge* all over.

The world is *mazenge* all over.

One who sings is singing for hers:

Answer please, grandmothers.

Yes, the year, let me sing the mouth.

My days when I still danced it!

Jumping as if we be two, chiefs.

I have no sister's child here.[22]

As she leads the song the soloist draws on a stock of proverbs, fixed phrases, and original couplets. The song as a text thus seems elliptical and disjointed. In this song, the soloist, Badlanje, laments her old age; to become old is to become the object of hateful whispers. Doubting that she has long to live, she bids her juniors farewell. But, grieving that they wish her dead, she asks them to let her live until she is through hoeing. Then they may remain eating what she has hoed. "You have already taken my chest," she tells them. "Now I am grown old, let me sing as I can, with my mouth only. Once I jumped as if I were two dancing; now I totter about like one holding her knees."[23]

Badlanje voices self-pity and represents herself as the object of ridicule; people think her drunk when they see her possessed. But out of her self-pity she challenges those who would laugh—tomorrow the Lion will find them and they will feel pain when they too become hosts. Indeed, she, a kinswoman, is being jeered at by women who themselves have *mazenge* yet never become possessed, an allusion to the wives of the hamlet. Yet these are not exclusively singled out as her enemies. Ranged against the possessed hosts, "grandfathers, chiefs, and bulls," are the "grandmothers," a chorus that may include daughters of the hamlet and guests as well as these wives. The soloist accuses them all of being like secret enemies: the grandmothers do not gather their hearts together in support of her and deliberately sing in discord.

Throughout her song, the soloist urges the chorus on, to dance

Figure 14. Stamping Grain.
Women of a Kalanga homestead
maintain a rhythm while they
cooperate in stamping grain.
The block upon which their poles
pound, a most familiar object
upon which their daily lives
depend, is the master symbol in
domestic possession.

more fervently, and to lift up the song that it be heard. "For do they think they are dancing for the possessed and the afflicted? No, they are dancing for themselves." She compares their dancing to stamping grain and warns them to dance as if they were stamping for themselves. In this and other songs, women are frequently enjoined not to remain mere onlookers, mountain women who sit unstirred. "There are the red buttocks, the buttocks red like a baboon's," is a refrain often used by hosts as a farewell song. And, as this is sung, the dancers hop mockingly backwards to display their buttocks to the onlookers, thus deriding as seated baboons those who have not danced. Here Badlanje concludes her song, grieving that she is like one without kinsmen, without a sister's child to defend her against those who laugh at her.

In similar vein, an old and childless widow sang the following song at a performance on behalf of a sick elder, who was her sister's son (and thus her "child" also). The chorus is the first two lines, and it is repeated after each line:

Oh go-between,
Oh go-between, having *mazenge* within.
Let us stamp.

Where we have danced.

Let us stamp.

I tire, I cannot cope.

Where we have danced.

The chief of the black string of bast.[24]

Oh lions, you defecate shit *[matoko]*.

Awe, the creeping, creeping.[25]

The divinity *[ndzimu]* of others falls.

Mine is like the stamping block's.[26]

About to be stamped upon, it lies outside.

Most have ended, long ago.

My children died, long ago.

If only I could die myself,

If only I could die myself . . .

My child remained outside.[27]

Let us offer for the divinity *[ndzimu]* of father.

The divinity *[ndzimu]* of [the sick elder].

How is it mine is so hard?

Mine is like the stamping block's,

About to be stamped upon, it remains outside.

A lullaby stolen in, its owners not here.

Let us offer for the divinity *[ndzimu]* of father.[28]

This soloist's plaintive chant has its force through a coalescence of images and ideas. Her composition characterizes her personal lot in life and the events of the immediate performance, all by mutual allusion. Her emblem of rank, the black string of bast, is an emblem of affliction, for "string" and "cry" *(mukosi)* are one word and symbol, a symbol of black sorrow; the phrase represents her as the "chief of the black grief."

The next phrase, being highly condensed, must be unpacked at some length, for it colors the significance of the "chief of the black grief." We may say that it makes the givens of animal physiology serve as an anchor for the contrast between the chiefship of men in the public domain and the "chiefship" of women as hosts in the domestic domain. The soloist sings of defecating *(nya)* shit *(matoko)*. A Lion however, should defecate distinctively and ritually. She is fed on special food, preferably prepared by the wife of the homestead head. A Lion avoids porridge, above all. Having lost her personality as a woman, she avoids that with which her personality as a woman is most identified in daily provisioning, namely food processed by the stamping block. Instead, a Lion eats maize kernels, and fresh melons in lieu of dry ones, mixed with round beans in a lumpy mixture of groundnuts—a potpourri I was told no one else would otherwise eat. It is said of Lions, "Excrement has been defecated on the path." In contrast, I never saw any human excrement on any path near a Kalanga hamlet; the transgression is a bestial act that puts the pollution and "dirt" outside the homestead. "Those who defecate are the ones having mealies and lumps."

In the next phrase, joined to that image of chiefship in the performance of bestial "dirt" making, is an image of chiefship in the diagnosis of dirt (excrement). The bestial defecator is also the tracker of defecating beasts, who knows them by their excrement and its location, before seeing them. In this image, the Lion is the pursuer and tracker who has to make patent what is unseen and hidden. Here the phrase "creeping, creeping," *manyawi nyawi,* used for awe, plays upon the term for "you defecate," *manya.* It conveys the animals' frenzy, excitement, and terror—their exaggerated self-confidence, which is unseen and yet known to the tracker. The creeping of the flesh, the awesome feeling *(manyawi nyawi),* is a sensation of the hair standing on end, Kalanga say. A host ought to feel *manyawi nyawi* at the onset of possession, when she must act overcome by the urge to dance and fall possessed. The host alludes, threateningly here, to this feeling, which ought to be in another host, who is present but not yet possessed.

The chiefship of black grief, excrement, and awe are thus brought together in a single image of the woman's role being ritualized. The nexus is then explicitly associated, in the next phrase, with a basic, everyday aspect of domestic life, one upon which it depends, and which is the special preserve of women, namely the daily provision of meal. The soloist calls upon a junior host, who is reluctant to join her, to let this neglect (lying outside) be like that of a stamping block about to be used and thus left around in the compound. Her step pounds on the floor of her kitchen in the rhythm of the pole on the block, and she sings of her dancing as stamping; the rhythm of the ritual is the everyday rhythm of provisioning. She alludes to her childlessness (the children she bore died) and she comments on the conduct of a kinswoman who is her junior and, ritually, her "child." In the ritual, too, she is "childless" for her "child" is hard, with the hardness of the block to be beaten, and denies a "father" (the patient and hamlet head) the ritual services he requires to be healed. The child refuses to fall possessed; she is warned that she must not deny *mazenge,* for that is death, and not for herself alone.

Formalization and Improvisation

This account of the hosts' creative use of counter-images, and their ritual use of song and dance for the authoritative construction of significance in their personal circumstances, leads me to the important problem of formalization in ritual. By formalization in ritual, I mean the repetitive practice through which the use of symbols and ritual substances is restricted, the speech is formulaic, and the song and dance are stylized. In brief, I refer to the limits upon improvisation and upon highly personal expression.

In his influential and important essay, Bloch reminds us that acts of discourse have to be explained in ways that take account of the mode of communication, be it song, dance, or speech (1977; 1986:182). The continuum he recognizes, somewhat after Bernstein (1972:474), is distinguished by extremes of formalization; that is, from the most freely unrestricted or informal style (or "code," in the usage of Bernstein and Bloch) to the opposite. Bloch goes on to oppose non-ritual and ritual on the same continuum, as though all ritual were similarly impoverished of meaning by formalization.

It is as if the fixity of form were such that ritual is unable to tolerate individual creativity. Historicity, or meaning that is specific to individuals or to peculiarities in their life circumstances, is abolished in ritual. Even though it is possible that some ritual does fit such an extreme, it would be very unlikely for this to be so throughout the whole of a ritual, although it may be true for a part. These issues have been discussed in a stimulating essay by Bloch (1977). The outcome of Bloch's argument is a view of ritual as impoverished symbolization (for my critique of the impoverishment view of oratory, see Werbner 1977d, and for related criticism, see Irvine 1979; on the transformative effectiveness of ritual, Kapferer 1984; La Fontaine 1985; Schieffelin 1985; see also Bloch's revised view 1985:182). Against that view, the actual richness of a ritual in individual creativity and historicity has to be recovered. One way to achieve this is to consider the continuum *within* ritual and to relate that to the mode of communication, such as song and dance.

For the sake of clarity, let me represent schematically the nub of the difference between Bloch's argument and my own. In the following, Bloch's model is shown by a single continuum, and my own by the alternation models, (A) exemplified by Kalanga sacrifice, and (B) exemplified by demonic possession:

SINGLE CONTINUUM

	Ritual	*Non-Ritual*
STYLE	Formalization	Improvisation

TIME	Ahistoricity	Historicity
REALITY	Authorized reality	Unauthorized reality

ALTERNATION OF PHASES

(A)	Main Rites	Play interludes
STYLE	Formalization (intent A)	Improvisation (intent A)
TIME	Ahistoricity	Historicity
REALITY	Authorized reality	Unauthorized counter-reality

(B)	Main Rites	Ritual interludes
STYLE	Formalization (intent B)	Improvisation (intent B)
TIME	Ahistoricity	Historicity
REALITY	Authorized counter-reality	Authorized reality

Bloch's impoverishment view is unhelpful not so much because it gives wrong answers, but even more because it prevents us from asking the most useful further questions about degrees of formalization. When is formalization in ritual greater or lesser, in interludes or main phrases? How does it vary sequentially and from mode to mode, from speech, to song and dance, to the use of the silent language of symbolic substances?

In demonic ritual, it is only the main phases that are to any considerable degree removed from the events of a particular time and place. That is so insofar as demonic rites verge on being, or rather are expected to be "nothing but repetitions" (Bloch 1977:78), and therefore virtually the same for all, irrespective of present differences in the lives of healers or afflicted individuals. The ritual progresses from disorder to order through a fixed sequence that follows its own logic, and always includes highly restricted alternatives in the main phases.

After each of these more formal main phases, marked by formulaic speech and the silent language of substances, the demonic ritual returns to the less formal and to the more unrestricted discourse of the song and dance of an interlude. Then the imagery resonates with the particularity of personal circumstances. Although hosts do learn songs from one another, and some songs become sufficiently widespread to be sung in many personal variations, a host's song is very much her own. I have heard one host rebuke another, "You sing yours, and let me sing mine." Despite such attitudes, conventions exist in the composition of songs, in the use of similar devices, similar points of irony or parody, and even similar cliches. I stress the need to appreciate the repeated shifts between contrasting styles in demonic possession. Thus, what the main phases temporarily suspend or even abolish—historicity and individual creativity—the interludes restore. Without the interludes, demonic ritual could not be so highly valued for its particularity, and for its specific assertions about people who can see, know, and make demands upon one another; but with the interludes, demonic ritual registers the current flow of relations between kin and affines, and commends their enduring relationships.

The congregation's symbolic discourse is rich in propositional significance. In other words, it has what ritual should not have, in Bloch's view, namely the power "to corner reality by adapting communication to past perception and connecting this with future perception" (1977:67; and see also his more recent appreciation of the propositional force in ritual 1986:182). Drawing upon linguistic philosophers like Searle (1969), Bloch gives his own reading of a distinction between "propositional force" and "illocutionary force," or the force *in* locution and in performing the speech act itself. Bloch goes on to argue that the two types of force or meaning vary inversely, and that the propositional force decreases most in ritual (for a critique that makes points similar to my own, see Tambiah 1985:155). In demonic possession, rich propositional significance goes along with great illocutionary force; in the communication of the discourse, much is done through the very inclusion, in the communication, of matters such as making promises, accomplishing the renewal of amity, or proving trust. To understand a congregation's subtle and inclusive deployment of the symbols, with rich propositional significance and great illocutionary force, one must be an intimate and(or) relative. Conversely, one is required to deploy these symbols in expression of one's relationships of intimacy and domesticity. The symbols advance the relationships, and the relationships sustain and carry forward the symbols.

Further implications of the continual shift between styles can be appreciated by comparison to a similar shift that occurs during sacrifice. The shifts in the interludes of both demonic possession and sacrifice are toward improvisation, within recognized limits, of course. However, the recognized intent of improvisation is opposite in each case. In the case of demonic interludes, wholeheartedness and unity of purpose is demanded— the intent is commitment to the moment of truth. This is not required during the interludes in sacrifice, where people may distance themselves from the improvisation and view it as mere entertainment. Consequently, the intent is non-commitment. Such opposition in intent must be given full weight in analysis, for along with this opposition in intent goes a corresponding contrast in the reconstruction of reality.

What sacrifice renews by means of highly formalized ritual is consonant with the authorized reality of everyday life. The precedence of elderhood is ritualized above all. Counter to that ritualization come anti-rites of play that suspend the authorized reality and, in so doing, complete its reconstruction. Demonic possession proceeds the other way around. Through its highly formalized main phases, the ritual constitutes the reality of the demonic, which is alien and wild and, as such, not consonant with everyday life. Against that dissonance, the interludes as dialogic ordeals reinstate a consonant reality, consonant with an ironic perception of the main subjects' own personal and domestic circumstances. Where sacrifice alternates between consonance and dissonance, demonic possession does the reverse, for their starting points, like their objectives, are opposites. Each makes use of formalization and improvisation, but for quite different purposes; any attempt to explain the effects of formalization without regard for intent within a social process is doomed to failure.

POSSESSION AND STRATEGIC ACTION

The strategic construction of reality by means of possession ritual is best seen in the light of an actual case. To contextualize the following case of the homecoming worker, I introduce it with some brief comments on occult attack, kinship and locality. The case also raises certain issues about the changing roles of women that I consider toward the end of this chapter, where I discuss labor migration and the perceived divide between town and country.

In the kinship range of the occult attack, both demonic possession and sorcery accusation have a similar nil incidence and approximately the same distribution. I know of no instance of a daughter accusing her mother; and a mother ought not to "awaken" *(musa)* her daughter's *zenge* in initiation. Otherwise, to be a mother, a sister, a mother's sister, or a father's sister is to be exposed to possible accusations of sorcery. There is a bias toward accusations of the old by the young, of seniors by their juniors, or between members of the same generation. Roughly the same pattern holds in terms of occult attack in host–patient relations. Within this range, however, the separation of roles is marked, and the situation is not like that found among Lugbara, for example, where invocation and accusation may involve the same individuals, possibly from different viewpoints (Middleton 1964). A host cannot give her ritual services on behalf of kin who accuse her of sorcery. To do so would run against the assumption upon which the role of *dombo* is predicated, that she is a go-between and has both sides' interests at heart.

Given the local restriction of accusations—a person is usually accused by others within an immediate vicinity of neighbors—the separation of roles has another important implication. At an external performance away from that immediate vicinity some kin, particularly kin accused by a sponsor, can be excluded from the congregation, while included in the dialogue of the occasion. Such kin are not excluded from knowledge of the specifics of the ritual healing in their absence. There is a usual expectation that excluded kin will become aware of what has transpired and will be under some pressure to modify their conduct accordingly. Those present in the congregation are required to pledge themselves to carry their relationships forward in amity. In agreement, they have to reconstitute a highly specific universe of meanings about their occult interdependence.

THE CASE OF THE HOMECOMING WORKER

I recorded the following case of a labor migrant and her kin, illustrated by Figure 15, during my fieldwork in 1964–65. Baka Siya,[29] a labor migrant and not herself a host, sponsored a ritual on her own behalf. She was the patient and the sponsor, and her father's sister was the possessed host. Along with Baka Siya and the host, Baka Siya's mother, her brothers, the sons of the host (Baka Siya's paternal cross-cousins), and one of their wives met as the congregation at the most exclusive events of the ritual. Baka Siya's offerings included a red, white, and black mantle to cover the possessed host, beer, and a goat for sacrifice.

The ritual was delayed one night. The host was aggrieved about neglect by her own children and manifested her grievance in her reluctance to become possessed. First, *tukana midzimu,* "scolding over the divinities" took place, in which her children were berated for the neglect.

Baka Siya had consulted a diviner in Johannesburg while she was ill and after her loss of employment as a cook and a nursemaid. She went to several diviners, she told me, to some alone and to others with her boyfriend, a Kalanga. "They all said I don't give anything to the father's sister. I was so ill my ears couldn't hear well. But when I remembered that I ought to go home, my ears were opened." She also

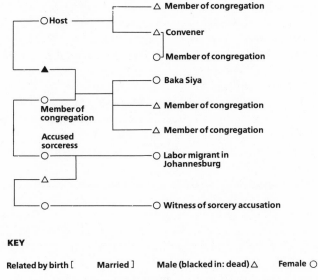

KEY

Related by birth [Married]   Male (blacked in: dead) △   Female ○

Figure 15. Congregation at a Ritual and Witness at a Sorcery Accusation.

divined that her mother's younger sister and her daughter had practiced sorcery against her.

Her own fault for neglecting a duty of kinship was central in Baka Siya's divinations. If she had needed to gift her kinsmen in the congregation excessively, to compensate for a past lack of generosity, her sponsorship of the ritual would have been of another kind. But it is no paradox that her acceptance of responsibility meant both a declaration of her dutifulness and an assertion of obligations owed to her. In one respect she had in the past neglected none of the principals in the congregation, including her father's sister. All were obligated to her for the money, blankets, clothing and other goods that she gave them each time she returned on vacation from her work. In times of scarcity she was the mainstay of her natal family; her brothers largely depended on her cattle and goats, and prided themselves on her bank account in Francistown. What she divined she owed her father's sister was a ritual offering within the congregation, although giving it was not a substitute for other dutiful acts. The offering was the binding embodiment of these acts.

A threat to Baka Siya's standing within her local kin group came from her parallel cousin, the daughter of the suspected sorceress. This cousin was a potential rival. Baka Siya had got her young cousin a job in Johannesburg several years earlier, and the cousin was beginning to prosper while Baka Siya, now reaching the end of her career, had trouble finding work. The cousin, unlike Baka Siya, had yet to invest substantially at home. In saving from her earnings, the cousin did not try to sustain her natal family. When Baka Siya sent bags of grain home during the drought, the cousin did not; the cousin's family battened on Baka Siya's and, Baka Siya's family believed, occasionally pilfered from them. Thus, in effect, the claims of Baka Siya's kinsmen forced Baka Siya into an indirect subsidy of her rival. As Baka Siya saw it, her mother's sister was envious of her and wanted her daughter to "surpass" *(pinda)* Baka Siya.

Shortly before the ritual, this mother's sister caught Baka Siya visiting me. Baka Siya tried to hide by my hut; her mother's sister pursued her, ostensibly to greet me, and surprised her. The mother's sister began a little homily, after the pleasantries of welcoming Baka Siya home, and spoke allusively through proverbs, the most choice of which was "The going, going jackal returns with a brace of hounds." The mother's sister drew out the meaning: "The great traveller comes home with faults *(milandu).*" After this she got up to go, but as she rounded the enclosure outside my hut she began to complain that Baka Siya had excused herself from coming to visit her at her hamlet, yet had gone much farther to her mother's brother's hamlet (Baka Siya had sent her brother to say her feet ached too much for her to travel and visit). Baka Siya replied, sadly but sharply, "Well, I fear you." *(Gala ndomuchya.)* Her mother's sister continued, "Yes,[30] is it so? Then why have you not come to my hamlet, since you were sick?" Baka Siya responded, "I fear, when I reflect on many things." There was a pause, then a few words of seemingly trivial banter were exchanged, and the mother's sister left at a dignified and unhurried pace. Baka Siya remained with me, complaining about her feet and telling me of her mother's sister.

Baka Siya's neighbors expected her to do more on her return home than sponsor a ritual. They spoke of the meeting outside of my hut and of another, and, as one said, "Ah you see, she's telling her now; she [Baka Siya] cannot just go and not tell her plainly *[patjena,* 'in the bare']." However, on both these occasions there was innuendo, the allusions were veiled, and the mother's sister gave no less than she received. The suspicion was spread, however, to enough neighbors, the right ones, for the mother's sister to hear of it, and try to clear herself, as she repeated, against a "going, going jackal."

The force of such suspicion is that it does spread, and can corrupt the closest relationships, so long as it remains ambiguous, not overt and yet not fully covert. Suspicion is forceful and threatening, particularly where no relationship is immune, where an accusation raised in one relationship can be taken up in others, until it fills a bundle of these and becomes a number of direct accusations. One of my closest neighbors was such a suspect, and accused; her sister-in-law, her brother, her daughter-in-law, her son, and others had all accused her on occasion, and they continued to do so, to the day her mother died, and then the scandal of blame for this rocked the vicinity where I lived. During the time of Baka Siya's brief visit, her suspect's son refused to remain with his mother in their hamlet, and went to the hamlet of the woman who became the witness of Baka Siya's accusation; he told me in confidence of his fears of what his mother and his sister (the labor migrant) might be doing, and that it would come back to them in the lightning of vengeance.

The suspect, for her part, tried to provoke Baka Siya into a direct accusation in front of responsible witnesses, who could later testify without supporting Baka Siya at a moot. Suspicion and insinuation would then have been turned into an actionable charge and slander. There is a procedure for combatting this, a hearing within the kin group that follows, or is followed by, a divination attended by a congregation representative of the interested parties and the responsible kin. Baka Siya was not ready for this, and the suspect knew it. Baka Siya told me that she intended to pursue the matter in the future. "Some day I will go with her to a diviner and we will see together."

Within her mother's kin group, where a moot would have been held first, Baka Siya could not rely on agreement about her mother's sister. Her suspect was trusted by her mother's brother, trusted especially by contrast to Baka Siya's mother. Her mother had been held to blame for the death of this kinsman's wife some twenty years before, and been beaten severely by him with a stool a few years earlier; after Baka Siya left, Baka Siya's mother was suspected once more of causing him a lingering illness, through sorcery. The brother then showed his trust in Baka Siya's suspect by leaving his own hamlet to seek refuge while recuperating in this sister's hamlet. Just as neighbors gossiped about her mother's sister in relation to Baka Siya, so too they gossiped about a counter-accusation against Baka Siya's mother and another sister. This other gossip was that they were trying to make "dolts" (*chihema*) out of their brother's children in order to inherit all their mother's goats as well as his property.

The first ritual action Baka Siya took on her return from work was to bring her natal family to the hamlet of her father's sister. This paternal kinswoman was not related directly by kinship to the suspected sorceress who, along with other maternal kin of Baka Siya's, was neither invited to attend nor came to the ritual. Before Baka Siya returned to Johannesburg, shortly after the ritual, she accused her mother's sister of sorcery. Baka Siya accused her victim directly, in private, baiting her. I was told that none of the congregation at the ritual was present at the baiting. The only witness was another woman, a close friend of Baka Siya's and an affine of the accused who also blamed her for other acts of sorcery. Other neighbors and kin considered this accusation, as they told me, "an affair of the women."

Baiting—I stress that this was the mode of accusation, direct and private, because it is essential to distinguish one mode from another; sociologically, each differs. An accuser need not bait her victim with the accusation of sorcery, or denounce, or sue on a charge.[31] When an accusation is made indirectly in gossip it is an insinuation; made directly in public, it is a denunciation; and raised in a legal or forensic context, it is a charge.

Baka Siya's choice of a ritual venue away from her own hamlet effectively excluded the mother's sister, whom she suspected, from the congregation. An alternative choice, which Baka Siya could have made in divination, would not have achieved this exclusion. Her mother's other sister was a host, living in a nearby hamlet in the same ward as Baka Siya's natal family, and belonging to the same local kin group under the leadership of Baka Siya's mother's brother. If Baka Siya's divination had fixed on this host, the mother's sister would have been able to join the congregation and raise her complaints against Baka Siya for neglecting her in the past and avoiding her. She was a "junior mother" and had a claim to attention and visits from a nearby "child." In a similar case, Kalanga explained to me, "the Lions of that place have been defeated by her long ago."

Instead, Baka Siya's natal family had to join her in a congregation outside their own ward and apart from the rest of their local kin group. Only an external relative, her father's sister, could, as a host, have furthered Baka Siya's campaign to separate her natal family from her local kin group. For other reasons also, this host was the ritual focus that Baka Siya required. In her father's sister, Baka Siya secured a go-between, indebted and grateful to her, and without cause for blaming her. Moreover, limiting the composition of the congregation to some of Baka Siya's paternal kin and her natal family assured that grievances against Baka Siya within her local kin group were not raised during the ritual. Thus her divinatory choice anticipated crucial consequences for relationships among her close kin. Baiting her mother's sister enabled Baka Siya to reject kinship obligations to this kinswoman without compelling Baka Siya's natal family publicly to be parties to the accusation, or involving others of the local kin group. At the same time, by publicly focusing upon the *zenge* of her father's sister, her choice rallied her natal family and other kin around her and promoted her own cause.

An important point about placement as strategic action in the locating of ritual must be stressed, for it is basic for any right understanding of demonic possession. Without benevolence, amity, and trust, demonic possession cannot proceed to bring the afflicted patient and the wrathful host together. For the sake of healing, Kalanga require these positive ideals to be actualized in deeds faithfully done during ritual. But where is the place for a particular person where benevolence, amity and trust actually hold true? Even if very close kin should ideally be benevolent, full of amity, and trusting, no one expects or finds them all actually to be so. Hence the location of a ritual in one place or another, avoiding the hostility of enemies as far as possible, is a matter of strategic choice for a sponsor. But to be cynical or deliberately manipulative in making the choice is to undermine the intent of ritual healing. It would be to stultify oneself in advance by a denial of the very ideals that must be actualized. Instead, making the choice through divination mystifies its strategic nature, especially in the eyes of the choicemakers themselves. In their eyes, the discriminator for the proof of amity, benevolence, trust, and for favoring a performance by certain kin in a certain location is the divinatory source of true knowledge, not the sponsor.

POSSESSION AND THE CHANGING DOMESTIC DOMAIN

Where the divide between town and country is perceived to have become radically narrowed, as in parts of rural Zambia (Colson 1984:11), one observed response has been that possession rituals formerly restricted to the countryside are performed in towns. However, based on my information and observations, which largely come from rural areas, Kalanga continue to perform demonic possession exclusively at home, in the countryside. Regarded from the countryside, the divide between town and country is still a meaningful one in terms of behavior that fits one or the other, although the divide is, of course, not absolute. In no way, however, would one deny a change in the last decade in the significance of demonic possession and, indeed, in the divide between town and country.

Rather than extending to town and increasing its importance, demonic possession has become more limited within the countryside. In my earlier writing about demonic possession (1971b, 1972), I did not appreciate a long-term trend against recruiting young hosts. The halt has become almost total in the past ten years (i.e., 1975–1985) in the areas I know best. Throughout the twenty-five year period of my study of demonic possession, the rule has been: once a migrant worker, never a novice host. In the four wards of my census and elsewhere, no women have, to my knowledge, become initiated into the status of host after a period of work in town. Some women, initiated before working in town, returned home for a visit, or permanently, and resumed the role of active host. Other roles among the principals have been played by previously uninitiated women who have been working away from their rural homes. As in the homecoming worker's case discussed earlier, such working women have been prominent among the patients and sponsors of the ritual; they are the ones who ritually pass property or on whose behalf it is passed to other women. Yet, how are we to account for the virtual avoidance of cult membership by the young and what are the main implications of this avoidance?

Kalanga themselves give various reasons. One is that young women prefer to join the "churches of the spirit" where, in congregations of kin and non-kin, they speak in tongues and are moved by the Holy Spirit. Such churches reject demonic possession as a backward thing of the past and worse still, a thing of the devil. Another reason mentioned is that young women are unwilling to undergo the initiation, given its nasty treatment and stink of the wild; it is held to be demeaning and ill-becoming by women who have been educated at school.

In the past, young novices were in the main elite women. At present, such women are often themselves schoolteachers, nurses, or other migrant workers, who are not primarily identified with domesticity in the countryside, or at least domesticity as it has been linked to the role of *dombo*. It is crucial to appreciate that the change equally has affected relations between older and younger women, and between women and men; in addition, the change is linked to kinship, rather than exclusively to gender. In the past, initiation established a long-lasting dependence between senior and junior kinswomen. The ritual services of the junior could not be given apart from the senior or without her permission, for the period of dependence. This dependence ended with the senior's death or with the payment of "bridewealth" (also called *malobola)* to the senior by the junior's husband (or son). Hosts who had been initiated by the same kinswoman formed bands. When they performed together, they deferred to one another; they observed a nice etiquette of seniority, according to birth and genealogical position. All members of a band were not always summoned; on occasion, no more than one or two hosts would become possessed, for various reasons. But as a host aged, her status was highest in the cult, and her authority extended through the greatest number of her junior hosts. At present, that dependence and authority can no longer be sustained. Currently, performances tend to focus on a single host, an old or middle-aged woman, with a chorus of younger women, kin, and affines, but without the band of juniors who, as hosts, could sing and dance about their own circumstances in the domestic life of the present.

CONCLUSION

We have seen that demonic possession is tied to the reconstruction of the domestic domain by Kalanga women. The possessed, who are women only, give their most important ritual services where women as active agents have their legitimate authority within the homestead. They perform in the kitchen, around the hearth in the compound, by the granary, and always at home, whether at their own or a relative's, but never in a strange place, such as in town. The master symbol in the demonic ritual is the stamping block, the mortar from which the staple of domestic life is produced by the pounding upon it of a pole as pestle.

The reconstruction of reality in the ritual is achieved through exchange and boundary-crossing. During demonic possession, Kalanga transfer "dirt" and purifying substances by means of go-betweens, in sacred exchange, between the domains of the domestic and the wild. Through the ritual treatment they seek to empower domestic life, "home," with something from beyond itself. Hence, during performances, they represent to themselves an image of existence in which the antitheses of everyday life are transcended.

Throughout the ritual, the demons are expected to disport themselves in ways that other divinities, such as the divinities of the dead, never do. The image of the demonic is centered on the lion as the predatory ruler of the wild. It is an image created around the bodies of possessed women dressed in imported luxuries, trade beads, and trade cloths. The wild and the alien are brought together around the women. The women are the agents of a domestic life, endangered in its commodity relations. The symbolic action of the hosts is more than mere resistance to encroachment from without, to "the penetration of capitalism," in an all too-familiar phrase. It is an empowering of domestic life that is actively creative of social reality.

During the interludes of demonic possession, Kalanga reconstruct social reality by counteracting a negative image. It is domestic life as it should not be. The demonic interludes are dialogic ordeals that include moments filled with mockery and humor alleging the bestial carnality of relatives. Home truths of domestic life are confronted. Relatives must share these moments of truth, and they alone can fully appreciate the irony and the subtlety of innuendo about the hidden and unknowable in their lives (for the contrast to Ndembu cults of affliction, see Werbner 1971b).

Upon the basis of a holistic, transformational analysis, we have advanced to an understanding of how the key idea of the ritual relates to its progression as a whole, to its higher order organization. Our understanding encompasses a view of ritual as coordinated action, the coordinates being the basic terms for agency and its characteristic qualities or various states. In making this advance, we have also kept the need for situational and symbolic analysis in perspective in order to show, through an actual case, how ritual can be regarded as strategic action.

ACKNOWLEDGMENT

I wish to thank the Fulbright Commission, the University of Manchester, and the Economic and Social Science Research Council (formerly SSRC) for grants and leave for research.

CHAPTER 3

KALANGA SACRIFICE

The Restorative Movement
of Divinities and People

UNDERLYING CONCEPTS

Like demonic possession, Kalanga sacrifice is a healing ritual. The rituals are alternatives, however. The difference between them is not so much in the nature of what they treat, but in how they heal, for each reconstructs reality in a distinct way. Both are performed to treat affliction as more than mere symptoms of a physical kind. What is manifest in the affliction Kalanga understand is occult disorder. The disturbed state is physical, and therefore evident in symptoms, and at the same time metaphysical, being the occult disturbance of aggrieved divinities. When aggrieved, divinities are "aroused" *(musa)* and "rise up," whereas they must "settle down" *(gadza)* and be "cool," if people too are to be "cool," and "healed" *(pola)*. In both demonic possession and sacrifice, an appropriate reconstruction of social reality is required to fulfill the quest for physical and metaphysical treatment. In both, satire, joking, and fun contribute to that healing reconstruction, during interludes set aside for them, although each make their contributions in ways that are as unlike as the rituals themselves.

In cattle sacrifice, satire, joking, and fun, though essential for the healing reconstruction, have no proper part. They are not recognized as obligatory rites or strictly ritual events. Instead, they belong to the anti-rites of play. Occurring as interludes between obligatory rites, these anti-rites, seemingly spontaneous yet always performed in the same style, suspend realities otherwise upheld in the ritual.

This contrast in the healing reconstruction of reality extends further to the alternative domains ritualized by demonic possession and cattle sacrifice. For sacrifice, the alternative is the public domain under male authority, of which the apt master symbol is the fence pole *(bango)*. Men control the sacrifice of cattle to *midzimu,* superior beings with whom men and women have a relation of filial piety. Even when a woman of a senior generation takes over the task of letting the blood of sacrifice pour in the wind, the ritual's most important act, she does so at a man's behest, within the forecourt. That, as the most public space within a homestead, remains under the legitimate authority of men. Overall, cattle sacrifice creates, and is itself a creation, in the public domain, where men dominate. In Kalanga ritual, that the public domain is above the domestic is as natural to the order of things as the knowledge that the pole as pestle is above the block as mortar.

The inequality between the public and domestic domains is an ideological reality. Within it, cattle sacrifice and demonic possession are constituted as variations of each other, the former superior and the latter inferior. There are: *(a)* alternative spaces and domains for performance, each requiring contrastive ritual movements; *(b)* alternatives in gender-specific authority; *(c)* alternatively located manifestations of divinity (the demons are also divinities) in alternative perpetual relations with people; *(d)* alternative kinds of interludes; *(e)* alternative ritual concerns, associated exclusively with guilty indebtedness, or with guilty indebtedness and pollution. All of these vary according to that ideological reality of superordination between domains; it informs the variation's alternatives and they, in turn, sustain it as part of the given order of existence.

In this chapter I devote my main attention to the second of the alternatives, cattle sacrifice and the public domain. Demonic possession and the domestic domain, discussed in the previous chapter, is here in the background, apart from salient features that I highlight briefly to illuminate the interrelation. At this point, for the sake of an early overview, a bare list of the alternatives is useful, even at the risk of some initial oversimplification.

	SACRIFICE	DEMONIC POSSESSION
Domain	Public	Domestic
Authority	Male	Female
Master Symbol	Fence pole	Stamping block

Orientation	Setting sun	Rising sun
Divinities	Divinities of dead	Demons
Relationship	Receivers of filial piety	Givers of impish irreverence
Concern	Debt	Pollution and debt
Interludes	Anti-rites of play	Rites of dialogic ordeal

Finally, for purposes of this introductory comparison, given my earlier discussion of commodity relations, gifting, and demonic possession, I must comment briefly upon the importance of sacrifice for decommoditization. Just as labor migrants offer goats for sacrifice in demonic possession, so too as older men do they offer cattle for sacrifice, usually one beast toward the climax of a career of labor migration. The cattle, like the labor migrants themselves, are important in "the good faith economy" (Bourdieu 1977:172). For example, they are paramount as investments and assets in social exchange, in the actual payment of bridewealth, and in commodity relations (the cash value of a single, mature beast may be nearly or even more than half of a labor migrant's annual wage). The decision to sacrifice cattle is an allocation of major wealth for home consumption in "the good faith economy" at the expense of its withdrawal from commodity relations. Hence, sacrifice, like demonic possession, is part of the management of labor migration as a social and symbolic process that changes a person's moral status and a person's moral condition (on the distinction, see Middleton 1979:184–86).

Repeated journeying back and forth between home and distant workplace moves the labor migrant between the moral status of stranger and that of homecomer (Schutz 1945). But the oscillation in moral status may be even more than that. If perceived at home to be of intrinsic value as a relative, friend, or neighbor, away from home the migrant risks being perceived as primarily a marketable commodity. The labor migrant who, over a long career, invests at home and earns at a great distance, is bound to be concerned with more than the management of material resources. In themselves such resources are often of minimal worth or yield unless around them the labor migrant can create unambiguously in the eyes of people at home what Bourdieu calls "symbolic capital" (1977). Hence it tends to be that the greater the labor migrant's investments at home, the more he or she is obliged to perform there public acts that can be seen unmistakeably to be highly charged in terms of generosity, selflessness, in short, the sociality of the home. Failure to meet this obligation puts the person at risk of being seen to be in an unfavorable moral condition. This is what cattle sacrifice counteracts since it is a means by which a man gives and significant others demonstrably receive an earnest of both commitment to a certain hierarchy of values and also attachment to home over any other place. In this respect, therefore, we may say that cattle sacrifice, with its pledging of support for "the good faith economy," becomes a part of the defense, renewal, and reconstruction of that economy.

Sacrifice: A General Model

In Hubert and Mauss' general model of sacrifice, the victim moves, when sacrificed, between the world of divinity and the world of living people (1964). In such communication, the victim is used for mediated contact between worlds. The victim is a vehicle by means of which sanctity is brought from the world of divinity or returned to it; and it may be a means by which sin is transferred from the world of living people. Whether the move is in one direction or the other, and thus whether the transfer is from the world of divinity or that of living people, depends on the prior condition of the sacrifier.[1] If the sacrifier is already invested excessively with a religious character, the expulsion of a divine element may be sought. If not, the purpose may be to endow the sacrifier with sanctity, moving the sacrifier closer to the world of divinity.

What the model does not represent is any move by divinity itself, coincident with the move of sacrifier or victim.[2] If such a model were to apply even where the divinities are unmoving or virtually unmoveable by human operation, it would hardly be a general model, because such divinities are no more than a special instance, at one extreme of a whole continuum. We may say that the model of Hubert and Mauss is Brahmanic or perhaps even Semitic, but it is not generally African; and certainly it does not hold for Kalanga, whose purpose is to move both divinities and people, through the personal sacrifice of a victim. Given the dual intent of such sacrifice, divinities have to be moved farther away and people closer together, with each movement being a condition for the other. In other words, the model, to be general, must comprehend, among other things, a double movement in opposite directions, and not merely a single movement in one direction.

My point is simply this: the subtlety of transformation in movement across ritual space escapes Hubert and Mauss' model. Hence, the first challenge to be addressed in this essay is a rethinking of movement in sacrifice. A model is needed that enables us to appreciate both the logic that underlies the movement and the experience that sacrifice reconstitutes. A second challenge arises from the limitations of Hubert and Mauss' general model. This concerns the processual form of ritual in sacrifice, its patterned movement from rite to rite. The conception they introduced has dominated the literature ever since. This dominance is evident not merely in studies of sacrifice, but in much of the literature concerned with various kinds of ritual that has built upon the related contributions of Van Gennep (1960) and most recently Turner (1967, 1982). Hubert and Mauss' conception of the processual form is tripartite. In the beginning is a phase of entry, next a central phase of consecration, and finally a phase of exit. The scheme is elaborated in their model along with their ideas about the distinct functions fulfilled in each phase.

A simple objection has to be put to their model. Here I am indebted to Stanner (1959) and Maddock (1985) in their efforts to rethink the processual form of initiation in the light of their comparative views of sacrifice. The objection is that the tripartite division collapses what are two quite distinct and unlike phases into one central phase. In symbolic behavior, the phases are contrasted and, in analysis, they need to be distinguished as well—hence the utility of a four-phase or, more fundamentally, a contrastive binary model.

It is not a matter of number, of one more or one less, that is at issue. Rather, our concern is with the processual form in an appropriate transformational analysis. If we follow Van Gennep and Turner, as well as Hubert and Mauss, and take the processual form to be tripartite, we tend to regard the ritual as if it were informed by a certain logic of mediation. We would say that from one extreme phase to the other, the sequence flows by way of a bridging transitional phase. That would be the much considered liminal phase which confounds or suspends the conditions of both the beginning and the end. Moreover, just as the bridging transitional phase would itself be in between the extremes so, too, would the ritual subjects be in a betwixt-and-between condition.

In a binary processual form, however, neither liminality nor the logic associated with it need figure. Instead, the sequence switches between alternatives; it goes from phase to contrasting phase in a dialectical progression. The same holds true for the condition of the ritual subjects, which switches and alternates without a confounding of extremes. The underlying logic is contrastive and reflexive. Put by way of introduction, the suggestion about the binary processual form is necessarily abstract; and to make it concrete in a more developed form, I must turn to the details of personal sacrifice of cattle among Kalanga.

In basing my argument upon an analysis of the ritual's processual form, I follow Hubert and Mauss in that I distinguish among the roles of the victim as the animal killed, the sacrifier who is the donor and prime beneficiary, the sacrificer who ritually offers the victim, and the divinity to whom the offering is made (1964). This distinction illuminates Kalanga practice, which, in separating the roles, creates a dependence of sacrifier on sacrificer. No man can be animal sacrificer on his own behalf. Instead, he must always rely on others, a senior and a junior relative, who in turn act on his behalf during the ritual. In Kalanga practice, this dependence has many implications; I examine these in due course.

Kalanga do perform other kinds of bloody sacrifice of domestic animals. The continuum includes the communal sacrifice of black bulls and oxen to a male manifestation of God Above, and of cows to the female manifestation of God Above (see Chapter 7), as well as the sacrifice of goats to *mazenge,* as alien demons of the wild (see Chapter 2). Regarding that whole continuum, however, I say here only what is required for my main account. Moreover, the sacrifiers I discuss are men, because women do not donate sacrificial cattle on their own behalf and they are limited to offering goats to *mazenge.* A further limitation is that I do not discuss the sacrifice at the founding of a kin shrine over black river stones, when a dead father or grandfather is received home as a divinity. To understand this calls for an account of an elder's succession and inheritance, and that is beyond my present scope.

Blood, meat, bones, dung, and chyme are all the stuff of sacrifice of a domestic animal. As such, much must be said about them. But in a sense each part is not a symbolic object in itself, since it is always treated as a component in a synthesis (see also, Firth 1973:245; Lewis 1980:33). Over the course of a bloody sacrifice every part, in turn, has to be recombined with its material antithesis, be that stone, beer, or water. Moreover, if certain symbolic relationships are to be balanced anew, and the bloody sacrifice is to succeed in its intent, transactions with significant others, living and dead, must be completed, in which the recombined antitheses are both given and accepted.

Each body part is a means for physically embodying symbolic relationships and inner or moral states, such as being at ease, free of debt, and "cool." Thus, the body part is a means for reconstituting, through external physical manipulation, what would otherwise be internal and inaccessible; but the body part is, in sacrifice, merely a component means.

In a sense, the sequences of sacrificial rites are tightly integrated around the victim's body as a dominant image of an organized interior space and as a metaphor for kinship and the self.[3] In such bloody sacrifice, however, the body has to be broken down, the parts brought into contact with antithetical things of the exterior, for the sake of a fresh synthesis, above all, a new inner state of being.

Underlying the break in contact and subsequent recombination is a process of deconstruction and reconstruction (see also, de Huesch 1985), which calls for close discussion of the sequencing of contact and part-to-whole relations, and the relations of metonomy in the ritual. But to avoid misunderstanding, I want to make it plain, from the very beginning, that I do not agree with Lévi-Strauss' view of sacrifice (1966:223–228). Lévi-Strauss argues, mistakenly, that sacrifice is metonymical in orientation. I would rather argue, following de Huesch, that sacrifice has both metonymical and metaphorical aspects, both of which have to be and are examined in my account.

All the same, given the very great importance of metonomy in sacrifice, a simple illustration of it in a single rite is useful to introduce certain key issues. Later, I contextualize the illustration more fully in the sequencing of the sacrificial rites as a whole. The rite is one of the first, and it is often said by Kalanga to be the most important thing in a sacrifice: letting the victim's hot blood spill by pouring it or allowing it to drip over cool stones.[4] This release is said to cause *midzimu,* the divinities of the dead,[5] to be cool and slow, rather than hot and quick to anger toward the sacrificer. The blood is said to be a dangerous thing. Hence tempering the blood and thus controlling the danger is as important in the rite as releasing the blood and the life associated with it. In the rite, excessive heat is brought together with cool, and an animate fluid with an inanimate solid. We may say that this operation has at least two dynamics: the first, the thermal, is intended to cause a change in heat, and the second, the kinetic, a change in movement.

I find it useful to regard the whole class of such metonymical operations under the notion of "ritual tempering." Ritual tempering is intended to modify unsuitable, perhaps excessive, states or qualities by a favorable combination with their antitheses. The ritual operation is metonymical and a matter of contiguity in that it is accomplished by bringing antithetical substances into contact, often by surrounding one with another.

Ritual tempering is, of course, a class term. As such, it covers many differences that could well do with further systematic conceptualization. Kinetic, thermal, chromatic, acoustic, or other dynamics may be produced separately or in any of a multitude of combinations in ritual tempering. The variation can be great, it hardly needs to be said, from culture to culture and even from phase to phase of the same ritual. The comparative problems involved go well beyond our present scope (see also, Beck 1969; P. Werbner 1986).

Nevertheless, it is worth pointing out that there is a special domain for analysis which may perhaps be usefully called "the synergetics of ritual." Its subject is the way that metonymic transformations operate together and constitute some movement in the ritual, such as a modification in the moral condition and other state of being of a person or group. In studying the synergetics of ritual, we may gain an understanding of how people use substances in sequences to modify their experience, and not only to rework their concepts in the fashion of Lévi-Strauss' bricoleur, as it were reconceptualizing a static whole with "the logic of the concrete."

For our purposes, the main questions of ritual synergetics are about *(a)* sequences of substances, *(b)* modifications in the states of the congregation, sacrifier and sacrificer, and *(c)* the processual form of sacrifice. Over the course of a personal sacrifice, how and why does the ritual tempering progress or alternate in space and sequence? With regard to different kinds of symbolic relationship, what is conveyed conceptually and made manifest in felt experience by thermal, kinetic, and other changes in substances? Finally, given the vast literature on theories of bloody sacrifice, no discussion of the subject can fruitfully ignore questions of communion and communication, of the sharing or giving of oneself. Thus, such questions are also considered in my account along with the related questions of synergetics.

Sacrifice: Semantics and Imagery

For the appropriate symbolic behavior among Kalanga, I use the word "sacrifice." Sacrifice is not an exact translation of any single Kalanga word, however. Most commonly, Kalanga speak of "stabbing" *(baya)*, which is, of course, not reserved exclusively for sacrifice. Similarly, other terms, such as "giving to divinities" *(pa midzimu)*, "driving away divinities" *(tatha midzimu)*, "consoling" *(fupa)*, "interceding and imploring" *(rapela)*, "spilling or pouring" *(tebula)*, all are used for other occasions, including the seasonal offering of grain and unfermented beer before sowing.

Words are, of course, notoriously bad hints of concepts; and the lack of a lexical distinction does not in itself stand in the way of a conceptual distinction that is operationalized and made evident in behavior. But one implication of this is that our account must concentrate on imagery and what is actualized in ritual sequences, rather than

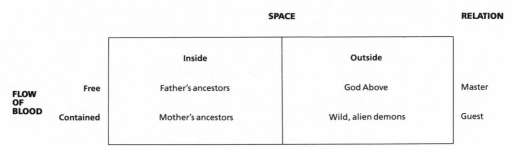

Figure 16. *Forms of Sacrifice.*

on the semantics of words. The release of blood is the imagery we must begin with, and return to repeatedly, given its paramount importance for Kalanga (see Figure 16).

Binary alternatives in the imagery are the basis for operationally distinguishing each of the four forms within the whole continuum of Kalanga sacrifice. According to where and how the blood is offered, contrasting relations with divinity—or rather different kinds of divinities—are represented. In spatial terms, the offering is made either within the hamlet, as a personal sacrifice to the dead as divinities, or outside the hamlet, either to Mwali, God Above, in a communal sacrifice, or in personal sacrifice to the *mazenge,* the alien demons of the wild. The relation expressed is thus with divinity as internal in the case of the dead, or external in the case of God Above and the alien *mazenge*. The relations vary with the alternative imagery of release. The blood of sacrifice can be free flowing or uncontained, as in the case of sacrifices made for God Above, as well as one's paternal ancestors or, alternatively, it can be the blood contained by a bowl or within a possessed person who has drunk of it (respectively, in sacrifices for the matrilateral ancestors and the demons in a perpetual matrilateral relationship). In this way, the bond with divinity is further imaged as either with a divinity as the master *(mweni)* freely owning the space, or as the guest *(mwezi)* temporarily contained within it.

Guilty Indebtedness, Balanced Reciprocity, and Communication

The usual motive for sacrifice also varies according to the space and imagery of release. Where the relation is internal, as in personal sacrifice to the dead, the general motive for sacrifice that is culturally stressed is "guilty indebtedness," to use Lienhardt's apt phrase for one form of

Dinka sacrifice (1961:150). The guilty aspect is a matter of having "forgotten" *(kangangwa)* or "neglected and abandoned" *(lasha)* one's forebears *(bobatategulu,* grandfathers, ancestors).

The mitigatory personal sacrifice is not piacular, however. The concept of sin is absent, and there is no rite of expiation. It is where the relation to divinity is external, as in the case of God Above or the alien *mazenge,* that sin and expiation feature in sacrifice. Even in personal sacrifice to the dead, the sacrificer or an extension of himself, such as his family and dependents, is seen to be suffering from the presence of *midzimu,* divinities that act upon the self from without.

The human condition, which is a manifestation of "the awakening of divinities," corresponds directly to that. It may be something quite general, such as unease, sleeplessness, anxiety, discord, or a lack of domestic peace; or it may be quite specific, such as the inability to keep a job or to have children who survive. But in every case, there is a debt *(nlandu)* to be paid, an obligation to be fulfilled; and the occasion for payment comes unwilled by the sacrificer as debtor. The idea is that it is the dead as creditors who determine that occasion by means of affliction which, in turn, has to be interpreted through divination.

In response to my telling about Americans landing on the moon, in Kalanga eyes an act of arrogance overreaching the human limits given by God (also *ndzimu),* an elder called Madzilumba challenged me as an American to affirm our common mortality and our common spiritual cycle with divinities. In demanding that affirmation from me, he gave the following basic ideas about divinity, the soul, flesh, and bone. I quote Madzilumba at length because the ideas he put are central in my discussion,

When a man breathes, we say it is the *meya,* soul, spirit. And when he dies, we bury his bones. But we do not know where his soul goes to. Then we divine *(kandila),* and we are troubled. We say it is *midzimu* (divinities, wrath) and we say it is wind *(pehpo).* A shrine *(Shumba nlume)* is established. He returns without our seeing him, and we ask, "Is it that there is wind coming?"

So I ask you, "At your home, when your fathers die, do they not return, being divinities *(buya midzimu)?* Whether we are red as you are now, or black as we are, are we not still one?" And so I say it must be so, that your fathers like ours do come back. We are all flesh together.

Similarly, in commenting upon the blood in sacrifice, an elder who was a diviner linked two ideas: to exist is to eat, and life is the flow of blood,

When a person dies, he grieves, saying that: "I have left the country and no longer eat." But we let him know that we still spill this blood for him so that it goes as the wind and mixes with the wind. Then he says, "I eat also," for he has eaten the blood that spilled to the ground.[6]

Bloody sacrifice emphasizes balanced reciprocity toward the dead to whom one owes one's possessions. The stress is on a filial relationship, which reverses over time. Children are the receivers of food and the very means of existence from their parents; in their turn, with the reversal of dependence, children become the givers.

Another elder told me, "These cattle we have, we have from our forebears; and if we do not give any to them, they will not give us again." Along with this is a notion of surrendering cattle as the most highly valued good, for the sake of a higher good, life itself. It is an idea of giving the life of a domestic animal to preserve one's own life and those of one's dependents. The cattle should thus come preferably from one's own herd, and not be bought specially for the occasion. Moreover, the idea of the substitution of the animal for its owner, if usually present, is sometimes dominant.

For example, Ta Mayenda came home as a labor migrant to sacrifice to the spirit of his mother's mother after having had several children die in infancy. On the advice of a diviner he consulted in Johannesburg, in the presence of his sister and brother, Ta Mayenda sacrificed a cow of his whose calves never survived weaning; that is, the sacrificial victim's condition was Ta Mayenda's own.

Such maintenance of balanced reciprocity over the giving of life is predicated upon a certain cultural conception of the appropriate distance between the living and the dead as divinities. Ideally, it involves a good measure of separation. Personal sacrifice is the means of restoring that. Once awakened, the dead as divinities come too close; they have to be driven away if the living are to rest easy.

In this respect, Evans-Pritchard's view of Nuer sacrifice to God holds true for Kalanga personal sacrifice to the dead. "It is made to separate God and man, not to unite them" (1956:275). The intent toward divinities is communication, not communion; the living give and the dead as divinities receive, but they are not brought together to share in the same experience or in some essential fellowship. While both feed on the victim, and the blood is said to be the feast *(madjo)* that the divinities demand, the living and dead could hardly be moved further apart in and through their feeding. Each feeds in a separate space on different parts of the victim's body ritually tempered in different ways, in different rites, and at different phases of the ritual. In due course, I say more about the nature of these differences and their implications for, among other things, a general model of sacrifice such as that of Hubert and Mauss.

The intent of communication with divinities is highlighted in the very choice of sacrificial victim. The victim is expected to cry out, when killed. In ritual, as in daily life, a child's crying out moves a parent to take pity and care for the child's wants, the sacrifier being in a filial relationship to the awakened dead and the victim's crying out being on the sacrifier's behalf. The victim is also expected to be a means for the communication to divinities of fellow feeling over loss at death. Kalanga recognize that "Just as we cry when a person dies, so too cattle cry when their fellow dies." The sight and smell of the victim's chyme makes other cattle cry. It is thus left in the pen so that the cattle remaining there bellow and moan the dead, just at the time when people, around the hearth and about to eat, ululate in thanks to the divinities.

Opposite sounds from people and their domestic animals are used to communicate to the divinities an acknowledgment of life giving at the expense of life taking. The giving of life by and for the people is recognized to be at the expense of the taking of life from the domestic animals. In accord with the victim's signal role in communication, the one domestic animal Kalanga do not sacrifice is the sheep. The sheep dies dumb, without crying. Thus it fails as a means of communication. Inarticulateness is incompatible with sacrifice.

Sacred Communion Among the Living

That said, however, it would be grossly misleading, and contrary to my later argument, to leave the impression that I agree with Evans-Pritchard's view of the meal in sacrifice, or rather, that it is the same for Kalanga as apparently for Nuer. For Kalanga sacrifice, at least, it is quite wrong to say, as Evans-Pritchard does for Nuer, that the eating by the living is "not a sacramental meal but an ordinary commensual act of family or kin which, moreover, falls outside the sacrificial rite" (1956:274).[7] Among Kalanga, the dead as divinities are expected to attend upon and have an interest in the meal of the living. While each portion is being shared out, the men who serve appeal to the divinities to return to their shade *(ntuzi)*, their place and condition of being cool. *Rapelana midzimu* (interceding and imploring with divinities) by a congregation as a whole *(gubungano)* is what is required on the sacrificer's behalf. But only when the living are well and generously satisfied can they accomplish such mediation. Hence they are urged by the sacrificers to rejoice while eating. All present are expected to form a moral community, with mutual understanding *(wanano)* and without fighting. Indeed, as Kalanga put it, the very eating and being satisfied together as a congregation is itself intercession by the living with the divinities.

Until the living have fulfilled their part in the meal in amity, the dead as divinities cannot complete theirs. The most important thing in the feast of the dead as divinities, the blood, is offered first and raw. But the living have to cook and then strip away the flesh by eating it, before the dead as divinities can get the rest of what they want, namely the body reconstituted as a clean inner whole. Only then can the victim's bones be recollected for the divinities and brought to them in the river, away from both human habitation or burial, in a cooled condition. Such a reconstituted unity as a whole of enduring bone, bare of the flesh that rots, is intended to be a consolation for the dead, and I would add that in Kalanga "bone" and "console" are the same word, *fupa*.

In the communication with the dead, which is not and cannot be communion, certain things must be rendered. The dead as divinities, and thus no longer mortal, want the blood as the substance that gives life, and the clean bone as the substance that lasts after life. The communion and fellowship of the living is in the sharing of flesh, as befits their mortal condition, all alike being liable to rot. I should point out that in Kalanga, flesh and meat are one word, *nyama;* and thus in self reference for ego, one says *"Imi ku nyama"* (I to my flesh), that is, "I myself;" but more will be said about ego and, indeed, the reconstruction of ego in sacrifice, below.

A general point needs to be stressed here. Communion and communication are sometimes put forward as though they were the basis for alternative theories of sacrifice, the one derived from Robertson Smith, the other from Hubert and Mauss. In Kalanga sacrifice however, both are important. Instead of being theoretical alternatives, communication and communion are phases, each essential for the other, in a cumulative and encompassing ritual transformation. It is a transformation that requires a step-by-step exposition, to be fully grasped as a whole.

Toward the dead, and in turn toward the living, there is a contrastive sequence. In this sequence communication and communion are juxtaposed, as are balanced and generalized reciprocity. The dead are thanked and implored to be thankful for the feast they receive as repayment on a debt. By contrast, the living must not give thanks to the sacrifier for the sacrificial flesh they eat; to do so would be an impious act. This marks the sacrificial meal apart from an ordinary meal. It is an imperative obligation for a guest to give thanks in an ordinary meal, and I found Kalanga to be very careful about that, always thankful for food at ordinary meals. The living owe nothing for their sacrificial meal, and they are under no obligation to repay it. Indeed, many never themselves manage to become sacrifiers; but if they do, it is again a matter of generalized reciprocity toward the living, rather than balanced reciprocity. There is no debt, but there is a relationship in which ritual service is rendered.

A familiar correlation underlies the contrast we have been discussing. It is the correlation that Sahlins suggests holds between social distance and forms of reciprocity in a spectrum (1972:196). At the extreme of closeness comes generalized reciprocity, and with greater distance, balanced reciprocity. We may say that in Kalanga personal sacrifice the use of correlated forms of reciprocity follows the dual intent of the ritual, namely achieving greater closeness with the living and greater distance from the dead as divinities; hence, generalized reciprocity toward the living, and balanced reciprocity toward the dead as divinities.

But how are we to understand as a sequence the juxtaposition of communication and balanced reciprocity, on the one hand, with communion and generalized reciprocity on the other? What transformation is effected through the sequence of contrast in symbolic modes along with contrasting forms of gift? To answer these questions we must follow the sequence in greater detail through the whole course of sacrifice from acts of deconstruction to rites of reconstruction. The latter, the most elaborate rites, include communication with its phases of entry and exit as well as communion with its phases of separation and aggregation.

THE "AROUSAL OF DIVINITIES" AND COSMOLOGY

Before I attempt to describe the whole course of cattle sacrifice, I must give my understanding of a Kalanga assumption about movement in the cosmos. It is an assumption upon which their concept of "the arousal of divinities" and, indeed, the entire course of cattle sacrifice is predicated. It is one of the assumptions about which we need to take special care in cross-cultural interpretation because it runs against what, in the West at least, is now usually taken for granted. It is, indeed, most like an assumption that is basic in the East (see Dumont 1970). The assumption is that the higher, ultimate state of existence, represented by the "cool" (pola) of composure, is properly inactivity, not activity.

Such primacy for rest, which is associated with the contrast between seniors or superiors and juniors or inferiors, is imaged as a cardinal feature of Kalanga divination, a feature upon which diviners readily comment (see Werbner 1973). The four divining lots are distinguished by seniority and sex. The seniormost and primary tablet, the Old Man, is known by a metaphor for endurance, and it is praised in a verse about a rock that sits and sits and does not budge. The contrast is to the Old Woman, who "trails after" or leaves a trail behind, and to the other juniors, the Young Man and Young Woman, who are even more active or aggressive.

Being still, immobile, at rest, and not the opposite, as in a Western assumption, is the superior condition. It is thus calm that befits superiors and seniors, such as the divinities, when the cosmos is in order with all things and everyone where they belong. Failing to give the dead their due puts things where they do not belong, with juniors at the expense of seniors. Hence it is incompatible with the superiors' rest, immobility, and being still; the disturbance is the superiors' arousal, which is unease, unrest, and turbulence.

Given this non-Western assumption valuing rest over motion, we can better appreciate how Kalanga see the dialectical process in which cultural reality is reconstructed at a sacrifice. What exists before the performance, and provides the occasion for it, is the disturbed condition of unease, unrest, and turbulence, which is "the arousal of divinities." In the first half of the sacrifice, the acts of deconstruction, in which the animal is killed and butchered, break down what was a whole being into its parts. The acts are disjunctive, exaggerating a breakdown of the order that sustains life. Next, in the second half, the making of the cosmically compatible distinctions in existence for the living and for the dead is ritually accomplished through the sharing out and receiving of cooked or uncooked food. Finally, after the ritual, there is the reign, however brief, of restored stillness and coolness, when the calmed divinities of the dead are powerfully beneficial towards their succeeding generations among the living.

THE CONTRASTIVE BINARY MODEL

This leads me closer to my detailed description of the ritual and, in turn, my transformational analysis. Another step is needed, however, for the sake of clarity, because, in my view, Kalanga sacrifice has a processual form built upon a contrastive binary model. This binary model, with its increasingly more inclusive contrasts, is illustrated in Figure 17.

Put abstractly, the binary model is a hierarchy of antitheses from action to counteraction. In other words, the major division of the

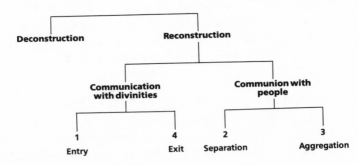

Figure 17. Binary Processual Form of Sacrifice.

whole sacrifice into halves is constructed by action in opposition to counteraction. Within that major division, the same relation of opposition is true for the subdivision of sets of phases; and in turn, for each phase and counterphase. More concretely, in the major division, which is the highest order antithesis, acts of deconstruction and rites of reconstruction are juxtaposed. Next, within the rites of reconstruction, the antithesis is between rites of communication with divinities and rites of communion with people. In turn, within the communication rites, the antithesis is between the rites of entry and exit; and, also in turn, within the communion rites, it is between the rites of separation and aggregation.

The sequencing in ritual performance, which has this hierarchy of antitheses, moves through oscillation. Ritual performance thus becomes a progression that surmounts the antitheses. I would stress that it is only in ritual performance that the antitheses are surmounted. The spiral in Figure 18 is a schematic illustration of a progressive oscillation through the rites of deconstruction.

Very briefly, in advance of my detailed description, this is the course of the oscillation. During the communication of the first and last rites, the movement is toward exclusion. Starting near the hamlet entry or the shrine of stones, which with its altar *(dala)* may be regarded as a kind of anti-hearth and home center for the dead, the divinities are sent away in coolness to cool waters, beyond human habitation, to where a river may ultimately find them in their remoteness. By contrast, during the communion of the rites in-between, rites 2 and 3, the switch is to and from inclusion. The elders remain at the hearth as a center of the living and are joined by their juniors around them. This, as I have already argued, follows the dual intent of the ritual, that is,

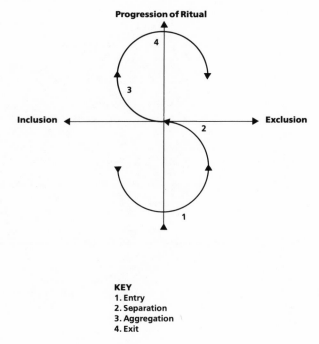

Figure 18. Oscillation in Ritual Sequence.

to move divinities farther away and people, closer together. I would go further and suggest that the way this sequence oscillates and turns back upon itself is a function of reflexivity in ritual.

PHASES IN SACRIFICE

First, in the early morning or late afternoon, come the acts of deconstruction. These take place outside the sacrificer's home, either in the pen or beyond the fence and in the frontage to the west. Later, moving eastward, come the rites of reconstruction within the sacrifier's fenced domestic space. These are the rites of (1) entry, (2) separation, (3) aggregation, and (4) exit.

To begin with, in that external space, the beast is slaughtered, skinned, bled, and cut up into pieces. The carving is done while the victim lies on its hide, resting on its back in the posture of an immobilized being. Usually, the sacrificer himself is absent; he simply tells the

Figure 19. A Newly Built Shrine Before the First Sacrifice. Built at the front of the hamlet, which is on the edge of a millet garden, the shrine has four posts bare of bark, that support a platform. Below it, on the right, *are the two black stones, embodying the returned dead, that have been rolled from the cool of the river. Maintaining this cool is the evergreen planted next to the stones.*

slaughterer in advance which beast is the victim, and only a few people are present. Men say they do not like to watch beasts die, their own or those of others.

The slaughterer, who may use a knife or a spear, but not a gun, is preferably a senior son or close junior kinsman. No special person is needed to perform the butchery. The operation is a menial task fit for a man other than an elder; it simply requires someone skillful with a knife. Moreover, the butcher need not be the slaughterer or sacrificer. He need not be, in other words, the person who takes charge of subsequent events during the meal and eventually completes the sacrifice by giving divinities the bones in the river.

Great care has to be taken during the deconstruction, in certain cases, to collect the blood in a bowl, always to separate distinct parts, and never to mix categories. For example, at one sacrifice, the butcher was a Bushman who unwittingly cut into the rumen and let the chyme, which is for the divinities, spill over the fatty tissue, which is for the elders. Outraged, the sacrificer screamed at the Bushman that he was cutting and spoiling like a wild animal. Another man grabbed the Bushman away by the scruff of the neck, rescued the fat, and took over the careful division of the beast into its separate parts.

Figure 20. A Libation of Unfermented Beer. This libation, poured over the two black stones, at the far right, by a senior and close kinswoman along with her uterine kin, was the first at a sacrifice during the installation of an elder at his new shrine.

With regard to a view of sacrifice as a ritual with four phases, we may say that only the four rites of reconstruction are the ritual proper. In a narrow sense of ritual, deconstruction takes place prior to the rites addressed to the divinities and it does not begin with any consecration. Another Kalanga ritual includes a rite of dedication that sets a bull aside for a divinity. The bull then incarnates a dead father or grandfather, after whom he is named and addressed, until he is eventually sacrificed or simply dies. But in personal sacrifice there is no initial act, such as rubbing ashes or the laying on of hands, that would impart sanctity to the living beast and perhaps, as Evans-Pritchard suggests for the Nuer, thereby devote the beast's life to divinity in substitution for the life of man (1956:261).

Before the sacrifice, or at least before the release of blood, some offering of grain should be made. Here I want to say about the grain offering only as much as is necessary for my main account of blood sacrifice. The offering, which is performed by both men and women, consists of three rites. In the first, the sacrificer's close kinsmen and kinswomen line up together, according to seniority. Facing west, each in turn takes a calabash in the right hand and, moving counterclockwise around the sacrifier, pours white unfermented beer over the

Figure 21. An Offering of Millet Seed. The kin stand, with their arms crossed, according to genealogical position, around the shrine at the installation sacrifice. They make an offering of millet seed, which they broadcast in anticipation of their future harvests. Behind them, and at the extreme left, with arms folded, stand the wife-receivers who built the shrine, brought its stones from the river, and never make offerings at it.

black stones of an elder's shrine.[8] Amidst the ululation of the women, the offerer invokes or berates the divinity on the sacrificer's behalf. Among the invocations I recorded are:

Let the child of my mother get well, the person who has long been suffering. For you divinity, what sort of divinity would you be without making it cool [i.e., what is wrong with you, if you are not to cause healing]? These are yours, Grandfather, the foods about which you have been complaining that "I am in the country and there is nothing that I eat." You have heard, Grandfather.

In the second rite, all the kin together cross their arms, and then, while uncrossing them, broadcast millet seed about themselves, the sacrificer, and the shrine. They are exhorted to act in unison. Again, similar invocations are made on behalf of the sacrificer, such as, "Let him heal. You have heard, Grandfather."

Finally, the grain offering is concluded, after it is said, "There are your foods, Grandfather." Each of the kin then drinks from the calabash, once again taking turns according to seniority, although this time an onlooker, such as I was, will be urged to drink as well, after the kin. That is done immediately before leaving the shrine, after the pouring of blood and chyme. Care is taken, with repeated instructions from the most senior of the kin, to make sure that the calabash is returned and left ready for use, upright on top of the black beer pot that contains the rest of the beer. Emptied of chyme, the relish pot is also left upright, but the sifting basket for the millet seed is turned over. It is a matter of respect for the divinities, out of due recognition that the beer is the divinities' and that they are to remain behind drinking it. Hence, sharing in a drink of the beer at the shrine is the closest that people come to communion with the divinities during the ritual as a whole.

Viewed abstractly, in terms of processual form, there is an alternation in these offering rites. The sequence switches between giving to divinities and taking by people; and within the giving to divinities, it switches from the representation of inequality among individuals to collective equality within an undifferentiated unity. As the following discussion demonstrates, the same logic, one that is contrastive and reflexive, underlies both blood sacrifice and grain offering.

As for the rites of reconstruction, these usually begin within the sacrificer's home, starting with private communication over blood between an elder and divinities.[9] This first ritual act is performed during the rite of entry, which takes place near the hamlet's public entrance to the west. At the other extreme, the end of the ritual takes place late in the final night, with an even more private, virtually secret, communication over the bones between a junior kinsman and divinities. This final ritual act is done during the rite of exit by the river, after a junior kinsman has carried the bones out of the hamlet's private exit to the east.

In the beginning, toward evening or at dawn, the blood is offered by an elder who is either the sacrificer's mother or father or, failing them, a surrogate (one of their siblings or siblings' children). The choice of elder and time depends upon the divinities that are being addressed; those on the mother's side are addressed at evening dusk, those on the father's side at dawn. In either case, the divinities are of the dead whom the elder could have known in life, usually within two generations. A linked variation holds for the place and pouring of the blood offering. If the divinities are of the father's side and the hamlet has a shrine of dedicated stones for them, the blood offering is allowed to flow from the portions of flesh hung above the stones. These are the portions later consumed by the elders. According to orthodox practice, if the divinities are of the mother's side, the offering should be poured on the ground from a bowl in the shade of a tree. However, where there is a shrine, Kalanga tend to use it, even for the offering to the mother's side.

In making the offering in the front within the hamlet, the elder may be alone. If highly visible to others busy elsewhere in the hamlet, the elder speaks in a way that may not be easily overheard. His or her brief speech is addressed to the known dead in a specific relationship, such as father or mother's brother.

The following is an example from a matrilateral sacrifice, the blood of which was offered by the sacrificer's mother:

Mother's brother and your sister, you should cool the children. They divine and they say that it is you who troubles us with divinity, so that we do not work, we do not awaken well. I entreat you, my brothers.[10] Today he has given you a feast, the feast that you seek. Today you should thank, my

Figure 22. A Senior Kinswoman Empties the Red Relish Pot of Chyme.

Figure 23. An Elder's Shrine Following the Completion of the Sacrificial Entry Rites. Above the platform is the victim's head, along with his hide. Below it, around the stones and the evergreen plant covered with the blood and the libation, is the dung-smeared floor. The elder's hide blanket is folded inside out upon his stool, next to the libation pot and, beyond the sacrificial floor, the sifting basket for the millet seed offering.

brothers. The congregation will be tomorrow; people will entreat you on my behalf, my divinity. Today let that little bug of yours[11] go well in the country; let it be beaten by the wind. I can be very thankful, my brothers. It is finished, my brothers; I can be very thankful.

Finally, in a last sacrificial act at the shrine, the officiating elder pours out chyme from a red relish pot and announces, "There are your foods, Grandfather."

After this, at the hearth and cooking yard, later in the evening (for a matrilateral sacrifice) or that morning (for a patrilineal one) comes the first rite of communion, which unites an inner circle of elders, the sacrifier's closest kin, neighbors and friends, and sets them apart from everyone else. After they or their juniors roast the liver, this small number of elders eat it, and then drink beer, the men and the women separately.

The rest of that evening or morning is taken up by a playful interlude, in which the intimates of the home, and not only the elders, drink and make merry. In a totally spontaneous way, men and women take turns singing and dancing. Songs of scandal, church hymns,

*Figure 24. Elders Share the
Roasted Liver along with Beer
in the Communion Rites.
The hearth for roasting is behind
the elders.*

popular ballads, or land-shrine chants, all are part of the medley as they may be in any socializing at a beer drink; and the aim is to perform for the sheer fun of it in a way that makes people rejoice and be happy.

Sometimes, an elder may do a take-off in a ridiculous performance. For example, at one such interlude, the sacrificer's paternal aunt, notorious in the family for her ill-temper and sorcery, was asked to give a mock sermon. She delivered it in the full-blown style of Zionist preachers, all to the great amusement of everyone around her.

On that day or the next, after the heat of the day has passed and the flesh has been cooked, the communion meal begins for the widest congregation.[12] It includes neighbors within the vicinity as well as kin and friends invited from a distance, all of whom are, for this purpose, the sacrificer's *zwalani,* "people who give birth together" or "mates." In this rite of aggregation, elders come together with their juniors, while being appropriately differentiated from them. Each gets a certain share in a certain place according to what befits the relationship with the sacrificer. Roughly, the more distant the relationship, the farther away from the hearth and cooking yard the person is likely to be when served during the meal. At the center of it all, by the hearth in the cooking yard, are the elders and those the sacrificer would honor as the closest of kin and friends. Homage *(svoba)* is paid to them by giving them a piece of flesh on the bone. They are, above all, next to the divinities who ultimately get all the bone.

During the meal, the flesh is made a metaphor for kinship and other relationships between generations. According to their roles in procreation and nurture, the father is given the thigh and front leg to share; the mother, the buttocks, backside and belly, and if the victim is a cow, the udder as well. According to their order of birth, a brother is given either a front or a hind leg, being like the leg either before or after the sacrificer. A sister, along with her family, gets a shoulder. Finally, according to seniority between generations, the elders as superiors have the head, including the eyes. Sometimes, as inferiors, children of the hamlet and other youngsters may get some of the lower part, including the tongue, jaw, and mouth.

The distribution also recognizes the emotions and capacities that ought to distinguish elders and juniors. The elders get the liver, one diviner told me, "because it is a thing that can calm down the soul *(gadzikanya meya)*"; the heart, "because it is something that can remember many thoughts and reflect very much *(alikanisa)*"; and the brain, "because it tells us what to do and what to think, working with the heart." Similarly, juniors are sometimes given the spleen, which is "the stick of the lads," because of their quickness to anger and fighting.

In the rite of aggregation, as in the preceding rite of separation, the communion meal culminates in beer drinking, the difference being a matter of scale and quantity. For the large congregation, the beer is laid on lavishly, and vast quantities are consumed. The subsequent playful interlude, which goes on until rather late at night, is a time for very high spirits, once again celebrated with spontaneous song and dance, often comic or satirical, and always performed with the license that indicates it is for sheer entertainment.

The next day, as is usual in any beer drink, Bango (the fence-pole, the master symbol for the public domain),[13] the drink of beer to clear the head of a hangover, is shared among the intimates and close neighbors. At this time the head may also be eaten. But the ritual itself is concluded with the exit rite by the river, before dawn, immediately after the playful interlude.

Describing this rite, an elder told me that the river carries the bones away to "grandfather" *(batategulu);* and when I objected, for the sake of exploring literal-mindedness, that the waters do not usually run on the surface of the river, it being a sand-river, the elder replied, "That does not matter. Once we have put them in the river, even if a dog comes and takes the bones away, there is no fault *(nlandu,* debt), for we *have* put them in the river."

The act is a free release with an intent of amity. Were the intent the opposite, the bones could be buried in the ground as an act of aggression or retaliation against sorcerers in the congregation. Done secretly in the dead of the night, the rite cannot be undone by people tampering with the bones for their own purposes. The sacrificer may make a final speech, "We are pouring away the bones of your cattle, Grandfather, those from which people ate."

PROGRESSION AND SIMULTANEOUS TRANSFORMATIONS

There is a progression from phase to phase in the overall sequence. That progressive totality has to be broken down, for purposes of analysis, into the distinct, though concurrent, sequences that constitute it. Only thus can we understand how the simultaneous transformations are built up as a whole. In this method, we consider each series separately: *(a)* the victim's substance and its processing; *(b)* the subjects performing the ritual; and *(c)* the spatio-temporal series.

In substances, the move away from the entry rite to the separation rite is a shift from *malopa,* "blood for the dead," to *chilopa,* "liver for the living elders." Here the semantic contrast around the root *-lopa* is between the notion of an aggregate of many, i.e., *lopa* with the *ma* prefix, and the notion of a diminutive, i.e., *lopa* with the *chi* prefix. The contrast implies a diminishing in substance that continues throughout the sequence. Similarly, the processing goes in a series from precooking to post-cooking. Thus the entire series is: initially, from the raw plenty for the dead, to the roasted little snack for the living elders, to the boiled away blood from the flesh for the whole congregation's meal, and finally, to the bloodless bones for the dead. It is as if rite by rite the blood is drawn away and the vitality totally released, until only its extreme opposite, bone and lifelessness, remains. The flesh is consumed as the mediating substance between blood as the substance of life and bone as the lifeless substance.

If we now regard ritual subjects, we see that they too follow in series. It goes from an elder acting alone as "the owner of divinity" *(mweni we ndzimu)* (or, in some instances, in the presence of immediate kin) in the first rite. Next is the second rite, where that elder is joined by other elders. In turn comes the third rite, which includes these elders together with the sacrificer and their juniors. Finally, the conclusion is the fourth rite, which is performed by a junior alone.

In reality, of course, vitality declines with increasing elderhood. In the ritual sequence, the contrary occurs: as elderhood yields to its opposite, youth and juniority, vitality also declines. At the same time, the giving of the substance of life yields to the giving of the lifeless substance. Taken together as a single progression, the two series, in subjects and substances, constitute a reversal of reality, or rather a symbolic counteraction of reality. From this we can see that one important transformation in the ritual is the revaluing and revitalization of elderhood at the expense of juniority.

That said, we must qualify our suggestion immediately in order for it to be rightly understood. Each relation in action has its antithesis within the dialectical progression of Kalanga sacrifice. Transformation is opposed by counter-transformation, sequences of animal substances by counter-sequences of non-animal substances, rites in phases of ritual by anti-rites in counterphases of play (on the notion of the anti-rite, see Douglas 1968). If one stage of our analysis requires that we break each relation into its components, the integrity of our interpretation depends upon how we build up the counterrelations. For the sake of holistic interpretation, certain counterrelations need to be recognized now; the completion of the analysis, with the sequences in space, will be undertaken later.

Each animal substance in the sequence is tempered in the ritual by a non-animal substance in a concurrent counter-sequence, the former being from blood to flesh to bone and the latter, from stone to beer to river water. Where the animal substances go from liquid to semi-solid, the non-animal sequence reverses that order. If, as we have argued, the animal sequence embodies one transformation, the revitalization of elders and elderhood, we may infer further that the opposite and reverse sequence constitutes a qualifying counter-transformation. The implicit cultural logic is that the awakening of divinities is controlled by elders and their condition, the divinities always being closest to elders, and that it is above all elders who must be distanced from divinities to ease the affliction—hence the desacralizing of elderhood as a counter-transformation to the revitalization of elderhood.

To appreciate the whole that is constituted by such simultaneous transformations, we need to say more about the alternation in symbolic mode not only within ritual—i.e., between communication and communion—but also between ritual and play. The alternation involves contrasts of an increasing order. We have already discussed one order of contrast, namely between communication and communion. The swing from entry to exit rites takes place, we have seen, by way of the communion rites, which switch in the course of an inversion of that swing. What we must consider now is the higher order contrast between rites of ritual and anti-rites of play.

The alternation in symbolic mode reaches its peak as a complete dialectical progression by means of a central juxtaposition of ritual and play. In the middle phases, after each rite of communion comes a playful anti-rite, on a progressively greater scale. In the anti-rites, joking, levelling sociability, spontaneous symbolic activity without a standard or highly organized pattern, all take over from the opposite in the rites. Elderhood is no longer elevated, as it is in the rites. What Douglas suggests in general for the joke as anti-rite holds true in particular for the Kalanga playful anti-rite, ". . . it is an image of the levelling of hierarchy, the triumph of intimacy over formality, of unofficial values over official ones" (Douglas 1968:366).

Kalanga sacrifice would not be complete without the anti-rite. It is the anti-rite which, in image and experience, regenerates what the rite cannot regenerate. The essentials that it provides are sociability without regard for the authority of elders; and informality and unofficial values, instead of the official values of elderhood. Such counter-regeneration restores a balance in the relations between elders and juniors; together, they participate in distancing themselves from certain potentially threatening aspects of elderhood. In effect, the anti-rite, given its counter-regeneration and distancing, makes it experientially valid, and not merely appropriate, for someone other than an elder to bring the ritual to its conclusion. This takes place in the final rite of amity, which releases all that remains for divinity.

To complement our account of the rebalancing of relationships towards divinities, elders and juniors, we must now regard the transformations during the rites in the person as a symbolic self. At the beginning of the communication rites, the ritual tempering is through blood and stone and, at the end, through bone and water. Here blood is said to be "the very person" (see Note 6), and it has the force of life upon which personhood depends. Imaged in the stones is *masimba*, "strength," and "power and authority," particularly of an achieved kind.

In commenting upon the stones, a diviner remarked,

When you die, they show people that your strength was like that and you worked like that. A youth has no "power and authority," he is just a child, with nothing of his own. The stones "stand for" [*anomila*] someone who has matured and come to have "power and authority," with his own homestead. He works for himself, he has a name.

I quote this and other texts at some length in order to document the ways that Kalanga themselves, in conceptualizing certain basic ideas, speak about their symbols as "standing for" or representing agency and qualities of agency (i.e., the stones for someone of maturity, power and authority). Pointing to the fence-poles *(Bango)* around his homestead (see Note 13), he went on:

When the soul *[meya]* has already left, is it not that my strength [power and authority] is what is fixed here? Therefore, when the souls awaken and return again, the stones are taken because the person had become strong.

Thus, what death separated, the first sacrificial rites bring together: in blood—the life force, and in stone—the person's achieved power and authority as an elder.

The final communication rite reaches an extreme alternative, combining bone and water. Bone is the usual metaphor for descent; it is used for shared substance, whether a relationship through the mother or father. For example, to get the order right according to birth, cognates at a grain offering invariably comment upon "who is senior according to the bone" *(wola ku fupa)*. By contrast, water, rather than being ascribed by birth as bone, is associated with culture in the mother–child bond, and with the first humanizing act in which the person emerges as a distinct being. With water, even before giving milk, the mother feeds and washes the newborn. Thus, in bringing bone to water, the rite puts descent and shared substance within a frame of cultural filiation.

In the communion rites, by contrast, the ritual tempering is first achieved through a juxtaposition of liver and beer, and finally, flesh and beer. In terms of the person, the first combination is of a substance that "can calm down the soul" (water) with its very antithesis. In the following combination, flesh is the ego that undergoes the experience of mortality and that defines everyone as an individual apart from all others. Its antithesis is beer, which is the We of heightened sociality. In beer, the self and other selves impinge upon or even merge with each other, with the extreme of *laladza,* "losing consciousness, getting drunk." The rites of communion are thus a reconstruction of ego through ritual tempering, whereby the ego of individuality is favorably modified by the We of heightened sociality. In experience, as in imagery, the person of the sacrifier is moved toward fellowship with the people at his home.

The last of the simultaneous transformational sequences to be analyzed is the spatio-temporal series in the movement within and around the sacrifier's home. So far the emphasis has been upon elders and elderhood; and the analysis has shown how transformation is controlled through counter-transformation, i.e., revitalization by desacralization, along with the regeneration of anti-hierarchy. Following the logic of the argument leads to certain corollaries of the transformational propositions. The corollary about divinities and divinity is that the expulsion of divinities as a transformation is controlled by a counter-transformation, which is the rebirth or renewal of divinity.

A view of contrasting planes of movement illuminates this suggestion and sustains it through further analysis of movement sequences. The first is the microcosmic plane, which is in and around the homestead and human settlement; the second is the cosmic, which extends to the wider universe (for a related distinction between macrocosm and microcosm, see Horton 1967). On the microcosmic plane, the sacrificial movement is a familiar passage from front to back, from entry to exit, which progresses toward secrecy and the hidden.

Such movement reenacts a feature of the coming and going in everyday life. The homestead is laid out with the most public, formal space in the front, the space of intimacy in the middle, and the space of secrecy in the back, around the granaries and the private exit. This reassertion of everyday domestic movement in the ritual is, nevertheless, a transformation in that it achieves the expulsion of divinities and modifies their condition from being closely manifest in affliction to being remotely hidden at rest. On the cosmic plane, however, the passage is back to front. Rather than being in harmony with everyday life, it is a counter-movement against the diurnal rhythm of the universe. From day to day, the progression in the rites reverses the direction of the sun's path by going from west to east; and in the instance of matrilateral sacrifice, the order also reverses the succession of events from rising to setting sun. Instead, matrilateral sacrifice goes from rites before the setting sun at dusk one day, to rites at afternoon the next and, finally, rites toward the following pre-dawn.[14]

The transformational significance of the counter-movement, calls for some comments on birth, burial, and return after death. Some days after birth and the feeding and washing of the newborn infant with water, the newborn is taken out of a hut that faces west, this being the usual direction for a door. After death, when buried, the person is oriented in the opposite direction, toward the rising sun and away from home. The head is buried to the east. At death, water is released once again, this time from a gourd shattered over stones. At the death of an elder, his sons-in-law or wife-receivers place the stones above his buried head. With the return of the dead, the sequence is continued with stones and water, but the next operation using them is reversed in space, back to the orientation of birth. Instead of toward the east,

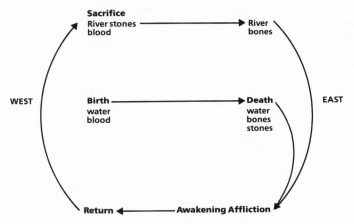

Figure 25. Spiral of Existence.

wife receivers place stones cooled by river waters to the west, in the front of the hamlet. The dead are then recognized to have returned from the east as divinities. Moving from the west eastwards, from the giving of vitality to the giving of lifelessness, the sequence in sacrifice completes a redemptive cycle between life and death. The counter-movement turns the return after death back upon itself in an endless spiral which is, to use Fernandez' apt phrase, a "saving circularity" (1982:9). This endless spiral of existence is illustrated in Figure 25.

Personal sacrifice among Kalanga does not reenact a cosmogony in the way that, in some African societies, sacrifice does when it is for divine kingship or high office (see de Huesch 1985). Nevertheless, Kalanga personal sacrifice does have a cosmic significance, for in transcending the very opposition between life and death, it creates a cosmic order, namely the endless spiral of existence. We may say further, in ontological terms, that Kalanga personal sacrifice makes a meal of existence and uses food or feasting metaphorically and metonymically for purposes of presenting the order of being and, indeed, for knowing its very nature.

To say this, however, raises a question. My view is that rituals that follow a contrastive model proceed by action and counteraction, transformation and counter-transformation. How does feasting fit such dialectics? In Kalanga sacrifice is feasting not a linear activity in which food is offered and consumed?

The answers lie in considering the two inner substances of the victim that, though significantly dedicated to the divinities, I have mentioned in passing, but not taken into account. One is the stuff of pre-digestion, the chyme; and the other, the stuff of post-digestion, the dung. Neither is stuff for ordinary feasting, and neither is regarded as part of the people's sacrificial meal. Thus, before the sacrifice, fresh dung *(dope)*—the evidence, Kalanga say, of a sated beast—is smeared on the earth, making a hard floor around the stones. This is done preferably by the senior wife of the hamlet head's senior son. After the release of blood, an elder pours out the chyme and announces the end of the meal for the divinities.

It can be seen that this sequence from post- to pre-digestion, like the cosmic countermovement, runs opposite to the natural order, and it is counteraction. In terms of associated ideas, "stale dung" *(tudze)* conveys actual increase; and Kalanga speak of "stale dung" when they refer to the share a herdsman gets from the increase of cattle feeding under agistment. My inference is that chyme is associated with the potential for increase.

If this is correct, then one may say that in sacrifice Kalanga overcome the linear nature of feasting by, as it were, letting divinities have their cake and eat it. Beginning with post-digestion and the stuff of actual increase, they go on to have their feast for the divinities; and after it, they return to pre-digestion and the stuff of potential increase. Eating, which is the outcome of sacrifice, is anticipated in the act prior to it, post-digestion. Here the dialectics are achieved through the use of anti-food along with food within the same symbolic cycle and through the inclusion of a linear progression, feasting, within its inversion, the undoing of digestion (for an illuminating contrast, see Walens 1981).

In effect, the events before and at the end of the divinities' feast counteract the feast. That is why the rite ends not with the consumed but with the about to be consumed or, in ontological terms, with existence in becoming, rather than in being. The end is a beginning once more in the spiral of existence.

A GENERAL MODEL FOR COMPARISON

On this basis, we can now begin to see the processual form of the ritual in a comparative perspective within a general model. To do so calls for a major step forward from Hubert and Mauss' model. Much of the theoretical interest in their model was due to its yield in dynamic propositions of a broadly comparative kind. The model seemed to be both generative and transformational. For example, given the sacrificer's intent with regard to a moral condition, say to be rid of an excess of sanctity, their model led us to expect, among alternatives, certain phases in a certain progression. In this instance, we would have expected a progression beginning with little or no entry phase (the sacrificer being already consecrated with excessive sanctity) and moving towards an exit phase of desacralization, in which the relations around the victim were dissolved. It would be a step backward from Hubert and Mauss' model, however, were I now to construct, on the basis of my analysis, another ideal type for sacrifice and simply substitute new contents for old.

We might do that naively by a more elaborate division of the middle or liminal phase in two. The ideal type for sacrifice would thus be *(a)* entry, *(b)* separation, *(c)* aggregation, and *(d)* exit. Instead, a higher order of comparison of the ritual dynamics and sequencing is required.

An even more general model and broader perspective enables us to comprehend what seem to be disparate rituals, such as sacrifice and exorcism. In the following, I attempt such a higher order comparison, on the basis of an abstraction first of Kalanga personal sacrifice in relation to demonic possession and subsequently an abstraction of Kapferer's analysis of Sri Lankan exorcism (1983). The discussion sets the model in relief, in general terms, and at once puts it to test.

The key idea dominant in the ritual is the starting point for this model. In the case of Kalanga personal sacrifice, the key idea is a quality of beings in existence, namely the idea of the divinity of the dead becoming powerfully favorable to kin in succeeding generations. Kalanga did not put this key idea abstractly to me, nor did I begin my interpretation with it. Rather, I arrived at the key idea after much analysis of the ethnography and upon the basis of my study of the ritual as a whole.

Further analysis leads me to see the key idea as itself a structure relating elementary terms for the state of being and the person or agency in a way that each term implies the others. One kind of key idea, with which we are ourselves perhaps too familiar, is the simple binary opposition, such as between Culture and Nature or even, divinity and non-divinity. The Kalanga key idea is unlike that in that it is a serial triad, with *(a)* initial, *(b)* middle and *(c)* final terms. The terms of this triad are: *(a)* divinity in divinities, *(b)* elderhood in elders, *(c)* juniority in juniors. Each is a term for a person's or agency's state of existence; the order is the order of succession between states and persons, according to the way that Kalanga themselves recognize succession.

It might be objected that the key idea is a static concept whereas the ritual is a sequence of events. Of what use is the key idea when it comes to making sense of the dynamics of ritual? My suggestion is that the key idea organizes the sequencing of the ritual. In other words, the phases of the ritual are governed as a definite progression by the combinations of the successive terms of the key idea. Hence, from the terms, we can generate a model to which the sequencing conforms and that enables us to account for variations in processual form according to variations in the terms.

To illustrate for Kalanga sacrifice, let us follow the order of the serial triad by combining the successive terms of the key idea. Taking the terms as shown on the axes of Figure 26, with the middle term as a pole for each axis, generates the following four combinations: (1) divinity in divinities with elderhood in elders; (2) elderhood in elders with elderhood in elders; (3) elderhood in elders with juniority in juniors; (4) juniority in juniors with divinity in divinities. Conforming to these four combinations, and in that order, are the four phases shown for Kalanga sacrifice. In the light of this we can appreciate further why it is that such ritual has four phases, rather than the three described in so much of the literature. If the key idea were an elementary opposition, the ritual could progress in three phases from one extreme to another by means of a mediating middle phase that might confound or combine both extremes. It follows that we might expect liminality where the ritual's key idea lacks a complex structure (for an example, see Chapter 4 on masquerade and liminal rites).

Given a serial triad, however, liminality fails to surmount the antitheses. Four phases are required. Ritual performance in four phases completes a progression that surmounts antitheses and that expresses and enacts the key idea as a whole with a complex structure. In other words, my argument is that the processual form of the ritual must conform to its key idea: the greater the structural complexity of the key idea, the greater, as well, will be the complexity of the processual form.

To develop this further, we must say more about the terms in relation to the sequencing. It can be seen that each phase is synthetic, incorporating a distinct combination of terms. In the Kalanga ritual, for example, the first phase, entry in communication about elderhood and divinity, is an interaction between elders and divinities that involves unwanted closeness and *dangerous* blood. By contrast, the final phase, exit in communication about juniority and divinity, is an interaction between juniors and divinities involving *wanted* distance and *safe* bones.

From this, it can also be seen that one term is problematic. It

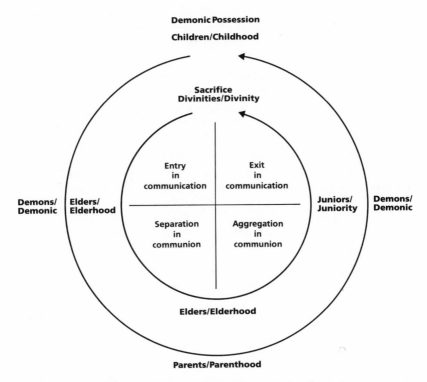

Figure 26. Axes of Processual Form: Kalanga Personal Sacrifice and Demonic Possession.

constitutes certain combinations that are dangerous, unfavorable and, as such, no longer wanted. This problematic term—elderhood in elders, in the Kalanga case—is the one which, introduced in a dangerous combination at the beginning of the ritual, is eliminated before the final phase. By way of conclusion comes a fresh synthesis, recombining the other term of the beginning, divinity in divinities, with the unproblematic alternative, namely juniority in juniors. As for the dialectical sequence as a whole, that proceeds through the terms in order, beginning with the combination of the initial and middle terms through to the combination of the final and initial terms. On Figure 26 that progression is shown by a counter-clockwise rotation from the axis with divinity back to it.

Also on Figure 26 is the comparable representation for demonic possession, around the inner ring. In sacrifice, what is problematic is parentage in the conjunction between elders and divinities; in demonic possession, it is anti-parentage in the conjunction between children and demons. Hence, in sacrifice the movement is primarily a distancing of divinities and elders, whereas in demonic possession it is a distancing of the opposite extreme, of demons and children.

It can be seen that, just as the terms are alternative variations, so too are the sequences of ritual and their contrasting symbolic modes. Given a constant cultural logic, the rituals differ according to the differences between their key ideas. The key idea of demonic possession concerns anti-parentage and the counter-filiation of children, whereas the key idea of cattle sacrifice concerns parentage and filiation. The variation can be put simply in this formula:

Demonic possession : Cattle sacrifice
::
anti-parentage and counter-filiation : parentage and filiation

The ideological significance of this variation must be stressed, for the formula represents not simply differences between alternatives but the inequality between them. Of the two key ideas, one is implicitly understood to be the superior, with a corresponding inequality between the rituals. The key idea that contains the culturally higher value is understood to be a given of social life, something in the very nature of human order; and the superior ritual sustains the endless spiral of existence. More particularly, the idea of parentage and filiation is taken to be axiomatic for human order; it is valued over counterparentage and counter-filiation. Cattle sacrifice is accordingly the superior ritual and demonic possession, the inferior, involving the Great Lion *(shumba wulu)* and the Lion, respectively. A notion of hierarchy is implicit, and it is related to the culturally assumed reality of a hierarchy of domains of social life. With the superior domain goes the superior idea and the superior ritual; and each along with its interrelation with the others is ideologically constructed as a natural reality, something to be taken for granted in the order of existence.

For purposes of comparison, let us now turn things back to front and see how our model enables us to regard the alternative dynamics arising from a transposition of the terms. Instead of beginning with a combination of the initial and middle terms $(a + b)$, the contrary progression begins with the initial and final $(a + c)$ terms and proceeds to the initial and middle terms $(a + b)$, through the terms in order. In this progression, the final term, (c), is culturally problematic and

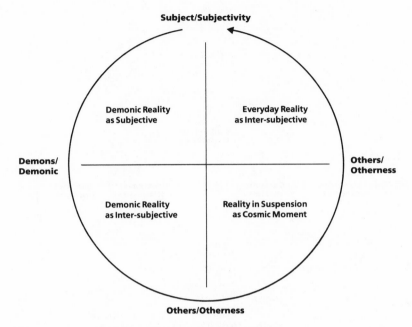

Figure 27. *Axes of Processual Form: Sri Lankan Exorcism.*

eliminated dialectically. Such a progression is shown in Figure 27, illustrating Sri Lankan exorcism.

To unpack this comparison, we have to appreciate how Sri Lankan exorcism, like Kalanga personal sacrifice, has four phases of ritual, and in its processual form conforms to the complex structure of a key idea composed of terms in a serial triad. An obvious similarity—though one that hides an important difference—is that both have the intent, among other things, to expel mislocated beings. As I understand it, and I make no claim to being able to distill the full subtlety of Kapferer's interpretation, the terms in Sri Lankan exorcism are: *(a)* subjectivity and the subject, *(b)* otherness and others (which here subsumes or is subsumed by the divine), and *(c)* the demonic and demons, the last being the problematic term.

As shown by the counterclockwise rotation on Figure 27, in the first phase comes the construction of the demonic as subjective reality. Next comes the elaboration of the demonic in a phase of intersubjective reality. After that follows the dissolution of the demonic reality in the cosmic moment. Finally comes the reconstruction of an everyday reality whose public hierarchical order is under the deity.

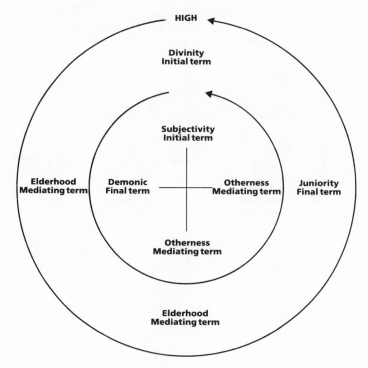

Figure 28. Dynamics of Sacrifice and Exorcism.

With regard to our comparison of sacrifice and exorcism, it can be seen that the key ideas of the rituals turn each other top to bottom. In the Kalanga ritual, as we have seen at some length, superior, more powerful beings are involved as divinities whose reality, properly restored, has the beneficial promise for peaceful order and sociability in everyday life. The Sri Lankan ritual is dominated by the contrary idea of human beings in a relation with inferior and weaker beings whose reality threatens to destroy social order and isolate human beings from their social relationships of everyday life (Kapferer 1983:205). Plotted on high and low axes for the beings in existence, the comparisons in the movement of the rituals movement are shown on Figure 28. This reveals that a common tendency governs them both. Both rituals revolve around a higher existence and lead away from its problematic manifestation toward its beneficial restoration; hence the return to divinity in sacrifice, and to subjectivity, instead of the demonic, in exorcism.

My suggestion is that just as the rituals' key ideas are relative to the hierarchy of beings in the order of existence, so too their sequences must be relative; and thus each has a different problematic term and each returns to a contrasting starting point. This tendency is, of course, only one of a number of possibilities which the underlying model enables us to consider. And I put it forward to begin the comparative discussion of the connections between the key ideas, problematic terms, and processual forms of ritual.

CONCLUSION

We have seen that Kalanga cattle sacrifice, which is focused on the public domain, has a typical progression. Cattle sacrifice culminates in the symbolic restoration of a higher, more powerfully beneficial order; it restores calm for divinities and thus healing for people. As a general type, the progression is not distinctive of sacrifice as a special kind of ritual. In various kinds of ritual, including exorcism, there is a similar type of progression, which involves action and counteraction, and which I would call contrastive oscillation, because of the way that it gains its momentum during performance.

In saying this, and in presenting my view of how Kalanga ritual is programmed by a binary model, according to a certain key idea, my concern is, in part, with form. But that is not all, of course. The appreciation of processual form, though necessary, is hardly sufficient when it comes to understanding the motive power of a dialectic in performance. That is why in this chapter, continuing from the earlier one, I have given an account of how actual performance moves between anti-rite or play and ritual, and between the deconstruction and the reconstruction of cultural and social reality.

ACKNOWLEDGMENT

I wish to thank Pnina Werbner, Don Handelman, Bruce Kapferer and the participants in my Colloquium on African Religion and Ritual at Satterthwaite, particularly James Fernandez and Maurice Bloch, for commenting on this chapter.

CHAPTER 4

UMEDA MASQUERADE

Renewing Identity and Power in the Cosmos

INTRODUCTION

Transitional festivals celebrate the passage from the old to the new year
with rites that play tricks with the realities of everyday life. Persons
and things are no longer represented in their usual places or in familiar
shapes. Everyday life is suspended, but it is not for a brief, playful
moment, as it is in the rituals we have been discussing so far. For most
of the time in such transitional festivals, people indulge themselves
in pretense and joking, sometimes devoting almost all the rites to
masquerade. In this chapter, my interest is primarily in masquerade as
self-caricature in a male-dominated yet otherwise highly egalitarian
society.[1] With certain questions in mind, I want to interpret specific
sequences of disguise and play in an actual festival, that of *ida,* which
is centered in the village of Umeda in the New Guinea Lowlands. I
base my own interpretation of *ida* on Alfred Gell's culturally sensitive
account (1975, 1978, 1979, 1981) and on a more recent study, by
Bernard Juillerat, of *yangis,* the version of *ida* performed by the nearby
Yafar (1986, n.d.; see also Werbner n.d.).

How do the sequences of disguise and play involve a construction
of both personal identity and cosmic order? What experience do they
give people of their own bodies and the space around them? How and

149

why do they emphasize reproductive sexuality, aging and certain other organic processes?

The festival of *ida* is performed annually for regeneration and growth. A major purpose of the performance is to enable men to act powerfully upon the plants and animals on which they depend for survival and which are revived symbolically around them at the sacred centers of a village. *Ida,* which is sometimes loosely translated as ritual (Gell 1975, *passim),* has the sense of "undergoing." What is "undergone" in the festival is a "labor" of cosmic rebirth.

Ida is an elaborate festival. An overview is essential. I begin with one that is necessarily sketchy yet sufficient to introduce the acts and scenes of the masquerade, its characters and players, and its surrounding rites. The masquerade dance of *ida* as a whole sequence is a rebirth. First comes a preliminary act, the very delivery from labor, with a novice passing through his mother's brothers' legs. This preliminary act, birth itself, is somewhat like a "flashback" as we know it. What the preliminary act anticipates is the outcome of the following action. Its main sequence is composed of three acts, each containing two scenes. The order is:

Act I Copulation,
  scenes: (i) defloration, (ii) ejaculation

Act II Gestation,
  scenes: (i) multiplication, (ii) womb confinement

Act III Parturition,
  scenes: (i) womb contraction and (ii) womb release

Scenes II(ii) and III(i) are scenes of clowning, during which the clowns invade and interfere with the dancing of gestation and parturition. After women and children drive away the clowns, heroes complete the performance.

More generally, the whole of the masquerade can be seen as a sequence of liminal rites between rites of separation and rites of incorporation. The rites of separation set the players apart as masqueraders, transform them into cosmic and primordial beings, and empower them, momentarily, with life beyond death. In the rites of incorporation, which culminate in a sacrificial hunt, "shooting [wild] pigs," the players are restored to their mortality. In my view, in brief, the festival as a whole follows the form of a *rite de passage.*

At the beginning, in the rites of separation, men are divided by the substances they own, by their "having" (see de Huesch 1985:202–04 on "having" and "being" in ritual). First, each bush association or set of territorial partners (see Gell 1977:45–46 on bush associations; see also Chapter 5 on territorial partnerships), then each festival hamlet of the village performs on its own, emphasizing the multiplicity of territorial or property-owning groups. By the end, however, the men are all "pigs," united in their identity through shared blood. They wash away as "dirt" *(nsak)* the self-decorations that distinguished them. Their becoming one in "being," one body with one blood, a united whole community, is the transformation in social identity that the men enact in the concluding rites of reincorporation.

The transition from the "having" of the many to the "being" of the one is effected through liminal rites in which men individuate themselves, each a variation upon the other, in powerful harmony with the flux of cosmic forces. In disguised caricature, each man reveals his character to be that of a person in social or anti-social relationships, with or without a moiety partner in his masquerade role. Such revelation is active and transitive into the formation of community around the sacred center of a village.

The festival passage in identity that we have been discussing can be put simply in this way:

SEPARATION RITES	LIMINAL RITES	REINCORPORATION RITES
Non-sharing of identity	Revelation of identity	Sharing of identity
by undifferentiated men	by differentiated men	by undifferentiated men
Disunity of "having"	Disunity of "having" in varieties of "being"	Unity of "being"

This is passage in identity as a social transformation; its analogue on a cosmic plane is a transfer of occult power. During the liminal phase, the men turn themselves into primordial creatures or immortals in command of the most potent substances of regeneration, such as the inner white heart of the palm, its sacred substance for growth. Each mask is a vehicle for movement between the present and the primordial worlds; and all the masks together are a means for the transfer of occult

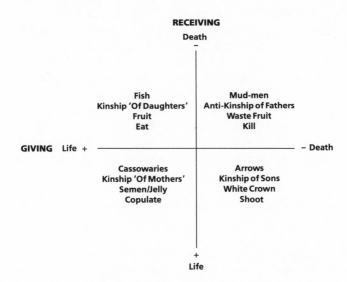

Figure 29. Relationships Epitomized by Categories of Character.

power from the latter to the former. Once having gained the dominant and regenerative power of the occult, the men restore their own mortality. They accomplish this restoration by taking control of the mortality, the lifeblood, of other beings like themselves. In pig's blood, they reincorporate themselves as "pigs," as hunters turned victims, "reborn only to die" (Paz 1978:141, see below on the dialectic vision in this reincorporation).

If we recall our discussion in the earlier chapters and examine the key idea here, we may say that it is constituted by an elementary opposition of binary and not triadic terms, and that it has a simple structure, as expected with liminality.

The characters of the masquerade are an elaboration of binary oppositions in the exchange of life and death (see Figure 29). Four to a category in each of four categories, their total is, of course, sixteen characters. Of these categories, three are the heroes —*(a)* the Cassowaries (Act I, scenes i and ii); *(b)* the Fish (Preliminary; Act I, scene i; Act II scene i); and *(c)* the Arrows (Act III, scene ii); and one is the clowns' category —*(d)* the Mudmen (Act II, scene ii, and Act III, scene i). In terms of kinship they represent, respectively, the relationships of *(a)* the mothers (life-giving), *(b)* the daughters (life-receiving), *(c)* the sons (death-giving), *(d)* the fathers (death-giving). Fuller details of the action

KEY

	Mode of Experience	Category of Character	Microcosm	Macrocosm	Space	Time
I.	Eat	Fish	Head	Eating Partners	Insiders	Youth
II.	Shoot	Arrows	Arms	Hunting Partners		
III.	Copulate	Cassowaries	Penis/Pelvis	Sexual Partners		
IV.	Kill	Mud-Men	Torso	Killing Non-Partners	Outsiders	Age

Figure 30. Microcosm and Macrocosm of Masked Categories.

according to the categories of character and kinship are provided in the Appendix that concludes this chapter.

The villagers have a conceptual grid of concentric concepts that cover both space and time (see Figure 30). In space, in terms of social distance within the widest universe, the concepts classify the separate horizons around ego. The concentric classification starts from the innermost horizon (I), within which ego *eats* and shares food with insiders, to the next (II), within which ego *shoots* and hunts, to the next but one (III), within which ego *copulates* and finds a wife, to the outermost (IV), within which ego *kills* outsiders, including women and children. Corresponding to that extension in the macrocosm is the classification of the microcosm, ego's own body, in these concentric zones, from top to bottom: head, arms, penis and hips, torso. In time, the same order is a sequence. Each horizon is associated with an age or generation, the most remote being the most aged. Similarly, at the level of the microcosm, the successive body zones are linked to increasing maturity, according to a man's growing competence from the beginning to the end of the life cycle.

These four concentric zones of cosmic space-time are embodied in the masquerade characters, and the relations between them are represented by the masquerade's four categories of character. Respectively, from the innermost and earliest, the categories are Fish, Arrows (called Bow Men by Gell, which wrongly shifts the emphasis from the masculine to the feminine part of the arms), Cassowaries, and Mud-Men (my term, and not to be confused with Highlands ritual performers who are known by the same name in the literature).

According to this order, a man may act the leading character part that epitomizes each category. Thus as a young man, he becomes the epitome of *eat, Tetagwana Tamwa,* the Fish of Cucurbit. Next, somewhat more mature as a hunter, his leading part is *Ipele,* the Arrow, which epitomizes *shoot.* Reaching seniority and full maturity, he performs *copulation:* he then may have the most orgiastic and thus most prestigious part of all, *Eli,* the Cassowary. Finally, his last leading part is *Sebuha,* the Old Ogre, epitomizing the killer. In brief, the leading festival roles follow a man's life-cycle and are played in an order of increasing seniority and maturity.

In dance, and through props, paint or coverings, an appropriate part of the body is stressed as the most important and powerful for each category of character. The head, arms, penis and pelvis, or torso is stressed, in turn, according to the order of categories from the innermost and earliest. For the Fish, the stress is on eating and the head, through the wearing of the most complete coconut fiber mask, which is thus associated with the most highly valued and luxurious food. Shooting is stressed for the Arrows as are their arms, bearing bows and arrows; and for the Cassowaries, copulation and their genitals, through the wearing of the "pig-bone" (materially, bird-bone) pelvic girdles and the elongated penis-gourds. Finally, certain Mud-Men alone have "dirt skins" and torsos covered with mud, rather than body-paint of living or organic substances, and the stress in dance and props is on war or killing.

COSMIC JOKING, ALTERNATIVE ORGANIZATION,
AND A MAN'S TRUE SELF

The villagers engage in verbal and visual double entendres when they celebrate their transitional festival. Their joking is from a male point of view, and it is primarily of and about sex and sequence, maleness in relation to femaleness, the contained in relation to the container, and the greater or second in relation to the lesser or first. More abstractly, it is a play with a logic of pairing and non-pairing, and of mating and mismating.

All of this implies a sense of the absurd that has a broad, cosmological significance. What is real and what is apparent becomes equivocal in and through the double entendres. In effect, the very opposition between reality and appearance is put in suspension. Moreover, in the festival's masquerade, a metamorphosis of forms and figures is presented in which everything becomes its opposite, outside is turned inside, and inside turned out; virtually everything comes into being as an unstable unity of opposites.

At the same time, the villagers act to recover an alternative order of space and place. The men take elaborate care, symbolically and at a high cost in feasting and in the consumption of luxuries, to give that order its cosmic significance. They use a mask that is a model of a palm as a cosmic Tree of Life. It is an instance of the general form about which Eliade writes, "The Tree reveals the World as a living totality, periodically regenerating itself, and thanks to this regeneration, continually fertile, rich and inexhaustible" (1954: 202).

Each kind of life, according to its origin, has its own Tree (i.e., the coconut palm in the village for the villagers themselves, and I infer, sago in the bush for certain others). The myth is that Toagtod, the first man, emerged from a coconut palm. In a state of bliss, he had around him an endless supply of all the things and creatures that men value, such as game. Recklessly breaking a taboo, one of his children invaded his storehouse and let the game loose. In a reversal of the myth, his descendants annually return to a euphoric state, for a brief time. They reenter coconut or sago palm trees as masks, and they reenact the parts of cosmic characters, above all, that orgiastic and most grossly phallic prey of the wild, the Cassowary.

For the villagers, the reversal recovers the primordial state of inexhaustible plenty, when all the prey were lodged together, not loose in the wild. But in the festival at the year's end, the villagers cannot make a transformation without negation: after the bliss of abundance, they also reenact, ironically, the release of the prey back into the wild.

Thus they swing the pendulum of time forward, as it were, from having gone backward to the beginning.

Year out and year in, the old gives way to the new, with the renewal of the workaday world, away from the height of bliss. By masking, a man effects a symbolic transition across time through space.[2] Inside the mask he enters the inner space from which life came at the beginning of time—one tree or another, according to the origin of a primordial being—and thus reversing space and time, he himself becomes a primordial being, such as the Cassowary.

Masks are used, recreating the division of insider from outsider, to effect a transition that is at once material and organizational as well as symbolic and personal.[3] Men who are outsiders to each other's territory exchange masks. In this way they turn themselves into insiders and thereby gain access to each other's inner space. For most of the rest of the year, they spend their lives virtually contained within contiguous strips of land, members of "bush associations" or territories in partnership for certain purposes of production. Anywhere beyond such a territorial partnership is normally beyond their usual limits for personal security and safe passage.

During the festival, however, they expand their limits; other territories are crossed, and villagers come together at central hamlets to enjoy whatever abundance has been accumulated for the celebration. There the men create perpetual contact between their hamlets, by means of the masks and women, which they exchange in coordinated, ranked spheres according to a fixed arrangement (see Chapter 5). The women, like the masks, are containers for the men as insiders, although each container is restricted to its own insiders. The mask is the male womb, the woman the female womb.

As partners, hamlets exchange one kind of womb or container, either masks or women, but not both. One can either provide the continually fertile, rich and inexhaustible source of eternal life—the mask as Cosmic Tree—or one can provide a woman. She, too, is vital; but in herself she consumes a man. Even more, in her precarious fertility, she is the source of children who, as the origin myth goes, are so greedy for the good things in life that they make them scarce and hard to find. Because of children, man cannot remain on the heights and, in a euphoric state, get all he wants effortlessly at home in the village; instead, having to descend into the bush, where he slogs away gardening sorghum, he must hunt game in the wild.

One inexhaustible, the other exhausting, the mask and the woman as objects of exchange are mutually exclusive; they cannot be traded for one another. Yet contact through either of the moveable objects of exchange frees men from other limitations in space. In and through the festival, and above all in its masks as containers of eternal life, the villagers create both the place where a man truly belongs and the space that a man can enter in personal security.

In the performance of the masquerade, the festival is an occasion for each man's true self to be made known. As befits a man's personal experience and phase in life, so does he trick himself out during the masquerade: the outside is the man inside (see also M. Strathern 1979). Or rather, as a man dances, so may he be; for not only is there a rite of initiation for a neophyte, on first assuming his penis sheath and thus his manhood (the preliminary rite of delivery, birth itself), but there is also the opportunity for gross and competitive sexual self-display, through which men sometimes manage "to ensnare the heart of a nubile widow, or a discontented wife" (Gell 1975:193).

The total number of distinct masquerade characters, each with its own costumed figure, is sixteen. But these are so differentiated that each man, whether neophyte or elder, can suit himself with an appropriate caricature, according to his age, marital status, reputed virility, aggressiveness, prowess in hunting or killing, and so forth. Moreover, in performance, the characters are so doubled and redoubled that at least sixty-four men take part in the dancing. Given the fact that even a large village has roughly eighty men at most, a part is assured for every adult male. Even more, the participation of all is virtually essential. Such total participation makes the festival, I would suggest, a grand occasion for self-awareness among men, for them to know and feel what all the significant others in their community currently accept as the essential character of each in relation to all. The masquerade is an occasion for men to recover themselves, above all.

THE MASQUERADE WITHIN THE FORM OF A *RITE DE PASSAGE*

I have suggested that the festival as a whole follows the form of a rite of passage. I must now review this suggestion and comment on the course of the masquerade as a part of the whole festival, culminating in a sacrificial hunt. In the festival, three distinct types of rites follow in sequence, each according to van Gennep's classic model (1960). Predictably, according to that model, the masquerade forms the liminal rites in between contrasting rites of separation and aggregation or reincorporation. The discussion by the ethnographer Gell about the *rite de passage* model and time in *ida* is somewhat confused, with mistaken suggestions for comparative analysis, because he misconceives the masquerade as if it were a *whole* ritual, although it comes between the initial and later rites (1975:336ff.).

To begin the rites of separation, men return from the festival site to the deep bush, with their neighbors who share access to the same territories and thus belong to the same "bush association." There men collect "leaves," "a euphemism for the various magico-ritual materials about which the women must know nothing" (Gell 1975:170). When the men go back to the village, the separation between them and the women is maintained; the women must leave so that the men may collect coconut fiber unseen by the women.

In none of the rites so far discussed do men act as one body of villagers. In the bush, they gather their materials as separate parties of neighbors, and in the village they collect as members of separate hamlets. Only then, when they have their own separate substances to contribute, do they come together. They "form columns by hamlets and converge from all directions on the site where the ritual enclosure is to be established, coordinating their movements by ululating" (Gell 1975:171).

After planting aromatics and "penis-like" rootlets in a brief rite, itself a symbolic copulation, they clear an area of undergrowth for the site of the "spring," the cosmic source of being. They then make the masks, paint the performers' bodies, and also construct the "dam" around the "spring," which is thus screened from the women by a fence.

At the start of the rites of reincorporation, the men return to the bush, once more, apart from the women. This time, the object,

. . . is to shoot game—no hunting having been done while the rites are in progress—to obtain blood. When game has been killed—preferably pig . . . the blood is preserved in small bamboo tubes. Blood having been obtained in this way the men proceed *in a body* to bush streams where they wash. They then anoint themselves with blood. This washing and anointing is said to be to remove the dirt *[nsak]* of the ritual and allows them to take up normal life again. (my italics, Gell 1975:208)

During these rites, the symbolic accumulation of secret power and control proceeds in stages that women must not see. Such powerful symbolic accumulation begins with "collecting leaves," in the rites of separation. The next secret and exclusively male stages come with "forcing Sago," in the first part of the masquerade, and "shooting bird," in the last part. Finally, the conclusion is "shooting pigs," which occurs in the final rites of reincorporation.

In the beginning, on collecting and handling the "leaves," the men purify themselves from the danger of contact with potent substances by washing their hands. From such purification, which is typical in rites of separation, they move in the liminal rites to the symbolic action the sacrificial hunt that they play on oppositions between species, to operate upon cosmic forces and thus to effect a transition. In this case, contrasting uses of substances are also transitive both for bringing about cosmic movement, in particular the renewal of the life force for some at the expense of death for others, and for forging social identity (see Whitehead 1986:86–87 for a comparative discussion of Lowlands substance use for the ritual forging of social identity).

THE COSMOS AND GELL'S INTERPRETATION

In order to clarify the basis for my interpretation, I must comment on my source. One of the great strengths of Gell's study of *ida* is his visually acute observation of the fine spaces of life. Illustrating his perception through drawings of an organic analogy between men, plants, and society, he provides essential detail with a felicity that is all too rare in studies of ritual. What we get to know so well is how the people map the body, whether of man or plant, and embody their mapping in ritual, or in their immediate universe of kinship. His description, however, extends well beyond his analysis. What we do not get to know, within an analytic framework, is how the map of the body bears on the map of the wider world, and how the performance of the festival creates and recreates this bearing of microcosm on macrocosm, of organic life and ego on the world around them. Microcosm and macrocosm are never quite brought together in a single perspective—to do that is one aim of my interpretation of *ida*.

Related to this aim is the problem of cosmic time. Gell has much to say about the intricacies of various other kinds of time.[4] As a process from generation to generation, time is given pride of place in his interpretation. He goes so far as to suggest, "If there is a sociological interpretation of *ida,* this is surely it: the acting out, on the ritual arena, of idealized role-complementarities between members of the senior and junior generations" (Gell 1975:331). But nowhere does he consider analytically the original time of the cosmos in myth and masquerade.

The neglect is fundamental. It leads to a wrong view of how *ida* achieves the "regeneration of the total society" through the inversion of time. In Gell's view, *ida* as ritual simply violates linear time to create cyclical time. I would argue, however, that in each masquerade performance, it is the direction of cosmic time that is reversed, back to the beginning, for the old to give way to the new. In myth, the end of the primordial cosmos was the beginning of the present workaday world. Thus the eternal return to the first Old Man's bliss, when the year is old, is concluded by the reenactment of the scattering by his

of discharge or liberation. Throwing or ejaculating in
liminal rites and shooting in the last enact the alter
potential during the masquerade. Initially, "forcing S
an individual, long after sunset, to make him involunt
the air the potent substance of sago jelly/semen. Finall
as Arrows, men shoot into the air at sunset, facing v
the sun, and they voluntarily release the innermost s
crown—the substance that is sacred for its power over
Their archery shooting growth substance is selfless.
risk to their lives, since the substance makes arrows
and is identified with their very being as Arrows. Af
ping their red bows (which are retrieved by spectators
to the enclosure as if their lives depended on it" (Ge
archery, restoring the wild creatures to the bush, ma
avoidance on hunting during the ritual, and the men
shoot pigs.

The passage in these exclusively male rites ca
among other things, a development in the men's p
selves as well as over others. Beginning with their gi
substances in the rites of separation, the movement c
phase is from vital yet forced giving to giving that
selfless. The development is carried forward to its
shift from the symbolic "bird shooting" to the actu
the rites of reincorporation.

In these rites, men, "pigs," and "birds," above
the dominant birds of the liminal phase, are linked
tions. What they are linked to is the mother's br
relationship, which, in my view, is also the ritual's
relationship between giver and receiver of life valu
themselves as "pigs" when they remark upon their
to sorcery in a mother's brother's village (Gell 19
hunter becomes, in turn, the mortal victim faced w
of life through poisonous debilitating attack. The
between man and Cassowary has the appropriate v
alternative is the cosmogonic attack from which spr
brothers. Their ancestors slew a Cassowary from
the men of their mother's brother's village, and from
the women (Gell 1975:226).

These rites are about cosmogonic power, a h
tionships with certain non-human species, and the
of substance. In at least the first two of these respec
forms of the sacrificial hunt in Africa, about wh
written so illuminatingly (1985:38–47). It is typica

child, the New Man, of the Cassowaries, fish and other creatures "back to the bush where they belong" (Gell 1975:294–95).

A further problem concerns sacred clowns. The difficulty here is that Gell does not take sacred clowns seriously. Heroes are his métier. It may be one of those tricks that good rapport plays upon a fieldworker (the masquerade working *modes,* its tricks, on the observer, too). Unfortunately, Gell dismisses in analysis what the people dismiss in action—the unruly clowns who do not fit in, who come out of place and out of time, who threaten to disrupt the proceedings, and who have to be driven away by the very people they most threaten, not the men as heroes, but women and children. In my view, the clowns are barbarians in their behavior, ghosts up from the dead; their condition and appearance epitomize "matter out of place."

The difficulty about clowns is, in fact, threefold. First, there is a matter of method. Although Gell's structuralist approach has been the subject of a recent debate about "misconstrued order in Melanesian religion" (Brunton 1980a, 1980b; Juillerat 1980; Johnson 1981; Jorgensen 1981; Gell 1981), that debate does not quite come to grips with Gell's work on its own terms. The question of whether Gell's interpretation stands or falls by the structuralist criteria that he sets for himself, following Barthes, is not raised. For such structuralist decoding, the heart of the matter is this: the solution must account for all the bits, somewhat in the way of a jigsaw puzzle. Not taking clowns seriously, Gell lets his interpretation slip, by his own criteria. Missing from virtually all his figures, the clowns are most importantly absent from his tabular design of *ida* as a whole (1975:216). Their bits are similarly not among the bits of characterization (masks, color, body-paint, dance style) which he considers when he argues that the course of the ritual is, visually, a "metamorphosis of cassowaries." In brief, his analysis of serial transformation is incomplete, and thus not valid in its own terms, whether or not it represents misconstrued order in any other sense.

It is not that Gell, in my view, has the wrong aim. I concur in the correctness of his goal of illuminating the masquerade by applying a structuralist method inspired by Lévi-Strauss and Barthes. His method is above all appropriate for reasons that are specific to the people studied, rather than for the usual theoretical justifications that are said to be universal to men everywhere. The people of Umeda have a binary view of the universe; they represent their society in dual oppositions, in both diametric and concentric forms. Appropriately, the structuralist method focuses, as is well known, on binarism.

Even more specifically, the masquerade is a coherent unity. Its impersonations are permutations one of another. Each is a combination of contrasting bits that are of certain kinds only. The same kinds reappear throughout, but are significantly varied in their manifestation as particular bits to suit the distinct character of each impersonation. Such coherent combination and permutation is best studied by a holistic method that respects combinatorial regularity while it reveals its rules.

Man disguised in many guises, each the same and yet different, distinct and opposed, and yet continuous and alike, portray the comic philosophy embodied in the masquerade. In my view, that philosophy of the absurd is best understood in the light of a method that focuses on the relation between negation and affirmation; that is, the structuralist method as a *dialectical* method. What it enables us to see is how the masquerade embodies, in Paz's words, "the realm of dialectic which ceaselessly destroys itself and is reborn only to die" (Paz 1978:141).

A second concern about Gell's treatment of clowns arises from the fact that *ida* takes the form of a classic *rite de passage*. The comparative evidence suggests that when clowns appear in a rite of passage they are transformers; they play a crucial part in making transitions and in making people aware, reflexively, of what it means to be in transition (P. Werbner 1979, 1986; Handelman 1981). Hence in their jokes and tricks clowns reveal, as well as conceal, what the rite of passage is all about. It behooves us to take the characters they represent seriously; they belong at the very center of our analysis, and we need to understand when, about what, and how they joke.

The remaining part of the difficulty concerning clowns leads back to the very beginning of our discussion. If clowns and clowning are given short shrift—if, "on the whole, they do little more than provide comic relief" (Gell 1975:281)—we ought not to expect an emphasis on the absurd, on nonsense, and on poking fun in the ritual. To the men who perform it and know it from within, *ida* is play *(modes)*, a game, a joke *(mokus)* (Gell 1975:219, 227–28, 276). This must be taken seriously. That Gell does not, is why the model he provides does violence to the sensitive factual observation upon which it is based.

SACRED CLOWNS AND THE ORDEAL OF CLOWNING

At first sight, the behavior of these sacred clowns would seem to be very much like that of such clowns elsewhere (see especially Crumrine 1969; Hieb 1972; Makarius 1970; Handelman 1981). As is typical elsewhere, these clowns emerge by contrast to heroes, and in turn, the heroes appear in contrast to the clowns. While both perform at the sacred center, the heroes, but not the clowns, are by their nature of the sacred center. If the clowns belong anywhere, it is somewhere outside the sacred center. But they go where they do not belong and, being insolent buffoons, they sometimes burlesque the heroes' dancing. Moreover, whereas the heroes are social beings, who always perform in pairs with one from the male moiety and the other from the female, the clowns are asocial, independent, and individualistic; they nearly all perform as isolates, without any partner. If the heroes evoke respect and admiration from spectators, the clowns arouse fear and hilarity, or ridicule.

From a man's point of view as an initiate, however, even a hero is tricky and up to deception. A hero, too, plays a game *(modes)* with the women who are "tricked" *(mankus)*. If, as is usual in many forms of masking in other parts of the world, the game is a form of hide-and-seek (see Grathoff 1970:136–38), in Umeda it is not played by hiding the performer's identity from the women. That is well-known, easily recognized, and, in the fish masks, even stressed in heraldic marking. The trickery is about what the person is as hero or clown, not who he is. The truth is hinted at, but the full and inner significance of the masking is hidden from women. Only men can appreciate the full significance, because men alone collect and secretly put together all the elements used in masking. Moreover, they alone are allowed to witness and act in all the masquerade's events, including its secret climax and release of jelly/semen by the Sago. A deliberate attempt is made by the men to tantalize the women about the significance of what they are seeing, and they are expected to take for the reality what is an appearance on the surface. Thus in one village, some heroes painted as fish appeared with mud on their feet, in effect disguising themselves to seem to be somewhat like mud-men clowns.

But do the sacred clowns transform in relation to the heroes, as is common elsewhere? For example, in his discussion of Hopi clowns, Handelman points out that the summer solstice rites culminate in reconciliation between the clowns and the heroic deities, the *kachina*: ". . . *kachina* and clowns begin to *exchange attributes* of their respective types. Now their contrast and opposition are stressed less and their similarities are emphasized more" (1981:351, italics in the original). No such exchange of attributes occurs between clown and hero in *ida*. Not only are they unlike and irreconcilable, but they must remain so. The very movement of the masquerade itself depends on their irreversibility. For the clown in *ida* provides a major service in effecting that which he can only give if the disjunction between clown and hero is insisted upon, to the very end. Makarius's general observation fits the clown in *ida* throughout his performance: "It is necessary that he should be conceived as 'the other,' in opposition to the group, even though he acts on their behalf" (1970:54).

Threatening to disrupt the progress of the heroic dancing with grotesque antics, the clown does the spectators the service of providing them with an ordeal. If they feel menaced and frightened by the clown, and by what he represents initially, they soon find themselves able to laugh him away. Then, aroused together as a mob, the women and children alone, without the aid of heroes or other men, get rid of the clown using matter that suits them as attackers and him as target. In a wild barrage directed at the clown, they cast out rubbish and dirt (perhaps ogre fruit?), and themselves expel the clown along with all that he represents. Any doubt that the clown and what he represents might overwhelm the sacred center or give it a character other than its own is dispelled by the clown's expulsion.

The ordeal by clowning makes the women and children change from being casual spectators to forceful actors who are essential. Their participation compels them to prove certain truths about themselves: first, their greater power as a mob, even against the most formidable of individuals (the Old Mud-Men) or a mob of youths (the Nettles); and second, their unanimity in rejecting what does not belong at the sacred center. The change is in the participants themselves, with the ritual clown playing the role of transformer, and not the transformed. In effect, the ordeal thus works a double transformation: it completes the active participation of the community as a whole in the renewal of the cosmos and, at the same time, it extends to all the consciousness of actually being needed to bring about that renewal.

Each person has an appropriate part. The men bring together the new, raw substances to display, contain, and change themselves *afresh* in the center. The male part initiates renewal. In response, for their part, the women and children are the discarders of waste. Their weakness turns into their strength in a job not fit for heroes. They throw away the center's rotten refuse while they attack the clowns, and thus return those perverse wholly other beings back to the bush. Thus as heroes, the men introduce the wanted, and as clowns, the unwanted; but the women and children mediate between the two and, as spectators turned participants, the women and children eliminate the unwanted with the remains of the wanted. If the parts are markedly unequal, with the leading parts for the men as heroes, all are seen and felt to be essential. Indeed, they are as essential as action and counteraction are within that cosmos which is a whole of unequal parts, according to a dialectical vision.

HEROES AND CLOWNS IN PROPORTION

Gell's model of *ida* is heroic, and disproportionately so. It is as if prestige were the paramount value dominating a celebration of heroes; the prestigious characters dominate the analysis, virtually to the exclusion of the others. The actors themselves insist that what is essential is the ludic or playful dimension, but it is the ludic dimension that Gell's model belittles (on the ludic dimension, see Handelman 1979, in press; Turner 1982; Babcock 1978:294ff).

At the very crux of Gell's argument is the location of the Cassowaries, in conceptual terms. On that location depends his view of the ritual as a movement from anti-structure, expressed by masquerade, to structure, expressed by exaggerated formality:

Masquerade goes with absence of structure, "communitas" in the Turnerian [sic] sense, and the sociological image of the cassowary, who threatens the boundaries between nature and culture. "Formality" comes with the renewal of the structure by the *ipele* bowmen [Arrows in my terms], specifically endowed with characteristically "cultural" attributes, the re-statement of both the idealized complementarity between senior and junior generations [*ipele/ kwanugwi*] and also of the complementary opposition between man and nature. (Gell 1975:338)

But why regard the Cassowary as a disorderly threat to the boundaries, as if he were a "Lord of Misrule" (Gell 1975:224) or humanity in its "wild" form in need of "domestication" (Gell 1975:230), or "dirt" (Gell 1975:296) in the sense of "matter out of place"? The inference is wrong. Misleading assumptions produce it, and I discuss the method immediately. The Cassowary is nowhere near being a dangerous invader or a representation of "matter out of place."

If we ask what a Cassowary is, part of the answer is that it is an earth-bound bird. Further, Cassowary has the sense of descent, of having come down from a coconut palm (the maternal Tree of Life) and of being the origin of all who come down (offspring). Following Gardner (1984), I would go further, and suggest that this idea of descent is closed; it turns back upon itself. It is an idea that includes self-sufficiency in production and reproduction. The Cassowary as a bird, like the Australian Emu,

is endowed with certain essential characteristics of both men [an erectile penis, a rarity among birds] and women [a cloaca, through which it defecates and reproduces] [and] displays the same capacity for self-sufficient and self-closing productive cycles. (Gardner 1984:14)

Calling a masquerade hero a Cassowary associates him with primordial origins, with masculine androgyny, with powers of, to use O'Flaherty's phrase, "unilateral creation" (1980:28) or autogenesis (see also Werbner n.d.).

A very brief description is helpful, at this point, to introduce the Cassowary as hero by contrast to a counterpart as clown, the Noxious Nettles. Cassowary is a hunted hero; he dances at the opening of the festival's masquerade, and is its most prestigious character. Simulating regenerative copulation for as much as eight hours at a time, with an elongated penis gourd, Cassowary is a masculine androgyne of enormous, sustained virility and erotic fulfillment; he lets himself go and come with orgiastic abandonment. His heavy mask, a tree, is feminized and "pregnant"; it is a male womb. By contrast, Noxious Nettles is a hunter clown. A grossly aroused figure of sexual frustration, his mask is light, without a feminine outer framework. His aggression against spectators and others like himself is futile, all show, and eventually he is driven off by the crowd of watching children, immediately before the finale of the masquerade.

It might be thought that, in his gloss on the Cassowary, Gell has fallen into the language trap of "backward translation" (Bohannan 1969:410–11). But saying that goes too far. It suggests that there is no representation of "matter out of place," or no invader's part, and that making the ideas explicit is a violation of the indigenous conceptual framework. Rather, in the masquerade, there is a disorderly threat to the boundaries, but it comes from certain characters who are Mud-Men: humanity in the mud is humanity out of place, "dirt" not to be affirmed. These Mud-Men are outsiders who invade the inside. So perversely unlike humanity, which is always paired in the reciprocity of moieties, Mud-Men alone come one-by-one from the bush, coated with mud from the river. The rest of the characters, including the Cassowary, literally spring from within, from the sacred enclosure which, itself a "spring," is a cosmic source of vital being.

This symbolic contrast between vital beings who come from or belong inside and other beings who do not, is fundamental. It makes contextual sense within the actual sequencing of the masquerade as well as within the indigenous conceptions of boundary relations. I return to that symbolic contrast later.

My immediate concern is Gell's method. His ethnography is rich and his translations acute; but his method of analysis is misleading, due to three mistaken assumptions. These are important in various ways in other structuralist studies, and my intent is to bring the general weakness into relief by criticizing Gell's study in particular.

The first assumption of structuralist method is that an argument can be put quite straightforwardly in terms of a general dichotomy between nature and culture. It is as if there is no need to proceed to the general level through an analysis of that indigenous conceptual framework for boundary relations that is also a framework for ego's experience vis-à-vis the environment (for a similar criticism of structuralist method, see La Fontaine 1982:*xxxii*).

Secondly, in this method, the indigenous logic is assumed to revolve around a single elementary dichotomy, culture versus nature. This assumption blocks analysis of alternatives, such as a mode of thought that operates using pairs of dichotomies on coordinate axes. In fact, the indigenous logic is axial (see Chapter 5). Moreover, it involves antithetical principles of social exchange, the giving and receiving of life and death.

I discuss the indigenous logic, its antithetical principles and polarities, in due course. Here, in advance of my argument, only a brief suggestion can be made, and it is this: What the indigenous logic is about, and thus what the masquerade is about, is not "culture versus nature," but relationships over life and death (see Figure 29). Such relationships are expressed in elementary forms of kinship, namely kinship of the daughters (life-receiving), of the mothers (life-giving), of the sons (death-giving) and of the fathers (death-receiving). In the masquerade there are four categories of character to match the four relationships. By means of the characters, the relationships are operationalized and symbolically worked through. Each movement or transformation in the masquerade is a movement in and through these relationships (see the Appendix; and for a related discussion of symbolic structures of ritual and elementary structures of kinship, see La Fontaine 1982:*xxvii–xxxii*).

This leads me to the third fault in Gell's structuralist method. He starts his analysis with a role, the Cassowary of the Mothers, which happens to come among the first *two* in the masquerade—the other initial role, the Fish of the Daughters, is disregarded for purposes of Gell's general argument. The reasoning is, apparently, that the beginning, or a part of it, constitutes an ultimate conceptual extreme, not merely an extreme within a sequence. Accordingly, the argument goes, the Cassowaries "represent a limit; a point beyond which spontaneity degenerates into disorder, 'communitas' into mere chaos" (Gell 1975:295). Succeeding dancers are mediators along the way to another conceptual extreme; hence the Metamorphosis of a Cassowary. The transformation is completed by the last role in the masquerade:

The ipele [Arrows] thus restore the accepted boundaries of the spheres proper to humankind and natural species, which the entry of the cassowaries (heralding an invasion of the cultural domain by natural species) threatened to overturn. (Gell 1975:295)

The basic difficulty with all this, I must stress, is that it is an argument that is metaphorically misinformed, at least according to indigenous concepts of boundary relations. The argument does not proceed from an analysis of the cultural systematics of metaphor for boundary relations. Hence, it cannot get right how the actual sequence in performance relates to the indigenous metaphoric framework that is conceptually prior to that actual sequence (see Fernandez 1985 on the systematics of metaphor in a ritual sequence).

Neither anti-structure, nor nature as anti-culture, is dramatized by the opening of the masquerade, despite Gell's assertion. In order to show further what the course of the masquerade does dramatize, within the festival as a whole, I turn now to analyze the indigenous metaphoric framework, and later in the light of that, I substantiate my interpretation of the course of the festival.

A SEXUAL PARADIGM OF PRIMARY EXPERIENCE

Without developing the point systematically in relation to *ida*,[5] Gell observes:

. . . Umeda language . . . has a single portmanteau-verb, *tadv,* whose meanings "eat," "shoot," "kill," and "copulate with" cover the entire range of sexual, aggressive and gustatory experience. . . . Ego's social field is demarcated by boundaries, across which relations are mediated by *tadv* relations. . . . *Tadv* relations are, in effect, the fundamental modality whereby ego and the group(s) with which he is identified relate to their encompassing environment. (1975:116)

Elsewhere Gell reports that there is a "passive" correlate to the *tadv* verb,

. . . a single verb *yahaitav* does duty to express a wide range of experiences of "boundary crossing," i.e., death, fainting, sleep, and ecstacy. The basic meaning of this verb is "to go soft." (1975:250)

The pairs are thus:

| *tadv* | eat | shoot | copulate | kill |
| *yahaitav* | sleep | die | faint | ecstacy |

The primary experiences of life and death are grasped and classified by these oppositions. Of necessity, each is rich in cultural significance, and I can barely begin to unpack that richness. My aim is to show that, rightly understood, these oppositions are the masquerade's conceptual *master key*. By a conceptual master key I mean a set of cultural oppositions that form an integral whole and that, as a structure of meanings, gives sequences of symbolic behavior overall integration. The conceptual master key is a classifying framework for the organization of rites.

Here, somewhat as an aside, I must say something about my own use of language in the interpretation of the Umeda portmanteau words and the conceptual master key. The words I myself use have to convey a play of meanings to be faithful to the playfulness of the masquerade. My words for the modes of experience such as shoot or eat are complex, pregnant with meaning, and ambiguous; all the more so because, *playful as in masquerade,* they are converted from one set of meanings to others by being used metaphorically. I ask the reader to appreciate the resonance and its aptness; I cannot avoid the ambiguity.

The coherence of the masquerade as a whole, like the coherence of its characters in all their fine individualization, depends upon the *tadv–yahaitav* oppositions. To get their specific meanings and their semantic structure very clear is thus essential, and in due course I show how the component oppositions are polarized as cultural antitheses. But the general meaning of the opposition between *tadv* and *yahaitav* has to be stressed first in order for us to appreciate the broad classification of experience organizing the masquerade.

Tadv, across its full range of eat, shoot, copulate, and kill, refers to an encompassing experience within certain boundaries. *Yahaitav,* which covers sleep, die, faint, and ecstacy, refers to "going soft," as in male sexual climax, and thus generally to passing away, or boundary crossing. The nearest approximation I can make for this opposition between the encompassing and the boundary crossing is, to put it colloquially, "having a go" for all the active and aggressive body functions of *tadv* and "letting go" for the passive or involuntary alternatives covered by *yahaitav*. Using this general opposition, the people themselves see sequences of action as alternatively *tadv* and *yahaitav*, alternating between the encompassing experience and the boundary crossing experience.

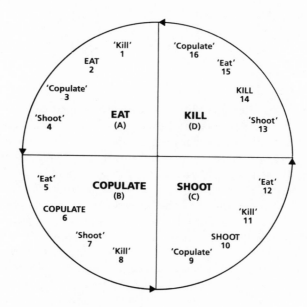

Figure 31. Serial Coupling of Metaphor.

THE METAPHORS FOR INDIVIDUAL CHARACTERS

Given the four primary categories of eat, shoot, copulate, and kill as primary terms, the rest follow quite simply by combination. From the primary four, sixteen varieties are produced by coupling the terms as metaphors in a sequence. This serial coupling of metaphor is a play on each experience, in turn, in terms of every other. In my view, such play is not random. If the masquerade is about anything, it is above all about reproductive sex, and time or age, from a dominantly male viewpoint. Dancing is a form of sexual activity, pounding the earth. Hence the metaphors, and thus the framework, are constructed in harmony with a conception of the normal passage of male sexual experience (Figure 31).

For the sake of clarity, I indicate each primary experience of *tadv*, such as copulate, without quotes, and its metaphoric variation with quotes, for example "eat." Also for clarity, the terms of translation I spell out are those of *tadv*, but the *yahaitav* terms are implied. For example, "shoot" in Copulation is "go soft," and "die," which is a term of *yahaitav*.

In the masquerade, as part of a festival dominated by men and designed for fertility and regeneration, the paradigmatic alternation, the *tadv–yahaitav* relations par excellence, are in male sexual experience. This is the course from *(a)* foreplay, to *(b)* play, to *(c)* climax, to *(d)* postclimax. The villagers' conceptual play on experience through masquerade has to be understood according to the course of Copulation, as it is erotically displayed by the Cassowaries. The first variety in terms of sexual experience, though not in order of appearance in masquerade, is *Ab,* the Wildfowl. His is not yet a body-painted figure (he and *Kwanugwi* of the Arrows are the only characters appearing in their own skins), but he is otherwise like the other Cassowaries, who all wear the elongated penis-gourd and pelvic girdle, but are unarmed. In a very brief dance, fit for a junior man, the Wildfowl scurries close to the ground, like a real wildfowl or a Cassowary about to be aroused.

Next comes *Eli,* the Cassowary par excellence. His is the prestigious part of a mature man, and I have already described his black-painted figure and sustained, fully aroused erotic display.

Third is *Aba,* the Sago, which is performed by a somewhat less senior man. Painted in flaming colors, red and yellow, as well as black, he appears and dances initially like *Eli,* while being watched by women. Later, unseen by women, the Sago dancer undergoes ordeals. First, he jumps over fire. Then his weaponless arm is seized to enact an ejaculation. Forced by the other men, he plunges his arm into near-boiling jelly (Sago that "dies," *yahaitav,* Gell 1975:183); coming up quickly, he releases his handful of jelly into the air over the heads of all the men present. It is a climax on behalf of all the men, since all contribute a handful of their own sago flour to make the jelly. This forced "coming up quickly" is said to make "the sago come up quickly" (Gell 1975:219).

Finally, as the postclimax, comes *Teh,* the Tinder, in Gell's terms "rotten wood" or "firewood" (1975:186). This is a part for a man of intermediate status. The *Teh* dancer has polychrome body-painting like the markings on bark or vines on trees; and his somewhat reduced and slightly altered "Cassowary" mask refers to a terminal phase in the life-cycle of trees (Gell 1975:257).

The four varieties of Cassowary epitomize the metaphoric elaboration of one experience in terms of each of the others. The serial coupling is this:

a	*b*	*c*	*d*
Ab Wildfowl	*Eli* Cassowary	*Aba* Sago	*Teh* Tinder
"eat"	Copulate	"shoot"	"kill"

yahaitav	*tadv*	*yahaitav*	*tadv*
boundary crossing	encompassing	boundary crossing	encompassing
foreplay	play	climax	postclimax

Literally, to eat is, of course, to consume food. But metaphorically, in the context of copulation, to "eat" is to arouse with high-value foods and aphrodisiacs, such as wildfowl eggs and fish. In our terms, it is foreplay. Similarly, to shoot is to release an arrow from a bow, but "shoot" as "dying," coming in the context of copulation, is ejaculation; it is the climax in our terms. Finally, as a metaphor in copulation, "kill" is the act of postclimax (hence the spent, no longer active, phase that the Tinder represents as the rotten wood consumed by fire).

Each variation can be seen as an alternation between boundary crossing and encompassing (cf. Gell 1978 on an alternation in *tadv*–*yahaitav* relations through the life-cycle). Thus the course of Copulation begins with "eating" and ends with "killing," a *yahaitav*–*tadv* opposition. In between, comes the opposition between copulation and "shoot." The former is the encompassing experience, the latter the passing away, the boundary crossing, "going soft."[6]

Given this fixed order as the paradigm for major categories of experience, the four basic terms generate sixteen varieties. Through an elementary rotation, each in turn becomes *(a)* foreplay, *(b)* play, *(c)* climax, and *(d)* postclimax. The whole can be seen as a metaphor cycle that returns back on itself. Below I list the varieties. Their numbers and letters correspond to the masquerade characters in Figure 32:

	(a) FOREPLAY	(b) PLAY	(c) CLIMAX	(d) POSTCLIMAX
Eat	1 "Kill"	2 Eat	3 "Copulate"	4 "Shoot"
Copulate	5 "Eat"	6 Copulate	7 "Shoot"	8 "Kill"
Shoot	9 "Copulate"	10 Shoot	11 "Kill"	12 "Eat"
Kill	13 "Shoot"	14 Kill	15 "Eat"	16 "Copulate"

Matched to the sixteen varieties of experience are the sixteen individual characters of the masquerade. As Figure 32 shows, each character represents a variety of experience in a systematic relation with the others. All the characters are generated in accord with the transposition of terms in the metaphor cycle.

Just as there is a cycle of metaphor, so too is there a cycle of characterization. The opposition between the characters is systematic, it is continuous, and it is in accord with the opposition between the

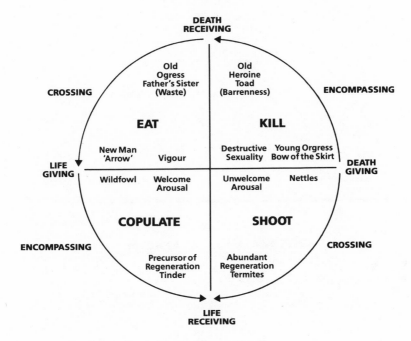

Figure 32. Continuous Opposition in Characterization.

basic modes of experience as terms and as metaphors. Eat, copulate, shoot, and kill form a continuous opposition in that order.

The antitheses are kill and eat, on the one hand, and copulate and shoot, on the other. One does not share food with enemies in war or eat one's own kill, and copulation is dangerous and debilitating for a hunter. In more detail, the extreme figures in the Kill series, Bow of the Skirt and Father's Sister, are opposed to the Eat extremes, Toad and New Man/"Arrow"; and so too are the extremes of Copulation, Wildfowl, and Tinder opposed to the extremes of Shoot, ending with Termites and beginning with Nettles (see Figure 33).

Unpacked very briefly, the oppositions can be seen as a play on sex and regeneration through the life cycle.

Mode	First Character	Imagery	Last Character	Imagery
Kill	Young Ogress	Sexual Attack	Old Ogress	Waste

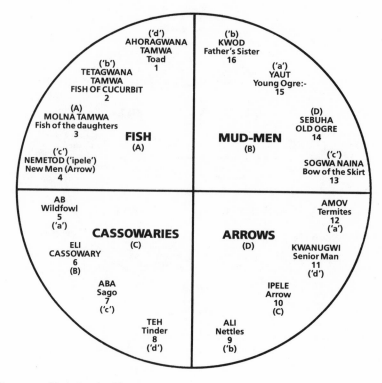

Figure 33. Variation in Character.

Eat	Old Heroine	Infertility	Neophyte	Potency
Copulation	Young Hero	Erotic Arousal	Mature Hero	Dessication
Shoot	Mature Hero	Fertility	Immature Clown	Unwelcome Arousal

Again, in detail, this is represented by the Kill–Eat and Copulate–Shoot antitheses in the following way. On the first antithesis: at the extremes of Kill are the Young Ogress, associated with sexual attack by means of her *vagina dentata,* and the Old Ogress, associated with waste (see Gell 1975:203, on the father's sister who is not a mother's brother's wife, and see my discussion below). These are opposed to the extremes of Eat, the Old Heroine associated with infertility, and the Neophyte, associated with youthful vigor and potency. Second, with regard to the other antithesis: at the extremes of Copulation are the youthful hero, associated with erotic stimulation, and the more mature hero, associated with dessication or the dried-out phase prior to regeneration. These are opposed, at the extremes of Shoot, to the more mature hero associated with abundant fertility, and the less mature clown associated with unwelcome arousal. Figure 33 shows the antitheses and the continuous opposition in characterization.

THE UNDERLYING VISION

It may well be asked, at this point, what the vision that underlies all this is, and what its essential principles may be. To sum up my discussion of the different orders within the conceptual framework may be useful before answering, for the sake of clarity. Just as experience and character are coordinated with concepts of cosmic time and space at the higher order of modes and categories, so, too, are the individual experiences and the individual characters geared to sexual time and space at the lower order of the varieties.

The conceptual framework of experience and characterization is a structure upon coordinate axes, according to a quite simple vision of opposing principles of exchange. It is a vision of the giving and receiving of life and death. I infer that the coordinate axes of the framework are the principles of giving and receiving, with life and death as the poles of the principles, as shown in Figure 33.

This figure illustrates the logic of the *yahaitav–tadv* relations as follows: First, Eat is an experience of boundary crossing in that it is a receiving of death, which becomes a giving of life. By contrast, Copulation is encompassing in that it is contained in life, both giving it and receiving it. In turn, there is boundary crossing in the experience of Shoot in that it involves life receiving through death giving. Finally, Kill is an experience of encompassing in that it is a receiving and a giving of death.

It is obvious that the Principle of Giving implies the Principle of Receiving—neither can exist alone, or without the other. What is perhaps not so obvious is that such co-implication is paradoxical. It poses a dilemma for the villagers when they annually renew their cosmos in masquerade. Human fertility threatens the abundance of game, and the more children a man fathers, the less he is expected to hunt or to be able to hunt. Similarly, killing vitiates commensality and, in the form of sorcery, becomes its ultimate perversion. In a festival for the best in eating, what place is there for killing? And in dancing, which is sexual expression, admittedly disguised in many ways, how is hunting to be given its due? In other words, the problem for the villagers is this: How are they to master the antitheses? All are essential, if the cosmos is to be renewed as a complete whole. Yet as antitheses, they are dangerous; one threatens to overwhelm or negate the other. The difficulty is not to be resolved by striking a balance. Rather, it is a matter of renewing the cosmos as an order containing its own imbalances, its priorities, its hierarchy of value as against an alternative (for a discussion of the defense of the cosmos elsewhere in the West Sepik province, see Huber 1975). In my view, the villagers resolve the dilemma primarily by recourse to humor and clowning, and by requiring the spectators to take matters into their own hands to overpower the dangerous beings in action. Their resolution fits a dialectical vision that sees that the cosmos is ceaselessly destroying itself and being reborn only to die.

This suggestion leads us forward to an understanding of the importance that a cultural nightmare has in the festival and in its sequencing. But first, an essential step is to think again about clowning and sacred clowns; we must go beyond the view that "they do little more than provide some comic relief" (Gell 1975:281). Their considerable importance in the renewal of the cosmos has to be recognized, for it is through the use of clowns that the villagers make sense of basic antitheses and manage a dilemma in their cosmology.

CLOWNS, HEROES, AND THEIR RELATIONSHIPS

Who and what are the clowns? Or rather, more in harmony with the villagers' own conception, who and what are the clowns in relation to the heroes?

The simplest answer is that the clowns are the heroes turned topsy-turvy in a perverse way. If the heroes are *symbolic types,* epitomizing basic categories of experience and elementary relationships of kinship and exchange, the clowns are *symbolic anti-types,* epitomizing the destructive antitheses.

The detailed account that follows demonstrates this point fully. It completes my discussion of the metaphoric framework for characterization. I begin with the four Mud-Men, who are clowns of the same kind, all being partnerless individuals performed by older men without wives; and I continue with the only clown from the other categories, the Nettles, a part acted by pairs from opposite moieties, usually frustrated bachelors. To provide an overview, the Table below lists the Mud-Men clowns by contrast to leading heroes in terms of experience and the version or perversion of a relationship.

OPPOSITION BETWEEN MUD-MEN, CLOWNS, AND LEADING HEROES

ROLE	CHARACTER		EXPERIENCE	RELATIONSHIP
Clown	*Sogwa Naina*	Bow of the Skirt	"shoot"	Junior female's perversion of matrikinship
Hero	*Ipele*	Arrow	shoot	Filial version of patrikinship
Clown	*Sebuha*	Old Ogre	kill	Fatherly perversion of patrikinship
Heroine	*Tetagwana Tamwa*	Fish of Cucurbit	eat	Daughterly version of patrikinship
Clown	*Yaut*	Young Ogre	"eat"	Junior male's perversion of patrikinship
Heroine	*Tetagwana Tamwa*	Fish of Cucurbit	eat	Daughterly version of patrikinship
Clown	*Kwod*	Father's sister	"copulate"	Senior female's perversion of matrikinship
Hero	*Eli*	Cassowary	copulate	Senior male's version of matrikinship

In the following account, I discuss the Mud-Men in the order listed, which is the order from foreplay to postclimax. The first is the clown Bow of the Skirt, whose antithesis is the hero Arrow; the clown and hero are opposed as "shoot" (the metaphoric action of perverse discharge in the context of kill) is to shoot. "Of the skirt" refers to the distaff side, the side of matrikin; its opposite is "of the penis sheath" *(pedana)*, the side of patrikin. But what is conveyed by Bow of the Skirt is something contrary to the positive nature of matrikinship. The bow's shaft is a euphemism for the womb, and in the Bow of the Skirt is embodied a negative kind of womb, with its horrible release. The penis that "feeds" the womb of a mother is turned, inside this ogress, into something rotten and disgusting, a worm. As a perverted form of a normal woman, the *vagina dentata* ogress uses her black bow–womb to attack. If the normal woman does not dwell in a tree—man having long ago descended from a palm—the ogress inhabits the black palm from which bows come. Similarly, her netbag is around her head, rather than suspended over her back. In performance, the barb of this role partly is directed against specific women in that their skirts are specially stolen to cover the dancer's genitals, and a woman's netbag is used to envelop his head.

In extreme contrast to that perversion of matrikinship and femininity, patrikinship and youthful masculinity is represented by the Arrow. The Arrow has the appearance of the young hunter, receiving vital potency. The Arrow's penis is itself treated as an arrow, or rather it *is* an arrow, with three sharp spines of black palm wood bound to it in the same manner as they are bound to a bamboo shaft. Attributed to the Arrow's head, arms, and genitals is the powerful and vital quality that is the very inner heart of growth. That is attributed by means of the white substance, otherwise avoided, that is used for the fringe of the Arrow's mask, for binding the arrow along with the red bow of his arms, and for the arrow of his penis.

Close attention must be paid to this white growth substance and its release by the Arrow. By contrast to an alternative substance, it conveys a conception of shoot or hunt and patrikinship, in contrast to the alternative, copulate and matrikinship. The white growth substance comes from the crown of the limbum palm. As food, it is forbidden, along with the crowns of other palms that resemble sago. In explaining their practice of avoidance, Lowlanders say that if such crowns were eaten, then the sago stands would not mature. Eating that interior white substance and eating sago are mutually exclusive alternatives, as are shooting or hunting and copulation. I infer, firstly, that the white growth substance is the solid, inedible counterpart of the liquid, edible *yis,* the semen/sago jelly; and secondly, that the release of one, the Arrow shooting an arrow of the inedible crown, is also the counterpart of the other, the Sago releasing sago/semen. Each action of release as symbolic discharge is vital, each is positive, and the fulfillment of a relationship; but they are counterposed as are the relationships of matrikinship and patrikinship, and Cassowaries and Arrows (see Appendix on involuntary giving in one relationship and voluntary giving in the other).

Among the clowns, with Bow of the Skirt as foreplay ("shoot"), and the Old Ogre as play (Kill), the next in turn is the Young Ogre ("eat") as climax. In appearance, somewhat of an immature version of the Old Ogre, with one club to brandish rather than two sticks, the Young Ogre wears a wood fern on the underbark around his head.

That identifies his descent, or lack of it; he does not belong to the humanity that has a common origin in the coconut palm and thus a common culture, based on exchange of coconut masks and women. Like the Old Ogre, the Young Ogre has a nature that is antithetical to what the Cucurbit (Eat) represents as the receiver of life. But whereas the Old Ogre is the perverse senior form, the anti-type of the father, the Young Ogre is the perverse junior form, the anti-type of the son, who represents a denial of normal descent or filial relationship.

Finally, the last of the Mud-Men clowns is the Father's Sister as postclimax ("copulate"). For the villagers, the relationship with a father's sister *(kwod)* is unwanted. It is an anomaly that arises from a woman failing to become a "mother's brother" *(na)* or a "mother" *(ava):*

Where a conventional exchange marriage has taken place, [the term for father's sister *(kwod)]* will not be used, since then the father's sister = mother's brother's wife, and will be addressed as *na,* by extension from the mother's brother, or more probably *ava,* which can be applied to any woman of the senior generation. . . . The father's sister can be classified neither as kin (in that her marriage associates her with non-kin) nor yet allies (as would be the case where FaSis = MoBrWi). The ego/*kwod* relationship establishes no ties, *kwod* are *awk*—outsiders as far as ego is concerned. Yet the connection is there. (Gell 1975:196)

The Father's Sister is an outsider and yet somewhat of an insider, a copulator who is still a hunter, a patrikinswoman not yet a matrikinswoman. The anomaly is embodied in the behavior and appearance of the Father's Sister. Dancing as an outsider, the Father's Sister

proceeds with a slow, bobbing step, to make a tour of the very edge of the arena, creeping furtively round and beneath the houses, menacing the spectators with tensed bow. (Gell 1975:195)

But rather than being covered in mud like the other ogres, who are invaders from without, the Father's Sister originates within, and wearing body paint, has a vital skin like a hero of the sacred center.

If subversive and centrifugal in action relative to the sacred center, the Father's Sister is identified with it in origin and, at once, is a party to its wasting away (i.e., as befits the failure to establish an exchange marriage). The dancer's penis is bound like that of the Arrow, and it is an arrow of growth, but one that is not and cannot be potent, since it does not come, like Arrow's, with the release of a bow and arrow. That which a patrikinsman would have productively, the Father's Sister has unproductively, as a patrikinswoman.

The Father's Sister does give the sacred center something totally unwanted by insiders. It is *yaut subove,* "ogre fruit," which is gaudy but not used in personal or ritual decoration. In throwing the ogre fruit away in order to plant it by the path *out of* the arena, the Father's Sister performs an act that is a perverse form of the mother's brother's giving nuts for the coconuts planted *innermost* within the festival hamlet. That wanted gift provides the potential for a future *ida,* for future exchange, and thus for the very culture of the festival. The ogress' useless planting merely memorializes the waste of a past performance. In short, all that the Cassowary represents positively in potency of mating, in exchange, and in life-giving, is negatively represented by the Father's Sister.

Earlier, I described the Nettles, the sexually frustrated, young clown, by contrast to the Cassowary, the sexually fulfilled, mature hero. At this point, I want to highlight what the Nettles represents as an anti-type: the youthful perversion of experience, which is "copulation" in the context of shoot. The Nettles is one of the Arrows and he is marked apart from the Mud-Men. If they are the clowns of the fathers, he is the one clown of the son and, as such, more hero-like than they are. Not only is he painted with the vital skin of a character from the sacred center, but he is paired with a partner from the opposite moiety, and he is not an isolated individual. Many Nettles perform in a mob at once. Characteristically, they do so in a rowdy, catch-as-catch-can manner, with their aggression directed both at spectators and each other. Frustrated and not mating normally, they wrestle with each other in their sexual arousal. They are disorderly and anti-social, and they dramatize the unwelcome contradiction of the young hunter as a would-be copulator.

Taken together, the four Mud-Men clowns are the very embodiment of hoary barbarism, from a male viewpoint. The cultural nightmare is an image of seniors and the aged, carrying on subversively beyond their time and out of their proper place. These clowns are like the old year during the festival; and like that, they must be got rid of, if the festival is to bring about rejuvenation in the new year. But as befits a dialectical vision, and the opposition of old and young, the first nightmare gives rise to a second. If child's play in comparison, the second nightmare is an image of the youthful barbarism that exists in coming prematurely, or not at all as desired. That nightmare, too, must be dispelled. But a single clown, the minimum role, is enough for the anti-type of the young, given the cultural emphasis on age and seniority as well as the timing of the festival, in welcoming the new year.

Here a qualification is in order. I suggested earlier that through the use of clowns, the villagers make sense of basic antitheses and manage a dilemma in their cosmology. But, in fact, clowns are almost entirely brought to bear on one half of that dilemma. It is the half that involves the antithesis between eat and kill along with the extreme opposition between inside and outside. The other half involves the antithesis between copulate and shoot (immediately antecedent and consequent), and only minimally is a clown used for that. Instead, one alternative resolution is avoidance. Thus the characters of each, the Cassowaries and the Arrows, are kept apart, respectively, for the masquerade's beginning and end. Moreover, the leading Arrow, who must not play any other part, is expected to remain secluded, until he emerges as the "new man" for the finale.

The further significance of this differential use of clowns can be appreciated, if we consider all the characters in relation to the two antitheses. The subsidiary characters follow the leading ones according to the following simple formula.

$$M_1 : M_2 :: C_1 : C_2$$
METAPHOR : METAPHOR   ::   CHARACTER : CHARACTER

A) copulate : shoot	::	Cassowary : Arrow
"eat"-copulate : "kill"-shoot	::	Wildfowl : Old Man
"shoot"-copulate : "copulate"-shoot	::	Sago : Nettles
"kill"-copulate : "eat"-shoot	::	Tinder : Termites
B) eat : kill	::	Cucurbit : Old Ogre
"kill"-eat : "eat"-kill	::	Toad-woman : Young Ogre
"copulate"-eat : "shoot"-kill	::	Fish of Daughters : Bow of Skirt
"shoot"-eat : "copulate"-kill	::	New Man : Father's Sister. ('Arrow')

I infer that the first antithesis, epitomized by Cassowary versus Arrow, is a relation of attraction and consequence, with the hunter following upon the hunted, the son upon the mother's brother. Such a relation is in the normal, and in that sense "natural," order of things and events. Its contrary—not following in the natural order of things and events—is the second antithesis. That is the relation of repulsion and inconsequence, epitomized by Cucurbit versus Old Ogre. In thus serving as a vehicle for the anti-natural and the perversion of the normal, the ritual clown is made to work for the renewal of the cosmos. Such ritual clowning is a way of passing off the negative extreme of the relation, which is contrary to natural. This is essential for the cosmology as a unified whole of positive and negative, natural and contrary-to-natural.

CONCLUSION

Bakhtin's general remarks about the mask of carnival are illuminating for the festival masquerade. The carnival mask, Bakhtin writes,

is connected with the joy of change and reincarnation, with joyful relativity and the happy negation of uniformity and similarity; it rejects conformity to one's own self. The mask is related to transition, metamorphoses, the violation of natural boundaries. (Bakhtin 1965:3, *cited in* Clark and Holquist 1984:304)

In commenting upon his observations, Clark and Holquist bring out Bakhtin's insight concerning the ambiguity and play on categories and classifications that is at the heart of masquerade and grotesque performance: "The mask is the very image of ambiguity, the variety and flux of identities that otherwise, unmasked, are conceived as single and fixed" *(ibid.)*. That is what the Umeda mask epitomizes as male womb, the variety and flux of identities.

Given the men's perspective of male dominance, my account of the masquerade and the grotesque shows how basic paradoxes, primarily of aging and sexuality, engross the men. Constructing physical and spatial caricatures, they exaggerate the most characteristic features of their bodies to achieve a series of cosmic and personal transitions. In other words, they relocate themselves in disguise, and thus the world around themselves, through "the logic of the concrete." Moreover, through the use of clowning and humor the men not only celebrate the total range of ego's experience in relation to his environment, but they also act to overcome the basic paradoxes in experience, because they provoke women and children into becoming participants and no longer mere spectators. The response includes everyone in the self discovery, which is a renewal of the cosmos. Thus what the men represent through their masquerade sequences is a vision of the cosmos as a total whole. But, nevertheless, it is an ironic and dialectical vision, in which one part after another continually has to give way to its alternative.

The masquerade puts everyday life in suspension. In general, that is true of the liminal phase elsewhere (Turner 1967:93ff). But there is an important difference, which supports this proposition: the form that liminality takes is relative to the social context of transformation (see also Hieb 1972:192ff). Thus, in hierarchical societies, liminality often involves the levelling of distinctions. By contrast, the same phase in this highly egalitarian society's rites exaggerates distinctions. The masquerade classifies and marks every man apart in a caricature of his own individuality. Each man's body is put into service for the embodiment anew of the cosmos as an integral whole, a total order of difference and resemblances.

The performance of rebirth recreates masculine fantasies about the fundamentals of human order. In the masquerade, playing upon masculine androgyny, kinship is recast in a primordial form—the kinship of mothers, of daughters, of fathers, of sons. Enacted first, in a male form, are the relationships which, as daughters and mothers, women mediate over the *receiving* and the *giving* of life. Then come the relationships that, as fathers, men mediate over the *receiving* of death and, as sons, over *giving* it. The movement of the masquerade, given its core metaphor of male reproductive sexuality, follows a masculinized order of kinship. Even more, it makes that masculinized order represent the cosmic truth of the giving and receiving of life and death, and it does so by a binary logic, using the opposition and inversion of features. But what is made known by and to the masqueraders is not merely something static: i.e., the way that relationships mirror each other. Rather, it is something dynamic. Each relationship is seen and felt, through ordeals and contradictions, to lead to its alternative, according to a dialectical vision of man and the beings around him. The male masquerade is an unfolding of primordiality, of masculine androgyny. It is as if men mask themselves in immortality only to recover their own mortality.

APPENDIX: CATEGORIES OF CHARACTER AND KINSHIP

The four categories of character are, in order of appearance, Cassowaries, Fish, Mud-Men, Arrows. The Cassowaries are masculine androgynes "of the Mothers" and along with the Fish "of the Daughters," they begin the masquerade. Relationships through women take precedence over relationships through men. The exemplary act of a mother's brother, giving from his own coconuts for his sister's son's coconut palms, is enacted in another form by one of the Cassowaries, known as *Aba,* the Sago, but also called the Cassowary. The Sago gives semen/sago jelly, somewhat involuntarily. I must stress that a man's agnates do not give him the coconut palms that he needs for the source of his most valued goods, although that source sustains and is sustained in their hamlet. At a man's birth, the coconut palms are planted for him by his mother from his mother's brother's nuts. Gell suggests that "The crucial symbol of 'culture' in the Umeda symbolic system is the coconut palm" (1975:270). If that is so, using "culture" in some loose sense, then "culture," or more simply life, is in the giving of the senior matrikinsman, and thus associated with the Cassowary as in his giving.

The contrast is to the characters at the end of the masquerade, the Arrows. I infer, although it is not explicitly said by the Lowlanders, that the Arrows' behavior, appearance, and name, all categorize them as "of the sons" and "of the growing point" of patrikinship (see Gell 1975:284 on *ip,* breadfruit versus coconut, and *ipud,* eldest son). In the culminating act of the masquerade, the act of parturition, the Arrows release the substance of growth, "shooting birds" with their potent arrows, and they thus "send the cassowaries, fish, *amov,* etc., back to the bush where they belong" (Gell 1975:294–95). In the masquerade, as in a myth of original time, that is the action of a junior patrikinsman; he is the child or "New Man" who scatters the game of the Old Man or original man. It follows that the Arrows are the positive counterpart of the Cassowaries, and thus represent the reverse: death and the wild as game in the bush, is in the giving of the junior patrikinsman, in contrast to what is in the giving of the senior matrikinsman —life and the domestic as seeded nurture.

As for the other contrast, that involves the Fish and the Mud-Men. The leading part among the Fish belongs to the mythic heroine, Cucurbit, who overcomes and destroys her ugly, barren elder, the war-painted Toad-Woman. Cucurbit herself appears as the young and beautiful image of fruitfulness and multiplication. Through her coconut fiber mask she is associated with the coconut, whose fruit may be eaten but no other part used for any purpose. The kinship "of the daughters" is thus positively represented, with the receiving of the coconut and thus "culture" or life, in exchange, through the daughters' successful reproductivity.

If my analysis is right so far, and the kinship of sons is opposed to the kinship "of mothers" (Arrows versus Cassowaries), then it is reasonable to suppose that the kinship "of daughters" is opposed to a relationship of fathers (Fish versus Mud-Men). In the leading part of the Mud-Men, the Old Ogre *(Sebuha)* is the very nemesis of what Cucurbit represents. The Old Ogre is said to have but one hair and one tooth, not the many coconut fibers of the fruitful Cucurbit. He appears with his head bound with the dead matter of underbark, and hobbles along, as if a not-so-human creature on all fours, with two sticks, which he also brandishes against people. He embodies petrification, "man into tree," in that unwelcome sense. It is thus the anti-kinship of the father that he represents, receiving death or "nature" as one who has aged beyond reproductive capacity or further growth.

ACKNOWLEDGMENT

I wish to thank Marilyn Strathern and Donald Tuzin for their helpful comments.

SACRED JOURNEY

CHAPTER 5

DUAL ORGANIZATION, AXIS, AND SACRED CENTER

Dialectical Representation
in the New Guinea Lowlands

INTRODUCTION

Umedas and other villagers in the Western Lowlands of New Guinea make an annual sacred journey from bush to village, from low to high season. They enact, as we have seen in the previous chapter, what Eliade (1954, 1974) would call an eternal return toward the beginning of time. It is a reversing of the course of recent history. Their quest is to recover a primordial state of powerful well-being and unity, a paradise of mature male dominance, by counteracting the move that lost that state. At the beginning of time, according to myth, Western Lowlanders were one. They lived in a single village, not apart as now. It was a time of integrity before the present fragmentation. All the good things in life were housed together around their common ancestor, not scattered between bush and village. Later, when people and goods became dispersed, the Umedas went downstream to the bush lowlands to the west. In counteraction, Umedas annually return to their village to the east, to an internal center near a symbolic spring or source of cosmic forces.[1]

In some societies, making the eternal return as a sacred journey is primarily a matter of cosmology, with little importance apart from

that. But among the Western Lowlanders, this is a counteractive movement that also has other dimensions, in social exchange, in the effective
limits of community and society, and in the social value of inequalities
in basic resources.

It is in making the eternal return by way of their fertility cult that
Western Lowlanders create community. The existence of community,
as in a village, cannot be taken for granted. It is something precarious.
Ambiguities about it arise at the margins, requiring symbolic and
organizational counteraction if it is to be sustained. Western Lowlanders are pulled into relations of cooperation and trust with one set of
fellows for certain purposes, such as production, and another set for
other purposes, such as communal ritual. The pressures on the Western
Lowlanders are contradictory, and their principles of dual organization
are in tension. Predicaments arise, and no easy harmony emerges to
resolve the tension, although symbolic means are used to impose an
appearance of resolution.

The ethnographer Gell argues, on the basis of what is, in my
view, a fundamentally mistaken dichotomy between action and the
expressive or ideational, that "the integration of the society provided
by the moiety organization is at the level of ideas, rather than the
level of action" (1975:83). Apparently, Umeda dual organization is
"important only in a ritual context" (1975:84). In this context it seems
to do no more than reflect basic aspects of social reality by raising
these to the participants' consciousness. Two moieties exist, for ritual
purposes, "as a symmetric opposition of identical and equal halves of
the total society" (1975:44). They are also opposed as insider is to
outsider, as center to periphery, being named "of the men" *(edtodna)*
and "of the women" *(agwatodna),* though of course each moiety has
men and women in it. No rule of exogamy fits both moieties. One is
exogamous, the other not. But somehow the moieties make possible
"the conceptualization of the total society as a single relationship of
alliance between opposed halves" (1975:42).

What Umeda dual organization lacks, at least in Gell's view, is
practical effectiveness. Reciprocity over access to land holds between
certain segments or hamlets. But this does not correspond to the dual
organization, nor is it regulated by it. Like relations over land, the
alliance pattern is itself a matter for segments or hamlets to manage.
Such management is subject to prohibitions on marrying an allied
group—prohibitions that separate the marriageable, preferably in "sister exchange," from those who can wear each other's masks at rituals
and are therefore allies. But again, to Gell, that has seemingly nothing
to do with dual organization.

Gell's perspective is simply that of "the total society," without regard for the relative perspectives of each segment or hamlet within it. In fact, as I show later, the named moieties are merely one—the most central and culturally stressed—of a plurality of cross-cutting dual divisions. Each such division has a hamlet's masking allies in one half and its marriage partners in the other. Hence, in identifying the native model of dual organization solely with the named moieties, Gell obscures their coordination with the rest of Umeda dual divisions. Gell's divorce of dual organization and alliance from economy and ecology is virtually complete, and it is fundamentally misleading.

One consequence of Gell's decontextualized approach to dual organization is the appearance of numerous anomalies and exceptions to an "ideal scheme," yielding moieties without exogamy, villages without moieties, and so forth. Another consequence is that binary principles seem to be irrelevant to the realities of production and distribution. Even the layout of hamlets and territories appears random, rather than bearing a binary imprint. In Gell's account, the inequalities in the physical environment—making territories better or worse for hunting or gardening, more or less accessible to enemies, more marginal or central—seem to be givens, beyond the people's organizational interests or capacities. Gell takes no cognizance of the organizational dilemmas that arise when people organize and reorganize reciprocity in relation to the environmental inequalities by using different forms of dualism. The dual organization, as Gell presents it, comes to be inert, without transitive features or the potential for alternative states of organization. Yet the society he studied is characterized by an annual cycle of transhumance marked by different forms of organization during successive phases. For Gell's finely detailed ethnography, the effect is fragmentary; he gives pieces for the sake of completeness in description yet includes too little that recognizably bears on dual organization.

To restore that bearing through a reanalysis of Gell's ethnography is one of my major aims in this chapter. The evidence needs to be examined closely, which is why I present it as fully as possible, within practical limits. My argument demonstrates the power of a *contextualized* semiotic approach. Here reciprocity over territory, women, and masks is crucial, for it is in this that the people coordinate production, reproduction, and redistribution. As well, reciprocity coordinates the sharing in accumulated abundance during a festival return to a condition of primordial plenty (see Chapter 4).

Environmentally differentiated segments are mutually coordinated in such reciprocity. I show that disparate tendencies operate in the patterning of their reciprocity. The first is a tendency toward homology, by which, among themselves, their networks of reciprocity are formally alike. Against that is a counter-tendency toward hierarchy and recognized differentiation among the segments. One of them, in various respects the most advantageous, is made the center of centers. It is at once the point around which the unity of a whole community emerges, and it is also the most important point for reciprocity beyond the community. In sum, therefore, my main aim is to develop an approach that illuminates these and other conflicting tendencies of Umeda dual organization by relating them to the environment in which the people produce, consume, and reproduce.

Debate about dualism and societies organized on binary principles is perhaps as old as anthropology itself. Yet we have only begun to understand how and why it is that people in such societies construct highly complex representations of social reality. Many studies overemphasize the importance of reciprocity or complementarity between the halves of a society. As a consequence, various seemingly unbalanced relations, such as social divisions in triads or other odd numbers, are seen as breaches of dualism, rather than further manifestations of it. Even when this complexity is recognized descriptively, much of it is often dismissed analytically, as patternless and irrelevant. Worse still, the analysis may dissolve the problem by suggesting an apparent pattern that has nothing to do with binary principles and the dynamics of dual organization. Hence, we are only beginning to understand how, within a single society, different forms of dual organization operate and, even more important, operate in tension with each other.

To move the debate forward we need to adopt a theoretical perspective that focuses on organizational contradictions. In dialectical societies, having different forms of dual organization, certain relations are typically in contradiction (on dialectical societies, see Maybury-Lewis 1979). These are, on the one hand, relations of simple dualism that imply balance or equivalence, such as between complementary moieties and, on the other hand, center–periphery relations, which imply imbalance and inequality. The imbalance occurs because one part, the center, is higher in value than the rest, which constitute the peripheries. Sometimes, the center also represents the totality to its parts. In addition, as in other societies, center–periphery relations are problematic in themselves, as they endure contradictory pulls toward and away from the center.

Let me introduce a caution, however. In context, the actual operation of forms of dual organization may be precarious and volatile (see Tuzin 1976:223ff). It is sterile, therefore, to treat binary principles in the abstract. The question that has to be answered is what use people actually make of binary principles in controlling and exploiting resources, in responding to demographic inequalities, and in constructing their cultural environment. My assumption, hardly novel, is that people use their binary principles selectively to grant cultural reality to certain social relations and to deny it to others. Which relations are selected and on what basis are open questions.

DIAMETRIC AND CONCENTRIC DUALISM
IN DIALECTICAL SOCIETIES

One of my further aims in this chapter is to extend to New Guinea the debate about dialectical societies which has so far been confined to South American examples (Maybury-Lewis 1979). The latter discussion has primarily been about world view, cultural categories and principles of social organization. Somewhat neglected are certain oscillations and ritual processes that, I argue, also characterize a dialectical society (for an exceptional analysis, see Hugh-Jones 1979:235ff), and which I discuss further in due course.

Much depends, of course, on how the dialectical society is conceptualized. A binary view of the universe and a dualistic mode of social organization are basic in Maybury-Lewis' initial conceptualization. The people consider opposition to be imminent in the nature of things. They strive "to create a harmonious synthesis out of the antithetical ideas, categories, and institutions that constitute their way of life" (Maybury-Lewis 1979:13).

The dual and the dialectical are, of course, quite different. But the difficulty is not simply that Maybury-Lewis' initial conceptualization stops short, leaving the difference between the dual and the dialectical largely implicit. Even more, his initial conceptualization remains too static and inert to be dialectical; he does not adequately cope with the transformation in dualism implied by the dialectical process.

Part of the difficulty arises because Maybury-Lewis does not distinguish between different forms of dualism. Having rejected Lévi-Strauss' distinction (Lévi-Strauss 1963a) between diametric and concentric dualism, he dismisses the problem of formal analysis, by arguing that no distinction is needed at all, stating: ". . . these antitheses are sociologically significant simply as oppositions and irrespective of the nature or structure of such oppositions" (Maybury-Lewis 1960:4). I agree that Lévi-Strauss' distinction needs to be examined and perhaps rethought, but some distinction between different forms of dualism is essential for purposes of comparison.

Lévi-Strauss leads us toward a more dynamic view in the course of his account of negation, complementarity, and balance among the Bororo:

They arranged and rearranged the contradictions they encountered, never accepting any opposition without repudiating it in favour of another, cutting up and dividing groups, joining them and setting them one against the other, and turning their whole social and spiritual life into a coat of arms in which symmetry and asymmetry are equally balanced. (1973:245)

In the world-view of a dialectical society, what is basic is not opposition as such, but a struggle between opposites and the transformation of opposition in the struggle. "The men kill the women and the women kill the men" is one way that New Guinea villagers state their underlying premise (Gell 1975:111). Our focus must be on the dynamics of negation, for it is through negation that the opposition between thesis and antithesis is continually made to collapse in favor of one synthesis. Later in this chapter I analyze how the Western Lowlanders use negation and its transcendence by asserting a hierarchy between antitheses.

Representations of Reality in Dialectical Societies

My analysis has the further aim of bringing together two strands of Lévi-Strauss' reasoning that to my knowledge have not yet been linked. One strand appears in his argument about alternative representations of reality in societies that have *both* diametric and concentric dualism, that is, dialectical societies (Lévi-Strauss 1960:45–54, 1963:132–63; and see also, Maybury-Lewis 1960; and for Highland New Guinea, Rubel and Rosman 1978:336ff). The other strand appears in his account of split representation and the aesthetics of mask cultures (Lévi-Strauss 1963:245ff, 1973:178–97, 230–31, 246).

Lévi-Strauss' arguments, although complex, are well known, and I am concerned here with only certain points. But it is worth mentioning, although it raises issues beyond my scope, that his distinction between diametric and concentric dualism relates to a contrast between static and dynamic oppositions, between a closed and an open system.

Lévi-Strauss argues that, in certain societies, no single form of dualism is adequate to represent the complexity of social relations (1963:134–35). Hence, alternative forms are used, which simplify or even conceal the complexity, and which generate multiple representations of reality. Having both forms enables people to engage in triadic or plural relations, which are serial, while conceptualizing them in terms of binary oppositions, which are simultaneous.

Complexity as such, however, is not enough to account for the disparate representations in a dialectical society. It follows from Lévi-Strauss' argument, first, that the disparity has to be understood as a surface manifestation of deeper, underlying contradiction, and second, that just as certain social relations are contradictory, so too are their representations antithetical. In my view, underlying the Western Lowlanders' disparate representations is a contradiction between relations for the production of luxuries and relations for their distribution and consumption. I suggest that, by having representations that are quite separate as well as antithetical, Western Lowlanders are able to sustain and overcome the underlying contradiction. I return to this suggestion later.

The diametric form of dualism represents the wholeness and unity . of a society as a product of the universal opposition between its halves, between the halves of its halves, and so forth, in a constant or static contrast. In concentric dualism, the basic opposition is to the environment; it is a representation of various ego-focused or sociocentric relations, such as those expressed in center–periphery terms. Concentric dualism is usually characterized by a series of oppositions (that is, in the series: center to margin to periphery). These oppositions are unlike and thus dynamic (see Crocker 1979:299 on complementary polarities among Bororo), and the structures, such as those of ritual exchange and marriage, cut across one another.

In light of the data from New Guinea's Western Lowlands, I would argue two additional points. First, having both forms of dualism constitutes a kind of transitiveness in relations that allows them to be alternatively ego-focused (in center-periphery terms) or universal (in terms of the halves of a social universe). Second, and more abstractly, perhaps one might say in terms of a deep structure, it is in the synthesis of both forms, transcending their opposition, that a society attains its dialectical character.

Mask Cultures, Split Representation, and Spatial Design

The second strand of Lévi-Strauss' argument is that, typical of a very widespread kind of mask culture is a stylistic opposition in visual art. One style simplifies and exaggerates, caricaturing reality. In the opposite style, split representation, reality is dislocated. The visual image of the subject is split repeatedly, composed and then decomposed, in such a way that the totality constitutes an ambiguous figure. Apparently in transformation, it is neither symmetrical nor asymmetrical, and yet somehow each, in turns. When a subject such as a face is represented, it is recognizable as a face and yet it is disfigured and deformed, with some elements transposed, and the usual axis of form rotated. In a sense, the transformational ambiguity is such that the usual appearance is at once embodied *and* transcended.

This style of split representation on masks is clearly related to social organization. Just as split representation is informed by a *tension* between two principles of dualism, symmetry and asymmetry, so too, the key to the related social organization is a corresponding *contradiction* between two principles, hierarchy and reciprocity or equality.

Even more strongly, Lévi-Strauss argues that split representation is a functional device for resolving, on a level of the imagination in art or aesthetics, a contradiction on the level of society. This resolution is a triumph for hierarchy over equality or reciprocity. In other words, split representation validates and justifies hierarchy; it is found on masks only in societies where "ancestrality," a relation to the dead or their spirits, is the basis for rank, titles, and privileges—in other words, hierarchy. This style is absent from the masks in most of New Guinea, with the apparent exception of the Sepik River, where egalitarianism and its representation prevails.

But what of the opposition of visual styles of caricature versus split representation? On the logic of Lévi-Strauss' argument, the possibility can be raised that in New Guinea's dialectical societies, caricature as the prevailing mask style does have its antithesis in other visual art. Indeed, I wish to argue that split representation, or something like it, prevails in Western Lowlanders' spatial design, i.e., the plan and layout of the spaces demarcated for marital exchange, ritual, production, and so forth.

TERRITORIAL PARTNERSHIPS

My discussion focuses on the Western Lowlands of New Guinea, where people who live in certain adjacent territories must maintain reciprocity and cooperate with each other whether or not they belong to the same community or even the same society. For purposes of production, primarily hunting and fishing, neighbors along a stream are interdependent. I refer to them as *territorial partners;* in pidgin, such a partnership between territories is called *wanbus* ("one bush," it has no indigenous name). The partners exchange relatively free access for tracking quarry, for garden help, and simply for visiting. For most of the year, apart from a brief festival period, the territorial partnership contains the widest universe within which a person feels secure and at home.

The partnerships do not all conform to binary principles within a form of dual organization. In other words, they are not all given cultural reality. Indeed, some of the partnerships, particularly between people living in the borderlands of hostile societies, have to be culturally dismissed. Hostility prevails. The neighbors' productive relations are not commutable by any sharing in consumption or any redistribution of resources other than land; the people explain away their actual reciprocity and cooperation with statements about history; the people say they are a survival from other times, when the territories or their people belonged to hamlets in the same village. Each territory has its own hamlet at a central site within a village community. Cultural reality is given within a form of dual organization solely to those relations of production that the people can, and actually do, encompass within a dominant field of social exchange. By the dominant field of social exchange, I mean the one in which the most highly valued transactions take place. In this dominant field, men exchange women as marriage partners; they exchange masks as vehicles for ritual services, and precious foods as consumable luxuries.

Within the Western Lowlands, the scale and span of social relations are quite limited in comparison to the much discussed exchange relations that are involved in the pig festivals of the New Guinea highlands. The Western Lowlanders in Umeda village and its environs raise virtually no pigs and they participate in little trade or direct ceremonial exchange of values. Their emphasis on collecting and hunting is such, according to Gell, that although they plant sago, their small-scale subsistence activity "can hardly be called agriculture, and bears a much greater resemblance to the life of 'hunters and gatherers' " (Gell 1975:18).[2]

"Your own pigs you must not eat" is a basic axiom of highland festivals but, in a sense, Western Lowlanders do just that: they consume their own "pigs" by sharing during their festival in the luxury foods, such as fish, fowl, and coconuts, that they themselves produce. Western Lowlanders do not produce for their festival either the kind or the scale of surplus food, luxuries, and high-value goods that Highlanders produce for theirs. The Western Lowlanders' festival might well be seen as an extreme on a continuum, along which the pig festivals of the highland agriculturalists (see Rubel and Rosman 1978:337ff) occupy the other extreme. But this is a major subject in itself, beyond my present scope (see also Whitehead 1986).

In terms of social exchange, territory and women are treated as antithetical providers and containers of the space of life, territory being immovable and women movable. Reciprocity over and exchange of a life-space container brings people into physical contact. And people can reconfigure their physical environment, the immovable surroundings, by their selection of the movable containers of life space. By exchanging women across the river in a fixed pattern, the Western Lowlanders reject the limitations and disparities of their territorial partnerships in strips of land that are parallel to the river (and thus perhaps relative to the movements of game and fish). This counteraction is an alternative configuration of the Western Lowlanders' life space, and it is a negation of their confinement within immovable surroundings.

The Western Lowlanders use a symbolic device in social exchange, however, to represent a transcendence of the opposition between relations over territory and relations over women. That symbolic device is the mask, which is higher in value than either a woman or a territory in that it contains immortal life, the life of a higher order of being at the very beginning of time. But the mask mediates between the other containers, and through the mask the opposition between the two is symbolically overcome. On the one hand, the mask, like a woman, is movable and on the other, like a territory, it relates to permanence. By sharing access to the space within masks, the Western Lowlanders establish a higher order of symbolic contact between territories that do not exchange women. Such territories symbolically meet and are identified with each other's mask-exchange partners, whether or not the territories are in contiguity or in territorial partnership with each other.

Alternation in the Annual Cycle

The organizational contradiction that arises in this dialectical society is managed by means of an oscillation in both time and space. Each year, the Western Lowlanders go through a cycle of organization and reorganization, and this is in accord with certain alternative representations of reality. At one extreme occasion during the cycle, the wholeness of their society emerges as a symbolic unity of complementary halves. The hamlets of a village form a community of equals participating in certain exchanges equally and in the same ways. Each hamlet has a balanced, symmetric universe that includes the same number of village partners. Moreover, each hamlet has an opposite, which halves that symmetric universe in reverse: where one hamlet exchanges women, the opposite exchanges masks and ritual services, and vice versa. Here centrality is at risk. Such balancing within the village community has to be, and is, counteracted by external exchange and social representations that focus on the center. Indeed, through the repeated performance of ritual during the annual festival, *ida,* a hierarchy of sacred centers and counter-centers emerges that corresponds with or, rather, coordinates distinct orders of community.

At another extreme in the Western Lowlanders' cycle, what emerges is the unequal fragmentation of the society. The social universe is represented as divided into a number of unequal parts; at the simplest, it is an asymmetric arrangement of three sets of territories, a tripartition that is, at first sight, a "breach" of binarism. The exchanges most characteristic of the alternative phase are blocked or forbidden during this phase of the cycle. Members are contained in inequality. Here the unity of the whole is at risk, with an excessive pull toward one or another part. For most of the year, villagers are dispersed in the lower elevations, where they produce luxuries such as smoked meat, that they distribute and consume during the brief period of their annual festival. During this festival period, they ascend from the lowlands and come together in the village at ridge-top hamlets.

In completing the cycle from dispersal to concentration, from fragmentation to symbolic unity and sacred centrality, Western Lowlanders bring their social life to a climax. They see their society as attaining a higher order, and their own experience of it as on a higher plane. Thus, from their viewpoint, the cycle culminates in a return to an original, higher mode of existence.

Viewing it abstractly, I argue that the oscillation represents alternative states of the same system of binary coordinates. Our own logic of dichotomies often works within a system of Cartesian coordinates, having two axes and thus four poles, a quadratic system. But for various reasons, the Western Lowlanders double that in their implicit logic; their axial system has four axes and eight poles.

This axial system has many surface manifestations: an eight-fold configuration of territories, three parallel sets of territorial partnerships, a triadic chain of villages, six hamlets in a village community, and many crosscutting moieties. My analysis shows how the Western Lowlanders configure and reconfigure their axial system, using different polarities and antitheses.

But why does a dialectical society have a double axial system? Part of the answer is that the axial system has to have certain *formal* properties, if it is to be adequate where alternative states are essential. In the case of the Western Lowlanders, the double axial system is the simplest system adequate for the required transformations in state; an elementary system of four coordinates would not suffice. The requirement is not primarily a matter of number. It is a matter of the more complex logic of relations between antitheses. In a double system, secondary antitheses can mediate, among other things, the primary set in an elementary system, as shown in Figure 34. Given that mediation, the double system has a potential for transformation that an elementary system lacks. Figure 34 shows one such transformation that represents, in concentric terms, the triadic relations between the middle and the extremes, or the center and its peripheries. In the Western Lowlands, the axial system is realized in various transformations: the coordinate points represent territories or hamlets as partners in reciprocity over access to territory and in the exchange of women, ritual services, or luxury foods. In the arrangement of territorial partnerships, the points are reconfigured; the eight territories are reduced to the parallel sets in a triadic pattern, which is shown by solid lines on Figure 35 (compare this with Figure 34). Notice that the pattern is at once symmetric and asymmetric, and that is has features reminiscent of split representation.

The Alternative Forms of Dualism and a Spatial Model

Of the alternative forms of dualism among the Western Lowlanders, the concentric is the dominant form in that it is the more pervasive over a greater variety of cultural realms, organizing relations of production, consumption, and exchange. Its surface manifestations tend to be intricate and highly elaborated. A great deal of analysis is needed to clarify this, and I devote much of this account to it. For the sake of clarity, however, I begin with the subordinate form, diametric dualism, which needs no lengthy discussion. It has none of the surface intricacy of concentric dualism, and it repeats itself, in halves of halves, in a familiar way—*within* versus *without* the society; *"of the men"* versus *"of the women"*; *original* versus *immigrant* hamlet; *original* versus *outsider* sides of the hamlet.

To the north, the mountain range is a major divide, at the limits of a Lowlander's moral universe from a Umeda perspective (Figure 36). Beyond and *outside* society are "rubbish" *(nsok)* or barbarians, with whom warfare involves merciless sneak raids, even against women and children. Between that range to the north and the next range to the south and along the rivers to the east and west are one's fellows *within* society, "the children of the coconut." The coconut signifies that the society is one of villages and hamlets, for the coconut is grown only on ridge-top sites, where it is the focus for a village's festival hamlets. In turn, a village is divided into immigrant and original (or owner) hamlets, roughly on a north–south axis relative to the mountain range. During the festival, the opposition is enacted by the dancing partners, "of the women" and "of the men." Finally, each hamlet has its halves. The outsiders are *asila* (garden) and the original occupants are *ivil* (breadfruit tree). Away from the festival sites for hamlets and around garden houses, groves of breadfruit trees are sited on ridge-tops, with the gardens themselves on the slopes. Thus, the opposition between *outsider* and *insider* is repeated along the *north–south* axis. In my view, this is the axis of *diametric* opposition: the society is a whole of opposed halves, with the halves of its halves, and so forth, in a constant, or static contrast.

The physical geography lends itself to a quite regular conceptual-

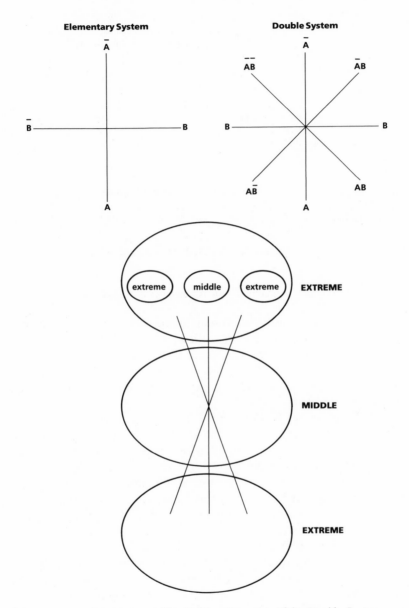

Figure 34. Axial Systems and Triadic Transformation of the Double System.

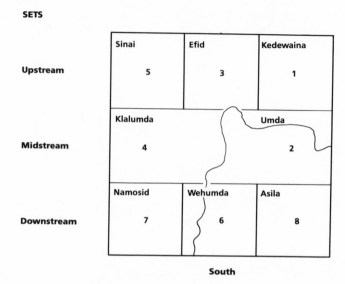

Figure 35. Territorial Partnership, Western Lowlands of New Guinea.

ization of society according to mountain ranges and river systems. But the Western Lowlanders' conceptualization is not a spatial model that merely corresponds to the fixed features of the physical geography. Instead it combines the spatial and the dual, in both diametric and concentric forms (on spatial and dual models in New Guinea, see Power 1966:274).

The multiple representations confirm Lévi-Strauss' argument. The diametric dualism is static; and insofar as it has transformations, one is like another. There is no overlap or reconfiguring of divisions, merely inclusion or exclusion according to social distance. By contrast, as I show later, the concentric dualism is dynamic; its transformations are unlike one another. In its disparate representations, center–periphery relations are reconfigured: each representation respects the spatial surroundings in its own way, and each uniquely reshapes them.

Hence, I am tempted to suggest that the Western Lowlanders' conceptualization of society is "split representation," that is, *somewhat* like split representation, in that it respects a physical reality only to dislocate and transform it. For convenience, I would call the form in the Western Lowlands *dialectical* representation. In the same vein I would also suggest a corollary to Lévi-Strauss' view about contradiction, in which split representation validates hierarchy. Rather than a hierarchy of persons, dialectical representation seems to justify a hierarchy of places, or rather, places in a personal geography that the people themselves code as persons.

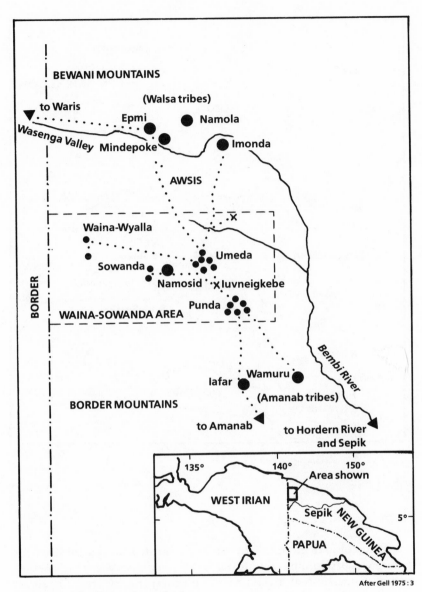

Figure 36. The Waina-Sowanda Area.

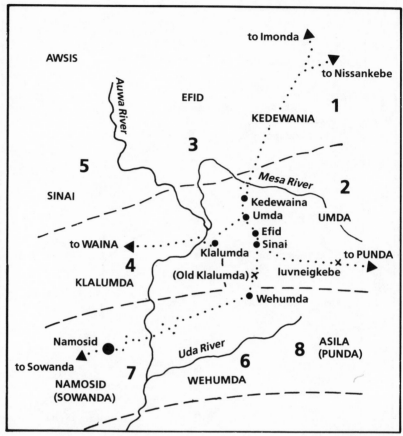

After Gell 1975 : 10

Figure 37. Umeda and its Environs.

The cultural modeling of reality is constructed on the basis of differences between physical features. Mountains serve for the orientation of diametric dualism and rivers for concentric dualism. The rivers in their flow provide a model for a flow in relations, for an opposition that is continuous and serial, whereas the mountains and heights are important for discrete opposition. By a simple analogy, the antithesis between the forms of dualism is represented by the antithesis between the physical features. For this suggestion to be understood rightly, I must say more about the kind of model a river provides for a dialectical society.

The river combines features of symmetry (in its opposite banks) and asymmetry (in its flow). The river has a middle and extremes, which suit the center-periphery opposition. Thus, according to the axial distribution and following the flow of the river, the territories are partners arranged into sets of three, two, and three, respectively upstream, midstream, and downstream. Furthermore, across the banks of the river, the territories' hamlets are arranged as opposites in perpetual exchange. Such an answer is crucially incomplete, however, for on that basis one might regard the river as merely a conceptual metaphor for concentric or perhaps axial relations. Yet the river, like the sun, with its daily rising and setting and its summer and winter solstices, is the kind of axial model that actually works, *physically*.

To put it more grandly, such a working model is a naturally operational analogue of space and time, by which people can understand the dynamics of their relations as they are coordinated with the working of nature. I would suggest that, in dialectical societies that have an axial system, the people are likely to rely heavily on such a naturally operational analogue for modelling purposes.

Counteraction: The Reversal of Time, Life Styles, and the Spatial Inversion

Every year, Western Lowlanders shift back and forth between a "high" and a "low" extreme in life style. The oscillation is evident in the Western Lowlanders' behavior and, to fit their actions, I call the extremes, "high" and "low." But I must stress that the Western Lowlanders apparently do not themselves label the oscillation at all, apart from the "bush"–"village" opposition. During the productive season, there is an annual dispersion to the lowlands, which are mainly below 900 feet. Families spend much of their time alone, by their gardens in the bush, and access to a hamlet's territory is restricted. At the other extreme, during the shorter season of village aggregation at the permanent hamlet sites, the move is to the east, to a high ridge. Visiting is then freer across territories and also across villages.

A brief list of the differences in the seasonal styles is useful. The low season is the humdrum time of (1) routine production by men and women, and processing mainly by women of the staples, sago, taro, and yams; (2) enjoined sexual activity for the legitimately reproductive, i.e., the married; (3) relatively monotonous diet, almost entirely of abundant, low-value foods; (4) accumulation and preparation for the next season's consumption of what are called "smokes," scarce high-value foods such as game and fish as well as euphorics such as tobacco;

(5) restriction on movement and on the flow of gifts and a reduction in the turn-over of exchanges, including marriage and remarriage.

As for the high season, it is the time, *par excellence,* for variety, diversity, and proliferation, all of which, as one would expect, are motifs in the masquerade of the festival itself. Thus, the high season is the time for (1) occasional and communal effort, such as the burning and clearing of forest after the festival, at the beginning of the new garden year; (2) productive sport uninterrupted by routine work, i.e., the diversion of frequent hunting and fishing without the monotony of garden work; (3) play on and about sexuality in the great village festival; (4) feasting and a highly varied diet of high value foods, including last year's coconuts along with "smokes" and sugar; (5) accumulation of next year's coconuts; (6) unrestricted flow of gifts and increased turn-over of exchanges. This is the season for a "high," for entering a state of consciousness outside oneself by chewing a narcotic *(areca)* during ritual, and also for being stimulated by the use of aphrodisiacs such as wildfowl eggs *(ab)* and fish, and euphorics such as tobacco. During the low season, a narcotic is also used for stimulation; but that season is most distinctively associated with the stimulation from wild nettles *(ako),* to ease aching limbs.

The spatial counterpart of the reversal of time is an inversion, again involving the bush–village antithesis. In contrast to time, the spatial rotation is from an east–west axis to a north–south axis. Thus, in contiguous territories in the Lowlands, three sets of territorial partnerships *(a)* 1, 3, 5; *(b)* 2, 4; *(c)* 6, 7, 8 run from east to west along a reach of the river (see Figure 35 and Gell 1975:10). On the village ridge, however, running roughly north–south, adjacent hamlets (1 and 2, and 4, 5 and 6, and another set of three) are paired as marriage and exchange partners.[3]

Reconfiguring the Surroundings and Inequalities in Basic Resources

Figure 36 shows the hamlets and villages of neighbors. At most, they are within about half day's walk from the villagers of Umeda, from whose perspective we regard the Western Lowlands. Figure 37 shows a narrower range: (1) Umeda's hamlets on the ridge-top to the east, (2) Umeda's territories, along with one territory of each of the neighboring villages on the Mesa River or its tributaries, (3) Umeda's recognized territorial partnerships. The people of Umeda recognize eight bush territories within their dominant field of social exchange; and these eight territories are numbered, for convenient reference. The territories are a cultural construction according to a binary logic, and they correspond to eight coordinate points on a double axial system.

The difference between territories relates to the social environment, which either cuts off ego's social horizon or extends it. To respect that difference and yet to override or displace it, through the creation of a reconfigured habitat is, I would argue, the paradoxical triumph of Western Lowlands social organization.

To illustrate, all but one of the northern territories are locked in by the mountains. The marginal territory of Kedewaina (1), which meets "barbarian" territory at the northern periphery, is the exception. From the perspective of the rest of Umeda, this border is even more confining than being mountain-locked, since it involves territorial partnership and association with barbarians, who are beyond the range of exchange and thus of the moral order.[4] In the south, around the village center, all the Umeda territories have direct river access to non-Umeda outsiders. In addition, all have at least one border with an outside territory belonging to an adjacent village, which further extends their horizons. And the extreme periphery in the south, Wehumda (6), is appropriately marginal, but is unlike Kedewaina (1); the outsiders who surround Wehumda as territorial partners are within the range of exchange and the moral order.

Both mountains and river, the one closing off the social horizon, and the other opening it out, are conceptually important. Western Lowlanders play with this antithesis, as they do with all others, in their characteristically dialectical way. Above, I discussed the mountain's association with the diametric form of dualism and the river's association with the concentric form.

THE CODING OF VALUE IN CONCENTRIC TERMS

Western Lowlanders encounter certain predicaments within their frameworks of territorial and village organization, predicaments related to inequalities in basic resources. The inequalities have a spatial distribution. On the Mesa River, a gradation in people and resources runs as follows. At the headwater is Punda, the least populous of the three nearby villages. Upstream are the smallest hamlets, the fewest gardens, the least fish and game, and hence, the least favorable fishing and hunting sites. As one goes downstream, the gradation increases, reaching its zenith at the major confluence of rivers, where the gardens are densest, and where the hunting is best, because the gardens attract the most wild pigs. At the zenith also are the contiguous territories of the largest hamlet in Umeda and its immediate neighbors.

For the sake of clarity about the conflicting interests in productive resources, I must emphasize the culturally defined value of these re-

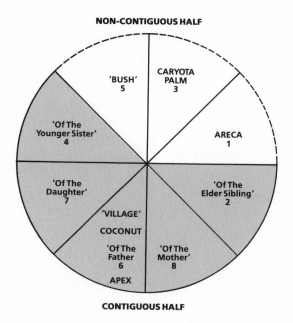

Figure 38. Personal and Plant Geography.

sources. Umeda villagers themselves recognize that their zenith territory (6) has the highest value of all; they treat its hamlet as their center of gravity, in various senses to be discussed shortly. Moreover, around that zenith territory they focus the terms that they use to represent all the territories in center-periphery oppositions.

Continuity with the zenith territory is represented in terms of perpetual kinship in a personal geography (see Figure 38). The opposite, non–contiguity, is put in terms of speciation in a plant geography. Relative to the focus, the underlying logic works with an organic analogy and a simple polarity between closer and more remote kinds of life (man and plant). The formula is this:

contiguity : perpetual kinship
::
non–contiguity : palm tree speciation

The coding can be given only very briefly here.[5] With the zenith territory italicized, the pattern is this in the contiguous half:

"Of the younger sister" (4) "Of the elder sibling" (2)
"Of the daughter" (7) *"Of the father"* (6) "Of the mother" (8)

In the non-contiguous half, again relative to the zenith, the coding is:

"Bush" (5) caryota palm (3) areca (1)
Coconut (6)
"VILLAGE"

PREDICAMENTS OF COMMUNITY

The zenith, an area of conflicting interests, poses a predicament for each of the three villages. Each village has only one segment that can enter into territorial partnership, as an equal, on the basis of the segment's own discrete tract of land at the zenith. Such exchange gains each partner a share in the whole of the zenith. But that gain conflicts with the interests of the village as a community. Those who make the gain get, along with it, a sense of security and home apart from all the rest of the village. In this respect, moreover, the most highly valued part of the village is the most peripheral: every other part is bound to at least one other member of the same village in territorial partnership.

As a consequence, there is a contradiction at the zenith between association and community: the territorial partnership in contrast to the village community. The former is based on equality in reciprocity over production, the latter on equality in reciprocity over the consumption and redistribution of goods. Equality in one runs counter to equality in the other. Each pulls people in opposite directions, and the gain at the zenith is, in effect, centrifugal relative to the village.

It can be seen that at each extreme, north and south, local interdependence is problematic for the territories whose hamlets make up the village community. To the north, contiguity and cooperation with barbarians pulls people away from the village. Similarly, the centrifugal tendency dominates at the zenith, to the south. The village community is precarious, especially at its margins. The villagers are able to sustain the village community only by overcoming powerful centrifugal tendencies.

Boundaries have to be imposed symbolically in order to create community and define the village. That is achieved through antitheses and, in turn, the symbolic transcendence of the antitheses. First, certain territorial partners are set apart physically as mutually antithetical. Next, alternative partners are brought together and, as we have seen in Chapter 4, vital substance is used to overcome their opposition, symbolically.[6] At the very beginning of *ida,* however, as people of one bush, one territorial partnership, parties of men go separately to the deep bush and collect the powerful substances for ritual contact. These substances are shared by men of the whole village to contain themselves in masks and body paint. The antithesis between territorial partners is thus transcended: vital substance is appropriated for all, from the zenith and the nadir alike, for the sake of the village as a whole. Moreover, from the perspective of the village's cardinal center, a formal symmetry of halves is established, with one set of six territories as the social universe for most of the year (during the productive season) and the village community of six hamlets for the rest of the year (during the festival season) (see Note 6). But at the same time, one half, that of the village community, is made to be the greater part, which symbolically appropriates the substance of the other and thus contains the whole in itself.

THE COUNTERACTION OF ORGANIZATIONAL PREDICAMENTS

As for the predicament at the zenith, Umeda's response is what one might expect in a dialectical society: counteraction standing the predicament on its head. The counteraction is centripetal. All the rest of the village comes to the most highly valued part, moving from the "bush" center to the "village" center on the zenith's land, for the alternative and final performance of *ida,* which culminates the festival. At this time the village reconfigures itself. Its outermost extreme is turned into the center of centers, and is, as it were, internalized, in accord with its actual value for the village as a whole.

A further predicament and contradiction arises in the management of two things together: the zenith predicament and the contradiction between territorial partnership and village community. The village represents itself as a global universe in terms of equality in perpetual exchange (discussed below), and yet the village is not and cannot be self-contained. In the exchange of women and masks, its members must have partners outside the village. Here a contradiction arises between the village as a primary community and as a component part of a wider order or greater community.

In managing this further predicament, villagers create a symbolic opposition that privileges the centripetal tendency and devalues the centrifugal one. Similarly, positive significance is given to relations with fellow members of the village community, and negative significance is imposed upon external relations with outsiders. The symbolic opposition is expressed in the following way: the village's internal center of centers has its antithesis in the external, inter-village center.[7]

The village's internal center is the place of the quest, specifically—if we are people of the same kind, we must return to seek the same center for vital exchange. This central place is the only one on the territory of the "father" of the original owners of the village, and the centripetal tendency pulls toward it as the center of gravity. Conversely, the external center is the original place from which our people came; it is now to be avoided; a place for no exchange at all, it is the focus for the centrifugal tendency. In brief, the underlying logic of this counteraction associates the external with avoidance, with flight from the center, whereas the internal is associated with preference, with the eternal return to the center (see Figure 39).

A further feature needs to be stressed. Movement and location have a positive or negative significance depending on the direction taken. Thus the festival journey to the village from the bush, when Umedas annually move east toward Punda, brings them symbolically to a restoration; they recover their original condition, as it was prior to their dispersal upstream and downstream. For Umeda, the village side facing Punda in the east has a positive significance in contrast to the bush side toward Sowanda in the west. Sowanda is the village in the negative direction of Umeda's dispersal.[8]

RECIPROCITY AND EXCHANGE

One predicament of dual organization readily leads to another, and in their response, the Western Lowlanders elaborate and counteract antithesis after antithesis. Given their binary principles, they find it problematic to sustain reciprocity and interdependence on the basis of contiguity. In response, they establish an alternative basis for reciprocity and set up an opposition between their relations over territory and their relations over women.

This social exchange has a definite pattern that is significant for village or wider community among the Western Lowlanders. In the next section, I consider different ranges of exchange, first within the village and then across villages. I suggest that what the Western Lowlanders create by means of perpetual exchange is, within the village, a community of apparent equals. Externally, across villages, they create the unequal relations that I call greater community and non-community.

Perpetual Exchange Within the Village Community

The exchange of women and masks generates social space within the village community, which is symmetrical and formally identical. Each participating hamlet is a central place with the same configuration

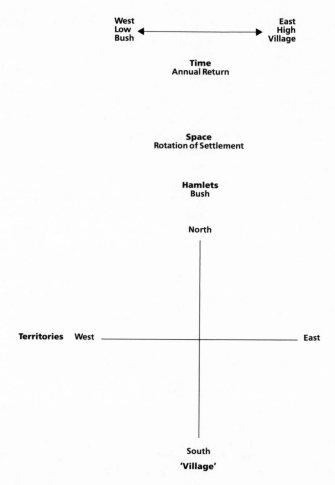

Figure 39. Counteraction in Time and Space.

of contacts with other members of the village. The general shape vis-à-vis ego, for every member, fits the simple three-step matrix of reachability shown in Figure 40. At one extreme is ego, and at the other, ego's opposite in exchange. In between come first the mask partners, followed by the marriage partners. The extension in social distance is from ego, as the innermost insider, to ego's opposite as the outermost outsider. The matrix is reversible, seen from the opposite's perspective; the opposite exchanges masks where ego exchanges women.

Order of Masking

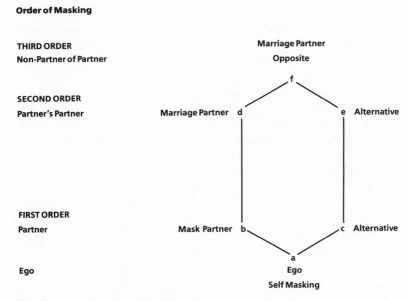

THIRD ORDER
Non-Partner of Partner

SECOND ORDER
Partner's Partner

FIRST ORDER
Partner

Ego

Marriage Partner
Opposite

Marriage Partner   d   e   Alternative

Mask Partner   b   c   Alternative

a

Ego
Self Masking

Figure 40. Matrix of Partners: Ego's Village.

Concentric dual organization emerges in the following way. The village is divided in halves relative to each hamlet as ego. One half has three hamlets, including ego, and the other half has three hamlets excluding ego. The moiety divisions are six crosscutting pairs, as many as the village's hamlets. The overall arrangement of moieties has an appearance of equivalence between members of the same community; and in this respect, the arrangement makes internal community seem to be a product of all taking part in dual organization in the same way.

Such features of a concentric form of dual organization are easily missed in analysis. The exchange, though regular and asymmetric, can be mistaken for something scrambled, not patterned; it can seem to have nothing to do with dual organization. Thus, in his report, Gell conveys the sheer intricacy of the surface appearance, but none of the regularity. The diagram (Gell 1975:49) given of "the ideal scheme of Coconut Compatibilities," mask partnerships, in my terms, is confusing, and Gell does not analyze the perpetual relationships as a pattern. Instead, ignoring dual organization, he uses an alliance theory with which he reconstructs a conjectual history as if it were causal sequence.

Derived from kinship terms and prohibitions, from first principles, as it were, Gell's reconstruction is what would be, *in vacuo,* a cycle of individual exchange, if each hamlet could act independently. His mistake is the same one that he admits, with refreshing frankness, and tries to correct elsewhere, "My mistake, in this instance, was to 'linearize' a situation which should properly be seen in terms of 'pattern' " (Gell 1975:275). Nevertheless, it is a hallmark of Gell's care in reporting that he himself provides the evidence for correcting his mistake. My criticism does not diminish that achievement; instead I make the criticism, lest it be thought that the error is mine, also. Mine is not a second-order abstraction, and it is not based upon a wrong first-order abstraction, namely the marriage-alliance structures or cycles that Gell adduces.

The questions are, on what basis does each member select partners for specific exchanges, either of women or masks, and what governs the selection as a whole pattern in the village? Predictably, in accord with a characteristic of dual organization, the governing rule is quite simple. It is this: masks are exchanged between directionally adjacent partners; and women, between directionally non-adjacent partners. As for the conceptual location of the partners, that is according to the orientation on the six-pointed axes as shown on Figure 41.[9]

The structures of perpetual exchange are, as the figure shows, regular and homologous; and they cut across each other, precisely in the way that Lévi-Strauss' view of concentric exchange would lead us to expect.

I arrived at my view independently of Gregory's analysis, to which a reader kindly drew my attention. Gregory constructs a model of an exchange pattern for six transactors in a Papuan gifts-to-men system (1980:643). This model disregards spheres of exchange and directionality. My Figure 31 is an instance of what he calls "a cobweb" *(ibid.),* his representation of circular, in contrast to linear, exchange as in the "rope" of *moka.* The difference is that my analysis takes into account ranked spheres of exchange that are alternatives and that are directionally located. The perimeter of the cobweb, and thus the encompassing circulation, is for the higher sphere, for ritual services and masks. Within the cobweb is the lower sphere, which includes marital exchange, and linking transactors of women.

It might be objected that such an arrangement cannot work, for various reasons. Perhaps most obvious, finding a wife from an appropriate hamlet within the village could very often be awkward, if not impossible. The hamlets are so small that very slight demographic variations could make for a lack of suitable partners. But such an objection turns a matter of perpetual relationships with regard to the environment into a matter of current affairs between individuals. To

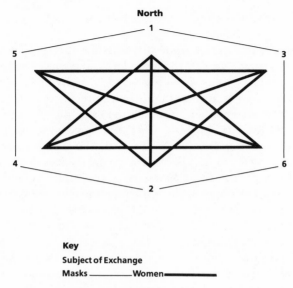

Figure 41. Intra-Village Perpetual Exchange.

a Western Lowlander, the arrangement is "something permanent, an immemorial and traditional arrangement" (Gell 1975:53), and we must understand it in that light, as something timeless. Basically, the objection is wide of the mark because the arrangement does not have to work, for certain purposes.

It would be misleading, also, to say that the arrangement is flexible or plastic, as has so often been said about kinship and other relationships in New Guinea. Rather than flexibility, what has to be appreciated is appropriateness.

There is a secondary elaboration of categories of membership, such as clan and subclan; what bearing such categories have for personal purposes is highly relative. By disregarding the hamlet of current residence, Western Lowlanders can make a marriage appropriate. Marriage partners are found according to more suitable categories of membership. They do this in the same way that they make a territorial partnership appropriate (see above on the "immigrant" part of Kede-waina (1), where partnerships with "barbarians" are justified as a survival from original times; for other examples, see Gell 1975:77–78). The category they bring to bear may stress a person's origins; these could be in another contemporary hamlet or one of its associated clans. Similarly, they could be in a former hamlet that is either a mere

memory from ancient times, or a sub-hamlet with a claim to past
independence as a hamlet.

In a sense, one might argue that to make such perpetual marital
and ritual exchange "work," the secondary categories, such as clan and
subclan, would have to be as numerous as the individuals involved, or
at least adequate enough to distinguish, in some instances, one man in
particular from all the others around him in a hamlet. In actuality, that
is the case in Umeda. In this village of about eighty men and fifty
women, there are nineteen localized agnatic clans, each an exogamous
unit of ritual action, with its own history, and its own distinctive body
painting during the festival. Moreover, some subclans or even clans
consist of one adult alone. Such highly individualized units of exogamy
would seem to be virtually essential, given the actual demographic
imbalance and the chronic shortage of women even in the wider community that includes Umeda and the adjacent village of Punda.

To pursue this argument involves discussion that is well beyond
my present scope. What I wish to stress, at this point, is that the
arrangement of perpetual relationships has a significant domain that
can be sustained in the face of the flux of current affairs. That domain
is what the Western Lowlanders see as the enduring relation between
community and environment; and they define it with regard to their
surrounding segments, hamlets and villages, and with regard also to
the distribution of value within their whole habitat.

Reconstruction of the Axes and the Inversion of Settlement

It can be seen that axial coordinates are the key to each of the separate
spheres of perpetual exchange: the sphere of the immovable—territory—on the one hand; the spheres of movables —masks and women—
on the other. There remains, however, the problem of understanding
the change from one key to the other. In other words, if one sphere is
a transformation of the other, what coordinates the transformation,
and how?

The problem is best understood with the help of Figure 42, which
illustrates the segments' locations in each sphere of exchange. For
example, Wehumda (6) is south on the territorial coordinates and
southeast on the movables' coordinates. The obvious question is what
fixes the segment's location in each case; and furthermore, what fixes
the actual location of a segment's hamlet site and, thus, its village
community neighbors in contrast to its streamside neighbors?

To effect the transformation, each segment needs only a bearing
on its extreme opposite, the outermost partner in terms of reachability
(see Figure 41). Pairing segments across the reaches of the river in the

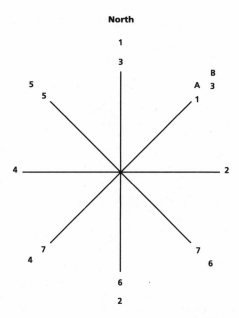

Figure 42. Location in Territorial Exchange (A) and Moveables Exchange (B).

order of river's flow gives that bearing. Each segment has a neighboring hamlet that is its extreme opposite in exchange. The transformation in spheres turns the relation to the environment inside out.

External Perpetual Exchange

So far, my account of the village community, relating it to the internal perpetual exchange, has shown the importance of formal equivalence or identity and symmetry in the concentric dual organization. To complete the account, I must now consider the external perpetual exchange and show how it extends formal equivalence and yet counteracts it with the opposites of identity and symmetry.

The external perpetual exchange is across the pair of villages, Umeda and Punda, which form a greater community. I infer that from an Umeda perspective, Punda is a mirror version of Umeda. In other words, just as paired villages are, mythically, an original inversion, one having gone upstream, the other downstream in primordial times, so too they are counterparts that annually reverse their conditions in an external return in opposite directions. Accordingly, the external

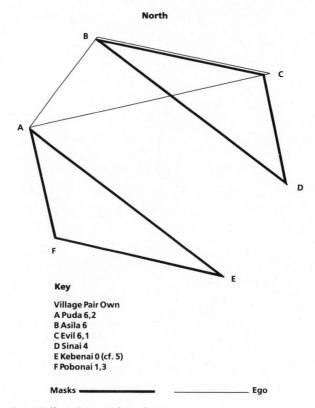

Figure 43. Inter-Village Perpetual Exchange.

perpetual exchange is a mirror version of the internal one, again, I must stress, seen from an Umeda perspective.[10]

From that perspective, the external community's axial coordinates would appear to be a mirror version, also, of the internal territorial coordinates. Here the primary rule for the external contacts between nonadjacent territories is that masks are exchanged with the partner opposite, who is thus ego's counterpart in the other village. In Figure 43, illustrating the external exchange pattern, the numbers refer to hamlets of Umeda that have the contacts across the villages. As shown in Figure 43, the paired village appears, like the mirror original, to have its own internal exchange and thus its own halves or moieties for masks and women.[11]

If the internal exchange can be said to level out differences in the environment of the territories, the external exchange across the villages can be said to respect the environmental differences and even to accentuate them. Here the asymmetry and lack of equivalence in the concentric dual organization is important. The territories are differentiated externally according to their masking contacts, and their central places form a hierarchy.[12]

Crosscutting moiety divisions are involved in the external arrangement, just as they are internally. But for external purposes, which involve differentiating the center of centers from all others rather than levelling, there is no need for six moieties, or for as many as the number of hamlets. What is needed is *only* as many, and in the simplest crosscutting pattern, as will suit the differentiation of a *single* central place.

Certain features of the external exchange are worth stressing. First, the exchange involves moieties of its own, counter to the rest, with which it completes a total intersection along the axes. Second, it differentiates a center of centers and entails a hierarchy of central places, with the most highly valued part of ego's village at the top of the hierarchy, just as it is at the focus of the kinship and species geographies.

More generally, it can be seen that concentric dualism has alternative and unlike appearances, as Lévi-Strauss' original argument would lead us to expect. In the internal context, used to model community relations, concentric dualism has the appearance of symmetry and equivalence. Used in the external context for intercommunity relations, concentric dualism takes on the appearance of asymmetry and hierarchy. The important point is that the appearance is secondary; the same form of dualism takes on alternative appearances according to context and the relation being modelled.

One final word about the perpetual exchange: Umeda's perspective is the only one given, as I have repeatedly emphasized. It may be obvious, but it needs to be said nonetheless, that from another vantage ground, such as from Punda, one would expect quite a different perspective on concentricity. Indeed, the very essence of the matter is that the representation of concentricity depends on the choice of center.

ON THE WIDER SYSTEMATICS

The question can now be raised about a heuristic model for further research on intercommunity relations in nearby parts of New Guinea that have similar festivals. What theoretical view can be put forward, on the basis of our analysis, to illuminate the wider systematics of such relations?

My basic hypothesis is that there are two principles that are fundamental throughout this socio-geographic region of New Guinea and
that these principles are contradictory. These principles are:

(1) The society is represented as having the simplest binary unity as a whole
of halves;
(2) Each community locates itself at the center of a universe of communities.

To resolve the contradiction, each community has to be a member of
both a pair and a triad. The pair satisfies the first principle, and the
triad, the second. Various surface differences appear in one way or
another, including variations in the number of hamlets or segments
(one possibility is ten, rather than twelve, for the widest universe
for the exchange of masks and women). Nevertheless, the resolution
involves certain regularities in perpetual relationships, and of the exchange of territory, masks, and women across separate communities.

To begin with the first principle and the pair, the wholeness of a
society is represented as emerging from the simplest opposition: our
community and theirs. Ours and theirs are counterparts; each coordinates its movement and its exchange of movables, masks and women,
on the basis of the same binary coordinate system. The separateness of
communities is taken to be reversible through the coordination. Two
communities thus constitute a society as a higher order of unity by
moving toward each other and, as it were, taking the part and the place
of the other.

As for the second principle and the triad, I want to suggest the
following points. First, each community locates itself, in space and in
terms of origins, as the midpoint between the extremes of a triadic
chain of communities. The chain is the usual range for men attending
others' festivals as visiting spectators. In no way does the existence of
a chain imply symmetry or homogeneity in the component communities, and it can be expected that the chain spans speakers of another
dialect besides ego's own. Second, this is a serial relation conceptualized
in terms of a binary opposition, such as mother–daughter. Thus according to origins and location, one community may be ego's mother
and the other its daughter. Third, ego sees itself as part of a particular
chain in accord with an intercommunity territorial partnership, as
between a segment of its own and a segment of two other communities.
Fourth, only one chain is recognized for a community's centrality,
although there is at least one more intercommunity partnership with
segments of other communities which are not part of the chain. Such
involvement beyond the chain is explained away as a survival from

ancient times. Thus, it is a matter for that segment alone as a former part of another whole.

It can be seen that this triadic relation in a chain is sociocentric and relative to one community as ego. Viewed from another community, the chain does not exist as such, since a part of it is seen in segmental rather than communal terms. In other words, if from community *X's* point of view another community, *Y,* is part of the chain, community *Y,* from its own perspective, need not recognize the chain of *X* or its own membership in it.

From the pair to the chain there is a disparity in the representation of social reality. But viewed abstractly, a certain fit can be seen in the social relations involved. Each community participates in a pair and in a nonpair; it has one community with which it is coordinated and another with which it is not, as shown below:

Nonpaired community	Paired community
	ego
Noncoordinated relations	Coordinated relations

In the wider field, which includes a series of such communities, there is thus an alternation, with first one kind of relation recognized between communities and then its opposite. In other words, extending across space, the alternation is from pairs in coordination to nonpairs in noncoordination.

Throughout this part of my discussion, I have used the term "community" rather than "village," because of the possible ambiguity or relativity in the notion of "village." Seen from the outside, a community may be considered as one village with two clusters of hamlets as moieties, but seen from within, each cluster of hamlets may be a village.

At this point, somewhat as an aside, it is worth remarking very briefly on the contrast with the classic segmentary system. That is a closed system, without reference to the environment and without systematic ambiguity depending on which ego is the focus. Segments have alternative relations with each other simply according to the principle of complementary opposition— us versus them, or us and them versus a more remote them, and so on. By contrast, in the model we have been discussing, the relations between segments depend on their location vis-à-vis the environment. The model is sociocentric or focused on a point or segment as ego. There is systematic ambiguity, since what is represented depends on the point or segment that constitutes the focus.

CONCLUSION

Few things have been given greater prominence in recent anthropological studies of New Guinea than social exchange, its tactics, and its strategies, from the viewpoint of the individual, usually the "big man" and, secondarily, the "rubbish man." Largely as a result of research in the highlands, we have come to think of New Guinea as a "society within which individual choice, uncertainty, and strategy are overtly recognised as important, and in which an important part of social relationships consists of networks of *individually* created and maintained exchange ties" (A. Strathern 1981:282, emphasis mine). However, the data from the Western Lowlands enable us to shift the analytic emphasis from the personal exchange network of the individual transactor to the perpetual exchange relationships of the community and its component parts.

Along with the shift in analytic emphasis comes the greater attraction of the semiotic approach, which has been developed in the study of dialectical societies in South America, and which raises broad issues of a theoretical kind. The objections to the semiotic approach include the allegation that the approach creates cultural logic as a self-contained and self-sustaining system, that it cannot cope with cultural ambiguity, or that the approach must treat culture as monolithic and is thus incompatible with a view of plurality and variation in structural and cultural frameworks (for a recent restatement of these and other objections, see Salzman 1981:244ff).

These objections undoubtedly have telling force against a certain kind of closed and mechanical structuralism. But a semiotic approach need not be that when it focuses on organizational contradictions and takes the relation to the environment as problematic. In such cases, the semiotic approach illuminates the coordination of access to key resources through dual organization.

Using a semiotic approach, I have shown that the people have alternative frameworks, one of territorial organization and another of nonterritorial or nodal organization, which they use for different purposes, at different times, and in different places. Viewed abstractly, the alternative frameworks are seen to be selected states of the same binary coordinate system. The people draw on the potential of this system to configure and reconfigure their perpetual relationships according to different kinds of binary opposition. Through their perpetual exchange relationships, the people reorder their physical and social environment, and make it conform to fundamental principles that are inherently contradictory.

By pursuing the connection between certain relations of production and those of distribution and consumption, my argument establishes the need for a comprehensive view of perpetual exchange relationships. Highlighted in this is the inadequacy of taking in isolation those relationships over women and ritual services that are usually associated with moieties. Much that has hitherto been regarded as patternless, or mere array, is thus seen to be patterned and a manifestation of binarism, no less than the more familiar "dual organization."

More generally, I am tempted to suggest that beyond the comparison of forms of dual organization we may well need a comparison of axial systems and their operation. A basic point is that the surface manifestations of an axial system need not appear to be obviously related. The surface manifestations include phenomena generally associated with dual organization, such as moieties, but include as well, various phenomena that conventionally are dismissed as irrelevant or contrary to dual organizations. Hence axial systems are theoretically important for enabling us to see disparate phenomena as expressions of dual organization and in the context of access to valued resources. What this view restores in analysis is the very basis upon which practice is predicated—namely, dual organization and alliance in conjunction with economy and ecology.

In the previous chapter on *ida* in the New Guinea lowlands fertility cult, we focused on ritual sequencing. The ritual passage in which men operate upon their "having" to alter their "being" was our major concern. We saw that men first gather separately and later pool collectively those essential possessions that are the powerful substances for self-differentiation and the regeneration of life. The transformation they bring about is in themselves, in their social identity, and in the cosmos around them. In this chapter we have turned to the sacred journey with its alternation between festival center and everyday periphery. We have regarded the sacred journey as a religious movement in which social exchange mediates relations between disparate local groups. The social exchange we discussed under the heading of "dual organization" involves ranked spheres and, in order from the lowest, the ranking is first, territorial exchange of access to game and fish; second, marital exchange of women, ideally "sister exchange"; and third, ritual exchange of masks. In the sacred journey as an annual return there is, of course, also the regulation of consumption, with the accumulation of luxuries for feasting on a grand scale. But what this kind of religious movement has not required us to consider is actual history, the change over time from one period to another in the aims and consequences of the sacred journey. And it is such change that I take up now in the next chapter and, indeed, throughout most of the rest of this book.

ACKNOWLEDGMENT

I began an earlier draft of this chapter in Jerusalem while I was a Visiting Professor at the Hebrew University, and I wish to thank my colleagues in the Department of Sociology and Anthropology for their comments, particularly Don Handelman, Uri Almagor, Erik Cohen and S. N. Eisenstadt. Pnina Werbner, Marilyn Strathern, and Donald Tuzin also made helpful suggestions for which I am grateful.

CHAPTER 6

"TOTEMISM" IN HISTORY

The Sacred Crossing of West African Strangers

INTRODUCTION

Religion and strangerhood transform together. Sometimes, it is a transformation toward greater inclusiveness. Various boundaries are overridden, and strangers and their hosts join together to refocus their ritual activities around fresh shrines or in long-established centers, with perhaps a new kind of deity. A classic view sees this as a Great Transformation. It is the view of religious evolution perhaps best, if not first, illuminated by Fustel de Coulanges in *The Ancient City* (1956). He argued that ancient religion with its "ineffaceable distinction between citizen and stranger" gave way to a "religion of the whole human race." With the rise of Christianity, the citizen was no longer, by definition, a man with access to the city gods and, in religion, set apart from the stranger, the one who had to be excluded from the gods' cult and protection. Citizen and stranger alike shared the world religion's communion. Thus the progression was from the maintenance of boundaries in and by religion toward religion's transcendence of boundaries. In other words, the religion of the microcosm gave way to the religion of the macrocosm.

The transformation that Fustel de Coulanges' work illuminated has deeply engaged the theoretical interest of historians and anthropologists ever since Maine (1861) wrote of a movement from "status" to "contract," and Morgan (1877), of a movement from *societas* (community) to *civitas* (state). In the nineteenth century, given the prevailing evolutionary bias, the movement was held to be problematic in one direction only. Anthropologists had yet to argue about processes of boundary redefinition—"retribalization" (Mercier 1965:486; Cohen 1967:Iff; 1969:92ff); "revitalization" (Wallace 1956); and "nativism" (Linton 1943). But now the theoretical interest is free of a preconception about one-way progress: movements have to be explained in either direction, toward *societas* or toward *civitas,* from boundary maintenance or from boundary transcendence. Moreover, the movements may be conceptualized in terms of a crossing in which those who move across cultural as well as spatial and political boundaries come to be strangers of one kind or another. Beyond their own *civitas,* they become external strangers or aliens without rights of citizenship, and beyond their *societas,* they become internal strangers with such rights but without bonds of community.

My approach to the cultural transformations in these processes uses an analogy to language. But the way this analogy has been widely taken for granted in studies of ritual and symbolic action needs rethinking, for many of these studies have largely passed over problems of alternatives, or problems of translation and recoding by the people themselves. Thus Munn puts the analogy simply, and in certain respects quite usefully, in her concept of "the cultural code," i.e., "a lexicon of sociocultural concepts or categories" organized in various ways for communication (1973:581). But, like many who use the linguistic analogy, Munn applies it with a link missed out, for she fails to allow explicitly for the systematics of translation or the use of alternative languages.

In *"the* cultural code," Munn's model is too parochially closed. No room is left for switching back and forth, either between codes or from source codes to a pidgin or creole (see Hymes 1972; Hall 1972). Yet people often do use several cultural codes. One they may regard as indigenous, traditionally theirs; a second may be held to be exotic and imported from strangers; and a third may be considered more a universal code, both ours and theirs.

The objection to the parochial linguistic model would be less critical were it merely a matter of saying the same thing, i.e., of changing the code but not the message. But switching introduces a fresh message about the making of messages, a meta-message, in Bateson's terms (1973:150), and it is of one kind or another, according to the codes used. The meta-message in its most general form is, "I am able to translate, to transcend my own culture." Contextually, the message may be "I am able to switch from an indigenous to an exotic code, to interpret and appropriate a specific culture of others," or it may be, "I am competent in the most inclusive or universal code; I am able to cope with the transcultural."

Obviously, it matters who makes the meta-message and to whom. Quite distinct meta-messages are conveyed in switching to an exotic or a universal code when the messages are between hosts and strangers of one kind or another, such as internal or external ones. In the parochial linguistic model, however, such meta-messages about communicative competence get lost, because one stranger, the anthropologist, assumes a monopoly on all competence to translate. But if understanding other cultures is the anthropologist's business, that is because it is also the native's. It is, perhaps, obvious that the translation of culture becomes a greater concern for the people themselves the more culturally diverse a cult's membership becomes. But rather less obvious is how a cult develops in accord with its relative capacity to focus relations while such a translation is being made.

My argument takes us beyond the single cult to an appreciation of a series of cults within a wider field, which itself has to be seen as a whole. These are rival yet basically similar cults that originated in the north from quite widely separated parts of Ghana, Ivory Coast, and Burkina Faso. Having spread south, toward the coast, they established southern client shrines, and promoted regular pilgrimages to and from the north. Their growth resulted in the routinized dissemination of ritual beliefs and practices. Eventually, to a large extent, they were displaced in the south by a "revival" of quite different cults, all of which claimed southern origins. But the direction of ritual importing was not reversed: none of the cults that had southern origins gave rise to client shrines in the north.

To examine this religious change across vast distances and among very different cultural groups, a number of steps are necessary. Therefore, after this introduction, I begin with one cult, the External Boghar, centered in Taleland, and then follow with an overall view of the shrine traffic and flows of other goods, services, and ideas across the northern and southern sectors of the wider field. My next step takes the argument forward to problems of code-switching. An important question is how the ritual and organization of the cults relate to the recoding of inequality and differentiation, from one phase of the field to the next. Answering this leads the discussion to problems of religious pluralism and conversion as well as the inner logic of alternative ritual forms. Finally, I put forward a hypothesis about encapsulation, boundary fluctuation and cult change, having demonstrated a connection between a broad political development in Ghana and a shift in religious pluralism within a part of it.

The West African ethnography raises a general point that I must stress from the outset. West African societies have had strangers living in their midst, often enclaved in quarters of their own, for centuries, well before modern colonialism. The crossing of strangers between communities and states, from one culture to another, is an ancient problem for religion in West Africa. Unlike a modern novelty, it must be studied in the light of historic continuity with the past (see also, Goody 1975:100). Indeed, one of my reasons for basing my discussion on the waxing and waning of West African cults is precisely this. It enables me to demonstrate how ancient and modern flows of strangers relate to each other as well as to the changing careers of cults.

PERSONAL SECURITY CULTS

In general terms, the kind of cult I discuss in the main is what I propose to call a "personal security cult," although it is usually labeled an "anti-witchcraft cult" (Debrunner 1959; McLeod 1975) or a "witch-finding movement" (Horton 1971; 1975; Fisher 1973). I prefer to speak of a personal security cult because my term sums up the following characteristics: the cult members are a security circle for each other. They are mutually harmless and bound together by a covenant and an ethic; they are purified, and under the same powerful protection of a shrine or spirit.

In certain personal security cults, communion is the substantiation—at once the test and the embodiment of a bond—and members regularly eat or drink sacraments. Whether such a cult is regional or non-regional varies—and I use regional in the sense given in the Introduction—but characteristically, the cult takes in strangers of one kind or another along with non-strangers, rather than being restricted in its membership as is the cult of a state, localized community, or kin group. Hence, while it is a cult of the microcosm, it is, by definition, quite unlike the one of the city in Fustel de Coulanges' ancient religion, which excludes external strangers. Similarly, it is also unlike the cult of the macrocosm or widest universe in his world religion, as it lacks its all-inclusive fellowship and its attention primarily to the Supreme Being. Each personal security cult takes in only certain kinds of stranger and uses a distinct mode of ritual and cult organization to do so.

The variation in these cults crucially depends on two things: first, who is converted into the cult's security circles—strangers of which kind along with their hosts—and, second, on how the conversion is done, for the conversion may be through a ritual that the hosts believe is exotic, borrowed from the stranger, or it may be done through ritual that the hosts believe to be indigenous. There are, of course, other permutations, but these highlight the need for my theoretical approach, which pays special attention to problems of the translation of culture. Such translation, I would stress, is a systematic feature of the personal security cult as a type characterized by the conversion of hosts and strangers.

The Boghar's Safe Crossing and Boundary Transcendence

Noting that cults of the earth were prominent throughout West Africa, Fortes observed:

> The pattern of doctrine and ritual practice of the Earth cult has a much greater uniformity over a wider area than that of the Boghar cult. . . . In the cult of the Earth identical beliefs and dogmas, norms of conduct, ritual conventions, and social settings hold throughout Taleland. Indeed, this is true of the whole of the Northern Territories. (1945:107)

What is surprising is the importance of the Boghar cult, as an organization operating across great distances in Ghana in modern times. The Boghar cult managed a highly organized pilgrimage traffic; it had client shrines and it directed the sacred journeys of strangers from quite disparate cultures and societies. Why did the Boghar cult have such importance, but not the Earth cult? After all, the Earth cult was characteristically transcultural and universalistic. But for the Boghar cult to become a major regional cult extending to the south of Ghana, and well beyond Taleland, in the north, a translation of culture had to be made. The Boghar cult was, and is, highly particularistic, exclusive, and even parochial, given its culturally distinctive ritual, focused on a primordial ancestor of certain Hill Talis.

Part of the answer is somewhat paradoxical, though it is a consequence of an earlier history. The Boghar cult had become a religion of a kind that bound people to a place and at the same time freed them to move from it, or perhaps, more correctly, *with* it (for the opposite view: that "place-bound religion" is incompatible with freedom of movement and bonds with strangers, see Tuan 1977:152ff).

A specific bond of substance put hosts and strangers, Talis and non-Talis alike, in contact with a protective power. Portable shrines were worn by travelers to secure their safe passage to and from the Boghar cult's sovereign shrines in the Tong Hills. Like the shrines fixed at clients' homes, the portable ones were concocted according to

a secret recipe, primarily of bits of substance from the sovereign shrine
and its soil. Throughout historical time, the Boghar cult has provided
a warrant for safe crossing and thus channelled the flow of trade
between potentially hostile and quite disparate centralized and non-
centralized communities. To a sovereign shrine in the Hills its clients
brought gifts of salt, cloth, and hoes; they paid for ritual services in
cowries. Hill Talis, ostensibly on ritual errands from a sovereign to a
client shrine outside the Hills, could sell chickens and buy grain or
yams in return. Specific client villages in chiefdoms of non-centralized
settlements outside the Hills had specific attachments to one or another
of the sovereign shrines and each sovereign shrine had "a well-defined
sphere of influence" (Fortes 1945:252), so the organizational principle
was not a matter of generalized inclusiveness.

Although it is somewhat of an aside, I would guess that sovereign
shrines may have had their early importance due to their location
within a "human buffer zone" (Goody 1967:183) between great states.
According to Wilks, in the nineteenth century, "the northernmost
outer provinces of greater Asante and the southernmost provinces of
Mossi were separated by a broad belt of rugged country inhabited
by stateless peoples [including the Tallensi among others]" (Wilks
1975:319). It may be that in the past the various sovereign shrines
remained fixed and independent points. Around them were highly
particularistic networks of communication and exchange. Each would
have been replete with its temporary imbalances. Such a network could
have formed and reformed with the rise and fall of chiefdoms or their
parts. The organization would have been highly responsive to the ebb
and flow in the fortunes of centralized and non-centralized areas of the
heartland.

I lack evidence to say whether, at any time in the past, one cardinal
shrine emerged as greater in some respects than any of the others.
Fortes reconstructs, in line with his axiom of past equilibrium, an
absence of inequality and imbalance, and thus no cardinal shrine before
colonial rule. What must be stressed, however, is that at the time of
his fieldwork a cardinal shrine did exist and was the focus for a monopoly on the long-distance pilgrim traffic. The full reconstruction of the
past must await the discovery of historical records: an argument for
past oscillations and even disequilibrium is merely the substitution of
one axiom for another.

Nevertheless, given its prior development, the External Boghar
cult, compared to the Earth cult, was clearly more suited to the focusing
of a twentieth-century region. It was also more suited to become the
kind of personal security cult favored under conditions of large-scale
immigration and colonization of cocoa farms, as existed particularly

in Ghana's southern hinterlands. To start with, the cult had specialized organizational devices for the management of center–periphery relations. These devices subordinated client shrines on the periphery to sovereign shrines at the center, even deriving the shrines' very substance from the center (for a general view of these devices in regional cults, see Van Binsbergen 1977). Perhaps most importantly, the cult had a highly particularistic arrangement for the protection of strangers and the licensing of their safe passage between culturally distinct and sometimes politically hostile communities. In effect, its apparently modern significance as a personal security cult in the south was a rather straightforward extension of its traditional significance within its heartland.

By contrast, the Earth cult was the kind of place-bound religion that made localness sacred, without ritually licensing crossings from place to place. The Earth cult was less compatible with the particularistic code and specific focus needed for more than a disparate series of independent, highly localized congregations, and it remained fragmented, as it lacked pilgrims coming from afar, or wide-reaching ritual collaboration around its shrines. Hence it is no paradox to say that the very universality of the Earth cult, its widely shared doctrine and practice, its stress on what Turner would call "a generic bond" (1974:224), its disinterestedness, and shared values—in brief, the cult's very inclusiveness—stultified its growth relative to the External Boghar cult.

The point is that people do not always turn to the widest, most generic bonds to transcend the boundaries of their communities. Particularistic relations are sometimes a more effective alternative that frees them to move safely, and with a highly specific and protected identity.

Traffic in a Wider Field

Shrine traffic and trade, along with the flow of labor, have intertwined for at least a century within a wider field across Ghana and its environs. In this chapter, I cannot say much about the past or present reaction of one on the other, although I do consider this to pose theoretical problems that are more interesting than the question of which came first. My hunch, and it is little more than that, is that a cult center's placement and importance in a major nineteenth-century trade route usually opened the way for it to become the cardinal center for a cult in the twentieth century (see map in Goody 1967:180).

A case in point is the Talis cardinal shrine of the External Boghar cult. Within the wider field, two ecologically unlike sectors are distinguishable, which shared a prevailing direction of trade and shrine traffic for much of the century before the 1950s. This was, for my purposes, at least, the field's first phase. The north sector is mainly dry, open savannah and the south, mainly luxuriant forest. Throughout the first half of the twentieth century, the import of shrines, like the migration of workers, was from the north to the south. As in the nineteenth century (and perhaps the eighteenth), with its parallel flow of shrines and slaves, the traffic was not the other way round, or reciprocal.[1]

Moreover, traffic was focused on a limited number of points, rather distant from each other, in present-day Ghana, Burkina Faso, and Ivory Coast. Shrines in the south, especially among Ashanti and other Akan peoples, were derived from the north's widely separated central places, such as, in Ghana, from the Tong Hill's Tong Naab shrine of the Boghar cult in the northeast, from among Lobi, from Senyon among Gonja to the northwest, from among Brong to the east, from the Dente shrine at Kratchi, from Burukung in the Chiare Hills, from the Tigari shrine at Wa, from the Nako Tong shrine among the Lo Dagaa of Burkina Faso, and from Kontrobi in Ivory Coast (Debrunner 1959:106–07; Field 1960:90; Goody 1961:201; 1975:100; McLeod 1975:110–11).[2]

This directional traffic was more than a one-way import of people and things, of labor and ritual substances. It was also an import of ideas, cultural codes, ritual activities, and even styles of ritual costume. To illustrate, I quote from Ward's account of the founding in 1946 of a satellite shrine in the south:

On the advice of a Northern Territories man who was labouring for him on his cocoa-farm [the founder] had set out for the Northern Territories to try to gain spiritual protection and salvation from his bad fortune. . . . Accordingly he "bought some of the medicine" from [a] North Territories priest and brought it home, setting up a small shrine in the clearing just outside the village. He then sent his nephew, a classificatory sister's son, to the Northern Territories to learn the *proper ritual* [and he later served at the southern village shrine] in Northern costume and following a Northern ritual. (1956:53, my emphasis)

Ward goes on to give an account of the ethic and exclusiveness of this personal security cult, and I return to this shortly.

The period of expansion of the northern cults among various Akan peoples of Ghana's south, such as the Ashanti, was a period of very rapid increase in the numbers and concentration of external or, in Fortes' terms "alien strangers" (1975:239). The category is one that "has been recognized in Akan society from the earliest time" (1975:239). It includes the strangers who "differ in language, culture and traditional forms of social organization and provenance from the Akan peoples" (1975:240). By definition, alien strangers are fundamentally unassimilable, excluded from intermarriage and barred from the rights of citizenship that Akan have in their communities as a birthright. Labor migration brought northern non-Akan alien strangers to the south in far greater swarms than even slavery did. Hired hands or sharecroppers, they came to work for and alongside Akan who were sometimes themselves immigrants to new areas that the Akan had colonized for cocoa farms (Hill 1970). The northern strangers' standing among Ashanti and other Akan is sharply described by McLeod:

Nowadays they provide nearly all the day or period labour for the jobs the Asante see as too menial or filthy to perform themselves. In allocating them such places in their society, the Asante are clearly treating them as less than fully human; they are despised and scorned and given tasks which no Asante will do. (1975:112)

Stranger quarters sprung up and, if another ancient feature of Akan societies, they became new, highly visible slums in areas where none had been before (Dunn and Robertson 1973:62–63). By appropriating imported shrines and rituals that had recognizable, diverse, and widely separated non-Akan origins in the north, Akan in the south were able, as it suited them, to acquire particularistic bonds with alien strangers in their midst, without marrying them, or granting them citizenship rights such as land rights. Significantly, this appropriation of the exotic was not a mutual transfer, and there is some evidence that Akan such as the Ashanti violently opposed mimicry by northerners (Dunn and Robertson 1973:367).

HOST'S RESEMBLANCES, STRANGERS' DIFFERENCES, AND DOMINANCE

So far my argument has stressed the gross direction of movement in relation to central places within a wider field. But, what was the significance of the readily recognizable differences between cults based upon the wide separation and marked diversity of major shrine centers? Two points must be made at this stage, and others toward the end of this chapter, when I have given an account of a shift toward cults that were also recognizably different but lacked an exotic and external socio-geographic reference.

The first point is a familiar one about "socio-logic" that Lévi-Strauss makes in his discussion of systems of transformations

(1966:75ff). In his critique of the illusion of "totemism," Lévi-Strauss
writes about animals and nature (1966:107). Put in terms of strangers
and exotic cultures, his point applies to our discussion, and I show the
substitution of my terms for his in brackets: "The differences between
[strangers], which man can extract from [exotic cultures] and transfer
to [his own] culture . . . are adopted as emblems by groups of men in
order to do away with their own resemblances." It is a process of
conversion which Ward reported thus,

> . . . contemporary groups, kinship and political, were tending to coalesce
> around different fetish cults, thus "cashing in," as it were upon this source of
> cohesive power. Members of the same kin-group tended to join the same
> fetish, and fission in the kin-group tended to be accompanied by a change of
> fetish allegiance. (1956:57)

Asante and other Akan "did away with their own resemblances" and
inflated the differences among themselves and others more or less like
themselves. To do so they acquired highly distinct exotic codes and
attachments to the socio-geographically quite disparate shrines, which
they mapped as the cardinal points of orientation for strangers.

The second point takes account of a structural inversion; and it
relates to the less appreciated half of what Lévi-Strauss considers to be
the dual character of "totemic" classifications. That is, it takes us
beyond the familiar point about the definition of internal differentiation, by which persons within the group, such as the Akan hosts,
are marked apart despite their resemblances. It takes us to the more
challenging yet complementary suggestion that:

> . . . one of the essential functions of totemic classifications is to break down
> this closing in of the group unto itself and to promote an idea something like
> that of a humanity without frontiers. (Lévi-Strauss 1966:166)

This suggestion applies to conditions of homogeneity within "tribal
frontiers," and I suggest that at work in conditions of heterogeneity,
with the inclusion of highly diverse strangers, may be a process of
"exotic reduction." It is a systematic transformation in which men
come to terms with the rich, perhaps too rich, diversity of the
exotic. There is a structural inversion, and nearby, small-scale
differences are encoded in terms of distant, large-scale ones. In the
field I discuss, the significance of differences and points of reference
is switched around as follows: the points and emblems of largest
scale differentiation in the north operate in the south for the smallest
scale differentiation.

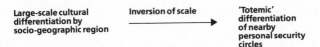

<figure>

| Large-scale cultural differentiation by socio-geographic region | Inversion of scale ⟶ | 'Totemic' differentiation of nearby personal security circles |

</figure>

Figure 44. Exotic Reduction.

Put less abstractly, what happens is this. In the south, a set of neighbors defines itself as a distinct personal security circle when it joins a regional cult, apart from those joined by other sets nearby. Each set acquires a derived socio-geographic reference point of its own, a client shrine, along with its own highly distinct, exotic code. Hence, what is significant in the north for the differentiation of culturally and spatially quite distant peoples becomes, in the south, significant for the differentiation of sets of people who live nearby as strangers and hosts. This systematic transformation allows people to domesticate the exotic by appropriating its specific forms within their personal security circles; they master the exotic by redefining it within their microcosm (see Figure 44).

There is more to this than the conventional wisdom about coding for coding's sake would lead us to see. Dominance and inequality must be kept in view, to get the "socio-logic" and coding right (see Godelier 1977:63ff). The southern hosts made it a prerogative of their own to appropriate exotic shrines and ritual. Mastery of the northerners' ritual, secret formulae, and even substances is what they shared with the northern strangers in their midst. Within each borrowed cult there was the semblance of equality and the leveling of distinctions between host and alien stranger, by including the landless along with the landed, and temporary, even seasonal, immigrants along with the more permanent residents. But this semblance was on the southerners' terms. The southerners acquired powers they believed the northerners had, without having to share their own. In accord with the basic facts of political and economic dominance went an assertion of cultural dominance through the one-directional borrowing of exotic codes and ritual. My general point is this: by itself the mere fact of communion and leveling in ritual is no guarantee of its significance. It may or may not imply merely what Turner would call *communitas* or some generic relation of boundary transcendence (1974:169). The direction of the appropriation of culture has to be appreciated in ritual action, for one-sided appropriation of culture encodes inequality and dominance along with privileged transcendence of boundaries.

THE SECOND PHASE OF RECODING AND CONVERSION

To draw "totemism" further into history and to take my argument a stage further, I must now distinguish two modes of cults, the "exotic" and the "indigenous" (for a related contrast see Cohen 1974:92ff). This enables me to pursue the displacement of the northern-based cults by southern ones and the historical recoding of relations with strangers. As for the exotic mode, it calls for a transcendence of boundaries with *external* strangers and an adoption of their cultural codes. In the case of regional cults, it also calls for organizational devices for the focusing of relations across great social and spatial distances. By contrast, the indigenous mode pays greatest attention to boundaries with *internal* strangers, people like us but not of us or our community, in certain basic respects. This mode calls for a renewal or revival of the beliefs and practices that are held by the people themselves to be traditionally their own, whether or not they are actually indigenous or novel. An extreme of the indigenous mode occurs with provincialism, where a super-tribal "tradition" emerges and thus, for example, things Ashanti may be taken to be their own by other Akan or Twi-speaking peoples.

Some ethnographic facts are in order, as a basis for the analysis of the displacement of the cults.[3] Field, whose 1958 observations provide the best evidence, wrote that "within the last few years the Ashanti type of *abosombrafo* shrine has spread [farther] south, outside Ashanti" (1960:89). It was a type of Ashanti shrine, which, in the 1940s, Ward considered had gone forever (1956:51ff). Once suppressed by law, according to Field, the shrine was "said to be a revival, in benign form, of an ancient type of 'executioner's' shrine which in the old days dealt out capital punishment to witches and other evildoers" (1960:80). Such a would-be ancient shrine was supposed to be "strictly in accordance with ancient Ashanti practice" in their "general set-up, priestly technique, festivals and routine ceremonial" (Field 1960:91). It was laid down "that all the traditional religious festivals of old Ashanti should be fully observed" (1960:103). The founder of such a shrine could derive it from no other; the shrine could come directly from a free-range divinity (on free-range divinities see Rattray 1923:145; Akesson 1950:237ff, 325ff; McLeod 1975:111). But in order to be guided "through the dangerous early stages of spirit possession" (Field 1960:92), the founder might go to an established medium or to a very ancient Akan shrine of another kind, perhaps an ancestral one whose priest would not himself be subject to possession. I infer from Field's account that in general the revived cults were not regional, although it remains somewhat unclear how far various shrines were linked together in a region centered on any single place in the south.[4] Nevertheless, at these shrines, people supplicated for health and prosperity and confessed to witchcraft just as they had in the earlier personal security cults.

Goody suggests that in West Africa the spread of Christianity and Islam is not usually a matter of conversion, but of identification, in which people "make an automatic identification of their own High God with the Allah of the Muslims and the Jehovah of the Christians" (Goody 1975:103). He goes on to argue in a way that confuses gods and Gods, and microcosm and macrocosm:

The Lodagaa [of northern Ghana] did not initially think of the acceptance of Christianity as conversion, because the introduction of a new cult does not involve a displacement of other gods. It is only when a religion says, "Thou shalt have no other Gods but me," when it becomes exclusive, that the problem of conversion arises, and this I suggest happens only with literate religions. (1975:103)

Contrary to Goody's view, in certain cults conversion and exclusiveness are aspects of the closure of a personal security circle against the unconverted, whether stranger or not. One of the difficulties with his suggestion is that it turns a special case into a general rule, unlimited except by literacy. It thus obscures the conditions under which conversion has to do with a god, not a High God, and the introduction of a new cult *does* involve a commandment against other gods, if not a successful displacement of them. In our discussion of personal security cults we have, in fact, been considering such conditions. Thus Ward reports in her account:

Anyone could become a cult member . . . by paying a small sum, taking a ritual bite or two of kola, and undertaking to obey the fetish rules, . . . mainly such precepts as "Do not commit adultery," "Do not swear against thy neighbour," "Do not steal," "Do not harbour evil thoughts against anyone," and so forth, and an injunction *to serve no other fetish but to rely solely upon Kune*. (1956:53, my emphasis)

Such ethics are the ethics of personal redemption through conversion to a cult that displaces others under certain conditions of religious pluralism. Under these conditions a multiplicity of alternatives, rival and disparate shrines and cults, and eventually Christian churches, all compete with each other. Over time, religious pluralism continues, but what changes are the modes the religious pluralism allows, and the relative prevalence of one or another, whether on the wax or on the wane.

ALTERNATIVE CULTS
AND THE CHANGING PREDICAMENT OF STRANGERS

To make sense of a shift from exotic to indigenous cults, change in the predicament of internal strangers has to be grasped. The internal strangers belong, along with their hosts, on the same side of a currently recognized ethnic boundary, the one that includes all Ashanti-speakers, for example. Yet they are strangers, because their birthplaces are beyond the boundaries currently recognized for certain political purposes by their hosts. To categorize them rightly a somewhat roundabout formulation, with the accent on current recognition, has to be used, because it is a predicament of unstable, relative, and complex boundaries. At some times and not others, it may become a critical predicament, with the people themselves caught on the horns of a dilemma. Skinner observed this to be general in West Africa:

Those African strangers who lived outside their home communities but within the borders of an incipient state to which they belonged, also found that the growth of the independence movement affected their status and role. (1963:314)

In the 1950s the rise of provincialism or quasi-nationalism made internal strangers and indigenous identity to be matters of concern far overriding the earlier concern about alien strangers and the exotic.[5] Quasi-nationalism is a broad political process that is closely linked with religious change. It is a process that has been most illuminated by Austin (1964) in his classic account of politics in Ghana in the mid-1950s and by Dunn and Robertson in their more locally concentrated study of political change in Ahafo within southern Ghana. My discussion is based mainly on their work.

In the 1950s nationalism and provincialism fostered each other, when many "nationalisms" thrived along with nationhood in Ghana. Provincial parties emerged, each in a different part of the country and each representing the interests and glorifying the identities of some congeries of peoples, collectively a quasi-nation within the nation. The definition of a quasi-nation was a political achievement that had to be won against opposition from alternatives, rather than being given from the past. Out of past state formation, the rise and fall of precolonial and colonial kingdoms, empires and confederacies came a rich complexity of political traditions (Tordoff 1965), and it was not a matter of one unquestionable, primordial, or tribal allegiance against another. An appeal to one traditional basis for quasi-nationhood was subject to a counterappeal on another opposed basis. But the point is that an appeal to *some* prior ethnic glory was the only basis, both legitimate and culturally evocative, for one provincial alliance in opposition to another and, even more, in opposition to any power in control of central government.

Politics might be, and was, about cocoa prices—how much should go to the primary producer and how much to the rest of the nation, for public or private gain—but economic dissatisfaction, however necessary, was not a sufficient basis for an alliance. In various parts of Ashanti, Austin points out that:

. . . each local grievance was encompassed by a general resentment against the CPP [the nationalist party then in power], based on the belief that Ashanti as a whole—as a people in history—were being "smothered" . . . by a rival nationalist movement whose principal leaders were non-Ashanti. (1964:267)

In effect it was that nationalist alliance centered in the south, primarily among townspeople of the coast (Kilson 1973:106), which helped to provoke a counteralliance in a movement among southerners in the interior. This movement, the National Liberation Movement (NLM), "was a Kumasi-centered, Ashanti movement, which appealed for support in the name of the Asantehene, the Golden Stool, Ashanti interests, Ashanti history, and Ashanti rights" (Austin 1964:265).

But what was "the Ashanti nation"? Who belonged to it, and for what purposes? Seen from the center, at Kumasi, the answer was one thing,[6] and from the periphery at Ahafo and elsewhere, the answer was several other things, for good reasons—both in terms of immediate local interests and traditional political glory. In the outer ring of chiefdoms, beyond about a fifty-mile radius of Kumasi, struggles against rule from the capital and campaigns to withdraw from a common political community, the Ashanti Confederacy, were longstanding. Not surprisingly, the NLM, in its turn, was also subject to opposition from among some of the very people within the political community whom it tried to rally as a part of "the Ashanti nation." In brief, the boundary of the quasi-nation was not merely relative, but ever more problematic.

It might be thought that under these conditions "Ashanti-type" shrines would arise only in areas clearly within the quasi-nation. After all, in such areas the assertion of Ashanti identity was beyond challenge, or virtually so. Moreover, in the environs of Kumasi, such shrines, with their revival of "old Ashanti religious festivals" and once suppressed Ashanti gods, would be in obvious harmony with the most stridently proclaimed patriotism and all the things most of the people held most sacred.

If this were so, we could look no further to understand the displacement of northern shrines than this: in the face of the enemy from without only a Durkheimian moment of solidarity, free of bonds with strangers, was to be tolerated. But, in reality, more is required. Field's evidence (see 1960:15 for shrines visited) shows that even among Brong, in Techiman at the quasi-nation's periphery, the "Ashanti-type" shrines proliferated at the expense of the northern shrines. Yet Brong were among those who opposed the so-called "true Ashanti states" and eventually had "a separate Brong region, with its own administrative headquarters, Regional Commissioner and house of chiefs . . . carved out of the western and northern district of Ashanti" (Austin 1964:296, note 81).

The position of landholders who were originally from Ashanti but lived at the periphery in Ahafo or in various Brong chiefdoms became more ambiguous as the boundary of the quasi-nation became more problematic. Sometimes more numerous than their hosts, they could be regarded as an ever more dangerous enemy-within, a people who would farm and exploit the land for the benefit of others elsewhere, and who had interests that led them to associate more closely with their original home communities. On the other hand, despite such suspicions, they often had, and were recognized to have, interests in common with their hosts', which set them apart from and opposed to Ashanti at the center. Therefore, in this period it was the power and danger in Ashantiness that had to be managed through cults.

THE CULT'S INNER LOGIC
AND THE MASTERY OF STRANGERHOOD

Two key changes in the focus and the primary emphasis of the cults are revealing. Both point to the inner logic of the alternative symbolism and ritual forms in the shift from one cult mode to another. There is first, the change of "old" gods for the new; the revival focuses on the free-range divinities, themselves of the sky as offspring of the creator, and associated with the unsocialized bush.

The waning gods are part of an alien environment. If not simply a swing from exotic culture to indigenous nature, the change from an emphasis on alien gods was a redirection of attention to the "wild" margins of the hosts' own universe. The change thus yields a fitting match: a concern with internal strangers and a concern with free-range divinities as powers against witchcraft, analogous to the concern with external strangers and alien divinities.

The second change that occurred moved from a primary emphasis on imported substances, such as the kola nuts characteristically eaten by northerners and, at shrines, consecrated by contact with bits of northern soil in the occult concoctions of northern origin, toward a primary emphasis on "wind or breeze," *honhom,* which "is related to the word *home,* to breathe" (Field 1960:79). In spirit possession, the form through which this alternative emphasis was manifested, the person was supposed to cease being himself and become another personal being. If we take the former cults as tendencies toward "place-bound religion" (Tuan 1977:152ff) and the latter as "person-bound," a convenient shorthand for the emphasis on person over place, then an inner logic can be read as follows:

exotic "place-bound" : indigenous "person-bound"
::
metonymic relation of substance and contiguity :
metaphoric relation of being and substitution.

In other words, just as a metonymic relation of contiguity is established with an alien divinity through substance in an exotic "place-bound" religion, so too its alternative, a metaphoric relation of spiritual being, is established through substitution in an indigenous "person-bound" religion.

The point is simply this: personal security cults are cults of the microcosm, and as such must change in mode with the need to redefine the boundaries of the microcosm differently and still control the transcendence of boundaries. No less than the exotic, the indigenous, too, has to be mastered, domesticated and, at times, reconstructed.

In one mode or another these cults continue to be concerned with inequality, strangers, and a cultural predicament in relation to them. What changes is the kind of stranger that is most problematic, and thus the kind of predicament that most needs to be grasped and managed in and by the cults. Hence, rather than being analyzed as a novelty, a "new" movement, the change in cult mode is better

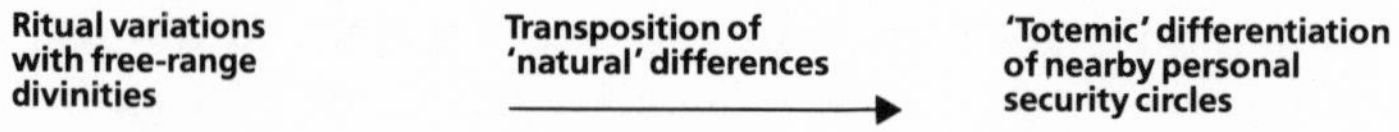

Ritual variations with free-range divinities	Transposition of 'natural' differences	'Totemic' differentiation of nearby personal security circles

Figure 45. Indigenous Reconstruction.

understood as a shift from one alternative process to another, from exotic reduction (see above) to indigenous reconstruction. A future shift may be in the opposite direction, with or without a return to focusing from non-regional to regional cults, i.e., with or without an associated change in organizational devices for the control of center-periphery relations. To say that religious change takes place in history is not to subscribe, necessarily, to a view of a progressive march of movements, whether "towards a purer faith" (Fisher 1973:31) or toward some other total transcendence of boundaries (see Figure 45).

Finally, before I conclude my argument, let me make explicit a debate that underlies much of my discussion. It is a debate about Horton's views on conversion and cosmology (1970; 1971; 1975). The nub of the matter is in his hypothesis that "where microcosmic boundaries are *weakened,* whatever the other consequences, increased attention to the supreme being is likely to be there as well" (1975:222–23, my emphasis). In this view, boundaries fluctuate, but in "strength" only; weak ones are cut across, and the weakest dissolve and disappear. It is as if change in their number or complication is irrelevant, and any ambiguity or indeterminacy in boundaries comes only with the dissolution of a microcosm. Yet the insights are applied to conditions of elaborate and highly fluid encapsulation (see Bailey 1969:144ff), kingdoms within kingdoms, super-kingdoms within empires, and, eventually, quasi-nations within nations. These conditions are alternatives for boundary fluctuation and redefinition in the present, all the more so because they are invoked as time-honored divides between strangers and non-strangers, between various definitions of "them" and "us."

The microcosm and its boundaries, rather than dissolving, may become more elaborately encapsulated, just as communities and states do, with an accompanying growth in the people's awareness of microcosms within microcosms, or alternative microcosms. Furthermore, whether or not one unitary cosmology emerges, in some sense a total whole rather than a series of partial cosmologies, is something that has to be both observed and explained theoretically, not assumed. Put briefly, my own hypothesis is that where encapsulation is radically made more elaborate, existing cults are likely to be displaced by their alternative kind: the multiplication and redefinition of boundaries is crucial for shifts in cult mode.

To begin to meet the need for analysis of alternative cults, waxing and waning within a wider field, a whole set of new analytic concepts has to be introduced, along with the rethinking of certain basic theoretical assumptions. Various flows and point-to-point relations have to be conceptualized so that the concepts may apply where each central place of a series of cults is a focal point within a field wider than a region. Such a focal point may be referred to as a socio-geographic pole in order to stress that it is an extreme reference point for movement, because it is mappable, both spatially and also in terms of ethnic differentiation. Just as a central sovereign shrine has its peripheral client shrines, so too the poles have to be conceived of as primary, or cardinal points, and derivatives, secondary or even tertiary poles. There is a broad process that can be spoken of as polarization in that it is the extension of polarity throughout a wider field, along with the derivation of other poles from primary ones.

Viewing the map of the wider field in terms of poles is helpful in that center-periphery relations can be analyzed without the need to make assumptions about defined boundaries, territorial or otherwise, that often enough do not exist. Sets of zones, heartlands and hinterlands, which may or may not overlap, are what become recognizable. For convenience, I would use the term "convergence" for the subprocess in which overlapping develops; conversely, I would use "divergence" for the development of zones that do not overlap. In no way does the analysis depend on fixing the circumference of any zone, and thus denying it the ambiguity and indeterminacy so important for a heartland zone such as "Taleland." Instead, divergence or convergence emerges, and has to be recognized, according to the placement of the socio-geographic poles and the flows of cults activities around them.

A schematic chart (Figure 46) illustrates the wider field that has been my main subject in this chapter. During its first phase the cults' heartlands were in one ecological division, the north sector of the field, and the hinterlands in the other, the south sector. The central sovereign shrines were distant, geographically and socially, whereas the peripheral satellite shrines of different cults were interspersed nearby each other. Correspondingly, the flows of cult activities diverged in each cult's disparate heartland, and they converged in the cults' overlapping hinterlands. As subprocesses, divergence and convergence were separate in space and complementary

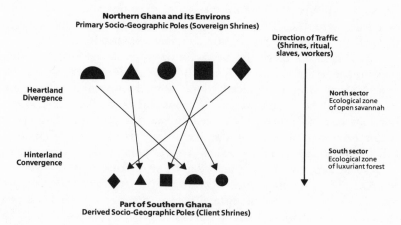

Figure 46. Schematic Chart of Wider Field (Phase One).

in center-periphery relations, simply because the broader process of polarization was directional, like the flow of imported labor, along with imported shrines and exotic codes, from the north sector to the south. And direction, as I argued above, can be shown to be linked to cultural dominance (on traffic across ecological zones and directionality in other regional cults, see my discussion 1977b:*xvii*).[7]

CONCLUSION

In so far as an emphasis of one kind or another freed West Africans to make their long distance pilgrimages in regional cults, the exclusiveness of a "place-bound" religion was the emphasis that prevailed. The importance of an emphasis on exclusiveness cannot be attributed to a lack of a more universalistic, less ethnically identifiable cult. The Earth cult not only stood for "common interests and common values" (Fortes 1945:81), but it was of a similar kind, whether among Talis, or other West Africans far from them in culture as well as socio-geographic space. Rather, exclusiveness was emphasized, because highly particularistic, not generic, bonds were required (contrast Turner 1974:184–85). Thus personal security and prosperity in the midst of various rather dissimilar strangers, both during and after pilgrimage, was ritually guaranteed through highly specific contracts, so specific that bonds of substance were made, from the very soil of a central place, in explicitly parochial cults such as the Talis External Boghar cult.

Yet the mere heterogeneity of the strangers, great as that was in terms of cultural differences, was not all that had to be mastered and domesticated in ritual. The strangers sojourning in their midst from beyond the hosts' own political community were regarded by their hosts as inferiors, fit for the most menial labor and temporary employment, but not fit, like a citizen, for rights to land within the hosts' territory. Hence cultural dominance was—I am tempted to say, had to be—asserted through the personal security cults, and it was done through an asymmetrical appropriation by the superiors of their inferiors' ethnically identifiable cults. Eventually, given major change within a wider field, other strangers, this time not alien or external but internal ones from other parts of the hosts' political community, became more problematic. Accordingly, the religious concerns changed as attention to inequality within the political community increased; and the prevailing mode of personal security cult shifted from the exotic to the indigenous, and from the "place-bound" to the "person-bound" religion.

More speculatively, I would say that a changing power relation structures the inner logic of the alternative ritual forms. The change could be seen from the viewpoint of hosts at the periphery of the Ashanti quasi-nation, who came to assert equality relative to their one-time superiors, internal strangers from the center. Formerly, toward inferiors, the alien strangers, personal security was coded unilaterally in terms of things, the bonds of substance. But, as the power relation changed toward one-time superiors, the internal strangers from the center, what was required was a ritual recoding of personal security in reciprocal terms of persons, the substitution in spirit possession (see Figure 47).

I have used regional analysis primarily to probe the connection between transformation in religion and strangerhood. But the approach is more broadly significant. Regional analysis brings to light the systematic alternatives in certain flows around central places. It opens the way to understanding historical transformations within a general theoretical framework. Applied to the study of cults of the middle-range, it enables us to make sense of their unstable resolution of opposite tendencies, toward exclusiveness and toward inclusiveness. Given its concentration on point-to-point relations rather than boundedness, regional analysis gives full weight to the ways that activities are focused and oriented within zones and wider fields whose circumference may be ambiguous or even indeterminate, rather than a known, essential prerequisite for analysis. Similarly,

Phase One 'Place-Bound' Religion	**Phase Two** 'Person-Bound' Religion
Emphasis of Substances ('Medicines' consumed)	Emphasis on Being (Spirit Possession)
Metonymic Relation of Ritual Contiguity	Metaphoric Relation of Ritual Substitution
Uni-directional Coding (borrowing in one direction)	Mutual Coding (within common Cultural Codes)
Exotic Mode of Cults	Indigenous Mode of Cults
External Strangers	Internal Strangers
Cultural Dominance and Subordination	Cultural Equality

Figure 47. Two Phases of Religious Change.

in its approach to culture, it presumes no box, no single or unitary cultural code within which all the flow of discourse must be contained. Instead, regional analysis recognizes the translation of culture by the people themselves, and takes as problematic their switching from code to code. Its utility is perhaps greatest where the transcendence of boundaries is most salient—in the conditions that are increasingly a major subject of research by anthropologists. The implication is not that "the little community" needs to be forgotten; rather, it must be brought into focus as one point to and from which people, goods, services, and ideas flow.

ACKNOWLEDGMENT

I am grateful to Malcolm Ruel for the invitation to give the first version of this chapter as a public lecture to the African Studies Centre, Cambridge University. Later versions were read to the Truman Institute in Jerusalem, the anthropology seminar at Tel Aviv University, and the African Studies Centre of Edinburgh University. I benefited also from conversations with Dennis Austin, Maurice Godelier, Nehemiah Levtzion, William Tordoff, and Wim Van Binsbergen.

CHAPTER 7

REGIONAL CULT
OF GOD ABOVE

Achieving and Defending the Macrocosm

INTRODUCTION

Southern Africans seeking the favor of God Above, *Mwali*, in Kalanga, go on sacred journeys to distant cult centers. Their quest takes them, in due season and at certain times of personal suffering, on sacred ascension, which they speak of as "going to Mwali." It brings them up to the central highlands of Botswana and Zimbabwe, the cult's heartland, and down to the surrounding hinterlands, to and from oracles and land shrines.

"Going to Mwali" has been practiced throughout this century, and perhaps for centuries before that, across much of southern Africa's great ecological zone of savanna or mopane[1] bushveld (see Keay 1959; Newman 1971:119).[2] The Mwali cult's domain has run, at its widest, from Botswana's eastern district across the south of Zimbabwe into Mozambique and the Transvaal of South Africa. Both as individuals and as whole congregations, the supplicants have come to the cult's distant centers from many culturally different communities. But whether they have been Kalanga, Karanga, Venda, Khurutse, Ndebele, or Ndau, they have all asked God Above for the same basic goods: fertility and the welfare of the land and people.

The stream of supplicants and their intermediaries, ritual substances, messages, and precious offerings has been immense. Great wealth has circulated between the relatively small number of heartland oracles and the innumerable land shrine communities. The capital accumulation at the disposal of cult leaders has, at times, also been huge. But above all, at least from an initiate's viewpoint, the bodies of cult dancers soiled by writhing on a land shrine's earth during possession by God Above have brought down the greatest goods. On their bodies has come that soil of the sacred places which, being ritually purified, frees the rain to sow the earth, as a blessing from God Above, without fear of the violation of the earth by mankind.

The shrines (daka) are many; God is one, Kalanga say. God Above's oneness transcends, in their theology, the recognized disparities, and even hostilities, between the communities that seek His blessings. What is represented in their conception of God Above is the macrocosm, the unbounded order beyond that of the congregation or any single community.

The right to free movement on religious errands across communal borders is basic. Such borders must not be closed against the cult staff or supplicants. Moreover, while any murder offends God, the shedding of the blood of an initiate or cult adept is a grave sin. The sin is tantamount to killing oneself, since it causes, or rather, is, a "standstill" (chamwi). Faced with such pollution, rain fears to sow the earth, and men die of hunger. Furthermore, the portion of the earth that individuals and communities have they hold from God, its Creator and ultimate Owner. In fighting over it (see Werbner 1975:109ff), they "spoil" (chinya); in our terms, they commit a sin, and this must be paid for.

The idea of a moral world order, indeed, a public quiet that must be conserved and defended, underlies the injunctions received from God Above. On a certain day of the week—different in each cult region—and at full moon, people must rest from work. They must not kill certain insects (a red one called mwali, after God Above, is one of the harbingers of rain), birds, or reptiles. They must not sell too much grain or certain produce, like melons, customarily given free. They must not play, especially during the rainy season, the incessant records that blare throughout sales at beer drinks. To this music God Above objects, as it brings turmoil and "wind" in the country—for when men and women dance together to the music, men take the wives of others.

Along with such negative injunctions are positive ones. People must settle a man's estate, fill his vacant office, and destroy his abandoned hut after his death. In brief, care must be taken by people to put things in their proper places, not to despoil the earth but to be non-violent and respectful of public order, lest God Above remain withdrawn, avoiding contact with the earth below. It is striking that pollution as disorder below makes God Above withdraw, whereas, as we have seen in Chapter 3, debt as disorder makes *bapasi,* "those of below," who are the divinities of the dead, rise up and come too close until they are "cooled."

There is, I infer, a favorable direction for divinities, including Mwali and other *midzimu,* to move toward men. The direction is downward, which in distance is closer in the case of God Above and farther away in the case of divinities of the dead. It is from the opposition between God Above and mankind below that the most fundamental religious predicament arises, to which much of the cult's ritual is and long has been addressed, i.e., how to overcome that opposition, given the readiness of mankind to err from the ways of God Above.

This is not to say that their conception of the cosmos as a moral world order represents a single wider society; in theological terms, this would simply reduce the macrocosm to a microcosm with its defined boundaries. Conversely, however, the microcosm must be sustained with respect to the macrocosm: the autonomy of communities must be acknowledged. Thus a person ought to die or at least be buried in his or her own community; i.e., preferably the person's home ward or, in a European's case, a hometown and not the countryside. Otherwise, the corpse becomes a *chamwi.*

More broadly, we may say that the Mwali cult is like other regional cults, which are also cults of the middle range, and thus more far-reaching than any parochial cult of the little community, yet less inclusive in belief and membership than any world religion in its most inclusive form. But the Mwali cult is one of those regional cults that has a certain dynamic tension, which affects its development from one historical context to another. As a cult of the macrocosm, it continually has to resolve opposite tendencies, toward inclusiveness and universalism, on the one hand, and toward exclusiveness and particularism on the other (cf. Werbner 1977a and the further development of this view in Sallnow 1987). The changing nature of that resolution and its expression in sacred exchange along with religious movement across space and time is a major subject of this chapter.

The conception of the cosmos as a moral world order is predicated upon certain axioms. Three of these need to be emphasized from the very beginning. We may say that the most fundamental is the axiom of cosmic creation, according to which God made the world and all that is in it, and according to which God's act of creation established the order for all things and creatures. To bring together, by force, what God separated in creation is *bushongole,* "arrogance, hubris," and it must lead to punishment, if not death. Thus I was told that Americans would all die out after they landed on the moon; God had made the earth and the moon to be separate, and bringing their soils together was fatal. Implied in this axiom is the stress on a Golden Mean and the avoidance of dangerous excess. For example, when men slaughter too many goats, their cries are said to reach God Above who responds and punishes men by stopping the rain, lest a kind of God's creation be devastated.

The notion that after the activity of creation, the Creator withdrew into inactivity, becoming an otiose deity, is widespread elsewhere in Africa. Such a God is never approached in regular ritual elsewhere in Africa. But the creation axiom must not be simply equated with that notion. Instead, of the three manifestations of Mwali—Shologulu, "The Great Head," as the Father, Banyanchaba, "The Mistress of Tribes," as the Mother, and Lunji, "The Awl," as the Son—the greatest, Shologulu, if now usually still and even immobile, is yet a manifestation of potentially boundless, uncontainable energy.

Most commonly, people mean the Son when they speak of Mwali. The Son is seen as the intermediary going back and forth between the Mother and the more remote, relatively immobile Father. Indeed, some people, not initiated into the cult as adepts, say they know the Son has a Father but do not know His name or who He is. Nevertheless, all three manifestations are regarded by initiates as being potentially active; they are the object of ritual and can be in communication with mankind. I was told by Vumbu, the high-priest of the cult's southwest domain, that in the time of creation, when the rocks were still soft, Mwali walked the earth and left an imprint on them. In our times, of course, God no longer walks the earth. But between God Above and people below, rocks and hollows constitute a sacred interior zone of mediation. Ossified, they now provide points of contact with the Creator, being the usual places and interior spaces where people can talk with God and hear God's Voice in response.

A second axiom is that of wider sharing. This is linked to the axiom of cosmic creation and its associated notions of the Golden Mean, God's active tendance, and to His direct speech about the current affairs of this world. According to the axiom of wider sharing, provision must be made for strangers and outsiders. Grain must be set aside for them. It is not enough to feed and produce for one's own family and community. Some produce, certain melons for example, are gifts of God and, as such, should be free to all. Moreover, every place where God speaks should have its own granary to feed shrine supplicants and other hungry passengers.

The importance of this axiom was driven home to me dramatically in 1977, during the guerrilla war in Zimbabwe. Mwali cult officials in Botswana told me they feared for the safety of a high-priest in Zimbabwe. They believed Rhodesian soldiers had arrested him and burnt down his huts. Whatever the Rhodesians may actually have suspected about collaboration with guerrillas, the cult officials themselves believed the arrest was made because the high-priest had opened the cult granary in his keeping to refugees and others fleeing from the Rhodesian forces.

As for the third axiom, that of the cosmos as a moral world order with safe passage for strangers, it may be understood through an image evoked in the verse that is chanted in praise of God's manifestation as the Mother, Banyanchaba. She is addressed as, among other things, the "hollowless mopane tree that saves the tired sun squirrel" *(Mpani usina pako yakanochidza sindi yanyala)*. In unpacking for me the paradoxical imagery of a sanctuary that lacks a hiding place, Vumbu, a high-priest said,

"Mopane" shows that it is a "metaphor" *[kufanisile]*. Banyanchaba is like a person. A person has no hollow. Once we come from the womb, we can't return to it. Once you have given birth to your child, he can't be swallowed again. Nor is the mouth a hollow: we can't enter to hide in it. Nothing can enter a person alive and come out alive. The mopane is trusted very much. It builds a hut that is strong, it gives firewood, and it is dry and hard.

Later, he added that if a tree has a hollow, the sun squirrel gets in it to hide and can be trapped there by a hunter, whereas the tree without a hollow provides shelter on its high branches. The image of a "Tree of Life" conveys God's special protection for the stranger "who comes from here and there"; who may be harmless yet weary from being hunted, like the sun squirrel. As I understand it, underlying this is an axiom of macrocosmic passage, of the protected movement of certain persons as strangers going across possibly hostile communities.

For our purposes, I want to stress that these axioms of cosmic creation, wider sharing, and macrocosmic passage all imply inclusiveness, indeed "a vision of humanity without frontiers" (Lévi-Strauss 1966:166). These axioms imply moral ideas of universalism and a transcendence of the political community along with the sovereignty of any state. What is not implied is a denial of what is owed to headmen, chiefs, and the state, or a rejection of the established order of tributary relations. Instead, these axioms assert a higher order, one that in some senses subsumes the lesser. God, too, is owed tribute. His is the highest, and its very payment is a ritual enactment of macrocosmic passage, imaged in the offering of leopard pelts. The choicest offering *(lunamato)* is the pelt of an elusive creature of the above. It is, like God Above, a mountain creature who, with the swiftest of movements, enters the most interior space, and preys on baboons and monkeys (which adepts are, according to their cult totem, if not their personal totems; see below on adepts and animal classification).

In this chapter I can only begin to describe the sacred places and the flows around them and across communities in southern Africa's most widespread indigenous cult of the macrocosm (see also Werbner 1977b). The people of the cult have organized sacred exchange in different ways at different times and places, and they have experienced marked changes in other religious movements within and across communities. My interest in that changing organization and experience leads me to interpret the central quest of the people, some of their religious ideas about world order, and its transcultural expression. In the following chapter I say more about other religious movements of the macrocosm, such as the largest African polyethnic churches within the same wider social field. This will enable us to appreciate the Mwali cult more fully within its changing context of religious pluralism. And it will lead, in turn, to a better perspective on the movements of the microcosm with which we began our discussion in the preceding chapters.

From the start, a caution is in order. Religious change in the cult is *not* an ahistorical process in which the cult's parts, such as regions or land shrine communities and congregations, make a closed adjustment to each other, subject merely to constraints of a political, economic, or ecological kind. People of the cult make conscious choices for religious change in the light of their knowledge and experience of alternative religious organizations, such as the polyethnic churches that I discuss in Chapter 8. Sometimes they make deliberate attempts to cooperate with other religious organizations.[3] Representatives go back and forth, on an *ad hoc* basis, between the staffs of various regions and the shrines and centers of different religious or ritual associations, such as diviners' unions, for example, the Botswana Dingaka Association (Mpaphadzi 1975a and b; Modongo 1975), and the Herbalist Association of Africa. Moreover, the opposition and rivalry between the religious organizations and ritual associations contribute to rivalry and competition within the Mwali cult itself. Because of this, a priest or would-be leader of a region has a changing series of managerial problems, some of which arise outside of his own cult or region. In due course, I discuss these problems, along with others that affect policy-making at an oracle.

REGIONS, ADEPTS, AND PRIESTS

My ethnography is primarily about the area that I know best, the southwestern region, formerly under the late priest Ntogwa Matafeni Dube and now under his son Vumbu. I describe first what regions are

and how their specific congregations change. I examine the southwestern region as a whole, its communal and personal traffic around the
oracle, the managerial activities of the priesthood, and the problems
of priestly succession.

Regions of the Cult

Every oracle of Mwali is the center of a considerable and ever-changing
part of the cult. It is consulted and speaks about the moral condition
of the land and the people in land shrine communities distributed over
thousands of square miles. For each oracle there is a regional network
of sacred central places, the oracle being at the heart of the network or
"region" (in my terms). Such a region develops across ethnic,[4] district,
and even international boundaries. A region is never a mere mirror
of tribe or state; nor can it be explained as a simple expression or
epiphenomenon of either. Indeed, boundaries as such are hardly recognized by the cult. There is no ritual performed for the sacred demarca-
tion of territory. The cult does condemn fighting over the land and
thus border disputes; but it sanctions no ritual for the resolution of
such disputes.

The region is somewhat of a patchwork, unlike a geographically
continuous whole, such as a territorial unit. In many, if not most,
instances the land shrine communities of different oracles come between each other. Land shrine communities tend, however, to be
mainly concentrated according to their oracle's location, for example,
in the cult domain's southwest for the southwestern oracle, the northwest for the northwestern oracle, and so forth. I describe below the
overall continuity in the number of cult regions and in the regions'
hierarchical relations.

Changes in Congregations

At this point, I consider the tremendous variation and fluctuation in a
cult region at the local level. My interest is in the nature of specific
changes in land shrine communities and congregations. The aspects I
want to examine are four in number. The first concerns progression
through the grades of shrine. Another focuses on investment and the
scale of assets, such as the donated fund and sacred offerings. The third
highlights sponsorship and the categories of staff, and the last regards
shifts in affiliation and the composition of communities. I take up each
aspect in roughly that order.

Every congregation goes through a career. As the congregation
waxes and wanes, changing its cult assets and investments, its fortune

is reflected in its shrine; therefore, it may be said that shrines vary from one grade to another. The shrine grades are (1) local, (2) interlocal, and (3) regional. Figure 48 lists the defining features of each grade whereas Figure 49 shows the current distribution of each.

Viewed as a simple process with advancement from the lowest to the highest grade, the progression is as follows. It begins with a phase in which a land shrine community emerges across adjacent administrative wards and the congregation defines itself around a local shrine. Next comes the phase in which the congregation transcends its communal boundaries; the community centers upon an interlocal shrine to which visitors also come. Finally, there is the phase in which the center of the community is a regional shrine and it sustains a major focus of ritual collaboration between congregations.

In actuality, so simple a process is rare. Very few congregations progress to the higher grades. None remain there for as much as two generations without interruption; they usually return to a lower grade or withdraw from the cult and cease to have a shrine. This holds true in the western regions and, I infer, elsewhere as well. The congregations that invest more than others attain the higher grades and accumulate the more enduring cult assets—goods such as huts, cattle, and grain, and personnel such as adepts. But even these are, in certain critical respects, fluid rather than completely fixed. They do not and cannot anchor a congregation permanently to a particular region, although they may delay a congregation's decline within the cult.

Nevertheless, lest I convey the impression of completely localized fluctuation, I must point out that the assets of congregations and regions are checked by the cult's central organization. Losses or gains in such assets—the slaughter of a black cow belonging to the cult, the death of a priest, an adept, a messenger or an affiliated chief, and their replacements—should all be reported to a cardinal oracle in the Matopo Hills. Moreover, a cult fine for such losses may be levied centrally.

The fortunes of shrine congregations wax and wane over time. Every level of shrine represents an organizational achievement, and is a source of prestige and honor within the community or region. Each congregation varies over time in span, kind, and composition. A chiefdom or any of its parts, one territorial community or several, may become one shrine congregation. The variation ranges from the kind of congregation that includes a whole territorial community (such as an entire chiefdom, a large or small division of one, or a single section or ward) to the kind which consists of a local cluster (for example, a select set of nearby, roughly contiguous communities, but not a whole territorial division). Examples are shown on Figure 49: a whole chieftaincy (Habangana–D); a section (the south of Musojane–C, Wards

	GRADE I - LOCAL	GRADE II - INTERLOCAL	GRADE III - REGIONAL
Distribution on Map 3	A18, A7, B3, C2, Tsamaya	C7	D3, A15
Kalanga Terms	Tanga (Nanga), 'Ring'	Gota (Daka), 'Hut'	Dombo (Ntolo), 'Hill'
Form	Clearing in ring around trees in fallows of local descent line	Clearing in ring; huts	Clearing in ring; more huts; oracle within congregation
Public	Mainly local (a ward or adjacent wards)	Local; some of near communities	Regional Representation
Adepts' Band	Own local band lacking or small	Local band; visitors	Local band; visitors
Circulation of Messengers	Own staff to and from oracles and other shrines	Own staff; occasional visits by nearby congregations' staff	Own staff; seasonal visits, at least, by staff of distant congregations
Offerings	Beer, rarely goats	Beer, goats, occasionally cattle	Beer, goats, at times cattle almost annually
Traffic in Supplicants	Absent, except rarely en route to regional shrine	Absent, except rarely en route to regional shrine	Continuous flow of afflicted and other supplicants

Note: Trees of shrines are Mpani (*Colophosperma mopane*), Nzeze (*Peltophorum africanum*), Nthula (*Sclerocarya caffra*)

Figure 48. Grades of Shrine.

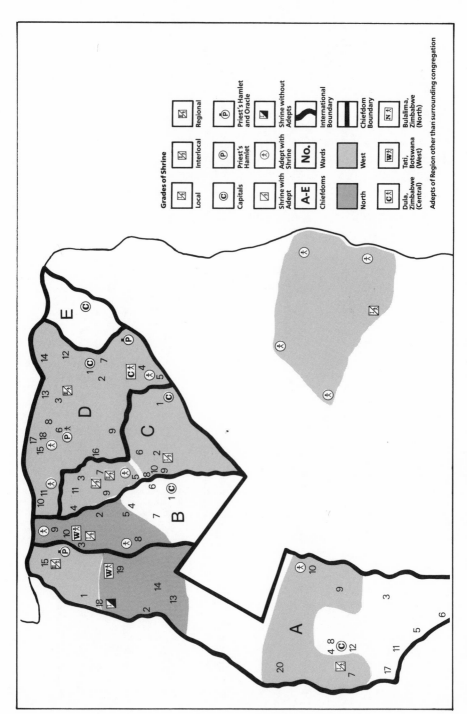

Figure 49. Congregation and Shrines of the Cult of God Above, Northeastern Botswana.

Figure 50. Women Carry Beer to a Local Land Shrine. At the front of the file of women, the community's messenger leads the way toward the tree at the center of the local land shrine on a bare stretch of his father's fallows. The place has an open arena for dancing, but no huts.

C1, C2, C6, C8, C10); a single ward (C9 of Musojane); and a local cluster (Wards B3, B5, B7, B8, B9 of Masunga).

Rarely does a congregation last as long as a generation with the same composition in territorial communities. Each congregation expands or contracts in accord with highly localized conditions, and these fluctuate from one small valley to the next (see Werbner 1975, 1982a and b). The process is highly sensitive to local shifts in population, in the support a territorial ruler can mobilize, and in his commitment to a particular priest or even the cult itself.

There are two categories of staff that are perhaps most important for change in a congregation. These are, first, the congregation's messenger *(ntumwa),* who is accompanied by one carrier *(nsengi)* or more and, second, the cult adept *(wosana* or *mwana wa Mwali,* "a child of Mwali"). A messenger explained the distinction between him and the porter thus: "I carry the truth; he carries the blankets." In fact, this messenger was slightly deaf, and at a public meeting, the porter gave most of the report about their pilgrimage to their regional oracle. It is common for a porter, in turn, to become a messenger.

The messenger is regarded as a courier, rather than a delegate who

Figure 51. The Messenger Oversees the Beer at a Local Land Shrine. Under the messenger's supervision, all the pots and calabashes of beer are collected in the middle of the dancing arena where their origins and destinations are discussed in preparation for the consumption in small groups. In the background, *women clap in a semi-circle, while an adept begins to sing and dance before the three drums.*

has independent authority. His errand is on a territorial ruler's behalf to communicate and carry out transactions with other congregations, shrines, and oracles. He carries offerings *(lunamoto)* to the oracle along with the congregation's petitions for rain, fertility, and seeds that are blessed at the oracle and then ritually treated with substances against pests. Besides the seeds, the messenger brings back from the oracle a declaration of Mwali's response according to the state of the land and moral order of the congregation, whether it observes and respects His injunctions. Daneel (1970:73ff) reports an instance of a prominent messenger who got the oracle at Matonjeni and its staff to take a side in a community's succession dispute. However, an oracle does not regularly declare the winner of that kind of political struggle; and it is not usual for a messenger to seek to have the oracle mediate a dispute over succession to territorial office.

The messenger is the cult official most bound to a particular land shrine community, its concerns, and interests. He owes his appointment to his standing as an elder within that community though he may also claim that his father was a messenger elsewhere. In some instances, a ward headman himself acts as messenger for his own ward and a set of others. Preferably, the messenger chosen at a meeting of the territorial ruler's relatives is a close paternal relative, a seminal brother or parallel cousin, or, under special circumstances, a close affine.

The cult incorporates land shrine communities that are diverse in their ethnic origins. It is crucial for such incorporation that a man may hold the messenger's office without regard to his ethnic origin or his kinship with a past messenger. Kalanga, Karanga, Venda, Khurutse, Ndebele, and Ndau, all hold this office on behalf of their own congregations, whereas the offices of priest and adept are more restricted. As the ethnic composition changes within the cult's total domain, so too may the composition of its messengers change, according to the petitions for affiliation by new congregations.

The messenger has a crucial part to play in the maintenance and growth of a shrine congregation. It is his duty to look after the collection of funds and livestock, to organize the brewing of beer for seasonal dances and shrine feasts, and to arrange for the annual repair of the shrine, if it has huts. On his efforts depends much of the local conversion of private goods into the cult's assets or its staff's benefits. A man stands little chance of becoming or remaining a prominent messenger, responsible for a prosperous or higher grade shrine, unless he is himself relatively rich and surrounded by numerous relatives. They have to be ready, along with him, to contribute substantially to the cult. Only when they become, like him, great investors in the cult, can his congregation transcend its boundaries, in various respects, by securing and sustaining the grade of shrine that requires the congregation's own band of adepts, or *wosana*.

Children of Mwali

The *wosana* are part of the more universalistic staff, and they are also a major channel for an index of local investment in the cult. Like a priest, and unlike a messenger, they may perform anywhere in the cult's total domain. Indeed, wherever invited, they may give ritual services. In their very bodies, they mediate between God Above and people. They pray and chant laments to Mwali[5] and sing of the oracles and famous adepts of the past and present. They mime things and memorialize events of broad significance to every congregation in the cult's domain. Dancing to three drums with a stick or a wildebeest's tail in a shrine's clearing or ring, they may mime a fatted cow, an eagle, a game animal or horse (in remembrance of a prophecy about the arrival of whites), an elder bent with age, a marksman or hunter with a gun, a soldier on military drill

Figure 52. A Band of Children of Mwali Make Obeisance. Upon first entering the arena at a regional shrine, a band of adepts kneel before the drums, lower their heads, and shut their eyes in obeisance to Mwali.

with a rifle (in remembrance of the "uprising" and white conquest), or an afflicted victim. After a bout of such dancing, they suffer stylized fits of dramatic, epileptoid possession. It is then that they are bound *(svungwa)* by Mwali ("a God who Binds," see Eliade 1961:177 on the symbolism of cosmic limits), rather than possessed by a lesser or ancestral divinity.[6] They writhe and roll about in the dust, like a person punished by Mwali's love. Some *wosana* perform feats. They rub hot coals from the fire on their backs and remain unburnt, as far as I could tell (on the significance of ash in sacred exchange, see below).

While their suffering is believed to be on behalf of each congregation as a whole, *wosana* are also offered gifts for the sake of individuals who seek a private blessing. Members of the public at a ritual donate beads, safety pins, or a few pence at a time, and make personal petitions silently or in a whisper to the adepts. For example, an old woman, whose daughter's breasts had run dry not long after childbirth, fixed a safety pin on a female adept's pleated skirt and whispered an appeal for milk to one of Mwali's three manifestations, Banyanchaba (The Mistress of Tribes),[7] whose one breast suckles all, mankind, animals, and birds.[8] More of the

Figure 53. A Child of Mwali at the Onset of Possession. The adept, wearing the black sash of recognition by an oracle, begins to be "bound by Mwali." The seizure makes her body totally rigid. With her head lifted up toward Mwali, her eyes are shut, and her fists are tightly clenched behind her back. She wears rattles from the cocoons of winged ants about her legs.

universalistic significance of the *wosana* can perhaps best be understood through an account of how and where the *wosana* is classified among God's creatures. All *wosana* are "monkeys" (sing. *shoko* in Kalanga; *ncube* in Sindebele). That is their "divinity totem" *(ntupo we ndzimu)*; and they are addressed as such for cult purposes, irrespective of their totems by descent, which they maintain for other purposes. The animals the *wosana* avoid are sun squirrel *(sindi)*, genet *(simba)*, *shuchi* (? a mountain cat), otter *(nyibi)*, and leopard *(ngwe)*. All of these are of one class. They are swift-moving creatures of the mountains (the otter is said to be also a creature of pools and the ocean) and hiders in holes and hollows. With the one revealing exception of the sun squirrel, the Mother's protected

*Figure 54. A Child of Mwali during Possession. Suffering the "love of Mwali,"
an adept rolls rigidly on the earth in the posture of the initial seizure. Within the
arena, another adept protects her from harm that might come from rolling violently
against the congregation.*

species (see above), these mountain hiders' pelts are all choice offerings
(sing. *lunamoto*) to God, left for him in the mountain hollows of the
oracles.

　　Within that class of swift-moving mountain hiders, the opposition
between sun squirrel and leopard is important for the difference between
wosana and high-priest as leader *(ntungamili)*. The sun squirrel is associated with the *wosana,* whereas the leopard is associated with the leader.
Only the leader wears a leopard skin on his way to and from the mountain
and when he enters the hollow to converse with God's Voice. In terms
of the animals' movements, the sun squirrel is said to be safe when it darts
about on the heights of the Great Tree (that is, Banyanchaba). It is in
mortal danger, however, when it enters a hollow where the hunter with
a stick can trap it. Its safety is in the exterior, not in the interior. By
contrast, as the high-priest himself pointed out to me, the leopard is the
one that gets safely into the hole of the ant-bear. It is of interest that the
"hole of the ant-bear" is "the hole of the divinity," since the ant-bear is
commonly referred to as "divinity" *(ndzimu)*. So too, for the *wosana,* the
hollow of Mwali is dangerous, whereas it is safe for the leader.

　　The underlying logic can be put this way: the dangerous space for
the *wosana* is to the safe space for the leader as the dangerous space for

the sun squirrel is to the safe space for the leopard. Thus the *wosana* is symbolically set apart from the high-priest as leader by a contrast in the safe spatial movement of the animals with which each is associated or identified, respectively the sun squirrel and the leopard.

So far I have spoken of the *wosana* as a human being. That does not exhaust the symbolic statements of the people themselves, however. Kalanga also say, "The klipspringer *(ngululu)* is a *wosana.*" No avoidance was implied; a human *wosana* was permitted to eat klipspringer. In a sense, the *wosana* is the leopard's prey, a symbolic statement about leader–follower relations of the kind that Kalanga make when they say that "a chief is a snake; he can bite his own offspring."

I was told, although I did not observe it myself, that there is, or was, a ritual hunt (on a parallel, see de Huesch 1985:386), which was said to be a thing of the past. For the hunt, Ntogwa, a southwestern priest, would send men to catch a female klipspringer by hand, without any hunting dogs. This feat in the ritual hunt symbolically implied Mwali's consent or willingness for the doe to be a *wosana;* it was not done by force. Unharmed, the doe would be brought to their homes and dressed in the black skirt of the *wosana.* After having her back rubbed with hot hearth ash, the doe would be brought back up the mountain to the shrine, shown to the oracle, and then let free. The rain would wash away the ash, and bring "cooling" *(tonodzwa).* The returning of the doe is *svoba,* an act of paying tribute. In no way, however, was the doe treated as a scapegoat for the confession of sins— no words were spoken to her.

In what sense, then, is the doe a *wosana* the way a person is? And what does this tell us about the wider significance of the *wosana?* Being also a creature of the mountains, the doe too would serve as an intermediary coming down from Mwali Above to the people below and going back up to God. Moreover, whether person or doe, the *wosana* could carry on their bodies, downward in one direction, the "cool" soil from the mountains where it rains, and upward in the other direction, the once "hot" hearth ash (i.e., the coolable remains transferred by rain's opposite, fire). Given their final destinations, we may say that the person as *wosana* is primarily the means of bringing the "cooling" and rain, whereas the doe as *wosana* is primarily the means of removing the "heat." More broadly, it follows that the *wosana* is both exchange vehicle and mediator. The *wosana* is at once a universal mediator in sacred exchange with God Above and also the physical means of effecting a wanted yet dangerous transference of opposite qualities, removing matter from one side to the other of the divide between Above and below.

More generally, I would argue that such sacred exchange on long-distance journeys is an important feature of much pilgrimage in Africa. The effort is to transfer qualities by moving substances embodying them from place to place, the direction depending upon whether there is a lack or an excess of the qualities. The hot–cold dialectic that the sacred exchange advances in "going to Mwali" and "returning from Mwali" must also be stressed in its broad significance, although it is, of course, only one dynamic among a number of others, and it is not an intrinsic characteristic of African sacred journeys.

The stress on wild animal symbolism in sacred exchange and pilgrimage also calls for general comment. It is striking, by contrast, how minimal the ritual use of animal symbolism is among people, such as Tswapong and other Tswana, who do not practice external sacred exchange across communities or even sacred exchange across the domestic and the wild or alien domains (see Chapters 1 and 2). Sacred exchange effects a change in people's moral condition that animal symbolism aptly images in ritual as a movement of one kind or another according to the animals chosen to serve as exchange vehicles.

The Organization of Adepts

Such universalistic aspects of an adept's role have to be understood in the light of highly particularistic criteria for the succession, recruitment, and seniority of adepts (see Figures 55, 56, and 57). This will also clarify a crucial fact and its implications: that an adept's status by comparison to a messenger's is restricted ethnically and more under a priest's control. A cult belief is that Mwali chooses each adept to succeed a close relative, and makes His choice known through possession after a more or less severe affliction. The symptoms in the roughly sixty cases that I recorded were severe anxiety, persistent headaches, attacks of hysteria, swelling of the elbows and aches all over the body, constant fatigue and weakness, crippling illness, and infertility.

Most adepts claim a predecessor who is an ancestor no more than one generation removed from the oldest living generation and at most three generations from Ego. The relationship claimed is usually through the adept's mother or father's mother, but the predecessor is not the adept's mother herself. In the cases I recorded, only fourteen out of sixty-two adepts claimed to succeed a patrilineal ancestor. These cases cover the adepts who resided or performed during 1964–65 in the former Tati Reserve, a part of the cult's domain shown on Figure 49 and all within about 30 miles of a priest's home and oracle. (For the distribution in detail, see Figure 55.) Kalanga say that a person must be of the "stock" *(ludzi)* of adepts to become a *wosana* of Mwali. This is a restriction that compels all adepts, irrespective of their own ethnic

Figure 55. Succession of Adepts (Wosana).

	EGO'S SEX	
DECEASED PREDECESSOR'S RELATIONSHP TO EGO	Male	Female
father's father	5	5
father's father's sister	0	3
father's father's father	0	1
father's mother	1	8
father's mother's sister	1	0
father's mother's brother	1	1
father's mother's mother	0	1
mother's father	4	4
mother's mother	1	9
mother's mother's sister	1	0
mother's mother's father	0	1
mother's father's mother	1	3
mother's father's father	1	0
mother's father's father's sister	0	1
mother's mother's mother	1	4
unknown	1	4
Total adepts	18	44

identities, to claim a predecessor within living memory who has a Kalanga or Venda ethnic identity. All adepts thus claim common ethnic *origins*. Significantly, whether to recognize this and a person's other qualifications, such as Mwali's choice through possession, is a matter for the priest and his oracle to decide; and I will consider this shortly.

The point that must be stressed is this: on the basis of a claim to a common ethnic origin, ethnically different people can be admitted to the status of adept. The cult is open to expansion and it includes ethnic newcomers as adepts. Indeed, matrilateral succession, the prevailing mode, fits and, even more, fosters such inclusion through intermarriage among people from the various patrilineal societies in the cult's domain. Above all, the succession and distribution of adepts represents the inclusion of newcomers' communities by their predecessors in the cult, for example, the inclusion of Ndebele or Khurutse by Kalanga and of the latter, in turn, by Venda.

Two further points must be made about restricted succession and

Figure 56. Recruitment of Junior Adepts (Wosana).

	EGO'S AGE AND STATUS RECRUITMENT			
IMMEDIATE SENIOR'S RELATIONSHP TO EGO	Unmarried Boy	Unmarried Man	Unmarried Girl	Married Woman
son	o	o	o	o
daughter	o	o	o	1
brother	o	o	o	1
sister	1	o	3	o
father	2	o	1	o
mother	2	o	1	o
father's sister	1	1	2	o
father's sister's daughter	o	o	1	o
father's brother's daughter	o	o	1	o
father's brother's son	1	o	o	o
father's mother's brother's daughter	o	o	2	o
mother's sister	o	1	6	3
mother's sister's son	o	o	1	o
mother's sister's daughter	o	o	1	4
mother's brother's daughter	o	o	1	1
mother's mother's sister	1	o	o	o
mother's mother's brother's daughter	o	1	o	o
unknown	o	2	1	2
Total	8	6	21	12

Figure 57. Recruitment of Senior Adepts (Wosana).

EGO'S AGE AND STATUS RECRUITMENT			
Unmarried Boy	Unmarried Man	Unmarried Girl	Married Woman
3	1	5	6

its implications for the inclusion of groups and communities. The first and immediate point illuminates how adepts and their kin connect within and across congregations. The second point needs to be considered later, since it concerns the extension of the priest's own connections, and requires a detailed discussion of how the adepts recruited are a selection who have close kin or origins in the priest's own home area.

Adepts enter the cult by joining bands of sets of relatives, in a series. Seniority is recognized thus: the earlier in the series, the more senior the adept, irrespective of kinship or other statuses. Usually, a recruit's closest living relative in the cult, listed as the immediate senior in Figure 56, is within the range of the recruit's first cousins and their parents (i.e., at least 38 out of the 47 junior adepts). In recruitment, one rather close relative usually follows another.

The band's composition, with its potentially wide extension through certain close links of kinship, depends on the composition of the land shrine community. Among Kalanga, at least, each congregation—indeed, each component ward—includes sets of relatives, related in a variety of ways, who change, of course, over time. Moreover, single descent groups do not remain in the overwhelming majority, or even the largest in a ward for very long (see Werbner 1971a, 1975).

To fit the highly variable and diverse composition of congregations, a band has to extend like a chain of short but cumulative links. The more the diverse sets of relatives meet the entry qualifications and, as will be seen below, the entry costs, the more comprehensive a band becomes. Similarly, as adepts change their residence, so too does a band change its local extension and thus the extension of ritual collaboration across congregations. Over time, members of a band form a network stretching across communities. Distance is an important factor. Usually the closer the adepts remain, the more regularly do they return to their original congregation's shrine and rejoin a band during a performance.

The genealogy shown as Figure 58 illustrates, for 1964–65, one band's series of adepts, shown in Roman numerals, and the current extension of the band in terms of kinship and wards, in Arabic numerals. The band belongs to the interlocal shrine located in Ward C7 of Musojane Chiefdom; it began in the early 1950s, when the daughter of its first messenger became an adept (see Figure 59).

Every adept has to be sponsored. Sponsorship is an important process, for sponsorship not only directs the connections within and between congregations but it also shapes the regional circulation of cult goods and services. It is usually a messenger who first acts as sponsor. The messenger establishes his congregation's band by sponsoring one of his dependents (his mother, sister, wife, son, or daughter)

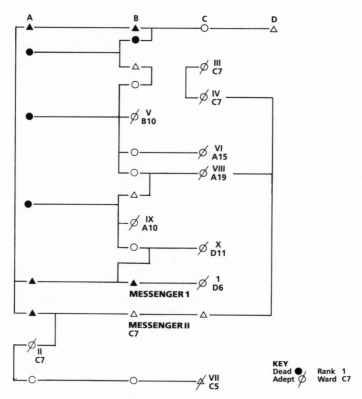

Figure 58. Genealogy of a Band of Adepts.

to become the band's founder and most senior adept. His kin and affines then follow his lead, and sponsor their own dependents.

The cost over time is considerable. At first, while reaching a decision to sponsor a candidate, not much need be spent: usually less than the smallest currency note and not more than a pound sterling or two in diviners' fees, paid by a close relative (a father, mother's brother, husband, or other elder with jural responsibility for an afflicted person) or, rarely, the candidate himself or herself. This or another relative makes the next, larger donations once a candidate gets endorsed and is urged to "go forward" at seances. The close relative who becomes the sponsor takes the candidate forward to the priest's oracle, preferably accompanied by an immediate senior or some other related adept. For the candidate's treatment and initiation, the priest receives an obligatory gift from the sponsor (*fupa,* "to give for ritual services"), often as much as ten pounds sterling. The priest does not charge a fee.

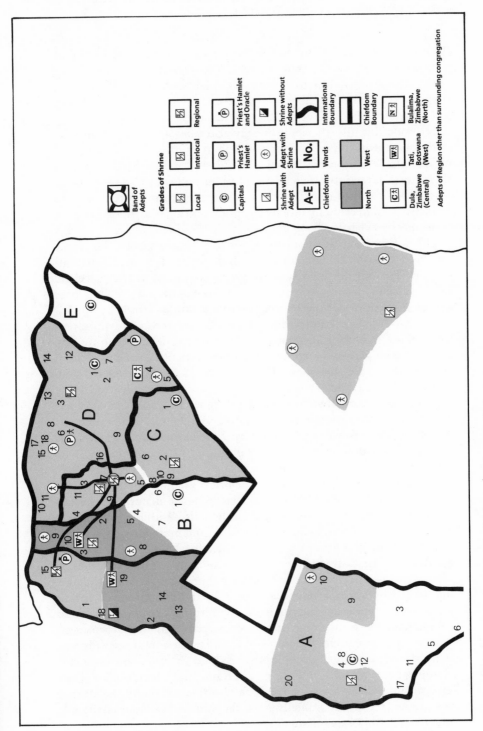

Figure 59. Interlocal Shrine and Band of Adepts, Northeastern Botswana.

Payment must also be made for the *wosana's* costume (which may become an heirloom), a kilt, preferably dark like a rain cloud, leg rattles, and strings of many brightly colored beads. From the oracle's supplies, the priest does allow the *wosana* a black sash *(limbo)*, a badge of recognition that is given at the oracle's command.

Besides his gift, the sponsor may also *namata*, "make an offering to supplicate for a favor" or "act as an adherent" (from *nama*, "adhere," or "cling to"), at the oracle and provide beer and perhaps a goat for slaughter. The sponsor then incurs a further obligation, to give a black cow to be dedicated to Mwali for the adept's sake and, eventually, to be sacrificed and eaten mainly by the priest and adepts, though anyone from messenger to anthropologist may be honored, as I was, with a thigh. Such giving by sponsors is not for one time only. The same man may sponsor as many as two or three adepts. Repeated donations of stock for sacrifice are expected over a period of years, especially from messengers and territorial rulers whose generosity sets the pace for the growth or decline of a congregation and its band.

Capital accumulation within the cult, like the accompanying circulation of prestige, depends upon largesse directed out of the community by the messengers and territorial rulers in particular. For this reason, among others, the cult cannot thrive where, as among Tswana, who live in highly centralized villages, territorial rulers have objected to the cult and had alternative sources of prestige. To some extent, their objection may be a rejection of tributary giving that is mainly centrifugal, when seen from the community's viewpoint, and which thus threatens the culturally valued centralization of the community.

Some of the cult expenditure circulates or remains within a congregation rather than concentrating in the priest's hands. Members of the congregation themselves thus have a stake in the material as well as intangible returns from investment in the cult. Within three or four years, depending on a *wosana's* participation and performances at home and elsewhere, the *wosana* may earn back for himself (or herself) a sponsor's initial cash expenditure. This income, which continues as profit, is earned in small sums from the public at performances, and is augmented by about a pound a year from the priest himself for an active adept. Similarly, the priest usually returns a pound or more to a messenger from the congregation's donated fund, for expenses en route to the oracle. He sometimes gives a larger sum and goods to a major donor, usually an important messenger or ruler. Ntogwa, for example, kept an oracle in Ward A15 of Ramokate Chiefdom for about ten years until the decline of its regional shrine late in the 1960s. During this period, the priest annually gave the ward's headmen about five pounds and a big sack of sugar.

Nevertheless, their stakes in the circulation of cult goods and investments are such that congregations may still shift from one region or priest to another. The stakes are not of a kind to stabilize a congregation's affiliation, irrespective of the succession of messengers and territorial rulers, and irrespective of adepts' personal preferences. The messenger who escalates the pace of donations and thus the importance of a shrine achieves a personal stake, materially and, in the spread of adepts as a band among his close kin and affines, also organizationally. This increasing personal stake attaches him more and more to a particular priest.

The greater the stake one messenger receives, however, the greater the hurdle for his successor. This is due primarily to change in the composition of the congregation, which also alters the set of relatives around the successor in that generation or the next. Despite such change, the successor is expected to begin with payments in accord with the established grade of the shrine, including a fine for his predecessor's death. He cannot gradually build up investment as his predecessor did. A decline in contributions and offerings readily becomes a matter for recrimination between the priest, messenger, and members of the congregation until, exasperated, the priest may announce that he has broken with them and that they may return to their former oracle.

Succession is thus rarely without some discontinuity; this contributes to the instability of regions and their congregations. A messenger often begins by continuing with his predecessor's priest and then shifts to another one or simply rests so that his wards, left without any messenger, may cease to be one congregation in the cult. Similar careers hold for adepts. All are free, as befits the universalistic aspect of their status, to serve the priest of their choice, though sets of adepts usually choose collectively. Some remain attached to their initial priest, despite their congregation's shifts. Others become dissatisfied, for various reasons, and press their congregation to change priest along with them. Adepts thus hasten or retard a shift. They are not a barrier against instability, either in regions or in their congregations. On the contrary, they are an essential force in the progress of a congregation through the grades of shrine toward increasingly wider ritual collaboration.

Ritual collaboration is no *deus ex machina,* and does not resolve or redress conflict between communities or congregations. Admittedly, "to settle down the country" *(gadzikanya shango),* to make peace with and on the land, is an avowed aim of an adept's performances; and though quarrels do sometimes break out, it is forbidden to disturb the peace of a shrine. However, it is not necessary for opposed communities, such as chiefdoms competing for territory, to collaborate in ritual. Such communities have an alternative to ritual collaboration—avoidance. A region is a set of scattered congregations, and opposed communities often resort to membership in alternative regions in order to avoid ritual collaboration with each other.

Occasions for ritual collaboration do, nevertheless, provide opportunities, and sometimes even the necessity, for testing and proving the relations between competitors. This is so particularly in those ambiguous border areas where people from different territorial communities come to be mixed together and interspersed (see Werbner 1975:115–17). For example, in a disputed valley, claimed by the chiefdoms of Habangana and Musojane (D and C on Figures 49 and 60), people from each chiefdom were so interspersed that no clear boundary divided them, until Habangana expanded across the valley at Musojane's expense. Ritual action as a phase in the competition was a test of strength. The people in the valley joined together in one congregation irrespective of their affiliation to either chiefdom, and thus proved that the valley was not divided within the cult. Even more, they anticipated the gain by one chiefdom, Habangana; they affiliated their congregation to the region centered on that chiefdom, where the chiefdom as a whole belonged. Thus a clear anticipatory definition was given through ritual collaboration across the valley, *before* the territorial and political ambiguity was resolved. Moreover, the other congregations of the losing chiefdom continued to avoid those of the winning chiefdom for several decades until after a further adjustment between the chiefdoms took place.

The Priesthood and Its Managerial Problems

How does a priest cope with the continual and sporadic changes in his region's many land shrine communities? How does he, at the same time, also accumulate assets and control adepts and their connections? The cult funds and offerings in a region generate varying opportunities to accumulate assets. Every household's adults are expected to contribute a few thebe or pence a year, voluntarily, to their congregation's fund, which is brought to the priest to be offered *(namata)* at his oracle. However, actual contributions are made more selectively.[9] As a congregation waxes and wanes, so does its funds and other offerings, such as grain for beer, or black cows or goats for slaughter at shrine feasts. It may happen that as many as ten or fifteen head of cattle are kept in trust by a priest for a particular community (Daneel 1970:41; Richards 1942:55). Nevertheless, even a few head are rarely kept in trust within the congregation for long; they are sacrificed, die naturally,

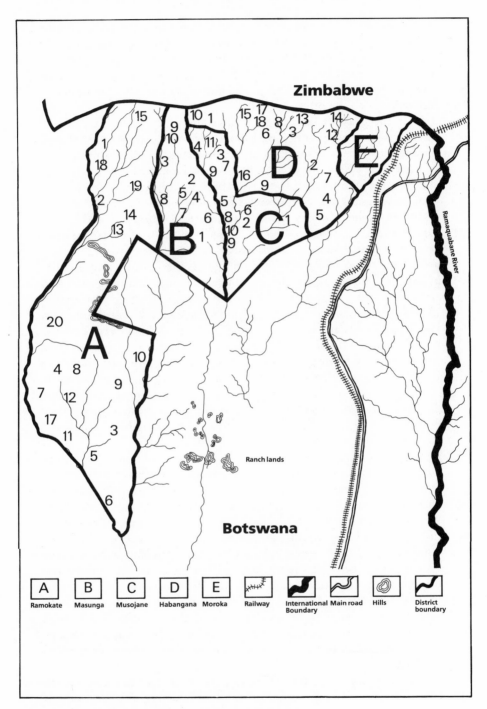

Figure 60. Territorial Divisions of Northeastern Botswana.

or are embezzled.[10] Similarly, every region ought to have at least one shrine at which a granary is kept full of grain for passers-by or supplicants at the oracle. However, only one in the western region, Manyangwa, now maintains such a public granary.[11] By far the greatest accumulation of assets in cattle, cash, and dependents is a personal one that belongs to the priest himself.

At the peak of his career, a priest may be rich in capital, the head of a very large family, and in charge of a great turnover in cult transactions. His riches usually invite the accusation that his main goal is profit, not "the work of Mwali." Ntogwa kept ten wives and their children, for whom he paid heavily in bridewealth, as well as a personal man-servant and many retainers as herdsmen. In 1972, at the time of his death in his eighties, he left an estate of hundreds of head of cattle, numerous two-hundred pound sacks of grain, a substantial bank account and large sums in small change, a donkey cart, a ruined tractor, and a greater assortment of consumer goods than most Kalanga could afford. His gross turnover in the cult can be estimated roughly, from the extent of his region during 1964–65 (see Figure 61). The region included at least seven communities in Zimbabwe[12] and fourteen in Botswana,[13] plus about half this total where his adepts lived in wards not affiliated to his region. Altogether this represents a considerable gross turnover from a catchment area well over a hundred miles in length. Yet to keep many dependents and be very rich, a priest needs a source of income besides messengers' congregational transactions and sponsors' gifts for initiation. From these, his gross turnover may be great, yet his net income low or inadequate for all his dependents, since he must return a share to the cult's staff.

A priest has a more lucrative source for his net income from the cult. He receives a great stream of gifts, often as much as ten each visit, from afflicted supplicants, who throughout the year consult the oracle about individual affairs, rather than seasonally about communal ones. The individual supplicants' traffic, so crucial for a priest's accumulation of great wealth, is not and cannot be divorced, however, from the congregational traffic—one sustains the other. A priest must manage both together, or risk a decline in both. This is so, in part, because the priest gets funds from the supplicant's traffic that he can use as he sees fit, to subsidize transactions with messengers and their congregations. Such funds enable him, for example, to continue to give five pounds to an important messenger, despite a shortfall or decline in his congregation's contributions (for example, the messenger from A15, mentioned above).

Yet, perhaps even more fundamental is the significance that one type of traffic has for the other in organizational terms. Each provides

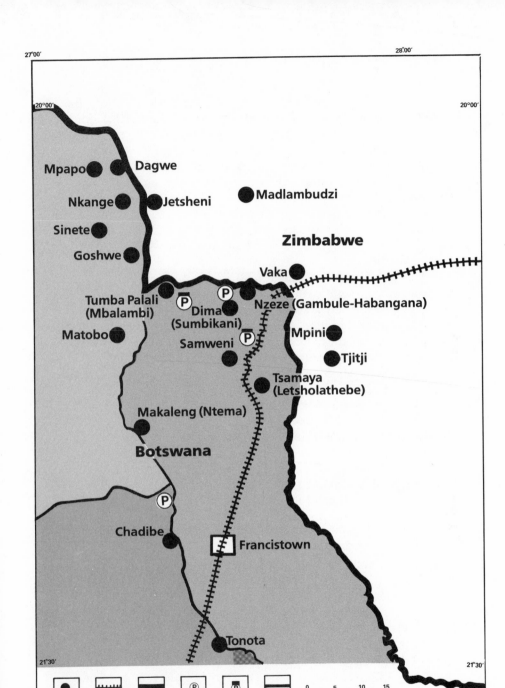

Figure 61. Congregations of Southwestern Region, Botswana and Zimbabwe.

personnel and contacts for the other; the seasonal and more fixed traffic for the continual but somewhat less dependable visits of afflicted supplicants, and vice versa. The more far-flung traffic, the personal one of the supplicants, seems, however, to represent a region's potential and may set limits for its variation. This personal traffic comes from well beyond a priest's current region, and brings to it some of its future staff. Thus members of wards about to form a congregation, or would-be messengers may first come to an oracle as individual supplicants; or a messenger from a congregation that is established in one region may throw out a feeler for an alternative while on a personal visit to another oracle.

This personal traffic, although somewhat more *ad hoc,* is directed, nevertheless, through regular channels. A supplicant, referred to the oracle by one diviner, may be referred back by it to another diviner elsewhere for further help and treatment. First, of course, the oracle may pronounce on the cause of the supplicant's affliction or misfortune. The diviners themselves may visit the oracle. There is, thus, a two-way traffic between diviners and an oracle, directed through specific referrals and carried on with authoritative advice and counseling.

The priest also maintains his contact with diviners and patients and receives firsthand, up-to-date information on local conditions through the frequent circuits that he makes round his region's congregations and beyond them. Even in very old age, Ntogwa visited most of his congregations at least once a year, and annually danced, for payment, at places hundreds of miles apart, from Gaborone, Botswana's capital, to Bulawayo in Zimbabwe. In the past, a priest carried out an additional role through such circuits: public witchfinder for a congregation. Kalanga elders recall an occasion when a priest such as the northwest's Njenjema, while on a visit to a community, spoke to an apparently empty hut from the front outside it and got a response from within in the oracle's voice. This accused someone by name or clan and ordered the person to cease the practice of sorcery. I observed no such occasion, although I accompanied both Ntogwa and later his son Vumbu on their regional circuits. Nor could I get adequate confirmation of claims, which I doubt, that public witchfinding is a thing of the past in the cult. Consequently, some important managerial problems in a priest's career must await further study, and can merely be indicated here.

What emerges clearly, nevertheless, is the nature of regional circuits as organizational resources. Perhaps even more than the major property from a priest's estate, which is inherited rather straightforwardly by rule *and* practice (the bulk for a senior wife's first-born son, in effect as an interested trustee for the family as a whole), a priest's successor needs to take over a major cult sphere. It is the sphere that the late priest managed through frequent circuits and long journeys, and it is one that is highly personal. It demands that a successor acquire intangibles of reputation, such as authoritative knowledge of the herbs needed for patients or to treat seeds, ritually, against pests. It also demands, of course, organizational expertise—effective first-hand knowledge of and contact with patients, diviners, and the other cult officials spread over great distances.

Reputation and organizational expertise, unlike inherited property, have to be gained gradually. Admittedly, they may be gained in good measure by a potential successor, before a priest dies, through the potential successor's service as his closest associate and companion on the circuits. But this gain hardly eliminates delays and disputes about the transmission of a priest's assets or about succession to his office. Indeed, such a gain may be the crux of delays and disputes, because a recognized heir to a priest's main property may have to come to terms with another potential successor, the closest associate and companion of the late priest.

Ntogwa's case illustrates the opposition between inheritance and personal achievement, and its consequences. For various reasons, Ntogwa relied more heavily, for cult purposes, on two of his daughters, Nlahliwe and Galani, than on his senior son and main heir, Vumbu. Nlahliwe was his first wife's first-born, who married and then separated from the northern region's priest. She went with her father on trips to the central oracles. Galani was his third wife's first-born, and she accompanied and helped her father on most of his other trips. She regularly took charge, on his behalf, of performances at shrines, and she became, after him, the region's most famous dancer; indeed, her father often sang, at shrines, "Galani is the senior" (i.e., of the *wosana* adepts). In contrast Vumbu, an accomplished dancer though not a *wosana*,[14] almost never accompanied his father. He was said to know little about his father's herbs, and he remained away for a long period working on the railway in Bulawayo, with only brief visits to his wife and children, who remained in his father's hamlet.

After Ntogwa's death, Vumbu was chosen to succeed his father by many of the region's messengers and rulers, led by Chief Habangana from Ntogwa's home chiefdom. However, some important messengers and rulers did not go to the selection meeting, notably Chief Ramokate from the chiefdom that rivals Habangana in size and other respects. For confirmation and installation, Vumbu was sent, along with Habangana's messenger and porters, to the cardinal oracle at Dula in Zimbabwe. He returned triumphantly with the black sash given by the cardinal oracle as a badge of recognition; but when he addressed his own region's oracle at Habangana Chiefdom, in the presence of a great assembly of messengers, he apparently failed at first to get a response from Mwali's voice. On his visit to Dula, neither of his prominent sisters, Nlahliwe and Galani accompanied him; a quarrel and bitter recriminations between him and Galani had already become public knowledge. Moreover, shortly afterwards, a member of the family insisted to me that the Voice would not be heard so long as they continued to quarrel and did not make peace with each other.

For a period after her father's death, Galani increased her prominence in the region through continued circuits around it, and by establishing a new personal base of her own. After a year's pause to mark his death, she resumed charge of performances at some Kalanga and Khurutse shrines[15] to the southwest, in the Central District. To the southeast, she chose a site suitable for a new oracle. She left the former Tati Reserve and her father's hamlet in Habangana Chiefdom, and moved south to an area of growing settlement—in fact, the region's area of greatest demographic growth—where she built her own hamlet at Thema Shanga. This site is next to a rocky kopje (a granite knoll) marked with Bushman cave paintings, and thus, as she told a confidante, especially suited to impress supplicants with its ancient significance. Her father's oracle had been in a Khami-type ruin of an ancient civilization. Moreover, the location in the State Lands gave her a contemporary vantage ground that was crucially comparable to that held by Habangana Chiefdom at the time it gained the regional oracle around 1914.[16]

At Thema Shanga, Galani had a base for the kind of shrine that only a major political community on the wax can sustain as the center of a whole region. However, it was essential for such a shrine that the territorial ruler, his messenger, and other local followers make a strong commitment of support along with considerable investment in the cult. Galani, for various reasons, failed to secure such support.

The problem Galani faced was primarily whether she could turn her personal base in the supplicants' traffic into a springboard sufficient to reach command of the congregational traffic. Besides her great organizational expertise, she had an important advantage due to her widespread reputation for mastery of her father's herbs, which she was said to have taken in great sacks to her own hamlet. At first she was visited not only by supplicants; would-be adepts also came to her for treatment. Following her father's death, she continued to initiate some new adepts from the region's periphery in the Central District, though not from its old heartland to the east in the former Tati Reserve. These, and some other adepts closely related to her, called her their leader (ntungamili) and insisted that she had to be recognized as a regional

*Figure 62. A Regional High
Priest's Sister Dances with a
Wooden Rifle.
The dancer is not an adept, and
thus does not wear the black sash
or suffer being "bound" by
Mwali during possession.*

priest. Along with them, a few rulers and messengers from the Central District, most prominently the Khurutse Radipitsi from Tonota, publicly took her side and invited her to take charge of performances at shrines. Others from the region's heartland, including the Khurutse Chief Ramokate, aided and encouraged her without such public recognition. But most continued to favor her brother Vumbu or began to throw out feelers for an alternative affiliation to the northern region. Only Vumbu had the backing needed for recognition by a cardinal oracle; and only Vumbu got the black sash and the witnesses to the recognition.

Opposition within the region's heartland, led by most of its messengers and rulers, forced Galani to develop her personal base by relying on the help of Apostolic churches, particularly the one heavily supported by Radipitsi and Khurutse. Through the churches she had access to local communities and organized bodies and thus an alternative to those represented by established messengers. In return, she had to make a greater personal commitment to the churches than her father had done. Even her father sent and received sufferers who went in a two-way traffic to and from certain churches. He attended their service, and included Christian prayers in shrine rituals.

*Figure 63. Vumbu, the Regional
High Priest of the Southwest.
Vumbu wears his Christian
costume, an innovation of his
own, for receiving visitors but
not for performance during the
ritual of Mwali. He designed this
costume to be like a bishop's or
prophet's in a Church of the
Spirit, with a white cross on a
black miter and a blue gown with
white stripes. His sash, which
proclaims him to be the leader of
the Wosanna contrasts with an
adept's; it is tri-colored, red with
white and black letters. His
costume for performing in the
dancing arena was a kilt of
spotted pelts, and a leopard skin
when he consulted the oracle of
Mwali.*

The further step Galani herself has had to make is the assumption
of an Apostolic church leader's role along with public conversion and
affirmation of church membership. It is a step she told me she was
forced to take to protect herself ritually against sorcery from closely
related enemies. However, this step, in turn, put another part of her
supplicants' traffic at risk and provoked further opposition, this time
from some of her father's other collaborators, who are opponents of
Galani's church and lead a diviners' union. In June 1975, they staged
an encounter with her because, according to their president's statement
in the *Botswana Daily News*, "she used a Christian church as a cover
up" (Mpaphadzi 1975a).[17] Their intention was "to set aside Galani who
self-installed herself as our god's chief minister" *(ibid.)*. Following the
encounter, Galani retained a personal base in the cult. But the threat
of her establishing a regional oracle seemed past. Her brother Vumbu's
ascendancy was gradually assured in the referrals to diviners as well as
the circuits around the region. By December 1977, when I accompanied
Vumbu around much of the region, the Voice of Mwali was regularly
heard in dialogue with Vumbu, and I was allowed by Vumbu to attend
seances. In response to the war in Zimbabwe, Vumbu was expanding
the region. Some congregations in Botswana, formerly affiliated to

Manyangwa's oracle in Zimbabwe, were reluctant to risk their lives on the journey through Zimbabwe, and Vumbu welcomed them at his own oracle. The interregnum was evidently over, with Vumbu as priest in place of his father.

THE WIDER CONTEXT OF REGIONAL ORGANIZATION

This history of the southwestern region needs to be understood within a wider context of regional organization. Each oracle is oriented within a central-place hierarchy. Roughly, the closer an oracle is to the center of the cult heartland, the higher its standing in recognized seniority. Moreover, the regularity in the oracles' standing conforms to ecological zoning and permanence in location. The three highest or cardinal oracles are placed symbolically and ecologically above the rest. Being innermost, they are located within an enclaved zone of somewhat higher rainfall in the Matopo Hills.[18] Their sites are moved the least, if at all.[19] The most central oracle is paramount in authority; and on each side of it, to the east and the west, is a cardinal oracle that is the senior in its line, consisting of not more than four oracles. In brief, the formal organization of the cult, at its widest, is concentric and also has diametric halves; the central-place hierarchy gives an ecological gradient its symbolic construction.

Every region within this organization has its own distinct land shrine communities affiliated to the oracle which is its cardinal central place (Figure 64). In this sense, regions are discrete. Yet regions may also be said to overlap, in that oracles are pilgrimage centers for individuals. Each oracle has a personal vicinity. This is the catchment area, within which supplicants come on their own behalf as suffering individuals, rather than on behalf of a congregation or land shrine community. Supplicants, who readily take part as neighbors in a single land shrine community, consult oracles in various other regions on personal matters, sometimes first in one, and then in another region. Hence personal vicinities overlap. It is a selective overlap, of course. Supplicants from a particular region prefer certain others, with oracles more in one direction than another. The existence of the personal vicinity for matters of individual affliction is important, among other things, for the waxing and waning of regions; and I discuss this later.

The patchwork nature of regions is also evident in what I call enclaves and borderlands. The enclaves are territorial communities that do not themselves join any region, although they are virtually surrounded by affiliated congregations of one oracle or another. Conversely, the borderlands are the territorial communities that block cult

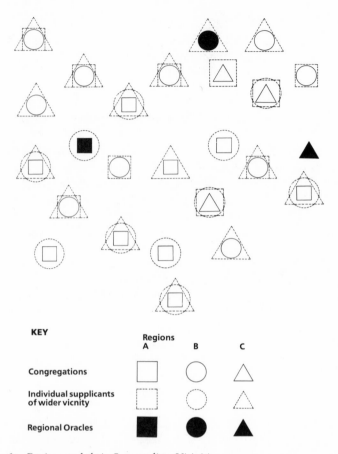

KEY

	Regions		
	A	B	C
Congregations	□	○	△
Individual supplicants of wider vicnity	□	○	△
Regional Oracles	■	●	▲

Figure 64. Regions and their Surrounding Vicinities.

expansion and remain at the outer limit, beyond any region. The enclaves tend to be less permanent; they fluctuate back and forth from non-affiliation to membership in a region, whereas the borderlands are more enduring as barriers against cult expansion.

With peripheral, and thus revealing exceptions (see Werbner 1977a:200), congregations are found only in areas of dispersed, though sometimes quite dense settlement marked by relatively mobile and ethnically heterogeneous populations. This virtually excludes the predominantly Tswana communities in the savanna zone's southwest, which are characterized by large nucleated villages that maintain cultural ideals of transhumance. The oracular *komana* cult found in the smaller, less strongly centralized villages of the southwest, in the Tswapong Hills, is addressed to the ancestral spirits (see Werbner 1977b). This cult is best understood as a cult of the microcosm (see Chapter 1) without the more universal concerns that the Mwali cult has as a cult of the macrocosm.

In more general terms, no simple correspondence between forms of society and religious movements is implied by my account. There is however, I would argue, a fundamental incompatibility blocking the spread of a certain type of religious organization. In the immediate case, the blockage operates against the spread of the external central-place organization of a hierarchical cult of the macrocosm. What cannot be incorporated are village communities where the dominant tendency is toward strong hierarchical organization around internal centers, such as at the village nucleus. Very broadly, there seem to be two central-place tendencies. One is toward hierarchical organization around external centers, and it is now usually found in the presence of weakly developed political authority. The second tendency is toward hierarchical organization around internal centers, and this is usually, or at least ideally, in the presence of strong political authority. The incompatibility would seem to be due to the fact that the central place tendencies are opposed, one being, from the viewpoint of the *community*, centrifugal and the other, centripetal.

Within the major ecological zone of savanna, regions compete for congregations and wax and wane in relation to each other (Figure 65). In this respect they are unstable, but they do not change arbitrarily. Congregations, which vary in themselves, gradually and continuously transfer their allegiance back and forth, from region to region. This transfer takes place even during the lifetime of the priest who leads the region,[20] often for several decades or more, though it is all the more frequent at his death. Indeed, after a priest's death, a long period often passes without a successor in full control of the priest's office. During such an interregnum, which may last a decade or more, the region appears to disintegrate and be partially taken over by others. Sometimes the disintegration lasts; somewhat new regions then emerge, without any increase in the total number of regions.

The cult's beliefs recognize and allow for such a constant flux. Even the site of the most senior oracle, now at Njelele (Snake Eagle),[21] is believed to be one site in a series that began elsewhere among Venda, who are now in the Transvaal to the south.[22] This oracle, like all others, is held to have ultimately come from a foreign site, though its origins were within the cult's total domain.

Any priest may resite his oracle and virtually every priest does. He may move it from cave to cave or hollow boabab tree, on one hill and then another. He need not keep to one site throughout his lifetime.

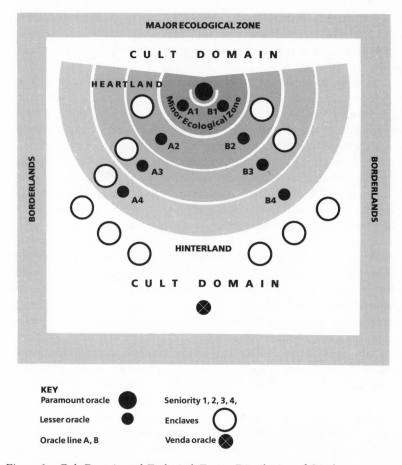

Figure 65. Cult Domain and Ecological Zones: Distribution of Oracles.

He may consult the oracle at a series in succession or at a pair of sites or more, during the same period. From time to time he may even leave his own center to live with another priest for months or perhaps longer.

Similarly, succession to offices is also variable, and people recall only a few successors. A priest's son is the preferred successor, or alternatively a brother (see also Richards 1942:55; Daneel 1970a:46). However, these are sometimes disqualified or lacking. The successor may then be another relative or a newcomer who may claim descent from Njelele's founder, Njenje, within a rather short patriline.[23] Usually, two generations is the most a priest claims in succession from his region's founder. However, no direct succession need occur within a region, and an oracle may end with its founder.

HIERARCHY, STABILITY, AND PRIESTLY PILGRIMAGE

Regions do not proliferate in the Mwali cult. I base this statement on my observations of the western regions over a twenty-five year period, on participants' memories, and on documentary sources for other regions from 1896 onward. The regions did alter relative to each other. This change was, among other things, in response to population increase, migration, war, the dislocation of individuals and communities under colonial rule, and other major political change. But it was their relative coverage and definition which changed, not their maximum number.

Figure 66 shows that no more than three regional oracles have survived for over eighty years in the west, despite a succession of priests and oracle sites. I do not have equally good evidence for other regions.[24] The available evidence also shows the continuity of three cardinal oracles: Njelele (Cockin 1879; Richards 1942:55; during an interregnum, Gelfand 1966:37), Matonjeni (Cockin 1879; Daneel 1970a:40), and Dula–Umkombo (Cockin 1879; under Maswabi III, Gelfand 1966:35ff; see also Daneel 1970a:47 on the priestess Kombo at Matojeni).

Such permanence is crucially an aspect of cult hierarchy. Far more checks the number of regions or priests than merely local conditions. Each cardinal oracle has its juniors. To be installed, with full authority, a would-be priest of a junior oracle requires a cardinal oracle's recognition, which may be given through the grant of a black sash. Among the western oracles under Njelele and Dula, the line of seniority, and thus of some authority, corresponds to their geographical location: the farther east and the closer to Njelele, the more senior. Traditionally, this line is a historical sequence: Mwali arrived at each oracle according to its seniority (see Note 20).

There are also kinship and affinal links between some priests, if not all. But these links do not provide a conceptual framework for relations between regions or oracles. A priest may claim, by reference to his kinship with Njelele's founder, that he has more or less personal seniority among other priests. Such personal seniority, however, does not locate his oracle in a line of seniority within the cult hierarchy. To illustrate, Ntogwa, the southwestern priest, recognized that his oracle was junior to Manyangwa's in the north. Personally, he claimed, he was senior to

REGION	DATES	PLACE	PRIEST'S NAME AND RELATIONSHIP	DOCUMENT SOURCE
	Pre-1896	(a) *Near Mangwe*; Bango Chiefdom? Zimbabwe	*Zviposa*. Child of Njenje.	On messenger Hobani, Burnham & Armstrong 1896, *in* Ranger 1967: 187)
I.	Early 1900s 1910 & INTERREGNUM	INTERREGNUM (b) *Jackalas*; (Shongwe Shaba) southwest of Habangana Chiefdom, Botswana	Baka Pasi 'Mother of Below' (Mantali) Grandchild of Njenje.	O'Neill 1920: 7–8, Cockroft 1972
S O U T H W E S T	Early 1920s	(c) *Nimakwali*; southwest of (b). (d) *Luswingo*; southwest of (c), Habangana Chiefdom, Botswana.	*Ntogwa*, 'Taken (by God)'. Grandchild of Njenje. (Bakapasi's Brother).	
	Late 1950s	(e) *Tumba Palale*; West of (d) Ramokate Chiefdom, Botswana.		Mpaphadzi 1975a & b; Modongo 1975
	1972 to 1977	INTERREGNUM		
	1977 –	(f) *Luswingo*	*Vumbu* Son of Ntogwa	

Figure 66. Western Regions of the High God Cult.

REGION	DATES	PLACE	PRIEST'S NAME AND RELATIONSHIP	DOCUMENT SOURCE
2.	1876	(a) *Maitengwe River, Mengwe Chiefdom?*	*? Unknown*	Holub 1881: 64
	1896	(b) *Dombo Dema*; South of (a) Nilikau Chiefdom (west of Tegwani River), Zimbabwe.	*Njenjema* 'Twinkles' (Variegation)—Child of Njenje.	Reed 1896: LMS 18/9/1896; Ranger 1967: 190
N	??	INTERREGNUM		
O				
R				
T				
H				
W	1930s	(c) – ? south of (b)	*Maboni* Son of Njenjema	Sebina 1947: 84
E				
S	?? early	INTERREGNUM		Modongo 1975
T	1950s			
3.	ca. 1904	(a)—East of Maitenge River, Nata Tribal Trust Land, Zimbabwe.	*Manyangwa I.*	Administrator's Office, S.R. 1904: AL 1/2/12/11, *in* Ranger 1967: 205
N	ca. 1920	INTERREGNUM		
O				
R	late 1920s	(b)—*Nkwasenga*, Matiwayile Hill, Nata Tribal Trust Land, Zimbabwe.	*Mandibenga* (*Palali*), 'You rejected me'. Son of Manyangwa I.	
T				
H				

Figure 66. Western Regions of the High God Cult (continued).

Manyangwa. Manyangwa I was a sister's son of Njelele's founder, that is, junior in kinship to Ntogwa. Ntogwa also boasted that his relationship to the founder placed him among the most senior priests, "We have no 'senior father' *(batatenkulu)* only 'junior fathers' *(batatenini)."* The late Tapa, another priest, with whom he had lived at another oracle (not of the western line), had been his "junior father" Ntogwa claimed.

The relations between the cardinal oracles themselves must be, for the moment, the subject of guesswork. I have yet to visit a cardinal oracle. I venture to guess, however, that the trinity of cardinal oracles—Njelele, Matonjeni, and Dula—stand in relation to each as do the Beings or manifestations in the cult's Trinity: Father, Mother, and Son. The earthly location of oracles in the hills corresponds to the celestial location of the Trinity: in the south, the Father and Njelele; in the east, the Mother and Matonjeni; and in the west, the Son of Dula. I was told by Mwali's Voice, during a seance at Vumbu's southwestern oracle, "Njelele is Shologulu, The Great Head. It is there that I arrived first, when I stepped in the country there, and when I left my footprint."

A pilgrimage from oracle to oracle in a fixed order, with appropriate offerings, is an essential part of the making of a high-priest. In recounting his own pilgrimage on the way to becoming a leader *(ntungamili),* Vumbu spoke of the journey's dangers and of first going wrong then right for safety. Alluding to the threat from an enemy (see above, on the succession dispute), he said that the elephant when he eats comes from the right to the left, so "go the other way round and he can't catch you."

As a novice, Vumbu went left to right and counterclockwise. He made cash offerings at each of the cardinal oracles in turn until he came to the lesser oracle of Tapa in the east (see Note 24 on Shangonyima–Jahunda). The current holder of the title Tapa, acting as his sponsor, then guided him in a right to left and clockwise circuit, while he again made offerings. A climax was, he said, at a beautiful mountain, called Bumbulo after its rock (The Roll, a sphere *without* an opening, perhaps a World Pillar, in Eliade's terms, but unlike the usual hollows for oracles), where it always rains and up which every leader is "elevated" *(tatisiwa).* There he left his largest offering of 200 Pula (then roughly US$200). He expected that he would go again "to help at Njelele" but he would "not go again to school" as it were, like a novice being trained and tested. The ordeal of the pilgrimage was, in the face of opposition from a rival (see above), to win the wider recognition symbolized by the award of a black sash from a cardinal oracle. The procedure, according to Vumbu's story, first tested his acceptability to each oracle in turn, and then confirmed it in the presence and under the sponsorship of the high-priest in the region most remote from his own.

Although it would be ideal to give a detailed account of the lines or oracles along with the hierarchical relations in the cult, less than the ideal must do, at present, for lack of information. The only list available to me that has been recorded at a cardinal oracle is incomplete (it omits Ntogwa and Njenjema), and it has no stated order.[25] Again, it would be ideal to spell out the transactions, rights, and duties that make the lines into a hierarchy, and to show how laymen and cult officials use the hierarchy. Unfortunately, too little is known for more than an initial sketch. Only two aspects of coordinated control and authority can be described briefly at this point. First, a junior priest is expected to take certain actions with his senior's consent, after consultation.[26] Above, I discussed various hierarchical relations in installation, in the required accounting for cult assets, and in the directed flow of replacement payments (that is, a cardinal oracle demands an "axe"–currently a cash equivalent–for replacement of a dead initiate or adept).

The second aspect is this: aside from such occasional cooperation, priests may meet and consult God Above in council, when they collaborate seasonally in ritual at a cardinal oracle. They are said to sit then in a semicircle, according to seniority, on both sides of the cardinal oracle's priest, in their midst (see also Cockcroft 1972). Such councils have yet to be studied. They do appear, however, to provide a central and collective check on the affairs of individual priests and their standing, along with an opportunity for the most general pronouncements on issues of broad or universal concern.

THE DEVELOPMENT OF A REGION
AND THE LIMITS OF ITS EXPANSION

The conditions that are perhaps most crucial for the southwestern region relate to emigration and territorial encroachment. During Ntogwa's long career as a priest, high rates of individual mobility (Werbner 1975:99) swelled into great tides of immigration toward the west and south. This was due partly to a higher rate of increase of human and animal populations, which resulted in greater pressure on land and, in places, severe land scarcity. But, fundamentally, migration has been due to the expropriation of the central highlands of Botswana and Zimbabwe for white-owned ranches. These divided or displaced numerous chiefdoms and led to the founding of others, such as Habangana and Musojane. Most importantly, the land available to their people was restricted, both in Zimbabwe and in Botswana (Werbner 1971a; 1982a).

Expansion from one chiefdom, Habangana, and migration from it to various others located as much as a hundred miles away, provided a flow of people whose connections were a network around which the southwestern region developed. As a youth the priest himself, Ntogwa, had been an immigrant from Zimbabwe, though after settling in Habangana Chiefdom, he came to be known as "a man of Habangana." Between 1914 and 1940, the Bechuanaland Protectorate administration repeatedly had to allow this chiefdom to take over territory, along with people, from its weaker neighbor, Musojane Chiefdom. The region's staff and oracle were thus drawn, along with the chiefdom, into problems of territorial encroachment and expansion. The expansion and emigration enabled Ntogwa to extend his cult connections widely yet retain some control over them through the selection of cult adepts with close kin or origins in his home chiefdom.

A halt to Habangana's expansion became, however, for various reasons, a threat to the further development of Ntogwa's region. What he did not do, though his children did, was marry anyone from the chiefdoms in the region's heartland (shown on Figure 49) other than from Habangana. In his old age he took his junior wives from the periphery of the region in the west (from Tonota, Chadibe, and Mathamngwane in the Central District, where he also established a hamlet) just as earlier he had married wives from the east (from areas of his youth in Zimbabwe).

Throughout the region's heartland, he spread his points of access strategically, in two ways. First, he distributed his wives and children in hamlets at the frontiers of each of the heartland's chiefdoms, and his oracle at a site accessible to a railway station. Second, he established an alternative oracle with its own regional shrine in the only chiefdom that had much room for immigration or more livestock, i.e., Habangana's greatest rival, Ramokate Chiefdom (A on Figure 49). However, this strategic placement and wide division of his family brought its own pressing problems, mainly due to local instability and succession disputes. After less than a decade, he retreated to Habangana, with his entire family except for his far western wives and children. Until his death, four or five years later, he continued to devote himself much more to the western areas than any others, and he admitted new adepts almost exclusively from there.

This account of Ntogwa's career and his region's development raises a difficult question, which calls for further research. What sets the limits to a region's expansion and extension? The most obvious part of the answer relates to competition between regions and to the priest's own perceptions. Much of Ntogwa's region was defined in a competition for congregations between his region and at least one other, mainly the north region of Manyangwa II. Significantly, this competition was absent in the far southwest, which may have been a further reason for Ntogwa's preoccupation with this area late in his life; he largely withdrew from the main areas of established competition. Yet it was Ntogwa himself who perceived quite early in his career that there had to be another region besides his in the whole of the west; he could not manage the total area.

Using a customary formula, Ntogwa reported to the cardinal oracle at Njelele that "All these people are too heavy for me." He requested another priest, asking "Give me another to help me." Ntogwa then insured that this other was a protégé of his own and closely bound to him. He trained his protégé, apparently a son of Manyangwa I; he brought him for confirmation at Njelele, and installed him in the north; he married him to his daughter, and continued to visit and help him for long periods.

When I asked this daughter (Manyangwa II's wife) about the interspersion of the regions' congregations, she insisted that the two priests never fought over the country. She said,

It is the black people themselves who did this. When they complained against father (Ntogwa), they went to Manyangwa and when they complained against him, they came here. We have our home in Botswana; Manyangwa has his in Rhodesia. But if people want to jump over from one to the other, it is all right; there is no fault.

The mutual definition of the regions is thus in part a product of cooperation and adjustment between the priests in response to their recognized and shared interests in the management of competition.

The evidence from the southwestern region suggests another part of the answer to the question of what sets the limits to a region. Ethnic links or historic ties and past affiliations are inadequate and are not in themselves enough of a basis for extending a cult region far into communities of large, nucleated villages. The inadequacy and limitation persists even when the cult's staff try to enhance these links and further various interests through their personal contacts and by heavy investments of resources.

This limitation by large, nucleated villages is not simply a matter of a lack of cultural familiarity with the cult. Kalanga themselves spread far and wide, among ethnically different people and beyond the cult's domain, into the borderlands' nucleated villages. Moreover, they have done so for at least one century and perhaps several. Kalanga have not managed, however, to establish cult congregations in the borderlands, with perhaps one peripheral exception (see Werbner 1977c:200), even though as individual supplicants, Kalanga come to the oracles[27] from villages such as Serowe, the Central District's sprawling capital.

Although ethnic and historic ties were inadequate as a basis for the extension of a region, conversely, in themselves, ethnic differences have not been a barrier to expansion over the history of a cult. Even though, at a particular moment in time, certain enclaves may be defined ethnically, this may not be permanent. An example of such an enclave is in the heartland of the southwestern region; it is the whole chiefdom of Moroka (E on Figure 49), which has no adepts or shrine, though the regional shrine in Habangana is virtually on its borders. The founders of Moroka Chiefdom and their descendants, along with a main body of Barolong immigrants who arrived after 1915, have largely remained ethnically separate from and, in some respects, opposed to the Kalanga among whom they live. The more the ethnic separation is modified through marriage, the more likely is the incorporation (or reincorporation) of this area into the cult, a process already well advanced, as shown by the marriage of the current priest, Vumbu, to a Barolong wife.

CRISIS IN HISTORY

An important conclusion follows from my historical analysis of long-term tendencies in the cult. It requires rethinking what I call the crisis conception of the cults. For the past ninety years, since the so-called rebellion in nineteenth-century Zimbabwe, the crisis conception has overwhelmed the literature on the cult (Selous 1896:14ff; Campbell 1926; Tredgold 1956; Gann 1965:14ff; Ransford 1968:8). Initially, this conception was fostered by white settlers along with their Ndebele allies or helpers to explain—or rather, explain away—the war's aims and inspiration. Yet, oddly enough, the modern version comes from Ranger (1967, 1979, for his revision see 1985). He is the British historian who has provided the most closely documented and masterly assessment of the earlier versions.[28] Daneel (1970, 1971), who insightfully reports clues contrary to this conception, nevertheless follows Ranger's lead. My immediate task is to make plain the inadequacy of the crisis conception, and put forward a better alternative.

In brief, the most modern version runs as follows. Toward the end of the nineteenth century, a grave crisis, the unprecedented catastrophe of white conquest, drove cult leaders to renounce their religious opposition to violence. Immediately after the onset of colonial rule, they

lent both their moral support and their organisational apparatus to the preparations for the rebellion. . . . *Curiously enough there is least evidence* about the

Njelele shrine, which all authorities agreed to be the senior and most influential. (Ranger 1967:148–49, my italics)

Fundamentally, this crisis conception of the cults is wrong because it obscures the fact that the diverse interests within the cult's domain called for a broad consensus in oracular policy. A war policy against white settlers, and thus for a restoration of a conquered Ndebele kingdom, suited the interests of people in no more than a small fraction of this domain. It was a fraction that included some non-Ndebele who were connected with the Ndebele regiments. One such example is that of the people in Belingwe, at the area's eastern fringe, among whom a small number of Ndebele also lived (Selous 1896:238).

The people in the rest of the domain had a different policy, and they were the ones who coordinated their action over the widest area. Their policy was one of protecting the white settlers, even fighting in their defense, *against* the restoration of Ndebele dominance. As seen at that time, this policy was more in the interests of the people who adopted it. They inhabited a great crescent-shaped area around the Ndebele kingdom's stronghold in the highlands of Zimbabwe that runs from east to west across Ndau, Karanga, Venda, and Kalanga country.[29] The cardinal and regional oracles of this vast crescent had to have–and *did* have–a policy in accord with that of their people; there is neither evidence nor reason to think otherwise.

Even before 1893, when the colonial conquest put an end to the Ndebele kingdom, the high priests and other staff of the cardinal oracles experienced political crises. They had concerns that were, in various senses, different from and greater than the Ndebele kingdom's. In some respects, each high-priest was dependent upon the king, but in others he was autonomous, and relations between priest and king were inherently unstable, with the king sometimes displaying his hostility and other times his attachment by wearing the adept's sash. The dialectic in their unstable relations was of the kind that has continued to characterize relations between priest and tribal ruler up to the present. Then, as now, the priest cannot escape his economic and political dependence on the ruler; nor can the ruler escape his religious and moral inferiority in relation to the priest as the Voice of Mwali. Hence priest and king oscillate between support and opposition, and the tension between them is dynamic.

In the nineteenth century, as in the present, the priests and their staff stood for God Above's hierarchy of authority, which was beyond, prior to, and much more far-reaching than that of a single king. They were thus accused of being presumptuous and of committing acts of lèse majesté. From their viewpoint, the king was dependent upon them; he needed them to make peace with the land. In order to punish them, the Ndebele king let loose against them his personal bodyguard (the Imbizu regiment, and also the Insuka regiment), and some of the cult staff were killed. However, to argue that cult leaders did not take part in the 1896 war merely because of their past history of conflict with a recently dead Ndebele king would be to clutch at a straw. What must be grasped are the underlying constraints and the predicaments at the very heart of their theology and their authority.

At the beginning of this chapter, I reported basic axioms and their conception of God's oneness, which transcends the divisions and divisiveness of mankind. While the earth is held by mankind in many portions, with each person having a home where he or she belongs and must be buried, the earth, for God Above, is one creation of which Mwali is the ultimate Owner. People "spoil" and violate the earth by fighting over it even though it belongs not to them but to God Above. If it is to rain, making the earth fruitful, a manifestation of God Above must come down and be in contact with the earth; but He "fears" and so avoids this earth of violence and violation.

It would be unwarranted to argue that such cosmological conceptions or even the whole of their theology dictated the actual responses of the cult staff in a crisis. Yet equally unwarranted is the insistence on another simplistic primary cause, such as a materialist view that disregards these cosmological conceptions. Such conceptions are significant factors in behavior because they enable communities to define their broadest consensus through them, irrespective of their differences, hostilities, and competition. In a crisis, the more inclusive the majority who can be rallied through the cults, the more comprehensive and fundamental will be the appeal to such cosmological conceptions. Even the minority, in its somewhat unsuccessful call for wider support during the 1896 war (the so-called *mass commitment,* Ranger 1967:353), had to recast these conceptions, rather than make radical religious innovations.

Thus a more fundamentally wrong view could hardly be put forth, in my opinion, than the following:

These hints justify us in finding in the risings of 1896–97 (including the war to the east among Shona), though in different proportions, the same elements which are so clearly detectable in the twentieth century millenarian movements with which they are in other ways so comparable. (Ranger 1967:354)

The need to respond to a broad consensus and the cult procedures for the discovery and definition of such consensus (for example, through councils at the cardinal oracles), together with the commitment to macrocosmic conceptions, all acted, and continue to act, as constraints on the cult leadership as a whole. Admittedly, the cult hierarchy was and is sustained through a capacity to collect, store, and allocate great resources and riches. But this capacity must, in turn, be sustained through voluntary consent to collaboration between communities. And it is here, in the winning of consent, that the predicament at the heart of the hierarchy's authority lies.

One last point about oracular policy-making must suffice here. According to the crisis conception, in its modern version, the cults' alternative to armed resistance has been, throughout most of the colonial period, a "sort of despairing passivity" (Ranger 1967:378) (see Note 5). Again the contrary is the case, as shown very clearly in the following account, which has numerous parallels elsewhere in the cult's domain:

Nyusa (Messengers) brought the instructions that [black people] were not to sell grain to white people except for salt, and then as little grain as possible, as Mwali desired them to obtain their salt at Brak [brackish] places or by burning salt grasses, as they did before the white people came. Should they barter grain for salt, they were to cover their baskets so that Mwali could not see it. [They] were told through *manyusa* [messengers] that Mwali would send a great wind and that all white people would leave the country in the night. On their departure, Mwali would introduce other white men who would charge 1 shilling tax only, and sell goods at a quarter of their present price. (Franklin 1932:82)

As seen by some sophisticated Kalanga, such as an ex-headmaster, "Mwali is a conservative God. He does not like change. He wants the old ways." Indeed, to some Kalanga, Mwali appears to have a devotion to customs for their own sake. Yet this appearance, though not a disguise, is nevertheless a cover for the enduring orientation of cult policy. It is conservative, but with economic and political concerns that are as basic in a neocolonial period as in a colonial one. The oracles' messages have repeatedly advocated resistance to the inroads of a cash economy. They have urged the people to store their grain, to rely on mutual aid in agriculture, to brew beer for the cooperative labor of work bees, and not to be at the mercy of sales. "Why do you sell all your grain, and not keep some to help the children?" As Ntogwa's daughter told me, "Mwali objects to sales, for the country is not sold. It is given to its owners." The oracles have insisted that the gifts of God Above must not be turned into commodities for sale. Moreover, in accord with the tide of popular opposition in Zimbabwe to measures for alien control of agriculture (in particular, through the making of ridges and fences), the oracles' messages have condemned the measures: they spoil the land and cause new "standstills" *(zwichamwi)* of rain.

Cult policy has been non-violent and yet directly active politically (rather than "passively despairing") in other respects also. At the time of the first elections prior to Botswana's independence, the messages warned of the dangers of party politics, i.e., that office is given by people according to law, and not fought over. Furthermore, in 1974, the message brought back to Botswana's shrines from the northern oracle in Zimbabwe was, "The rain is held back because of those who fight over the country, those of Smith, Nkomo, and Kaunda."

In November 1977, at the height of the guerrilla war of liberation in Zimbabwe, I was present in Botswana at the hamlet of the wife and son of the north priest (see above on this priest's marriage to the southwestern priest's daughter), when the message came that the north priest had been arrested by Rhodesian police and soldiers; he was later released unharmed. Despite this arrest, both the north and the southwestern oracles maintained their policy of non-violence, and continued to do so, to my knowledge, at least throughout the beginning of 1978.

Elsewhere in Zimbabwe, some mediums in cults of quite a different kind did sanction, legitimize, and even urge violent resistance, both in the nineteenth century and again in the most recent war of this century. There is a religious contrast between these mediums' cult of ancestors, which is a cult of the microcosm, and the Mwali cult as a cult of God Above. It is an important and illuminating contrast, but I can discuss it only briefly here. The mediums' cults are addressed to ancestors and heroes who conquered the land. Some of the ancestral spirits are more associated with the power of war than others. But, despite an emphasis on blood as polluting to themselves and the earth, all have a traditional history of having been forceful invaders (for a study of the mediums' innovation in political symbolism and their incorporation of guerrillas, see Lan 1985). In contrast to the validation of conquest in cults of the microcosm, particularly among certain Shona, the Mwali cult derives its authority ultimately from God Above's creation of the world. I have never heard people of the cult say that God Above is associated with the power of war or that He calls for armed struggle against a regime, however oppressive. Similarly, the press, which amply reported the backing of guerrillas by some mediums, made no such reports for oracles of Mwali. In cosmology, organization, and members' interests, the world creation cult of God Above is radically removed from the conquest cults of the ancestral spirits. In my view, it is a mistake to expect similar responses from such disparate cults, even though the crisis may be of the gravest kind.[30]

My observation of the cult in crisis and out of it leads me to a single conclusion. The central concern of the oracles' messages was and still is to conserve order in the world, and maintain the welfare of the land, its people, and their economy. Peaceful continuity is the policy of the cult of God Above. From precolonial times to the present, this cult of God Above has sustained its commitment in preaching and in practice to a theology of cosmos as world order.

It is not surprising that such conservatism is fostered by a cult that values a certain, lasting fixity in its hierarchical centralization. What is surprising is the combination of such fixity with instability in the coverage and definition of regions, impermanence in the sites of oracles, variability in priestly succession, and broad fluctuations in affiliated congregations and their staff. On the one hand, ranking is fixed in this cult of God Above. There is a small, limited number of ranked regional oracles. The ranking is in a stabilized, unified order according to a gradient within a central heartland. Similarly, the ranks of the cult's staff form a hierarchy that maintains relatively exclusive criteria for recruitment. The higher the rank, the narrower and more exclusive are the criteria, and recruitment to the inner circle of priests is on the most exclusive basis. On the other hand, at the local levels, an oracle's land shrines lack an overall pecking order. They are widely dispersed, highly variable in standing, and they pass through what I regard as three grades—local, interlocal, and regional. Like their congregations, they rise and fall in importance as the foci of ritual collaboration (and some disappear completely) in relation to local level competition between communities or their rulers.

CONCLUSION

The Mwali cult of God Above is one of those to which Turner seems to refer when he suggests that earth cults stress inclusiveness, rather than "selfish and sectional interests and conflict over them" (Turner 1974:185). Yet the Mwali cult fits no polar extreme in Turner's terms. Admittedly, its ritual never offers a straightfoward representation of the various political divisions within its vast domain. But the cult does thrive, nevertheless, on what I call indexical occasions (see Werbner 1977b:xxv), the very stuff of micro-politics, when the relations between competitors are put to the test of ritual collaboration or avoidance, or when the scale of local commitment and investment in the cult is proved, or when still unresolved territorial and political ambiguities are given a somewhat anticipatory definition, heralding new power divisions.

At the same time, its ritual represents images and memorializes events, such as the onset of white rule, that are broadly significant for every congregation, be it mainly Kalanga, Karanga, Venda, Ndau, Khurutse, Ndebele, or any other. Given its capacity to override or encompass quite marked cultural differences, the cult continually admits newcomers irrespective of their ethnic origins. Moreover, its theology directs attention to the macrocosm, the order beyond that of the congregation or any single community. Thus, highly sensitive and responsive as the cult is to micro-political change, it is no less concerned with "wider bonding, . . . disinterestedness and shared values" (Turner loc. cit.). It is the dynamic tension between inclusiveness and exclusiveness that gives the cult much of its momentum and renewed viability from one historical context to another.

The importance of this dynamic tension between inclusiveness and exclusiveness requires that we pay close attention in analysis to the organization of sacred and other social exchange in relation to cosmology. Over time, at any local place, there is a waxing and waning in the local giving to God Above, with more or less importance given the place as a wider center for exchange across communities. In a sense, we may say that the exchange contains within it the seeds of its own destruction and renewal. Sacred exchange is the means by which the little community or the local neighborhood gives actual substance to its wider bonding, and yet it is also the means by which the little community or the local neighborhood reconstitutes itself as a distinctly limited whole. Similarly, through gifts to God Above, social exchange is redirected externally toward capital accumulation outside the community and neighborhood. But it is also through gifts to God Above that prestige is defined within the community and neighborhood and the local eminence of kin-groups holding large areas of land is morally validated (for a case study of exchange relations, ritual organization, and the path to local eminence, see Werbner 1980).

If the cosmology is disregarded, giving to God Above might easily be confused by an outsider with paying tax, since chiefs and headmen have, in the past, been involved in managing the fund-raising for both. Given the cosmology, however, we see that only through the cult do tributary relations reorder moral conditions within a community while creating a higher locus of value outside it. There is an inherent instability in the relations of priests or cult staff and chiefs or headmen. Their oscillation between support and opposition is one expression of that dynamic tension between inclusiveness and exclusiveness that is basic in the cult.

A two-way process of politics has taken place. The cult has had its impact on changes in the distribution of power within various arenas and so, too, have nationwide conflicts and factional struggles, both within and between local communities and Christian churches, contributed to political competition within the cult itself. Territorial encroachment and the expansion of political communities and churches figure prominently in the cult's history, because individual and communal migration, in part due to the historic appropriation of much of the central highlands of Botswana and Zimbabwe for ranches, has been a considerable factor in the cult regions' politics. The dislocation has contributed to a growing shortage of land and increasingly diversified the regions ethnically.

In the southwestern region, in particular, related shifts in the flow of transactions have affected the control of assets and the accumulation of great wealth by the region's leaders and the leaders' heirs. It has been critically important to have a secure base in a political community on the wax in order to command a center for the region as a whole. It would be a gross error to turn the region's sequences of political competition into a series of successful manipulations by Machiavellian masterminds in collusion with each other or, on the other hand, to exaggerate the *ad hoc* element in decision-making in the cult. My argument avoided both these pitfalls by taking account of competitors' long and short term objectives, and not merely the highly pragmatic, situational adjustments which they make without any grand design in view.

It may be, as Turner suggests, that studies of African cults of the earth, most strikingly the Tallensi case, tend to have little to say about "factional conflict" *(idem)*. But the Mwali cult can hardly be studied adequately without a discussion of politics and policy-making in various arenas, from the most petty to one grand enough to embrace the cult's vast domain across southern Africa. In fact, as I have noted, there is considerable debate in the literature on the cult, though mainly from the viewpoints of white settlers, about how the cult responded in crises, especially the early war against white rule in 1896. I have suggested that even during crises, or rather then most of all, the cult has been constrained to favor political compromise in its widest policy—its cardinal oracles make pronouncements that do not commit the cult to one side only during a struggle—and that, in good measure, this balancing has been in response to the diversity of peoples and interests that the cult must encompass.

In no way does this suggestion deny the cult its part in rallying moral sentiment against exploitation and the abuse of power. Some of its songs ring with moral outrage against alien rule. Its oracles have urged resistance against the inroads of a cash economy. They have also warned about the dangers of party politics; such politics denies that office comes to a person by right. Rather, this suggestion takes account of the fact that the cult's ultimate dependence is on voluntary consent.

Its appeal is to the most general consensus, which it may focus but cannot invent. Even more broadly, the appeal of the cult is to a shared recognition of a fundamental need to go beyond one's own community for the sake of its very viability. The internal "heat" of one's own community, its unwanted moral condition, can be replaced by imported "cool," the ideal for vital rain, only if there is a higher order in the world, sustained by external sacred exchange and the highest giving of tribute to God Above. Thus, around the cult of God Above's high central places, the shared objective is ascension and transcendence, when people are mobilized in ways that enable them symbolically to revitalize their communities and the earth upon which they depend, from without and above.

ACKNOWLEDGMENT

Richard Fardon made helpful comments on the structure of my argument. I am grateful to the many Kalanga and Khurutse, cult officials and laymen alike, who helped me to understand the cult, especially the southwestern priests, Mr. Ntogwa Matafeni Dube and Mr. Vumbu Ntogwa Dube, Reverend Mongwa Tjuma, Mr. Mpubuli Matenge Ngulube and their families. Numerous messengers, porters, and more than sixty adepts kindly discussed with me their experiences in the cult. Public personalities and places referred to here are significant for the wider history of the cult's domain and too readily recognizable to be disguised. I have, therefore, not used pseudonyms, as I usually do, to protect personal identities.

CHAPTER 8

CHURCHES OF THE SPIRIT

The Argument of Images from Zion to the Wilderness

THE DYNAMIC INTERPLAY OF REALITY AND IMAGINATION

In meeting the challenge of radical change, the religious imagination often creates and recreates alternative images of space and place, of transition and passage in this world and the next. Even the most familiar locational imagery, such as that of the body or the home, is then given a new significance. A whole series of cults and churches may arise, each with its own specific imagery but often as variations on the same basic elements and themes. According to a widely accepted explanation, each religious movement is a way of restoring order. In other words, the movement is a kind of redressive mechanism; through it, people adjust to a changed social environment, and they find some consonance between otherwise contradictory experiences.

Criticizing Horton (1967), Fernandez suggests that in response to a change in the scale of social life, "images of adaptive conversion" make it possible for people to negotiate "the disorder present in expanding social relationships" (1978:224). On this view, the religious imagination invents or rediscovers images of an overarching order in the world, while striving to counteract the felt disorder and contradictions in experience. It is as if the religious imagination uses solely one kind of locational imagery. That kind is somehow consonant in itself, and in harmony with the changed social environment. Order is not imposed on experience arbitrarily, but through imaginative forms that are iconic or correspond directly with some external, social reality. The comparison Fernandez draws is between the play of imagination in folktales and the "argument of images" in religious movements:

> In religious movements, however, we discover imagination struggling with more challenging displacements in which the outer has become a greater reality than the inner . . . a more attractive reality. We miss the heart of such religious thought if we neglect the fact that this decentering and the acute sense of peripherality it produces is imaginatively negotiated in primary images of body and household, field and forest life. . . . (1978:229)

There is a danger in this view, when it comes to studying religious pluralism. The "argument of images" may be turned into something of a monologue, leaving aside the locational imagery of dissent and non-conformity. By this I mean the imagery through which people direct themselves and others, for the sake of spiritual regeneration, to remake their environment, rather than merely adjusting to it. I have in mind the imagery that, as I explain later, I would call disharmonic, with a view to its semantic structure.

Using disharmonic imagery, people may resist and reject the state; they may break away from one mode of production to seek another; they may abandon some existing economic or social niche in order to go about gaining a new one. What the people perceive as disorder, as something negative, is not here converted into order or something positive by the religious imagination. Instead, the disorder is recognized, even embraced for what it is, in images of pervasive dislocation: God's chosen people are wanderers in the wilderness (on the negative in religious imagination, see Fabian 1979:170).

As an illustration, the image of the Wilderness Church is illuminating. It shows what features the locational image of a religious movement has, and it also introduces this chapter's main discussion of the contrasting imagery generated by three Zionist or Apostolic churches in Zimbabwe. The disharmonic image of the Wilderness Church focuses on indefinite space, instead of either permanently or temporarily defined place.

God's chosen people are in exile. They are migrating toward the Promised Land, and wherever a congregation meets, it is the Wilderness. Bereft of any enclosure, the usual space for ritual is not marked apart in any way, but is boundless: the space for ritual must be in the open. God has no earth-bound house of substance, no material building temporarily or permanently set aside for ritual. Instead the house of God is personified. It is one of the Biblical houses, the house of Ham, and thus the house of all Africans, indeed all blacks. Similarly, the temple is the church leader, or other persons specially dedicated to God. Moreover, there is a passing vessel (such as an ark for the sea or, at a later period and more radically, certain virgins as sisters of the church) to carry God's chosen people. They are the pure who are to be rescued from among the exiled mankind, when the day comes for the great destruction of the powerful of the present sinful world.[1]

The use of sacraments is rejected; and while baptism in Jordan (i.e., in a flowing river) is essential for salvation, only the church founder has the power to baptize. Thus the church ritual is spatially transformative on the outside, not the inside, of the person. The ritual uses external lustration of the person only, without internal transformation through communion. Some local congregations in the countryside have their own places of ascension, but there is no height for regular, churchwide pilgrimage, no single place of ascension for the chosen people as a whole, until the founder's death and the reforming of the church's image.

This image of exile in the Wilderness Church is in an argument of images with others belonging to other churches, including one image that focuses on the eternal place for the Kingdom of God on earth, the New Jerusalem, and another that focuses on the ephemeral places of humankind on earth, the tabernacles of the Pentecost. My main aim in this chapter is to interpret that argument while developing a conceptual framework that enables us to explain it comparatively.

Field, Strangerhood, and Estrangement

I begin by putting the central problems of the chapter somewhat abstractly, by way of introduction, and then attempt to pursue them more concretely through a comparison of cults and churches in West and southern Africa.

First comes the problem of conceptualizing the social environment as changing, and as subject to change arising from the impact of the locational imagery. Conceptual weaknesses spring from the metaphors we ourselves use to interpret this interplay. Our metaphors may impoverish the locational imagery of the people we study. Our metaphors may also impose a simplistic social determinism. A critical example is the metaphor of increasing "scale" that is so widespread in the literature on religious conversion and African churches. Its use has weakened our understanding of the nexus between locational imagery and the changing social environment. My point goes beyond the usual criticisms that "increasing scale" lumps together quite disparate transformations, or that it imposes too neat an evolutionary bias on history (see Kuper 1979). Even more fundamentally, "increasing scale" diverts attention away from changes in the structural placement of part-societies, their variable center-periphery relations, and their evolving encapsulation within wider social fields. Yet these are the very changes in which, and for which, locational imagery so often matters the most. Hence such changes require explicit conceptualization and analysis no less than the imagery itself.

Secondly, we need to show how the imagery informs and is informed by certain culturally perceived predicaments and contradictions in experience. Displacement, or the cultural perception of a decentering of reality, is the broad predicament that Fernandez illuminates (Fernandez 1978, 1979, 1982). But this remains too broad for systematic comparison. Hence we need to see various alternative predicaments in terms of problematic conditions of personhood, and by that I mean conditions that bring into question the cultural definition of the person vis-à-vis significant others.

To explore the systematic comparison, I focus in this chapter on alternative predicaments that relate to movement in space, especially labor migration, and that fall within the polar contrast between strangerhood and estrangement. As developed by Skinner, the distinction between stranger and "estranger" conceptualizes the relative capacity of outsiders to convert their hosts into aliens in their own land and community. Skinner's concern is the colonial or postcolonial impact of different kinds of outsiders. On the one hand, there are the strangers who are able to remain as immigrants near their hosts yet somehow continue detached from them, without being able to dominate them. On the other hand there are the estrangers who, as conquerors and colonizers, have the power to dominate; they act as if they can determine who their hosts are and can treat the indigenous people as aliens on their own soil. Thus Europeans as estrangers "alienated the lands, resources, persons and even psyches of the indigenous populations, who eventually became subordinated to the interests of their conquerors" (Skinner 1979:282, see also Skinner 1974, cited in Sudarkasa 1979:145).

As put by Skinner, the contrast seems to exaggerate alienation as total. It inflates the capacity of colonizers actually to determine the condition of the estranged, rather than stressing their perceptions. Without that implication, but with an emphasis on the problematic relation between us and ourselves as mediated by dominant others, the concept of estrangement in contrast to strangerhood is illuminating (for a helpful formulation of stranger and estranger relationships, see also Levine 1979). For my purposes, it is especially useful, because it enables me to relate religious movements to the movement of labor migrants—as strangers, away from home, and as estranged homecomers, on their return. Moreover, as will be discussed, an important reason for distinguishing the predicaments of stranger and estranged systematically is that this helps in answering key questions: which of the predicaments have an emphasis on the microcosm in their associated imagery; which emphasize the macrocosm, and why? For the sake of clarity, I must explain further, at this point, that my notion of predicament allows for the possibility that the same individuals may know different predicaments, for example, predicaments of strangerhood and estrangement as well, and that they may express their consciousness of each separately, in distinct religious movements or cults. The notion does not necessarily imply a single predicament as being the exclusive one for a whole society or even for a single individual.

The Semantic Structure of the Imagery

In addition to a conceptualization of change in the social environment and in personal predicaments, the much neglected semantic context of the imagery needs to be explored. The temptation has been to turn directly to a relation with the social environment—i.e., the social field—and to ask how religious images correspond with or negate conditions in the social field. Or, put in Marxist terms, the question that easily takes priority at the expense of semantic analysis is: how are the religious forms in a relation of either correspondence, positive dialectics, or negative dialectics to articulated modes of production? (See van Binsbergen 1979:67) What this approach misses is the fact that it is on the semantic structure, the inner logic and relative coherence of the image that its force depends, *as* an image. Hence a semantic analysis is essential. In no way does this imply adopting an approach that divorces the forms and images from the sociocultural configurations out of which they arise.

For a start, in a semantic analysis, we have to identify whole patterns of imagery and their basic semantic elements, i.e., the semantic elements that recur in one guise or another, either in a series of successive images, such as those that belong to earlier and later churches, or in a set of images that are in contrast with each other as contemporaries. The underlying problem is a familiar one: to appreciate historical transformation—the changing pattern of imagery in a series; while accounting for contemporary dynamics—the patterns of permutation in contrastive sets. Only by doing both can we begin to say what makes a particular image forceful for consciousness of one kind, or another.

Part of the basis for comprehending the semantics of locational imagery is already well established in Eliade's richly insightful studies. Writing about the imagery that "archaic man" uses for the world around him, Eliade discerns what he considers to be two modalities, *Chaos* and *Cosmos,* with the imagery belonging in one or the other (see especially 1974:9ff and *passim.*).

Chaos refers to the part of the world that is perceived according to an exemplary model of the undifferentiated, formless, and ephemeral condition; an example is the flux of the wilderness or unknown seas. By contrast, the rest of the world takes on the reality of being Cosmos, the differentiated, the eternal, and all that is organized by forms and norms. A corresponding example is the sacred city, built after a celestial model, with its temple at the center of the world.

Eliade's insight advances our discussion if we take into account the simple fact that a single locational image may encompass *both* Chaos and Cosmos. Indeed, its very significance may arise from the tension in the imagery between Chaos and Cosmos, as I show below in discussing the disharmonic imagery of the Wilderness Church. Hence it is the polar aspects of an image, not its modality, that we need to consider in the light of Eliade's insight. Moreover, freed from the notion of "archaic man," the general relevance of the insight must be stressed, lest we seem to be distancing it from ourselves, with regard to a spirituality or mentality that is premodern, and therefore not shared by us.

In my view, the systematics of locational imagery can be better appreciated if we compare the structuring of the perceptions of Chaos or Cosmos in the images of a set or series. The comparison has to be made with regard to the general terms that are fundamental, and that serve as the coordinates of the imagery as a whole. Chaos and Cosmos are a coordinate's polar aspects or, one might say, relative values. Given the nature of locational imagery, I take such coordinates to be simply: "Person" and "Space" or "Space–Time," which is a shorthand for space and time-expressed-as-space (for a discussion of such "spaced time" see Sharron 1981).

Figure 67 shows the structural variation in the semantic harmony of imagery, according to whether the imagery has 'Person' and 'Space' with like values (the harmonic image) or unlike values (the disharmonic image).[2] Chaos is indicated by the negative value *(-)* and Cosmos by the positive *(+)*. Four structures are shown.

A caution is in order because my discussion is limited by what is relevant to the polyethnic churches. Thus my present concern is only

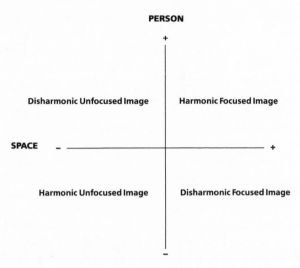

Figure 67. Harmony in Imagery—Person and Space.

with the two structures in the upper half of the diagram. The reader must keep in mind the existence of contrasting types, two harmonic and two disharmonic. My argument covers one of the harmonic and one of the disharmonic, not all four.[3]

To illustrate briefly, in advance of my main account, I refer to the image of the Wilderness Church, which is described above. In this image, relative to certain others, Space is unfocused and has the aspect of Chaos, with indefinite boundlessness, ever in flux. Person, however, is framed and has the aspect of Cosmos; it is as organized by forms and norms, in that the pure person is well set apart from the impure by baptism and other rites and rules of purity or purification. In other words, this is a disharmonic image, relative to certain others, for it is constituted by a tension, balancing Chaos as the aspect of one coordinate, Space; and Cosmos as the aspect of the other, Person.

The question must be asked: can Eliade's insight contribute to the kind of semantic analysis that is needed? It might be thought, for various reasons, that Eliade's approach runs counter to our project, as it views religious movement within sociocultural configurations in history, and that we are being misled into viewing the image as a discrete entity, somehow given significance by its internal aspects, in a void. Some may wonder what has become of the *argument* of images, the persuasive discourse generating and regenerating alternatives under conditions of religious pluralism. In response to the challenge posed by these concerns, I attempt, later in this chapter, to examine the nexus between the changing social field, harmonic or disharmonic semantic structures, and the varieties of consciousness which the images project.

For the sake of clarity, however, let me stress, at this point, a further difference between Eliade's approach and mine. Eliade views the image as static largely because he fixes attention on one kind of image almost exclusively. But my view, by taking in the wider set, recognizes that the image is dynamic in that there is a tension between Cosmos and Chaos and, indeed, Person and Space. Moreover, because the tension may be more or less *imbalanced,* the stability of the image varies, with the possibility of radical change and development. To give the most familiar example, Cosmos may tame Chaos and dominate both Person and Space such that a relatively *stable* image is generated. It is to this kind of image that Eliade gives his attention, repeatedly.

By contrast, my view directs attention to the images where the imbalance is not so certain. In such images, Cosmos does not dominate throughout, but has to contend with Chaos prevailing over Space or Person. The key problem is the direction that the tendency toward instability takes, with the possibility of a gain by either Chaos or Cosmos, and the reconstruction of the image as harmonic or dishar-monic. I would argue that the fulfillment of the tendency's potential is not a function of the image alone: it is not self-generating. In due course, in a discussion of organizational forms, I examine the influences that are exerted to determine the tendency's actual direction.

THREE CHURCHES: VARIATIONS IN IMAGERY

I turn now to my account of the specific imagery in large-scale and polyethnic religious movements of the macrocosm. My interest here is primarily in the three most extensive polyethnic churches originally founded in rural Zimbabwe and, in relation to them, the indigenous Mwali cult of God Above. Each church comes from a recognizably different yet quite nearby socio-geographic zone in south or eastern Zimbabwe, two from within the reach of the Mwali cult and one from beyond it. The church founders' homes are within a sixty-mile radius from the most central among them. The churches are, in order of closeness to the Mwali cult, from the south, to the southeast, to the northeast:

(1) Bishop Mutendi's Zion Christian Church (ZCC), centered in the Bikita District and, at its peak, extending across Zimbabwe and Zambia;

(2) The African Apostolic Church of Johane Maranke centered in the Mtare District which, at its peak, extended as far north as the Republic of Zaire; and (3) Johane Masowe's Apostolic Sabbath Church of God, with its founder's original home and burial place near Rusape and its congregations in Zimbabwe, Botswana, South Africa, Zambia, Malawi, Kenya, and Zaire.

In the same order, the churches are: (1) regional, having a permanently built central place and a locational image focused on the eternal Kingdom of God on earth; (2) regional, having impermanently built central places and a locational image focused on the ephemeral places of mankind on earth; (3) communitarian, migratory (see B. R. Wilson 1967) and later regional also, having, at first, no constructed central place and an image focused on temporarily defined places or undefined space.

From the outset of my account, I must acknowledge a major debt. The quite unparalleled richness of observation and insight into African churches in Daneel's work (1970a, 1970b, 1971, 1974, 1976) is the basis for the best part of my interpretation, although I draw on complementary studies, such as those by Sundkler (1961), Dillon-Malone (1978), Murphree (1969), Aquina (1967, 1969), Kileff and Kileff (1979), Jules-Rosette (1975a, 1975b, 1977, 1979), Ranger (1970), and others, as well as my own rather limited observation of the churches.

The Image of Place

A brief description of the church imagery is essential before I consider its systematic variation, and the varieties of consciousness that are projected in and through the images. The most harmonic, and as it happens the oldest, is the image of the ZCC. This image focuses on the eternal place for the Kingdom of God on earth. A great temple is built to last forever, and fixed sites are sanctified for the annual or periodic pilgrimages, known as Passovers. But all of this placement is concentrated at the Kingdom's center, the headquarters of the church. Reaching the center is a movement upward in space. The sacred journey is to the heights of a mountain or hill, with a corresponding ritual ascension from the communities of everyday life to the congregation cleansed of sin, by confession and acts of purification, and thus raised to the heights of holiness. The ritual is transformative of both the inner and the outer body; there is a sharing of food in communion along with the lustration, by means of total immersion of the body during baptism.

In between the most harmonic and the most disharmonic images comes the ambiguous image of the Maranke Apostles. This image focuses on the ephemeral places of humankind on earth. The Kingdom of God is in heaven, and if ever it is to come to earth, it is yet to do so. Each enclosure of space for ritual is makeshift. It may be a temporary fence of poles of seasonal branches. It may be no more than a wave in the air or a drawing on the ground. Instead of the one temple as the great church building, there are the many tabernacles, as impermanent, moveable sanctuaries and shelters, in which church members camp during their Pentecosts. Ascension takes place at various heights, and it is a sacred journey for even the smallest congregation, such as may come from within one local community alone. Nevertheless, this image, like the most harmonic, is a centralized one, insofar as the ascensions are ordered in importance, according to the congregation represented, from the local, to the interlocal, and to the regional, at the headquarters of the church. Moreover, as in the harmonic image, there is communion and lustration, internally and externally transformative ritual.

The most disharmonic image, that of the Wilderness Church, has already been presented above. I need merely draw attention to the fact that it represents an extreme contrast to the others. I am tempted to suggest that, of all the images, it is the most volatile, in part because of the tension in balancing Chaos and Cosmos within the image; over time it has a tendency to alter drastically, whereas the most harmonic image remains relatively constant for a considerable period of time.

The pattern of variation in the imagery of these three polyethnic churches is simple. From one image to the next, the Space coordinate is variable, whereas the Person coordinate is constant. Space is either focused as definite place (ZCC), ambiguously focused (Maranke), or unfocused as indefinite space (Masowe). In all three images, the Person coordinate is constantly framed in that the pure are well set apart from the impure by rules and rites of purity or purification.

Saying this does not deny that there are other differences from church to church. They do differ in the concept of the person, as seen in the relative openness to spirit possession, in the emphasis on internal versus external purity through lustration or eucharistic communion, and above all in the emphasis on healing in the ZCC and the Maranke churches by contrast to the emphasis on redemption in the Wilderness Church.[4] But in each of their images, Cosmos prevails on the Person.

In the imagery of certain alternative churches and cults, by contrast to these polyethnic churches, the Person coordinate is variable. Person is ambiguously framed or unframed in the alternative imagery, such as is usual in European missions or related Ethiopian-type churches, without the strong emphasis on food taboos, total lustration, and so on (on Ethiopian churches, see Daneel 1971:350b).

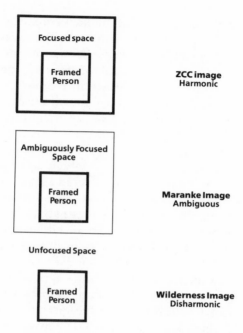

Figure 68. Images of Person and Space in Three Religious Movements in South Central Africa.

A set of box diagrams is a useful illustration (Figure 68). The first diagram shows an image that is harmonic in that it is both focused and framed, by Space and Person respectively. In the second diagram the image is ambiguous, framed but ambiguously focused. Last comes the disharmonic image, unfocused yet framed.

Put in terms of Cosmos and Chaos, the pattern is this: In the ZCC harmonic image, the imbalance is overwhelming, and Cosmos tames Chaos. In the Maranke ambiguous image, there is less of an imbalance, with Space ambiguously penetrated by Chaos; it is a more unstable image. Finally, the imbalance is least, without the certainty of dominance, in the disharmonic Wilderness image; it is the most unstable image. Having viewed these three images as a contrast set, as it were semantic structures out of time, I next regard them as a sequence of innovations in time in order to examine briefly the varieties of consciousness that the images project. And here the images must be contextualized in an environmental and historical relation, i.e., relative to a changing social field.

First, the ZCC harmonic image was the religious innovation introduced in the 1920s at a period of economic boom. The expansion in long-distance labor migration, especially to the Transvaal, was, despite some fluctuations, rapid and dramatic. As that boom gave way to slump, and too many workers pursued too few jobs, the next innovation was the ambiguous image of the Maranke church, and finally, the disharmonic image of the Wilderness Church. In effect, the innovation sequence is a changing construction, from a participant's point of view, of the shift in the field itself (see Thoden Van Velsen 1977) and it can be put, in van Binsbergen's terms, as a shift in consciousness from "acquiescence" (harmonic image), to "symbolic ambivalence" (ambigous image) to "protest" (disharmonic image) (van Binsbergen 1979:69).

It would take me well beyond my present limits to spell out fully how these varieties of consciousness are manifested in the churches' histories, in their differing relations to nationalism as well as the colonial state, or in their positive affirmation or rejection of wage labor and technological innovation for market-oriented agriculture. Very briefly, however, the ZCC was the most hostile to the nationalist parties, and was the most closely identified with the market economy and the existing state. Bishop Mutendi urged his followers to take part in government-sponsored agricultural schemes, such as that for master-farming in Purchase Farm areas. The Bishop preached, in 1965, "If you are true Zionists, you must never join any of these movements that go Zig-Zag (ZAPU and ZANU)" (Daneel 1976:88).

The facts are somewhat less clear with regard to the Maranke Church. Discussing various Apostolic churches, Daneel remarks, "During the political disturbances in the early 1960s the va Postori [Apostolic] prophets were presenting their fellow members with a choice of either burning their ZAPU or ZANU membership cards in public, or forfeiting their Church membership" (Daneel loc. cit.). However, when he comments on a trend toward elevating Johane Maranke to the status of a Black Savior, Daneel modifies his earlier comment, but observes that:

[the trend reflects] the pervading mood in Apostolic circles, which is more nationalistic, militant and decidely anti-White than in most Zionist groups. For instead of the frequently repeated plea for racial harmony in the Zionist camp, one hears with monotonous regularity the accusations of va Postori that the white race had killed Jesus Christ, that the Europeans had deliberately suppressed the message of the Holy Spirit and that their period of blessing had lapsed. (Daneel 1976:98–99)

Besides such political expression, the Maranke Church image

also sustains symbolic ambivalence economically in that, although the tilling of the land is still accepted as good, economic self-sufficiency and self-employment, rather than wage labor, is favored (see Jules-Rosette 1977:198–99).

As for the Wilderness Church, there is a radical consciousness in the form of protest, and I return to this later, after considering the link between the church organization and imagery. It suffices, at this point, to mention the welcome a Wilderness Church leader gave a visiting nationalist leader and ZAPU Vice-President, Dr. Parirenyatwa, "Since the foundation of our [Wilderness Church] movement in 1932, we have been struggling for the ideals which ZAPU stands for today, in our own way" (ZAPU 1962:2, this documentation was kindly made available to me by Professor Terence Ranger).

Throughout this series, there is a match between image and consciousness. I suggest that this match is not fortuitous: each image, with its own appropriate semantic structure, commands a suitable variety of consciousness, and the semantic structure of the image must be changed, if there is to be a change in the variety of consciousness.

Macrocosmic Imagery: The Continuity in Semantic Structure

Is there any continuity between church and indigenous macrocosmic cult in their locational imagery's semantic structure? Does our analysis hold for the Mwali cult also? In a word, yes; the proof must necessarily be brief, at this point, to maintain the main thread of our present discussion of the churches. It should already be evident that the Mwali cult's imagery of definite place is focused. In the previous chapter, I gave a full account of ascension to the Mwali cult's central places, their hierarchy and conceptual framework. Cosmos clearly dominates in terms of Space in the imagery of this cult of God Above. More must be said, however, to establish that this focused image is also framed, and that Cosmos also dominates in terms of Person.

To describe briefly, at initiation, the person of the Child of Mwali is set apart in a "cool" condition. The person is regarded as having had unwelcome "heat." The ritual, like that for full membership in the ZCC, is transformative of both the inner and the outer body. The same foamy preparation that is swallowed orally is used to wash and cool the joints, and thus the body as one whole.

A small, fired-clay pot is placed on the seated initiate's head. This is suitable for the cooking of porridge but it is filled with the ritual preparation. It is stirred from above with the special, four-pronged stick for stirring porridge by a senior female adept or the wife of the leader, until the preparation bubbles and foams over the initiate's head.

Figure 69. The Anti-Cooking of Cooling Foam for the Initiation of a Child of Mwali. The regional high priest's wife, using a stirring stick between her hands, makes the foam spill from the pot over the initiate's head, having treated each of his joints with some foam. The location is immediately behind the back of the high priest's homestead.

First, this covers the outer space of the skull bones. (This is the space for the infant's fontanelle and before the joint hardens Kalanga ritually splash *(dabiwa)* the infant's skull with another mixture. The treatment helps the person survive the dangers from meeting ritually prepared others during the first week of life.) Next, every joint is treated with the foam, from head to foot in turn. The preparation includes various herbs. One is *datha sindi* ("climb a sun squirrel," see Chapter 7 on the sun squirrel and *wosana),* and another is *mopasha* (a creeper with a white milky sap). The main herb is *Gadzi Gulu,* "the great calmer" (from *gadza,* "to settle" or "cause to sit"). It is also a favorite cleansing agent for the cooling of a "hot" patient afflicted by ancestral wrath (see Chapter 3 on "calm" and rest as the highest state of being). In itself, the foam is symbolically, at once, the froth of porridge and the froth at the source of rivers, and as such it is associated with the Mother of God Above, Banyanchaba.

We may say that the rite is performed as a variant of the image of cooking, but it is anti-cooking—with water not fire, and with cool not heat (see de Huesch 1985:209 on the hot–cool dialectic in ritual). Just as a woman cooks frothy porridge over fire, so too she symbolically "cooks" the foamy preparation over the "hot" person. In the succeeding rites, this theme of a woman's lifegiving capacity in nurture is amplified, while the total transformation of the person, internally as well as externally, is achieved through the use by a woman of foam, which is identified with staple food, the source of waters, and ultimately, the source of life itself. This transformation, along with the subsequent observance of food taboos and other rules of purity, clearly sets aside the person of the *wosana* as dedicated to God Above.

It follows that the imagery of the Mwali cult is harmonic, in that Cosmos dominates both Person and Space. In this respect, along with others, such as features of regional organization, which I discuss below, there is continuity between the Mwali cult and the polyethnic church that is geographically closest to it, and perhaps most in rivalry with it, namely the ZCC. As might be expected from our argument so far, both have highly stable images, enduring with relatively little change from generation to generation. Similarly, both emphasize conservation of the order God has established in this world, although at one time or another both (the ZCC at its early period, especially) have resisted the state and the abuse of power, from a conservative standpoint.

CHURCH TENDENCIES:
THE DIALECTICS OF ORGANIZATIONAL FORM

So far I have considered problems with regard to the changing social field, the emphasis on the macrocosm or the microcosm in cosmology, and the alternative predicaments of strangerhood and estrangement. A central concern has been the semantic context and structure of images— identifying their coordinates and relative aspects, and the varieties of consciousness that they project. It remains to link my discussion to an account of the major tendencies in the development of church organization. In the wider social field we have been discussing, the three most important tendencies are (1) territorialism, (2) regionalism, and (3) communitarianism. Each tendency emerges in that order, and at a specific phase in the development of the wider social field. A church tendency, once established, develops in a dialectical relation with the rest, in successive phases, so that the series as a whole is cumulative, increasing the elaboration of religious pluralism over time.

Initially, the conversion of church founders takes place in South African towns, within "Zionist" churches. The founding of the migrants' churches is done on their return home. After being converted, the founders, as migrants, convert others within Zimbabwe, while working in nearby or more remote towns, such as Mtare or Harare (then Salisbury); they then return home to found churches that they

Figure 70. River Baptism in the African Full Gospel Church. A Tswapong preacher in Botswana, wearing a miter and flowing robe, leads the congregation in prayer and song before the total immersion of the newly baptized. To the left is the author.

themselves tend to call Apostolic, after Christ's true disciples. Additional conversions of new communicants take place at home. They eventually form the bulk of a church's membership. The process usually culminates in river baptism away from town, when a migrant reincorporates himself on joining a home congregation, after—and not before—his return from labor migration.

What underlies much of this conversion and the growth of church membership is the religious assumption that the person has to be remade as a spiritual whole by the substitution of a new and total code of purity for the prior, indigenous code. The religious assumption of total regeneration and separation from one's former person becomes an absolute, when the congregation becomes a society within a society, and the church becomes communitarian.

The usual developmental path for the spread from home of a polyethnic church is as follows: The founding migrant begins it among his relatives and neighbors within the same rural socio-geographic zone, where ethnic differentiation is relatively minimal, but not reduced to homogeneity. Thereafter, the innovations are disseminated widely—and more or less modified in the process—from zone to zone and finally beyond Zimbabwe. Many major cultural boundaries are crossed, and the move is toward encompassing very great social and ethnic differentiation. Eventually, a polyethnic church is established, lasting more than a generation, and including urban as well as rural congregations.

Territorialism and Complementarity Between Church and Cult

To begin with, the earliest church tendency is the one that continues to dominate the religious order officially recognized by the colonial state: territorialism. Territorialism tends to match religion with a local or geographical division, and it arises with the establishment of missions that claim distinct "spheres of influence." Such an established territorial mission expects others not to poach on its territory for the saving of souls; it participates in the collective delineation of missionary territories at a Missionary Conference; and it comes into conflict with the established global mission, i.e., the Roman Catholic Church (Daneel 1971:187), as well as the unestablished mission, i.e., Pentecostalist bodies, such as the Watchtower, and the Apostolic Faith, among others.

Along with territorialism comes an appropriate central place hierarchy. The mission founds functionally ordered centers. The hierarchy is from the highest order center with the most elaborate services (the main mission station with its grand, often towering house for worship, its clinic, school, and so on) to the lowest, with perhaps a single service (the outstation with no more than a meeting place for worship).

As for Zimbabwe's earliest African churches, these design themselves according to a model derived from the established territorialist missions. They adopt the model from South African separatists, well-known in the literature as "Ethiopian" churches. In Zimbabwe, some of these churches become territorialized and serve as primarily urban churches; others, as rural ones. But, apparently, none of them provide the kind of sacred centrality around which a major polyethnic region can or does form. While they often try, especially in rural areas, to locate a sphere of their own by distancing their church building from a mission's, and by keeping a geographical divide, such as a river, between them and the mission center, their rural centers nevertheless remain, in effect, mission satellites or lesser order centers. Ethiopian centers are clearly secondary by comparison to the mission's higher order centers. Although they convey a more tolerant and perhaps more ecumenical attitude than the missions, Ethiopian churches put rather little emphasis on rules of purity. They do not require total immersion to divide the purified and the baptized from the rest of their neighbors. It is usual for their leaders either to "evade outright repudiation of the old practices [in the indigenous cults]; or [to] seek to justify [them] as a God-given institution" (Daneel 1971: 464). The ritual code of these churches is thus partial; it is not a total recoding of something already indigenous; and both church and indigenous cult codes can be kept, as it were, compartmentalized.

These territorialized churches tend therefore to complement, rather than be a substitute for the God Above cult. Organizationally too, the churches and the cult of God Above are not rivals; they do not attempt to provide the same services. Although from their beginning some of these churches have been based in the cult's heartland, their development of sacred centrality has been minimal. None has a sacred center and facilities for long-distance pilgrims seeking healing, fertility, relief from suffering or other services for their personal and communal welfare. No church place is raised above and apart from any other, as somehow a cardinal platform for a higher religious authority. There is no ascension to holy heights to replace the indigenous sacred journey, going up toward God Above through a hierarchy of hill oracles. Hence being a church member does not necessarily exclude a person from membership in the cult. Indeed, the Mwali priest who recently succceeded his father in the cult's southwestern region was a member of the African Methodist Episcopal Church before becoming a priest, and today continues to keep up his church membership. Mutual tolerance and overlapping membership have long been shared, characteristically, by these churches and the cult.

Regionalism and Central Place Competition

Church regionalism, is the tendency, above all, to center religion at sacred places, such as the tops of hills. Around these are focused religious centers and major networks of communication and exchange for ritual purposes, such as spiritual healing, personal redemption, and blessing for individual and congregational prosperity. The break from a model derived from the colonial state's established territorialist missions is radical. So too is the recentering and recoding of religion relative to the indigenous cults.

The socio-geographic zones near a church's center tend to be one—although not necessarily the only—main catchment area for church membership. Thus the church that starts within a cult region partly concentrates within it. But the region a polyethnic church generates never fits simply within a mission territory or a preexisting cult region. The church region is a product of church activity, just as the cult region is a product of cult activity, and thus has its own distinct, if somewhat competing, distribution. Moreover, the church regions themselves can be said to crisscross in that they draw people, goods, services, and even cultural orientations, from overlapping catchment areas.

Given the dominance of territorialism as the state-recognized and state-sanctioned order, a regional church seems to need a home or a starting place at some distance from a mission's functioning higher order center. This distance seems to be vital for the survival of the new Zionist or Apostolic church in its early growth toward becoming regional and polyethnic. Moreover, placement at the periphery seems to be an essential vantage ground, when church regionalism aggressively opposes cult regionalism, bringing church and cult into the kind of conflict that is an effective, zero-sum rivalry.

This leads to an important question. Where does the religious recoding and the recentering of sacred centrality by a church pose an effective challenge to the indigenous, large-scale cult of God Above? The answer is clear. The challenge comes from within the Mwali cult's hinterland, to the east, not far from those socio-geographic zones where the indigenous cults are non-centralized or weakly centralized; it is in such zones that prophets and spirit mediums have their transient clienteles and where a defined hierarchy of central places is absent (see Werbner 1977a:xxiii). The challenge does not come from the very heartland, around the Mwali cult's central places, which persist as its major stronghold.

The case in point is Bishop Mutendi's Zion Christian Church (ZCC on its Star of David badges). The ZCC is centered in the Bikita District in the eastern part of the cult hinterland. Here the church competes to turn its sacred center into *the* center, the New Jerusalem at Mount Moriah. Such a cardinal center is the one that is unsurpassed in functional comprehensiveness by any other religious center. Its long-term project is to reach the highest order of, as it were, a mission station and a pilgrimage center rolled into one. Its goal is to have a great church and school building, houses for patients and their treatment, as well as sacred spaces and a hill set aside for holy ascension by pilgrims. The organizational form of such a church can be seen as, among other things, the product of a completely hierarchical competition. The organizational form is within the parameters predicted by hierarchy in both the state-sanctioned mission and the regional cult.[5]

A general rule operates here. It can be put simply thus: the tendency toward regionalism develops in and through a certain church depending, in part, on central-place competition. In other words, it depends, perhaps most critically, on how the church enters or opts out of competition with an established mission's higher order center, or with an indigenous cardinal place, such as that of the Mwali cult.

The first case to be examined, involving the ZCC, is where the cult of God Above is present; therefore two central-place hierarchies are effective. Put somewhat more abstractly, the critical parameters for the tendency's development are, on the one extreme, a central-place hierarchy that accords with or corresponds to a colonial state-established order and, on the other extreme, a central-place hierarchy that runs counter to that order and predicates a higher, more enduring one.[6]

Quite different critical parameters operate in the absence of the cult of God Above. There is accordingly a systematic transformation in the form of church organization. This holds true in the second case of a regional polyethnic church, the African Apostolic Church of Johane Maranke. The Maranke Church starts just beyond the Mwali cult's periphery. Its origin is in one of those socio-geographic zones where the indigenous cults operate without a central-place hierarchy. This church's long-term project is, as a matter of faith and explicit credo, against the building of the church visible:

. . . the task of a true Apostle is to move about and spread God's word and not get involved in such time-consuming projects as building Churches and schools. (Daneel 1971:346)

In terms of central places, its organizational form combines hierarchy with non-hierarchy. The organizational form does that in a way that makes it an inversion of *both* established mission and indigenous cult. On the one hand, contrary to the non-hierarchical indigenous cult, it has a sacred central-place hierarchy for pilgrimage. On the other, contrary to the established mission, it has no higher order centers. Its functional elaboration of centers is minimal, so much so that one could speak of a central-place pyramid, rather than a hierarchy. The reason is that the difference from lesser to greater pilgrimage place for the pentecosts is primarily a matter of increasing congregational inclusiveness, rather than increasing differentiation of services and functions.[7]

What is somewhat arguable is the church's relation to quite a different kind of mission which is, at once, a precursor and rival. I refer to the unestablished mission. The unestablished mission is, in my terms, a form of church that lacks central places, and is in a negative relation with the state and its established religious order. Certain imported or European pentecostal churches are unestablished missions.

They continue to missionize while being blocked by the state from becoming established with their own centers. The colonial state forces the pentecostal churches to adopt an alternative form of organization "by refusing them facilities normally granted to the established Mission bodies, such as the entry of European missionaries into the tribal areas (reserves), the granting of land leases for mission sites or the permission to build schools" (Daneel 1971:403).

Two of my main sources disagree about the impact of European pentecostals, such as the Apostolic Faith Church, on African Apostles (for the view of minimal impact, see Daneel 1971:286–87; for the view of major impact, see Dillon-Malone 1978:9–14, 20–24). Nevertheless, a couple of points can be made that indicate the critical importance of pentecostals for the development of the African Apostles. First, the African preachers of the European pentecostal churches come to move about freely "under no apparent supervision" (Dillon-Malone 1978:9) and are especially active in "Mashonaland" just before the major African Apostolic churches are founded there. Despite being persecuted, or perhaps all the more because of the persecution, the pentecostalists make numerous converts, many of whom later become Apostles. Although the ZCC also became a competitor with unestablished missions in the decade after its founding, the major Apostolic churches had to compete with them from the very start, in the late 1920s and early 1930s, when conversion to pentecostalism was at a peak. Secondly, therefore, what may be called anti-hierarchy—the negation of central placement among the pentecostalists—became a critical parameter for the development of regionalism in the Apostolic case.

Communitarianism, Anti-Hierarchy, and Unstable Imagery

In my opinion, the third church tendency, *communitarianism,* is the one in which anti-hierarchy dominates. Communitarianism tends to decenter religion spatially. Church communities are founded, somewhat in tension with the rest of society, but without a sacred place as a focus or point of permanent anchorage. To escape persecution from the alien-ruled state—which they believe is damned to Hell, like the white rulers—church communities migrate from colony to colony. But they also migrate because none of the places where they sojourn are yet the sacred central place that they envision. The colonized become the colonizers on their own colonial mission.

The church does not merely opt out of central-place competition within any state. It goes to a further extreme in its rejection of the basis for that competition. The very tilling of the land or working for wages is held to be a danger to salvation. And note that it is the tilling of the land that is a matter for religious regulation in one central place hierarchy or another, mission or indigenous, and even in the unranked places of the non-centralized indigenous cults.

Hence for the communitarian church, the religious recoding itself implies a dislocation from the countryside and, at the same time, not the location then taken for granted in town. The church communities are to be self-employed, petty commodity producers, traders, and transporters; and wherever they live, they must be able to regard themselves as in the place, but fundamentally not of it. The more the church expands and becomes more prosperous, as its members successfully explore and generate an economic niche of their own, the more problematic becomes the lack of sacred centrality within the church. Ultimately, the communitarianism becomes regional: sacred central places are recognized, such as at the founder's grave or in a sacred grove around the homes of "virgins" dedicated to the church. Nevertheless, the fixing of a center for the meeting of the church as a whole does not end the migratory project: the search for an ultimate sacred place on earth goes on.

The case in point is the Apostolic Sabbath Church of God, founded by Johane Masowe (John of the Wilderness). To keep the contrast between the different Apostles well in view, I have called one the Maranke Church and the other the Wilderness Church. This usage, which is similar to members' labeling, locates them relative to each other in their early relations, both to the state and much else in their environment. Maranke is the title of the founder's maternal grandfather who, as his chief, enabled the church to establish itself at home and get the state's official sanction to evangelize. Chief Maranke sponsored the church before the colonial Native Commissioner. Thus "Maranke" places the church with its center at the founder's home, and invests it with state recognition and local legitimacy. By contrast, some months after his own conversion, persecution forced the Wilderness Church's founder first to return home—where he began to baptize—and then to flee from it secretly in order to evangelize. Whether or not pentecostal churches were an immediate model for the Church of the Wilderness, what is clear is that the state's officials regarded them in the same light. They were seen to pose the same political danger, the pentecostal mission being to blame for paving the way for the Wilderness Church; and they were similarly repressed by the colonial state.

The colonial state persecuted the Wilderness Church's founder. He was not allowed to remain away from home, in a peri-urban area in the east, on the outskirts of Zimbabwe's capital, near his earliest followers and close to the scene of his own conversion. Nor was he allowed to maintain his own home openly as a centre for pentecosts and holy ascension. It was too dangerous as a headquarters for preaching across the countryside about the end of white rule and for mobilizing Africans against it. The districts between Mtare and Rusape near his founder's home continued to be a main catchment area for converts. But during succeeding decades, the establishment of urban and peri-urban colonies of the self-employed, of Israelites not working "as slaves for non-Israelites" (Sundkler 1961:308), came to dominate the church's project, as it was harassed and driven out of Bulawayo, the major town in western Zimbabwe, to a series of towns in South Africa, in Zimbabwe, once again, and elsewhere.

Finally, the change toward the most complete relocation in religious as well as economic terms began once a colony reached a shanty-town in Zambia's capital, shortly before independence. In that new nation-state, the church, which negated sacred centrality within the state under European rule, began to generate sacred centrality under African rule:

Masowe worship and work life centres around their main prayer grove in the southern sector of Marrapodi [the Lusaka shantytown]. The homes of elders are located in a semi-circle around the grove. Inside the grove is a large house where the Masowe "virgins" said to have been the former wives of the deceased leader, now live. They embody the purity and sacrificial commitments of the Church as a whole and are insulated from the "world" by the grove and the ring of elders' homes. (Jules-Rosette 1977:197)

As compared to the cult of God Above or the other polyethnic churches, the transformation was a radical one: sacred centrality was fixed at a major political and economic center, and away from the economic periphery. Whereas the indigenous cult of God Above remained in tension with the colonial state, the Wilderness Church began to legitimize and sanctify the neocolonial one. The church's imagery changed accordingly, toward recentering instead of decentering, toward location instead of dislocation, and toward the harmonic rather than the disharmonic.

CONCLUSION

Taking a body of religious movements as my basic unit of study, rather than any single church or cult in isolation, I have shown how the religious movements can be understood as innovations in space. My analysis started with a view of the wider social field, in which there is massive extraction of labor from one sector to another. It is the change in such a wider social field that participants come to experience as contradiction, disorder, or dislocation, and that they confront through religious innovation. As a contrast to an earlier discussion of West African religious movements of the microcosm (Chapter 6), in this chapter I explored the Southern African counterpart, within a comparable, wider social field. Here, the large-scale religious movements of the macrocosm that I considered included three polyethnic churches and the indigenous cult of God Above. My hypothesis has been that, just as there is a nexus between transformation in cults of the microcosm and the changing predicament of strangerhood, so too are cults of the macrocosm linked to change in estrangement. Each predicament evokes its own kind of religious response and, in turn, responds to it, as the effect in its turn becomes a cause.

Two critical conditions are presupposed in all of this. First, my hypothesis refers to colonial or neo-colonial capitalism, to that kind of imbalanced social field in which, away from home, the person, or rather his labor, is often regarded as a marketable commodity. Secondly, I keep in view changes in predicament that involve changes in the perceived relations of power and dominance between outsiders, such as labor migrants, and certain significant others.

To understand religious movements as innovations in space, I find it necessary to give a comparative account of four interrelated dimensions, according to their variation from one church to the next within the whole body of religious movements. These four are the dimensions of (1) image, (2) consciousness, (3) project, and (4) organization.

As structured by its aspects of Chaos or Cosmos, the church image varies from the harmonic, to the ambiguous, to the disharmonic. Similarly, consciousness varies from acquiescence, to symbolic ambivalence, to protest. I suggest that within a body of churches, image and consciousness fit aptly. In other words, they inform and are informed by each other according to a regular pattern. In the body of churches that I discuss the regularity is this: the harmonic image and acquiescence are interdependent, constituting each other, as are the ambiguous image and symbolic ambivalence, and the disharmonic image and protest.

As for the dimension of project, the variation is from material establishment, to immaterial incorporation, to immaterial disestablishment. Thus, at one extreme in this variation is the priority of building the church visible within the existing state. In between the extremes is the priority, irrespective of the state, of creating solely the church invisible, in and through the reunion of more and more saved souls each year.

Finally, on the dimension of organization, it is central placement and hierarchy that varies regularly from church to church, the range being from the most highly centripetal and functionally comprehensive, such as in the New Jerusalem at Mount Moriah of the New Testament, to the more diffuse, such as in the encampments of the Pentecost, to the centrifugal, such as in the total communities of the migratory Wilderness. I would suggest, also, that the pattern holding between these dimensions, project, and organization, tends to be regular in the way that the pattern of the other dimensions is regular.

My approach presents the elaboration of religious pluralism as a dialectical process in which churches and cults mutually differentiate themselves in competition with each other. I reject the view that religious change, when considered historically, must be seen as a progressive march of movements or a unilinear evolution. Rather, shifts in the direction of religious change must be seen to be highly variable; they therefore pose some of the most challenging problems for analysis. It may well be once again in vogue to make evolutionary schemes of change, somewhat after nineteenth-century models. But such schemes cannot be allowed to sink what is still in a tentative, exploratory stage: the analysis and theoretical explanation of the shifting direction of religious movement.

ACKNOWLEDGMENT

I wish to thank Matthew Schoffeleers, Jean Comaroff, Terence Ranger, Hilda Kuper, John Peel, Bengt Sundkler, Don Handelman, Wim van Binsbergen and Pnina Werbner. They read an earlier draft of this chapter, and made suggestions for improving it.

CHAPTER 9

POSTSCRIPT

Religious Movement in History

This book represents a synthesis of different approaches, in studies from different ethnographic areas. In the early chapters I built my discussion around the sequencing of practice in ritual passages. In later chapters my emphasis was upon shifts in sacred journeys, from the situational and repetitive, to serial transformations in histories of religious pluralism.

I am aware that the method I have used, and the very nature of my theoretical interest itself, is open to criticism. My method has followed cases on an increasing scale, running from privacy or intimacy, as in wisdom divination and demonic possession, through the public reconstruction of the person in sacrifice and masquerade, up to the widest relocation, as found in large-scale cults and churches. As shown in this volume, mine is a cumulative view of religious movement, one that draws on spatial metaphors of passage and journey, and on the visual representation of form, such as that of coordinate axes. The criticism all of this invites is the one that Fabian (1983) has made against so much anthropology in general.

Fabian has discerned "a preponderance of visual-spatial presentation of the Other in anthropology" (1983:122). His accusation is that "visualization and spatialization," like the stance of observer toward the observed, prejudice knowledge. They are not merely reductive, but are strategies for distancing the Other. Anthropologists become observer-gatherers, exploiters of space, in other words. Their strategies function to deny that the producers and the objects of anthropological discourse belong to the same time and are truly "coeval." As strategies in the power relations of the West to the Rest, they reinforce dominance, political hegemony, and "intellectual imperialism."

I find the criticism mistaken. Accepting it blocks all understanding of the locational force of religious movement. It imposes a political censorship of its own upon studies of the visual and the spatial among *any* people, never mind the Other. In rejecting Fabian's criticism, I have pursued a transformational interest in location.

Among other points, I have posed the following salient questions as markers for my research: How do the people find themselves, over time, in a cosmos, whether microcosm or macrocosm? How, as homecomers, strangers, or the estranged, do they symbolically locate order and disorder in their universe? How, in ritually recreating the felt qualities of their experience, do they powerfully recenter or decenter, according to their own vision, a preferred version of reality?

The answers, like the questions themselves, call for anthropological knowledge that is informed by the people's own views seen in the light of comparative theory. My own *long-term* observation—and I use the word aware of how much I had to see in order to know—of "going to Mwali," in the most widespread cult of God Above in Southern Africa points to an important direction. I observed numerous, fine micro-historical religious changes in repeated fieldwork between 1960 and 1985. Many were in response to instability in local organization, continuing from the colonial to the neocolonial period. Among those changes that resulted from instability were fluctuations due to long-term tensions between priest and chief, between cult officials and tribal rulers, and between political community and religious organization across and between the components of political comunity. Most of these changes were not innovations—or rather, they were not what is dominantly looked at by students of African religious movements when they discuss innovation. Their concern has overwhelmingly been the religious responses to "the shattered microcosm," as van Binsbergen aptly puts it (1979:34).

All too rarely has there been any study in depth and over generations of the change through which people sustain, renew, and reproduce their own vision of a cosmos. My fieldwork has led me to begin to overcome that neglect. In Chapter 7, I demonstrated how it is that the cosmology of the Mwali cult has not become what Janzen would call one of "the exhausted paradigms of the culture" (cited in Fernandez 1978:225, for an alternative view of the cult see Schoffeleers 1979, and my reply in Werbner 1983). My account illuminates the importance of

conflicting tendencies toward inclusiveness and exclusiveness in relation to a characteristic image the people have of the macrocosm, of the
widest order overarching the known divisions of mankind, or in Lévi-
Strauss' phrase, "an idea something like that of a humanity without
frontiers" (1966:166).

In my view religious innovation in ritual passages and sacred
journeys cannot be contained by the periodicity of colonialism, or the
encounters of the West with the Rest. That is another reason why I
would argue that we must see beyond Fabian's view of spatializing the
Other. More positively, I extend my perspective to the reconstruction
of the microcosm and sacred centrality over a longer duration than
recent colonial history. This interest has led me to transformations in
West African personal security cults.

In the personal security cults, beginning before the colonial period,
there has been first a waxing and later a waning of sacred centrality.
During the waxing phase, northern-based shrines increased their importance as central places. Long-distance pilgrimage to them took
place, and they provided ritual protection, in the form of portable
shrine bits, for the peaceful crossing of strangers throughout the social
field. The shrines have continued to serve as the fixed points of focus
for particularistic networks of exchange, communication, and trade.

The shrines, however, also have become the cardinal points of
socio-geographic orientation for the social field as a whole. They have
served both the social field's north sector of savannah and its south
sector of forest. Later, in the waning phase, their scope narrowed to,
at most, one sector or the other of the social field. Thus southerners
tended, in the main, not to import satellite shrines from the north;
the long-distance pilgrimage from the south to the north declined
drastically; non-regional cults waxed along with the waning of regional
cults; and less attention was paid to the appropriation in ritual of exotic
forms from distant or alien socio-geographic zones.

For purposes of analysis, I found it essential to contextualize the
shifts in cults and cult modes. I did so by taking account of major
economic and political changes across the wider social field. One was
the colonization of southern cocoa farms. Another was the replacement
of a precolonial flow of slaves from the north to the south by a flow
of labor migrants, hired for a share of the crop, yet still coming to the
south as inferiors fit for menial jobs but not fit for intermarriage or the
local citizen's rights to land. In addition, the cults were effected by the
changes in processes of state formation, such as the emergence of super-
tribes or quasi-nations within the nation.

From one phase to the next, the personal security cults continued
to be linked to inequality between hosts and strangers and to a cultural

predicament of strangerhood. But at stake in the shifts in cult mode was the dominance and control over different kinds of strangers, as well as the cultural mastery of strangerhood itself. There was an interplay between cult change and change in the wider field. Much depended upon replacing the kind of stranger who was most problematic or dangerous and upon remaking the power relations between strangers and non-strangers or hosts.

This account led me to the inner logic of ritual forms in the successive cult modes. It is an inner logic that is best understood in terms of a ritual inscription of personal security. The swing was from the inscription of personal security in terms of *things* (namely through bonds of substance, including bits of soil from the central places, and through communion in commensality) to the inscription in terms of *persons* (by means of spirit possession).

My hypothesis is that there is a systematic connection between ritual inscription and problematic strangerhood. Secondly, I suggest that the inner logic works according to either a relation of *contact,* such as the metonymic relation between parts and wholes of things, or a relation of *resemblances and differences,* as in a metaphoric relation of *persons.* It varies whether a metonymic or a metaphoric relation suits the reinscription of identity within a personal security circle. When the most problematic stranger is the cultural alien, one with whom there is no prior bond of substance, the ritual passage toward personal security is embodied by means of imported things, and identity is reinscribed through the metonymic relation with strangers. Alternatively, when the internal stranger, from another part of one's own community, is the most problematic, the ritual passage involves intrusive persons (as spirits); in such cases, identity is reinscribed through the metaphoric relation with strangers.

On the basis of my account of polyethnic churches in Southern Africa, I would put forth a related hypothesis about religious movements of the macrocosm. My suggestion is that just as variations in strangerhood give rise to alternative religious movements of the microcosm, so too do alternative religious movements of the macrocosm arise in response to what I would call variations in estrangement (following Skinner 1979:282). This is one of the suggestions that I argue applies to the social field where colonialism co-occurs with a massive, capitalist extraction of labor from one economic sector to another.

My argument is about a whole range of alternatives concerned with recentering and decentering in response to the changing predicament of estrangement. These alternatives cannot be reduced to the single type of the protest movement (for a contrary view see Comaroff

1985, and my critique in Werbner 1986). Indeed, one church, the Zion Christian Church, eventually came to be typed as "conservative," at least by Africans active in the more radical political protest movements. Protest as a form of consciousness is important, and it is expressed in radical dissent by certain church members. But only in the most radically decentered of the churches has protest dominated the expression of consciousness. Such protest consciousness prevailed in the migratory church, which used the imagery of displacement in this world and which, until the postcolonial period, was without any sacred central place. The dominant form of consciousness expressed in the other churches has varied from outright acquiescence, identifying conservatively with the market economy and the state, to symbolic ambivalence.

An argument of images arose. Each church in a series differentiated its own version of the location of the person within God's space–time. The differentiation situated the saved by baptism along the way to God's promised land. At one extreme was the imagery of the church permanently at home in Zion. In-between came the imagery of the church in the temporary encampment of the Pentecost. Finally there was the imagery of displacement, of God's chosen people wandering homeless in the Wilderness. From one extreme to the other, a more radical dislocation pervaded the cosmos; what had been the cosmos was broken down by the dominance of Chaos. It is an argument of images in which, under conditions of estrangement and oppression, some people proclaim the promise of an end to estrangement in this world, and others envision the end of this world for the fulfillment of God's promise.

My aim in this discussion has been a holistic one. It has been to account for the differences as well as the resemblances within a whole set of religious movements, including indigenous cults. This aim has raised a conceptual problem of the kind we encountered in discussing processual form and the totalizing tendency in ritual passages. This problem is the use of a coordinate system for a comparative framework of semantic analysis. I find that there is systematic variation from church to church in the imagery each creates for locating the person within the cosmos. Using a coordinate system helps, in my view, to conceptualize what the systematic variation in locational imagery is as a whole. Moreover, it also helps us to appreciate a dynamic tension in semantic terms within the locational imagery. We are able to see how that dynamic tension is important for the relative stability or instability of the imagery in history, from the colonial past to the postcolonial present. Throughout this book I have exercised the anthropologist's privilege of cross-cultural interpretation, of writing about what comes from beyond my own culture, the alien, the exotic. But I also argue that, although we, as anthropologists, arrogate this privilege to ourselves, we can never monopolize it. Much ritual moves through the appropriation of the culturally alien; some ritual is a domestication of the exotic. Images of what does not belong to a culture are often as familiar as images of home and what does belong within it. Similarly, the pull of centers of value within the community or society is often great, but so too is the pull of the centers beyond it. Thus, if anthropologists are sometimes footloose strangers, the people themselves, at home and on their journeys, are almost always translators of culture.

NOTES

CHAPTER 2:
Kalanga Demonic Possession:
The Cultural Reconstruction of a Domestic Domain

1. I saw no young girls in full ritual costume and possessed. I was told that a host performs regularly only after becoming an adult. However, the following are the details told to me in the 1960s concerning the recruitment of hosts in the part of the eastern Botswana chieftancy that I know best: ten hosts were recruited as young girls before marriage; eighteen were recruited after marriage; and fourteen were recruited at a time unknown to me. In 1964–65, these forty-two hosts represented roughly twenty percent of the 208 adult women in that part of the chieftancy.

2. In the four wards I know best, I collected the following information on inheritance from the hosts themselves or from their immediate and knowledgeable kin: from the mother's mother, nineteen hosts; from the mother, three; from the mother's sister, two; from the father's mother, two; from the father's sister, four. I was unable to get information on the remaining twelve hosts in that part of the chieftancy. I asked the local diviners their opinions about which kinswoman is the most likely predecessor of a host. They all agreed that a woman was most likely to get her *zenge* from her mother's mother.

3. In opposition to the danger of a lion, and all that it represents, the homestead at its founding should be ritually encircled under the protection of a senior patrikins-man. The homestead's founder should invite a senior patrikinsman (a patrilineal

parallel cousin, brother, or father's brother) to draw the branch of a hardwood, *Mswazi*, for his children round all but the entrance of the new site, whereupon the founder and all his dependents enter. Long ago, Kalanga say, this was always done, so that a lion could not enter, but now the practice is often not observed. I did not see it done, although I did see diviners' herbs being used for protective purposes to encircle the space of a new homestead.

4. *Mana* also has the sense of forcing disproportion, squeezing a misfit.

5. *Mbvana* is usually the term in Kalanga. *Dombo* also has the sense of knoll, which is the inadequate translation I gave in an earlier publication (1972:249). The macrocosm has a go-between in the *hosana* (see Chapter 7). The *hosana* carries bodily, in one direction, ash and thus hot waste or impurity out of the community upwards toward God Above and, in the other direction, cool soil ritually in contact with God Above, and thus purity, downwards from God Above toward the community. The host as go-between *(dombo)* is to the microcosm and the demons what the *wosana* is to the macrocosm and God Above. Hence the two go-betweens in sacred exchange are counterparts, not twins. The *wosana* can be a person or a doe, but the host is always a Lion *(shumba)*. In bloody sacrifice, a relation with the wild is also recognized for men and the public domain. At the front, in the west, a man's shrine of stones for the divinities of the dead is the "Great Lion" *(shumba wulu)*. But, in that, the wild is fixed in place in an inanimate form, and lacks the personification of a go-between. The sacrificial victim I show in Chapter 3 is broken down into its parts; its vitality is released; it is recombined with other things; and it is reconstituted as something to be consumed in fulfillment of the reciprocity between living and dead.

6. Venda speak Karanga during their possession (Blacking 1986).

7. See Firth's discussion of the role of mediator and his suggestion, which evidence from Kalanga sustains, "that externalization of responsibility is an important function of spirit possession" (1964:64).

8. *Isvi tamudana. Tomubikila zvogwadza. Takandila tibata imwi. Ndimwi munomusila kaba. Ndiko timudana wali.*

9. *Hateli imi. Nde zve bawumbe ne bachembere na mme gulu.*

10. See my discussion of the smearing of an elder's shrine in Chapter 3.

11. This and plastering are important acts at a land shrine, and women are exhorted to fulfil this obligation for the community where they live.

12. Men have the duty of gathering up firewood struck in the wild by lightning, so that it does not become domestic firewood —a confusion of things. As matter out of place, it would be a "stopper" *(chamwi)*, blocking the rain from falling on the earth. Men gather the wood, while the women meet at a land shrine or near it, where they sing and dance in a ritually licensed and bawdy style. This is known as *mayile*.

13. One song of *mayile* that women sing, while the men are gathering wood struck by lightning and other "stoppers," is "My husband is a flute *(nyele)*. I fetch wood with him; I fetch water with him; I carry him round my waist."

14. Hosts who share the same predecessor may be spoken of, loosely, as "having the *zenge*" of the deceased: it "arrived" *(yasvika)* to each. But the secret and usually risible *zenge* name by which each host is summoned to perform is hers alone, not shared with anyone else. Close ties between kinswomen of adjacent generations limit the transmission of the role. In usual practice, only the daughter or own brother's daughter of a living host takes on the role herself. In no instances that I recorded did a host become recruited when she had only a mother's sister as a living host in the previous generation, although two hosts received a demon from a mother's sister.

15. Diviners told me that a mother ought not to *musa,* "awaken," her daughter's *zenge* during initiation, and that special herbs had to be prepared for her to do so. In the past, an initiator usually served for her sister's or brother's daughter, her sister and, in very special circumstances, for her daughter-in-law, but I found no case where a host did so for her son's daughter.

16. The shrine stones are to the returned dead as divinities what the gravestones are to the male elder as newly buried. It is prohibited to burn fire above either a shrine or gravestones.

17. The chase and seizure also represented a further fault and its ritual treatment. I refer to the host's initiation by her mother-in-law. The reluctant woman had married her cognate, despite the marriage bar. She became a customary prey for the demons because of this, whereas she would have been excluded from this band otherwise, as either a remote kinswoman or an affine. As both, she was anomalous and required a special initiation. Kalanga use such anomalies to circumvent prescriptions that would otherwise bar a woman, such as this senior elder's wife, from becoming a host. She had no living close kinswoman to initiate her, though she claimed that her mother had been a host.

18. The plural is used usually in referring to demons and divinities of the dead. A woman may have more than one demon.

19. That is, the demons and their wrath.

20. Her mother prefers going to a diviner to find an alternative explanation and treatment for affliction, rather than receiving the demon.

21. One host is reluctant to become possessed fearing other hosts.

22. Mr. Timon Mongwa transcribed this song in Kalanga during my fieldwork in 1961 in Zimbabwe. After he checked his transcription against a tape-recording, he translated the text literally; I revised his translation, slightly, only after discussion with Badlanje, the singer. The other *mazenge* songs and texts are my own translations from my fieldwork in Botswana.

23. I quote directly from Badlanje's exegesis of the song.

24. A senior host wears a black string of bast as a bracelet or necklace amulet, *psveko;* a senior elder wears a bracelet, *linga,* around his right wrist, having succeeded to his father's name and position. A patient may later wear a bracelet of red, white, and black beads. To remove it is once again to risk affliction and the wrath of demons.

25. "Creeping, creeping," *manyawi nyawi*, is gooseflesh, the creeping of the flesh.

26. "Mine" refers to her junior host and also the demon that she complains is refusing to be invoked; her junior host was reluctant to join in possession, and was denying the congregation her ritual services.

27. Again, in the immediate context, "child" refers to her junior.

28. The following is the text in Kalanga. I checked my transcription with the host herself:

> Ye dombo,
> Ye dombo ladzina mazenge.
> Tikwe,
> Pataka zana.
> Nadanyala, andinga kone.
> Pataka zana.
> She baka mukosi dema.
> Mashumba manya matoko.
> Manyawi nyawi.
> Ndzimu we bamwe inowa.
> Wangu inonga we duni.
> Linokwa likalala pazhe.
> Banji bakapela ntolo.
> Katsena kungafe imi.
> Katsena kungafe imi.
> Mwanangu kasala kuzhe.
> Tipile ndzimu we tate.
> Ndzimu wa Ta Tuelo
> Wangu wakasima chini?
> Wangu inonga we duni.
> Linokwa lino lala pazhe.
> Chimbo chikwibila beni basipo.
> Tipile ndzimu we tate.

29. The name is fictitious, to protect the privacy of individuals, and uses the convention, *Baka* . . . (Mother of . . .), and *Ta* . . . (Father of . . .).

30. To "fear" is to "respect," and the mother's sister turned the remark about, so that she could challenge her sister's daughter with failing to show respect in a visit.

31. For an analysis of charges as distinct from other accusations, see Schapera 1955, 1969. Colonial magistrates' records of sorcery charges, some involving Kalanga, are examined in Crawford 1967.

CHAPTER 3:

Kalanga Sacrifice:
The Restorative Movement of Divinities and People

1. In my terminology distinguishing the various roles in sacrifice, I follow the translation of Hubert and Mauss (1964).

2. In their description, as distinct from their general model and main argument, Hubert and Mauss mention the coming and incarnation of a goddess during the course of a sacrifice in response to human appeals (1964:42); they also mention the expulsion of a divine element in the form of a divinized bull (1964:55). They make the general point that "the expulsion of a sacred spirit . . . is a primordial component of sacrifice, as primordial and irreducible as communion" (1964:6). But this point has to be read in the light of their focus on the victim. In the victim is a spirit or religious principle or force, as they variously call it, which is released through sacrificial slaughter and thus expelled to the divine world. Also discussed is the sacrifice of a god who descends to enter a victim and be incarnated. But throughout their text what is not conceptualized is the movement of divinities who are not in the victim but who are yet too close to the sacrifier. Here I am grateful to Maurice Bloch for urging me to clarify my understanding of the text. An important exception is Evans-Pritchard's account of Nuer sacrifice in the four phases of presentation, consecration, invocation and immolation (1956). But Evans-Pritchard does not analyze the logic of the processual form; nor does he consider the implications of the four Nuer phases for the general model of Hubert and Mauss. That remains a task for that continuing industry, the reanalysis of the Nuer.

3. Although the hide is usually symbolically unstressed, it may be offered ritually by being suspended on the rack above the sacrificial shrine of an elder. After being dried, the hide becomes a resting mat for a grandmother or senior kinswoman and known as *thobo ya batategulu,* the "mat of grandfather." At a later sacrifice, that kinswoman may sit upon it by the shrine.

4. The blood is caught in a bowl for a matrilateral sacrifice or, in the case of a patrilineal sacrifice, allowed to drip from bits of the carcass which are hung on a rack above the shrine stones.

5. It has not been easy to find the best English equivalent for *ndzimu* (singular) and *midzimu* (plural). In earlier publications, I wrote of ancestral spirits or shades. Upon reflection, I consider such usage misleading. It tends to devalue the underlying religious ideas; it obscures their view of divinity as one and many. My present usage conforms better to the religious unity that Kalanga convey in speaking of *ndzimu* and *midzimu,* whether *ndzimu ye pezhugwi,* the divinity of above (God Above or Mwali), *ndzimu ya pasi,* the divinity of below (divinity of the dead), *ndzimu ye ngumba,* divinity of the hut (demon or *zenge*). Kalanga sometimes use the word *kaba,* "wrath"; for example, *musa kaba,* "to awaken wrath." Kalanga say, however, that this is a borrowing from the Tswana word, *kgaba* (see Schapera 1934). In borrowing the word, Kalanga have not borrowed the Tswana distinction between *Badimo,* "divinities," and *kgaba,* "wrath;" nor do they have the Tswana focus on color dynamics in settling wrath. *Kaba,* when used by Kalanga, is interchangeable with *midzimu,* except that *midzimu* also has a wider sense that includes possession by demons.

6. In the words of another diviner, "The blood is the very person, 'the vitamins' [in English]. Can a person live without blood? No, the blood is the very divinity."

7. As if to protect his own view, Evans-Pritchard allows that things may be different elsewhere in Africa. Thus Evans-Pritchard concedes too much to Willoughby's view that ". . . the fundamental meaning of sacrifice, according to Bantu thinking, is that of sacramental communion with the gods" (Willoughby 1928,

reprinted 1970:399). Despite Willoughby's knowledge of Kalanga practice and his considerable scholarship, he clearly was so overwhelmed by Robertson-Smith's view that he ignored the apotropaic aspects of sacrifice along with the separation of divinities and people in the eating of the meal.

8. On the color symbolism in the offering and concerning the sacrifice as a whole, I cannot comment in detail here. Within my present limits I must merely note that the entire sequence, covering grain offering and blood sacrifice, begins and ends with substances in a white/black opposition—i.e., first, white beer (called "water") on black stones and finally, white bones in black river water—and that, in between, there is a framing of red as the dangerous color. In time, however, the red also is present at the beginning and end, since the ritual begins either toward sunset or dawn and ends with the release of bone during the red of dawn.

9. Although an elder always officiates, pouring the blood and chyme, an inner congregation of close relatives may sometimes be present, such as when an elder's shrine is being consecrated.

10. She shifts between addressing her mother's brothers in her own relationship to them and in a relationship she would have as a host of *mazenge,* having received her *zenge* from her mother's sister (see Werbner 1972 and Chapter 2, above).

11. The bug of which she speaks is like the sacrificer, whose powerlessness and inferiority in relation to the divinity is thus avowed. This is the text in Kalanga:

> *Basekulu ne hazwadzi enyu, mutotodze bana. Bano kandila beti ndimwi unotika-taza ne ndzimu, hatito bereka, hatito muka zwibuyanana. Ndo murapela, baz-wadzi bangu. Nasi wamupa madjo, madjo gwa muno shaka. Nasi muboke, bazwadzi bangu. Gubungano inobe mangwana. Bathu bendi rapelesa kumundli, ndzimu angu. Nasi chiyende zwibuyana mushango ikonyana chenyu. Chilobwe ne phepo. Ndinga boka kwazwo bazwadzi bangu. Gwapela bazwadzi bangu; ndinga boka kwazo.*

12. The scale of the congregation differentiates the form of personal sacrifice in that the sacrifice of cattle is, of course, for the larger congregation, much larger than goat sacrifice.

13. *Bango,* the "fence-pole," is a dominant metaphor for authority and power in a homestead and its head as an elder. It is also used for the beer to drive away a hangover, which is drunk the day after a great beer drink and at the end of a sacrifice.

14. The hamlet is laid out along the sun's axis, a layout which makes it possible for both domestic movement and cosmic counter-movement to be simultaneous sequences. Or, rather, I am tempted to say that it is because both movements have to be simultaneous that the hamlet has to be laid out along the sun's axis.

CHAPTER 4: UMEDA MASQUERADE:
Renewing Identity and Power in the Cosmos

1. The "big men" who figure so prominently elsewhere in New Guinea are absent here.

2. The transition by means of the mask is illuminated by Jedrej's insightful comparative analysis (1980). I am beholden to Jedrej's general analysis for my own argument. But I do not agree with his view that *ida* masks are exceptional. Like others of the same general kind, the masks of *ida* "embody notions of transition, of boundaries between categories of space and time"; and it is a mistake to argue that these masks do "not mediate such categories but represent(s) them" (1980:228). Viewing the "cassowary Dancer as Tree," as Jedrej does, following Gell (1975:237), eliminates transition. Instead, in my view, man enters the Tree and becomes a Cassowary.

3. In effect, by holding the festival, villagers are able to sustain alternative forms of organization—one segmental in territories, the other nodal at central places—and to oscillate between them, while giving one a value higher than the other (on nodal forms of organization, cf. Smith 1977; Werbner 1983). The oscillation is also between two spatially and temporally separate sectors of the economy: the one of routine production, and the other of festival consumption and exchange. It is the ritual that establishes what the hierarchy of value is in terms of the alternative forms of organization and economic sectors. Thus in value, the nodal organization is ritually raised above the locally bounded organization, and consumption and exchange above production. This brief comment must suffice here, in the next chapter I give a full discussion of the economic and organizational oscillation.

4. He discusses the symbolic time expressed in the ritual's color sequences, duration, or the actual time in which the ritual is performed, and the organic process time or the succession in the human life cycle.

5. Elsewhere Gell weakens a dialectical view of these relations by collapsing the four distinguished here into three modes (1979).

6. The logic involves an inversion in the relations between categories. The extreme terms *(a, d)* are a mirror inversion of the other terms *(B, c)*, the means between the extremes.

CHAPTER 5:
Dual Organization, Axis, and Sacred Center: Dialectical Representation in the New Guinea Lowlands

1. My evidence comes from Alfred Gell's observations (1975, 1980), primarily of Umeda village, although I reject his model of Umeda society, which lacks a view of organizational contradiction and its management. Most of Umeda is at an altitude of about 900 feet, and for convenience, I refer to the micro-region around the village as the "Western Lowlands."

2. The similarity to hunter-gatherers is a subject for separate discussion. But it is worth noting that Lee's important generalization about hunter-gatherers would apply to the Western Lowlanders, ". . . central to all these cases is a pattern of concentration and dispersion, usually seasonal, and a set of rules and practices for allowing reciprocal access to, or joint exploitation of, key resources" (Lee 1976:91).

3. One hamlet has its territory in the north, the other in the south, across the river; and the mask partners of one are the marriage partners of the other. Moreover, in the extreme pair (Sinai, Wehumda), the antithesis is explicitly conceptualized: Sinai, to the north, is "in the bush" and Wehumda, to the south, is "in the village."

4. Umedas have to explain away that territorial partnership to fit their conceptualization of their other social horizons. The explanation is that this partnership is a matter of ancient history, or rather a survival from original times.

5. The apex in terms of perpetual kinship is the zenith territory, Wehumda (6); its people are "of the father." Around it are its bush partners, Asila (8), "of the mother," and Namosid (7), "of the daughter"; and by extension, their respective upstream and downstream villages, Punda and Sowanda as "mother" and "daughter" to Umeda village. Next, immediately upstream, are its juniors in the next generation, with Umda (2) as "of the elder sibling" and Klalumda (4) "of the younger sister." Only the territories immediately around Wehumda are located in this kinship geography.

The Umeda territories beyond the immediate reach of Wehumda are represented in concentric terms relative to Wehumda in the following way. In terms of palm trees, Wehumda itself is known by the greatest good, the coconut tree, which is kept at the very center of a hamlet, providing shade as well as fruit. Kedewaina (1), at the periphery with barbarians, is associated with the areca. This palm tree's name is the word for a fence to keep people or pigs out, its nut is a narcotic that is chewed during moments of transition. Planted at the fringes of inhabited sites, and a miniature of the coconut, the areca is of the inner periphery relative to the coconut. Coconut versus areca is thus an apt representation of the concentric opposition between Kedewaina and Wehumda. Similarly, the outer periphery, Efid (3) is represented by the Caryota palm. In pidgin, it is called *wail SakSak,* "wild sago," and it is virtually inedible except in a dire emergency. It grows wild in the bush, away from human habitation. Finally, the outermost periphery, Sinai (5) is simply "in the bush," as against Wehumda, which is "in the village"; and this opposition is beyond the coding in organic terms of human or tree life. (For the elaboration in myth, see Gell 1975:34–35, 125–30, on the heroes *(a)* Toag-tod, as Smoked-meat Man and the original man, *(b)* Pul-tod, Areca-nut Man and Toag-tod's younger brother/son, and *(c)* Naimo-tod, Caryota Palm and the providers of two wives *(d)* and *(e)* for Toag-tod. These heroes, *(a)* through *(e),* are respectively associated with hamlets 6, 1, 3, 2, 4, which thus covers the village community as a whole, with the exception of 5, the outermost periphery and an "offshoot" of 3.)

6. During the festival season, Wehumda (6) as the "village center," is set apart physically from its own pair of territorial partners at the zenith: they in turn are in the adjacent villages. For about eight months, during the long productive period of preparation for the festival, the reverse holds. Wehumda is then inaccessible to another pair, close to barbarians as the partners of its "bush" opposite, in hamlet (5), at the extreme north. This marginal pair, (1) and (3)—in coding, respectively the marginal "areca" and the peripheral "Caryota palm"—are forbidden to enter the territory of Wehumda "the coconut" until after the food is produced; then in *ida* itself they come together using the hamlet of the "bush" center (5) as mediator.

7. Around this intervillage center, at Iuvnugkebe ("the place of rotten houses") are

the paired villages, about half an hour's walk apart, in the greater community of Umeda and Umeda's upstream counterpart, Punda. As befits an external center, it is sited as a midpoint on the boundary, between the pair of villages, in no-man's land from an Umeda perspective (see Gell 1975:20 on the origin myth).

8. For my later discussion of concentric relations and the axial system, it is important to note also that Umeda locates itself as the middle between antithetical extremes of community and non-community. From its own perspective, moreover, Umeda is the internal community and Punda the external one; both together form the greater community, which is the limit for the perpetual exchange of masks and women. At the other extreme is non-community, which has no exchange of masks and no actual exchange of women between Sowanda and Umeda. But, conforming to the idea of dispersal, Sowanda is said to have received Umeda's daughters as wives, in ancient times, without ever having reciprocated. The relation is thus asymmetric and negative in accord with Sowanda's direction relative to Umeda. By means of this history, also, Sowanda is included within the dominant field of social exchange. Thus history is used to exclude (the territorial partnership with barbarians) or to include (the territorial partnership with the noncommunity of Sowanda) partners relative to the dominant field of social exchange.

9. Note that the axes are reduced. The transformation excludes the east–west axis, which is for the external hamlets (8 and 7) in neighboring villages, who are thus not participants in the internal perpetual exchange.

10. Further details are in order about this suggestion. The mirror has a "bend," as it were, to meet the particular locus of points and territories around Punda, as known to Umeda. For example, notice that the north–south axis is excluded in Punda, whereas in Umeda it is the east–west axis that is eliminated. This transposition fits the rotation in their situations, in terms of involvement with outsiders. Punda, by contrast, gets most of its wives from the north, and some from the south (Gell 1975:20). Hence, in regarding Punda as a mirror counterpart, for purposes of exchange, Umeda has to recognize an equivalent to its own north–south axis (Punda's north–south axis being the equivalent to the excluded east–west axis). I infer that this equivalent is the northeast–southwest axis. Hence, Umeda's north (Efid, 5) and south (Wehumda, 6) are partnered respectively with Punda's southwest (Pobonai) and northeast (Evil, i.e., "breadfruit," a name that conveys an original importance as an owner comparable to that of its counterpart, Wehumda).

11. This runs contrary to Gell's report that he "found no moiety exogamy rules in Punda" (1975:41).

12. The territory most surrounded by outsiders, Wehumda (6), of the "village," has the most masking contacts, followed by the other marginal territory, Kedewaina (1). Wehumda's mountain-locked "bush" opposite, Sinai (5), has no external contacts in mask exchange. Sinai can marry anywhere externally. The highest order center, the center of centers (Wehumda, 6) is in perpetual contact *(a)* with certain linchpin territories, *(b)* its external counterpart, apparently the original center of the paired village, and *(c)* its alter ego, which is also at the zenith and the paired village's largest hamlet. Moreover, through its alter ego, the center of centers has

the same kind of access across villages that others have only within the village community.

CHAPTER 6:
"Totemism" in History:
The Sacred Crossing of West African Strangers

1. Goody mentions some ancient movement in a different direction: one cult "is said to have migrated, together with its practitioners, from Techniman [on the edge of the Brong chiefdoms in the south] to Gonja [in the northwest] about a century ago" (1956:360).

2. According to MacLeod, "By the early 1960s anti-witchcraft powers were being sought and imported from as far away as Wogadougou or even Gao" (1975:113).

3. A word must be said about McLeod's account (1975), which is somewhat puzzling in the light of Field's evidence. McLeod appears to echo Ward's views based on observation in the 1940s (Ward 1956), rather than provide firsthand evidence, from his more recent fieldwork, on the import of shrines. Ward reported "Ashanti statements that the old gods did not know how to deal with witchcraft" (1956:42). Similarly, McLeod echoes,

> This intra-lineage maleficence, Asante believe, can only be combatted by imported and almost entirely Northern based cults, which not only offer to catch witches (as did the earlier ordeals) but to protect those who subscribe to them from the activity of witches. (1975:112)

He writes as if *bosom-brafo* shrines were things of the distant past (1975:108) and contends that the Northern cults "continue to be introduced into Asante today" (1975:109). However, he gives no account of such a cult or shrine being introduced from the north during his fieldwork, and merely presents, from hearsay, accounts of shrines imported in the 1940s and 1950s (1975: 113ff). See also Note 2.

4. More evidence is needed about those personal security cults from the north that were not completely displaced by the mid-1950s. A key case is Krakyi Dente with its "active shrines in Akim and Kwahu" (Field 1960:90). It may, perhaps, have been primarily limited to its own immediate "socio-geographic region," with pilgrims primarily coming from the adjacent Akim and Kwahu areas near the sovereign shrine. Its placement, the location of its sovereign shrine, and its heartland and hinterland, all appear to remove it from involvement in relations across great cultural and social distances from the north sector to the south. Tigare, the imported cult that seems to have taken the longest to decline, was also apparently a relatively early one, with its first shrine in northwest Ashanti, during the First World War (Field 1960:90). In the early 1970s it still had "two branches" in Winneba, the chief Effutu town, "although their importance had recently diminished" (Wyllie 1973:75). Note that Debrunner estimates that:

> Roughly speaking, there have been three main crests in the waves of anti-witchcraft shrines: before 1912, between 1924 and the economic crisis, and in and after World War II. At each of these times the influx of foreign ideas was particularly strong and the country had something of an economic boom. (1959:107)

5. A later swing in the opposite direction is apparent in the expulsion of foreigners from Ghana in late 1969 and early 1970; but this state-fostered intolerance of "aliens" is beyond the limits of my discussion (see Peil 1979).

6. Skinner observed that "relations between the C.P.P. and the strangers of Kumasi deteriorated when after the election of June 1954 many local Gao, Mossi, Yoruba, and Hausa chiefs declared themselves in favour of the newly created National Liberation Movement which was anti-C.P.P." (1963:313).

7. Polarization that is non-directional or multi-directional entails quite different relations between the subprocesses and, of course, a corresponding variation in the pattern of shrines, heartlands, and hinterlands. However, to consider these alternatives is well beyond the limits of this chapter.

CHAPTER 7:
Regional Cult of God Above:
Achieving and Defending the Macrocosm

1. Mopane *(Colophosperma Mapane),* also spelled "mopani," is an African ironwood tree that yields hard, durable timber.

2. The cult's domain also coincides, roughly, with the distribution of Khami-type Iron Age buildings (with the exception of Mtoko, in the east; for a map, see Summers 1961:9). The somewhat wider distribution of Zimbabwe-type buildings extends beyond the present cult domain into the Korekore-Zezuru areas to the north, where cults of local and territorial spirits have their domains (see Garbett 1977).

3. Daneel (1974:109) stresses hostility and opposition between Zionist churches and the cult's staff at the cardinal oracle of Matonjeni, though he also mentions more cooperative relations between the cult and Ethiopian-type churches. In Botswana, the southwestern priest, Ntogwa, cooperated in various ways with leaders of the Bethannia Mission Apostolic Church and J. E. Mtembo's Church of Christ.

4. Included in the cult are such ethnically different people as Kalanga (Holub 1881; O'Neill 1920; Richards 1942; Sebina 1947; Gelfand 1966), Karanga (Knöthe 1888; von Sicard 1952; Daneel 1970, 1971), Venda (Schwellnus 1888; Stayt 1931; van Warmelo 1940), Ndau (Daneel 1970: 57), Khurutse (Schapera 1971), Ndebele (Campbell 1926; Ranger 1967), and others. I am not sure whether Namzwa to the north, near Wankie, have congregations.

5. Ranger (1967:378) reads his own interpretation, somewhat mistakenly, into a cult lament which Mr. Timon Mongwa transcribed for me, and I translated with his help. The text is not "a despairing lament for the ruin created in the Shona world by the white man and the powerlessness of the defeated to do anything about it." Nor does it express "a mood of despondency" (Daneel 1970:35). It expresses moral outrage and complaint—a refusal to be defeated—as shown by the chorus and remarks at the time. The prevailing attitude of protest and complaint

in cult songs is explained thus by Kalanga themselves, "A child must cry so that his father will heed his suffering."

6. At a different time, and on a domestic occasion, an adept may act as a host of Mazenge and be possessed by a demon. (See Chapter 2 and Werbner 1964, 1971, 1972 and also Daneel 1970:51 on Jukwa possession in the cult of Mwari.)

7. Her husband, Shologulu (The Great Head), dwells in the sky to the south, Her Son, Lunji (The Awl), to the west; and She Herself, to the east. She and Her Son go back and forth and communicate with each other and Shologulu via a shooting star. Note that Kalanga bury a corpse, on the left side, oriented in accord with the trinity thus: its face toward the south, its head to the east, and feet to the west, along the sun's path.

8. When an elder, after reciting Her praise poetry, professed to me the conventional piety that She has one breast because that suffices for all, another elder interjected, "Tell him the truth —it's because she is too stingy that she has only one." Her parts are half a person's: one eye, ear, nose, arm, and leg. (See also Cockin 1879 for an early missionary's report.) She is an embodiment of unity where human beings embody duality.

9. The fund is conceived of as one whole from the congregation. Neighbors know, at the time, who contributes, since the collections are made or announced at public meetings. But it is taboo to make a permanent record of this public knowledge, by writing down a list of donors and contributions.

10. A close kinsman of a deceased cult messenger once boasted to me about the debt his kinsman incurred through such embezzlement.

11. Another is at a cardinal oracle in the Matopo Hills, which is called Dula (Granary), apparently after the shape of its rock. In the past, during the youth of the oldest living elders, valuables were stored at the senior cardinal oracle, Njelele, including durables such as hoes, and consumer goods such as tobacco, hides, and cloth. A ruler or locally important elder was, on occasion, given a hoe from the store.

12. These are: Chichi, Mapokani, Vaka, Mpini, Makwela, Jeshen, and Madlambudzi.

13. These are: besides the six shown in detail on Figure 59 (including Letsholathebe outside the Tati Reserve), Mpapo, Nkange, Dagwe, Goshwe, Sinete, Mzonga, and Matobo.

14. Vumbu was, like his father, a dancer of *hosho* (the gourd rattle) and a singer of its somewhat satirical ballads. This dance is performed for recreation and ridicule at rituals and also beer parties. It is the dance Mwali prefers to the Gumba-Gumba and pop music on records. Note also that Galani, too, never became possessed or wore a black sash, although she otherwise dressed and danced as a *wosana*.

15. From north to south in 1974: Mathamngwane, Tonota, and Mmadinare.

16. Just as Habangana had then, the territory surrounding the chiefdom currently enjoys a recently enhanced political significance, as well as room for immigration

and expansion (presently lacking at Habangana). Then Habangana was, in various respects, foremost among the set of newly independent Kalanga chiefdoms in the Tati Reserve (see Werbner 1971a). Similarly, Letsholatebe's new political community on the State Lands, formed under one territorial ruler by the Government, was potentially the most prominent in the region. It covers a large part of the State Lands (including Thema Shanga) acquired by the nation in 1969 from a colonial company; and it exceeds Habangana in size and perhaps in population.

17. I am grateful to Mr. Harry Finnigan for the *Botswana Daily News* references. In reply to my enquiries and at Mr. Finnigan's suggestion, the *News* reporter, Mr. Mishingo Mpaphadzi, kindly wrote an additional, unpublished, account for me.

18. This is a smaller zone of wooded steppe containing abundant Acacia and Comiphora.

19. Cockin, a missionary at Hope Fountain in 1879, mentions three oracles in the Matopo Hills (Cockin 1879, cited in Ranger 1967:145), as follows, *relative to his mission station:* Ematjetjeni (Matonjeni) to the east, Entjeleli (Njelele) to the south, and Umkombo to the southwest. (I am grateful to Mr. Richard Brown for supplying me with Cockin's full text.) Another oracle, contemporary with them, is mentioned by Holub for the northwest in 1876 at the Maitengwe River (Holub 1881:64). Note that all these oracles continue into the twentieth century. I disagree with Ranger's view of Cockin's report *(loc. cit.)*. Ranger eliminates one of the central oracles; he mistakes a lesser oracle outside the central Matopo Hills near Mangwe for a cardinal oracle.

20. At a cardinal oracle of Matonjeni, two offices are distinguished: that of shrine keeper, customarily a Venda, and that of priest, customarily from the Shoko (Monkey) clan among Mbire. This distinction is not maintained in the western regions. *Lumbi,* "minstrel," is the term that was commonly used for the priest, Ntogwa, who also spoke of himself as "Leader" *ntungamili.* Similarly here, unlike at Matonjeni, the term *wosana* is used for both male and female adepts.

21. Newman (1971) records, "In the Matopo Hills in Zimbabwe there is a remarkably dense population [of eagles], possibly the most concentrated eagle population known anywhere in the world." Note the snake eagle is a friend of man in that it preys on snakes. I am tempted to suggest that the two figures of the famous Zimbabwe figurine may be a snake eagle or a martial eagle and its prey, a monitor lizard.

22. According to Kalanga tradition, the oracle of Mwali came from: (1) Lutombo Lutema to (2) Bambudzi, (3) Zhomba, (4) Chizeze, (5) Mavula Majena, (6) Njelele, (7) Dula, (8) Manyangwa, (9) Njenjema, and to (10) Ntogwa.

23. In the region I know best, the priest Ntogwa succeeded his sister Mantali (Baka Pasi), and also claimed that Njenje was his paternal grandfather. His father, Matafeni, was an important official at Njelele. He claimed Venda origin for his patriline in a Zebra clan *(Dube* or *Ntembo).* Njenjema, a priest of the northwest, was said to be of the Monkey clan *(Shoko* or *Ncube,* praise-name Luvimbi), although this may be the cult totem, Zebra being his own clan. Manyangwa, the northern priest, is a Leya.

24. Other oracles apparently under Matonjeni are these two: (1) the oracle sometimes known as Magubu (perhaps a hereditary title), which has been southeast of
Fort Usher and under Mtabani then Magubu (Richards 1942:55; "Majuba," Gelfand
1966:35ff; Maguhu, Daneel 1970:41), and (2) the oracle at Shangonyima–Jahunda,
in turn under Tapa, Mike, and Kamba (Knöthe 1888; Schwellnus 1888; Posselt
1927:530ff; Richards, *ibid.*). The first oracle is the one that figures so largely,
indeed too largely, in Ranger's account (1967:149); the second has been especially
important for Venda in the Transvaal and in the Gwanda District.

25. Maswabi III told it to Gelfand (1966:40) as an account of attendance at Dula,
rather than as an account of the order in which oracles were established and thus
the order or line of seniority.

26. An example that is also significant for my analysis of policy-making illustrates
this. Ntogwa described three steps when he told me how Njenjema of the northwestern oracle rescued a missionary, Reed, before Ndebele warriors attacked whites
in 1896 (a rescue confirmed by Reed's letter 1 September 1896). Njenjema first took
Reed under his protection to Manyangwa, his senior *(wola)*, then reported *(biga)*
Reed, and finally brought him to the safety of a settlers' town, Bulawayo (see also
Reed 4 April 1896 in Ranger 1967:189). In anticipation of my later analysis, I must
stress that these priests, and later their oracles, acted in coordination, according to
a hierarchy.

27. Note that Kalanga, both from the cult's domain and outside it, also approach
the Tswapong oracle as supplicants; some Kalanga claim Tswapong ethnic origins.

28. Ranger (1967:187) misreports that I was "told that [a] high priest had been shot
at Mangwe in 1896 by a fellow American." Despite his assertion, it is not so that
"there can be little doubt that the man killed and called Jobani or Tshobani was *the
High Priest of Mwari for the southwest,* remembered by the Kalanga today under the
name Habangana" (my italics). Kalanga told me that during the war, Armstrong
murdered Chief Bango's *messenger,* his parallel cousin. Hobani (no connection with
Botswana's Chief Habangana of the same *totem,* Zebra, but not of the Bango clan);
Zviposa, the *priest,* continued to perform near Mangwe, clandestinely, even after
the war. His oracle was a *junior* southwestern one. In 1960–61, I observed that
Chief Bango sent adepts and a messenger to the cardinal oracle of the priest
Maswabi at Dula in Kubutu Cave. I must record also, sadly, that in 1984 Chief
Bango himself became the innocent victim of war; he was murdered, according to
his family, by soldiers seeking armed enemies of the new state. For further criticism
of Ranger's thesis, see Cobbing 1977 and the response to my own and others'
criticisms in Ranger 1979:*x–xii,* 1985.

29. Ranger (1967) misses the general accord in the crescent from Chilimanzi south
and eastward, and including Gutu, Chibi, Ndanga along with others, because he
isolates each instance and treats as exceptional any congregation such as Ndanga's,
which opposed the war (see Selous 1896:238).

30. Ranger modifies his views in the light of my earlier criticism (1977), but he
considers that I do not fully appreciate the difference between normal and crisis
times: "Werbner has seen the Mwali cult in operation 'normally'" (Ranger
1979:*xiii).* I did observe the recent crisis period while I was in Botswana, but the

history of the cult in Zimbabwe during the guerilla war is a subject for further research.

CHAPTER 8:
Churches of the Spirit:
The Argument of Images from Zion to the Wilderness

1. My interpretation differs somewhat from that of Hastings in his wide-ranging history of African Christianity. Hastings sees a continuing emphasis in the Wilderness Church on centrality and a house of prayer, albeit one that is a symbol of a pilgrim journey.

> [The church] centred around a sort of convent of nuns, "The Ark of the Covenant." The Ark was a house of prayer marking the true centre of the church, first at Korsten, then at Marrapodi and now in Nairobi. . . . As Ark, "this house" is both Noah's ark and ark of the covenant—the central symbol of a pilgrim journey, of salvation and divine presence. (Hastings 1979:249)

Hastings bases his interpretation primarily on Dillon-Malone, and I consider that this source favors my interpretation, the imagery being of a "carrier of God's presence" (Dillon-Malone 1978:64). On the saving ark as, first, an ark of wood and then, an ark of persons, "the mothers of the covenant"; and on the gradual shift in the notion of "house" and "temple," see Dillon-Malone (1978:65–67). Prayer "walks" through the "house," in the person of the Sisters.

2. The following discussion concentrates on the upper quadrants of the framework. To consider the developmental problems of shifts in image across the whole set would take me well beyond my present limits. But I must note that I know of no African church or cult that establishes itself permanently around the disharmonic image of total Chaos. Indeed, I am doubtful that it would happen, except perhaps as a transitory moment, given the usual tendency for churches to foster *some* quest for Cosmos in the imagery of Person or Space. The wholly chaotic image may suit conditions of self-estrangement that are beyond my present scope.

3. More concretely, the caution is this: The African church imagery that I do discuss here, and certain mission imagery that I do not, are in contrasting senses disharmonic. The former has Person positive and Space negative (a framed, unfocused image, in my terms) and the latter has Person negative and Space positive (an unframed, focused image). Ignoring the difference, van Binsbergen and Schoffeleers have tried to ask for the same answer to a question about mission imagery and African church imagery, despite their being structurally and significantly poles apart 1985:31). There is no point in confusing them.

4. Note that along with the Wilderness Church's relative lack of interest in physical healing goes a primary regard for the external person, as the subject of lustration, and a disregard for the internal person, through the rejection of eucharistic sacraments. Inner and outer are not at one here, and the inner is dislocated.

5. My impression is, also, that the churches differ in the relative emphasis each

puts on the divide between member and non-member, with the Apostolic churches putting the greater emphasis (see also Hastings 1979:77). In this respect, one might say that Person is emphasized over Space or place in the imagery of the Apostolic churches and conversely Space is emphasized over Person in the Zionist case.

6. A word is in order about the link to South Africa's ZCC. In many respects, Bishop Mutendi modeled his church along lines similar to the South African ZCC founded by Lekhanyane in 1925. At that time, Bishop Mutendi had already spent two years in Zimbabwe as a Zionist evangelist, and Lekhanyane, whom he supported in a schism, ordained him as a minister in his own right. He remained loyal to Lekhanyane until Lekhanyane's death. There was thus a personal link between the two church founders, but their two churches became virtually autonomous (see Daneel 1971:298ff).

7. The order of congregations is from the local *(kireke)*, which meets weekly with neighbors as members, to the interlocal *(sabata)*, which is the occasional weekend gathering of members of different nearby *kireke,* to the pilgrimage congregation of the annual *penta* or *paseka.* The *paseka* is the only occasion for a eucharistic communion and for exorcism rites, and therefore involves services not given at the sites merely for the *kireke* or *sabata.* However, the critical criterion for an annual pilgrimage congregation became not the place *per se,* i.e., the center at the founder's home or elsewhere, but the presence of Johane Maranke or later his son, in person. He performed the same rituals at the numerous remote *paseka* sites and at his headquarters, the major difference being in the size of his congregation, with a maximum of about 20,000 pilgrims at the main *paseka* in the Maranke reserve (see Murphree 1969:92ff; Daneel 1971:330–31).

REFERENCES

Akesson, S. K.
1950   The Secret of Akom. African Affairs 49:237–45, 325–33.

Aquina, Mary
1967   The People of the Spirit: An Independent Church in Rhodesia.
         Africa 37:203–219.
1969   Zionists in Rhodesia. Africa 39:113–137.

Austin, D. E.
1964   Politics in Ghana. London: Oxford University Press for the Royal
         Institute of International Affairs.

Babcock, Barbara A.
1978   Too Many, Too Few: Ritual Modes of Signification. Semiotica
         23:291–302.

Bailey, F. G.
1969   Stratagems and Spoils. Oxford: Blackwell.

Bartels, M.
1903   Der Wurfelzaüber südafrikanischer Völker. Zeitschrift für
         Ethnologie 35:338–78.

Barth, Frederick
1971   Tribes and Intertribal Relations in the Fly Headwaters. Oceania
         41:171–91.

347

Bateson, G.
    1973   Steps in the Ecology of the Mind. Frogmore, St. Albans: Paladin.

Beck, Brenda
    1969   Colour and Heat in South Indian Ritual. Man (N.S.) 4:553–72.

Bernstein, B.
    1972   A Sociolinguistic Approach to Socialisation, with some Reference
            to Educability. In Directions in Social Linguistics. J.J. Gumperz
            and D. Hymes, eds. New York: Holt, Rinehart and Winston.

Blacking, J.
    1985   The Context of Venda Possession Music—Reflections on the
            Effectiveness of Symbols. International Yearbook for Traditional
            Music 3:63–87.

Bloch, M.
    1974   Symbol, Song, Dance and Features of Articulation. European
            Journal of Sociology 15:55–81.
    1985   From Cognition to Ideology. In Power and Knowledge:
            Anthropological and Sociological Approaches. Richard Fardon,
            ed. Edinburgh: Scottish Academic Press.
    1986   From Blessing to Violence—History and Ideology in the
            Circumcision Ritual of the Merina of Madagascar. Cambridge:
            Cambridge University Press.

Bohannan, Paul
    1969   Ethnography and comparison in legal anthropology. In Law in
            Culture and Society. Laura Nader, ed. Chicago: Aldine.

Bourdieu, Pierre
    1977   Outline of a Theory of Practice. R. Nice, transl. Cambridge:
            Cambridge University Press.

Brown, J.T.
    1967   Secwana Dictionary. Lobatsi: Bechuanaland Book Centre.

Brunton, Ron
    1980a   Misconstrued Order in Melanesian Religion. Man (N. S.) 15:112–
            28.
    1980b   Correspondence. Man (N. S.) 15:734–35.

Burks, A.W.
    1948   Icon, Index, and Symbol. Philosophy and Phenomenological
            Research 9:673–89.

Campbell, A. A. (Mziki)
    1926   Mlimo: The Rise and Fall of the Matabele. Pietermaritzburg:
            Natal Witness.

Clark, Katerina and Michael Holquist
    1984   Mikhail Bakhtin. Cambridge: Harvard University Press.

Cobbing, Julian
 1977   The Absent Priesthood: Another Look at the Rhodesian Risings of
         1896–7. Journal of African History 17:61–83.

Cockin, J.
 1879   Letter to J. Mullins. In London Missionary Society Archives:
         Matabele Mission Vol. 4 L9/6/1/4. London: London Missionary
         Society.

Cockcroft, J.G.
 1972   The Mlimo (Mwari) cult. NADA 10:83–92.

Cohen, Abner
 1967   Stranger communities: the Hausa. In The City of Ibadan. P.
         Lloyd and others, eds. Cambridge: Cambridge University Press.
 1969   Custom and Politics in Urban Africa: A Study of Hausa Migrants
         in Yoruba Towns. London: Routledge and Kegan Paul.
 1974   Two Dimensional Man. Berkeley, Los Angeles: University of
         California Press.

Colson, Elizabeth
 1984   The Reordering of Experience: Anthropological Involvement with
         Time. Journal of Anthropological Research 40:1–13.

Comaroff, Jean
 1985   Body of Power, Spirit of Resistance, Chicago: Chicago
         University Press.

Crawford, J. R.
 1967   Witchcraft and Sorcery in Rhodesia. London: Oxford University
         Press for the International African Institute.

Crocker, J. C.
 1979   Selves and Alters among the Eastern Bororo of Central Brazil. In
         Dialectical Societies—The Ge and Bororo of Central Brazil. David
         Maybury-Lewis, ed. Cambridge: Harvard University Press.

Crumrine, N. Ross
 1969   Capakoba, the Mayo Easter Ceremonial Impersonator:
         Explanations of Ritual Clowning. Journal for the Scientific Study
         of Religion 8:1–22.

Daneel, M.L.
 1970a   The God of the Matopo Hills. The Hague: Mouton for the
         Afrika-Studiecentrum.
 1970b   Zionism and Faith Healing in Rhodesia. The Hague: Mouton for
         the Afrika-Studiecentrum.
 1971   Old and New in Shona Independent Churches. I: Background and
         Rise of the Major Movements. The Hague: Mouton for the
         Afrika-Studiecentrum.
 1974   Old and New in Shona Independent Churches. II. Causative
         Factors and Recruitment Techniques. The Hague: Mouton for the
         Afrika-Studiecentrum.

1976   Independent Church Leadership South of the Zambesi. African
          Perspectives 2:81–99.

Debrunner, H.
  1959   Witchcraft in Ghana. Kumasi: Presbyterian Book Depot.

De Jager, E. J. and O. M. Seboni
  1964   Bone Divination among the Kwena of the Molepolole District,
          Bechuanaland Protectorate. Afrika und bersee 48:504–11.

Devisch, R.
  1978a   Towards a Semantic Study of Divination: Trance and Initiation of
          the Yaka Diviner as a Basis for his Authority. Bijdragen,
          Tijdschrift voor Filosofie en Theologie 39:278–88.
  1978b   Perspectives on Mediumistic Divination in Contemporary sub-
          Saharan Africa. Paper presented to the Conference on Recent
          African Religious Studies. Leiden: Afrika-Studiecentrum.
  1985a   Perspectives on Divination in Contemporary Sub-Saharan Africa.
          In Theoretical Explorations in African Religion. Wim van
          Binsbergen and Matthew Schoffeleers, eds. London: Kegan Paul
          International.
  1985b   Symbol and Psychosomatic Symptom in Bodily Space-Time: The
          Case of the Yaka of Zaire. International Journal of Psychiatry
          20:589–616.
  1988   From Equal to Better: Investing the Chief among the Northern
          Yaka of Zaire. Africa 58:261–290.

Dillon-Malone, C. M.
  1978   The Korsten Basketmakers. Manchester: Manchester University
          Press for the Institute of African Studies.

Douglas, Mary
  1968   The Social Control of Cognition: Some Factors in Joke
          Perception. Man (N.S.) 3:361–76.

Dumont, Louis
  1957   Religion, Politics and History in India. Paris: Mouton.
  1970   Homo Hierarchicus: The Caste System and its Implications.
          London: Weidenfeld and Nicholson.

Dunn, J. and A. F. Robertson
  1973   Dependence and Opportunity: Political Change in Ahafo.
          Cambridge: Cambridge University Press.

Eiselen, W. M.
  1932   The Art of Divination as Practiced by the Bamasemola. Bantu
          Studies 6:1–29, 251–63.

Eliade, Mircea
  1954   The Myth of the Eternal Return, or Cosmos and History. Willard
          R. Trask, transl. Bollingen Series XLVI. Princeton: Princeton
          University Press (paperback ed. 1974).
  1961   Images and Symbols. London: Harvill Press. (Original publ. 1952)

Evans-Pritchard, E. E.
    1937   Witchcraft, Oracles and Magic among the Azande. London:
            Oxford University Press.
    1956   Nuer Religion. London: Oxford University Press.

Fabian, Johannes
    1979   Text as Terror: Second Thoughts about Charisma. Social
            Research 46:166–203.
    1983   Time and the Other. New York: Columbia University Press.

Fernandez, J. W.
    1967   Divinations, Confessions, Testimonies. Occasional Paper 9, Natal:
            Institute for Social Research.
    1978   African Religious Movements. Annual Review of Anthropology
            7:198–234.
    1979   On the Notion of Religious Movement. Social Research 46:36–62.
    1982   Bwiti: An Ethnography of the Religious Imagination in Africa.
            Princeton: Princeton University Press.
    1984   Emergence and Convergence in some African Sacred Places.
            Geoscience and Man 24:31–42.
    1985   The Feeling of Architectonic Form: Residual and Emergent
            Qualities in Fang Cult and Culture. In The Visual Arts: Plastic
            and Graphic. Justine Cordwell, ed. The Hague: Mouton.

Field, M. J.
    1960   Search for Security: An Ethnopsychiatric Study of Rural Ghana.
            London: Faber and Faber.

Firth, Raymond
    1964   Essays on Social Organisation and Values. London: Athlone
            Press.
    1973   Symbols—Public and Private. London: George Allen and Unwin.

Fisher, H.
    1973   Conversion Reconsidered: Some Historical Aspects of Religious
            Conversion in Black Africa. Africa 43:27–40.

Fortes, Meyer
    1945   The Dynamics of Clanship Among the Tallensi. London: Oxford
            University Press.
    1966   Religious Premises and Logical Techniques in Divinatory Ritual.
            Philosophical Transactions of the Royal Society of London
            251:409–22.
    1975   Strangers. In Studies in African Social Anthropology. Meyer
            Fortes and S. Patterson, eds. London: Academic Press.

Franklin, H.
    1932   Manyusa. NADA 10:77–83.

Fustel de Coulanges, N. D.
    1956   The Ancient City: A View of Greece and Rome. Garden City:
            Doubleday. (Original publ. 1864, transl. 1873)

Gann, L. H.
    1965   A History of Southern Rhodesia. London: Chatto and Windus.

Garbett, Kingsley
    1977   Disparate Regional Cults and a Unitary Field in Zimbabwe. *In* Regional Cults. R. P. Werbner, ed. A.S.A. Monographs 16. London: Academic Press.

Garbutt, H. W.
    1909   Native Witchcraft and Superstition in South Africa. Journal of the Royal Anthropological Institute 39:553–54.

Gardner, D. S.
    1984   A Note on the Androgynous Qualities of the Cassowary: Or Why the Mianmin Say it is not a Bird. Oceania 55:137–45.

Gelfand, M.
    1966   An African's Religion—The Spirit of Nyajena. Cape Town: Juta.

Gell, Alfred
    1975   Metamorphosis of the Cassowaries: Umeda Society, Language and Ritual. London: Athlone Press.
    1978   The Umeda Language Poem. Canberra Anthropology 2:44–62.
    1979   Reflections on a Cut Finger: Taboo in the Umeda Conception of the Self. *In* Fantasy and Symbol: Studies in Anthropological Interpretation. R. H. Hook, ed. London: Academic Press.
    1981   Correspondence. Man (N.S.) 15:735–37.

Giesekke, E.
    1930   Wahrsagerei bei den Venda. Zeitschrift für Eingeborenen-Sprachen 21:257–310.

Gluckman, M.
    1955   The Judicial Process among the Barotse. Manchester: Manchester University Press.
    1965   Politics, Law and Ritual in Tribal Society. London: Basil Blackwell.

Godelier, M.
    1977   Perspectives in Marxist Anthropology. Cambridge: Cambridge University Press.

Goody, J.
    1956   Anomie in Ashanti? Ashanti 26:356–63.
    1967   The Over-Kingdom of Gonja. *In* West African Kingdoms in the Nineteenth Century. Darryl Forde and P. M. Kaberry, eds. London: International African Institute.
    1975   Religion, Social Change and the Sociology of Conversion. *In* Changing Social Structure in Ghana. J. Goody, ed. London: International African Institute.

Grathoff, Richard
    1970   The Structure of Social Inconsistencies. The Hague: Martinus
            Nijhoff.

Gregory, C. A.
    1980   Gifts to Men and Gifts to God: Gift Exchange and Capital
            Accumulation in Contemporary Papua. Man (N.S.) 115:626–52.
    1982   Gifts and Commodities. London: Academic Press.

Hall, R. A. Jr.
    1972   Pidgins and Creoles as standard languages. In Sociolinguistics. J.
            B. Pride and Janet Holmes, eds. Harmondsworth: Penguin.

Hammond-Tooke, W.
    1981   Boundaries and Belief. Human Sciences Research Council
            Publication 74. Johannesburg: Witwatersrand University Press.

Handelman, Don
    1979   Is Naven Ludic?: Paradox and the Communication of Identity.
            Social Analysis 1:77–91.
    1981   The Ritual Clown: Attributes and Affinities. Anthropos 76:321–
            70.
    n.d.   Models and Mirrors: Towards an Anthropology of Public Events.
            Cambridge: Cambridge University Press. In press.

Hannan, M.
    1959   Standard Shona Dictionary. London: Macmillan.

Harris, Grace
    1959   Possession "Hysteria" in a Kenya tribe. American Anthropologist
            57:1046–66.

Hastings, A.
    1979   A History of African Christianity 1950–1975. Cambridge:
            Cambridge University Press.

Hieb, Louis A.
    1972   Meaning and Mismeaning: Toward an Understanding of the
            Ritual Clown. In New Perspectives on the Pueblos. Alfonso
            Ortiz, ed. Albuquerque: University of New Mexico Press.

Hill, Polly
    1970   Migrant Cocoa Farmers of Southern Ghana: A Study in Rural
            Capitalism. Cambridge: Cambridge University Press.

Holub, Emil
    1881   Seven Years in Southern Africa—(1872–79). London: Sampson
            Low Marston Searle, and Rivington.

Horton, Robin
    1967   African Traditional Thought and Western Science. Africa 37:50–
            71, 155–87.
    1971   African Conversion. Africa 41:85–108.

1975   On the Rationality of Conversion. I. Africa 45:219–35.

Huber, Peter B.
1975   Defending the Cosmos: Violence and Social Order among the
        Anggor of New Guinea. *In* War, Its Causes and Correlates. M.A.
        Nettleship, R.D. Givens, A. Nettleship, eds. The Hague:
        Martinus Nijhoff.

Hubert, H., and M. Mauss
1964   Sacrifice: Its Nature and Function. W.D. Halls, transl. London:
        Cohen and West.

Huesch, Luc de
1985   Sacrifice in Africa: A Structuralist Approach. Manchester:
        Manchester University Press.

Hugh-Jones, Christine
1979   From the Milk River: Spatial and Temporal Processes in
        Northwest Amazonia. Cambridge: Cambridge University Press.

Hymes, D.H.
1972   On Communicative Competence. *In* Sociolinguistics. J. B. Pride
        and Janet Holmes, eds. Harmondsworth: Penguin.

Irvine, J.
1979   Formality and Informality in Communicative Events. American
        Anthropologist 81:773–90.

Jackson, M.
1978   An Approach to Kuranko Divination. Human Relations 31:117–
        38.

Jedrej, M.C.
1980   A Comparison of Some Masks from North America, Africa, and
        Melanesia. Journal of Anthropological Research 36:220–30.

Johnson, Ragnar
1981   Correspondence. Man (N.S.) 16:472–5.

Jorgensen, Dan
1981   Correspondence. Man (N.S.) 16:470–72.

Juillerat, Bernard
1980   Correspondence. Man (N.S.) 15:732–74.
1986   Les Enfants du Sang. Paris: Editions de la Maison des Sciences de
        l'Homme.
n.d.   (ed.) Shooting at the Sun. Forthcoming.

Jules-Rosette, B.
1975a   African Apostles. Ithaca: Cornell University Press.
1975b   Marrapodi: an Independent Religious Community in Transition.
        African Studies Review 18:1–16.
1977   Grass-Roots Ecumenism: Religious and Social Co-operation in

two African Urban Churches. African Social Research 23:185–216.

1978   The Veil of Objectivity: Prophecy, Divination and Social Inquiry. American Anthropologist 80:549-70.

1979   Women as Ceremonial Leaders in an African Church: the Apostles of John Maranke. In The New Religions of Africa. G. Bond and B. Jules-Rosette, eds. Alblex Publishing Corporation.

Junod, H. A.
1925   La Divination au Moyen de Tablettes d'Ivoire chez les Pedis. Bulletin de la Société de Neuchatel du Géographie 34:38–56.
1927   The Life of a South African Tribe. London: Macmillan.

Kapferer, B.
1983   A Celebration of Demons. Bloomington: Indiana University Press.
1984   Introduction: Ritual Process and the Transformation of Context. Social Analysis 1:3–19 (reprinted from 1979).

Keay, R. W. J. ed.
1959   Vegetation Map of Africa. London: Oxford University Press.

Kileff, Clive and Margaret Kileff
1979   The Masowe Vapostori of Seki. In The New Religions of Africa. G. Bond and B. Jules-Rosette, eds. Alblex Publishing Corporation.

Kilson, M.
1973   The Grassroots in Ghanaian Politics. In Ghana and Ivory Coast: Perspectives on Modernization. P. Foster and A. R. Zolberg, eds. Chicago: Chicago University Press.

Knöthe, C.
1888   Kürzer Bericht über die Reise nach Bonyai. Berlin Missions Berichte.

Kuper, Adam
1979   The Magician and the Missionary. In The Liberal Dilemma in South Africa. London: Croom Helm.

La Fontaine, J.
1981   The Domestication of the Savage Male. Man (N.S.) 16:333–49.
1982   Introduction. In Chisungu. Audrey Richards, ed. London: Tavistock Publications. (1st ed. 1956)

Lan, David
1985   Guns and Rain: Guerrillas and Spirit Mediums in Zimbabwe. London: James Currey.

Laydevant, F.
1933   The Praises of the Divining Bones among the Basutho. Bantu Studies 7:341–373.

Lee, Richard
   1976   !Kung Spatial Organization. *In* Kalahari Hunter-Gatherers, Studies
           of the !Kung San and Their Neighbors. eds. Richard Lee and
           Irven DeVore. Cambridge: Harvard University Press.

Levine, Donald N.
   1979   Simmel at a Distance: On the History and Systematics of the
           Sociology of the Stranger. *In* Strangers in African Societies. eds.
           William Shack and Elliot Skinner. Berkeley: University of
           California Press.

Lévi-Strauss, Claude
   1960   On Manipulated Sociological Models. Bijdragen tot de taal-land-
           en volkenkunde 116:45–54.
   1963a   Do Dual Organizations Exist? *In* Structural Anthropology. New
           York: Basic Books. (Original publ. 1956)
   1966   The Savage Mind. London: Weidenfeld and Nicholson (Original
           publ. 1962).
   1973   Tristes tropiques. John Weightman and Doreen Weightman,
           transl. London: Jonathan Cape (Original publ. 1955)

Lewis, Gilbert
   1980   Day of Shining Red. Cambridge: Cambridge University Press.

Lewis, Ioan M.
   1971   Ecstatic Religion: An Anthropological Study of Spirit Possession
           and Shamanism. Harmondsworth: Pelican Books.

Lienhardt, Godfrey
   1961   Divinity and Experience: The Religion of the Dinka. Oxford:
           Clarendon Press.

Linton, R.
   1943   Nativistic Movements. American Anthropologist 45: 230–42.

Long, Norman
   1986   Commoditization: Thesis and Antithesis. *In* The
           Commoditization Debate: Labour Process, Strategy and Social
           Network. Norman Long, Jan Douwe van der Ploeg, Chris
           Curtin, and Louk Box, eds. Papers of the Department of
           Sociology 17. Wageningen: Agricultural University Wageningen.

MacCormack, C.
   1980   Nature, Culture and Gender: A Critique. *In* Nature, Culture and
           Gender. C. MacCormack and M. Strathern. eds. Cambridge:
           Cambridge University Press.

McLeod, M.
   1975   On the Spread of Anti-Witchcraft Cults in Modern Ashanti. *In*
           Changing Social Structure in Ghana. Jack Goody, ed. London:
           International African Institute.

Maddock, Kenneth
  1985   Sacrifice and other Models in Australian Aboriginal ritual. *In*
          Metaphors of Interpretation (Festschrift for W. E. H. Stanner).
          Canberra: Australian National University.

Maine, H.
  1861   Ancient Law. London: Murray.

Makarius, Laura
  1970   Ritual Clowns and Symbolic Behavior. Diogenes 69: 44–73.

Maybury-Lewis, David
  1960   The Analysis of Dual Organization: A Methodological Critique.
          Bijdragen tot de taal-land-en volkenkunde 116:17–44.
  1979   Dialectical Societies: The Ge and Bororo of Central Brazil.
          Cambridge: Harvard University Press.

Mendonsa, E. L.
  1982   The Politics of Divination. Berkeley: University of California
          Press.

Mercier, P.
  1965   On the Meaning of "Tribalism" in Black Africa. *In* Africa: Social
          Problems of Change and Conflict. P. L. van den Berghe, ed. San
          Francisco: Chandler.

Middleton, J.
  1960   Lugbara Religion. London: Oxford University Press for the
          International African Institute.
  1979   Rites of sacrifice among the Lugbara. *In* Système de Pensée en
          Afrique Noire. Cahier 4. Le Sacrifice III. Paris.

Modongo, T.
  1975   Over 100 Attempts to Trace "Mwali". Gaborone: Botswana Daily
          News (June 11th).

Morgan, L. H.
  1878   Ancient Society. New York: Henry Holt (1st ed. 1877).

Mpaphadzi, M.
  1975a   Bid to Solve Mystery of God in Dead End. Gaborone: Botswana
          Daily News. July.
  1975b   Report to the District Officer. Author's Archives (courtesy of Mr.
          Harry Finnigan). Francistown

Munn, N.D.
  1973   Symbolism in a Ritual Context: Aspects of Symbolic Action. *In*
          Handbook of Cultural and Social Anthropology. J. J.
          Honigmann, ed. Chicago: Rand McNally.

Murphree, M. W.
  1969   Christianity and the Shona. Athlone Press.

Native Commissioner Plumtree
    1914   Letter, Ref. N3/31/1-5. Harare: Archives of Zimbabwe.

Newman, K.
    1971   Birdlife in Southern Africa. Johannesburg: Purnell.

O'Flaherty, Wendy
    1980   Women, Androgynes, and Other Mythical Beasts. Chicago: University of Chicago Press.

O'Neill, J.
    1907   The Kalanga Belief in Spirits and Witchcraft. Zambesi Mission Record 3:35–39, 223–27.
    1920   The Natives of S.W. Matabeleland and Some of Their Religious Customs. *In* Proceedings. Rhodesian Scientific Association 19:3–11.

Ortner, S.
    1974   Is Female to Male as Nature is to Culture? *In* Women, Culture and Society. M. Rosaldo and L. Lamphere, eds. Stanford: Stanford University Press.

Parkin, D.
    1982   Straightening the Paths from Wilderness. Paideuma 28:71: 83.7.
    1985   Reason, Emotion and the Embodiment of Power. *In* Reason and Morality. J. Overing, ed. London: Tavistock.

Paz, Octavio
    1978   Claude Lévi-Strauss: An Introduction. New York: Dell. (1st ed. 1970).

Peek, P., ed.
    n.d.   African Divination Systems: Ways of Knowing. Forthcoming.

Peil, Margaret
    1979   Host Reactions: Aliens in Ghana. *In* Strangers in African Societies. William A. Shack and Elliot P. Skinner, eds. Berkeley: University of California Press.

Posselt, F.
    1927   Some Notes on the Religious Ideas of the Natives of Southern Rhodesia. South African Journal of Science 24:530–536.

Pouwer, J.
    1966   Structure and Flexibility in a New Guinea Society. Bijdragen tot de taal-land-en volkenkunde 122:158–169.

Ranger, T. O.
    1966   The Role of Ndebele and Shona Religious Authorities in the Rebellions of 1896 and 1897. *In* The Zambesian Past. E. Stokes and R. Brown, ed. Manchester: Manchester University Press.
    1967   Revolt in Southern Rhodesia 1896–97. London: Heinemann. [1987 2nd ed., with a new introduction].

1970   The African Voice in Southern Rhodesia 1898–1930. London: Heinemann.

1985   Religious studies and political economy: the Mwari Cult and the Peasant Experience in Southern Rhodesia. *In* Explorations in African Religion. Wim van Binsbergen and Matthew Schoffeleers, eds. London: Routledge and Kegan Paul International.

Ransford, O.
1968   Bulawayo: Historical Background of Rhodesia. Cape Town: A. A. Balkena.

Rattray, R. S.
1923   Ashanti. Oxford: Clarendon Press.

Reed, G. C. H.
1896   Letter from Dombudema. London Missionary Society Archives 18/9/1896. London: London Missionary Society.

Richards, J. B.
1942   The Mlimo Belief and Practice of Kalanga. NADA 19: 51–55.

Roberts, N.
1916   The Bagananoa or Ma-Laboch: Notes on Their Early History, Customs, and Creed. South African Journal of Science 13:241–56.

Rosaldo, M.
1974   Women, Culture and Society: A Theoretical Overview. *In* Women, Culture and Society. M. Rosaldo and L. Lamphere, eds. Stanford: Stanford University Press.

Rubel, Paula G. and Abraham Rosman
1978   Your Own Pigs You May Not Eat. Chicago: University of Chicago Press.

Ruel, Malcolm
1987   Icons, Indexical Symbols and Metaphorical Action: an Analysis of two East African Rites. Journal of Religion in Africa 17:98–112.

Sahlins, Marshall
1974   Stone Age Economics. London: Tavistock Publications.

Sallnow, Michael J.
1987   Pilgrims of the Andes: Regional Cults in Cusco. Washington: Smithsonian Institution Press.

Salzman, P.
1981   Culture as Enhabilment. *In* The structure of Folk Models. L. Holy and M. Stuchlik, eds. Association of Social Anthropologists Monograph 20. London: Academic Press.

Saunders, L.
1977   Variants in Zar experience in an Egyptian village. *In* Case Studies in Spirit Possession. V. Crapanzano and V. Garrison, eds. New York: John Wiley and Sons.

Schapera, I.
1934   Oral sorcery among the natives of Bechuanaland. *In* Essays
        presented to C. G. Seligman. E. E. Evans-Pritchard and others,
        eds. London: Routledge.
1938   Handbook of Tswana Law and Custom. London: Oxford
        University Press for the International African Institute.
1953   The Tswana Ethnographic Survey of Africa. Part 3. London:
        International African Institute (reprinted with supplements 1976).
1955   Witchcraft Beyond Reasonable Doubt. Man 55:72.
1969   The Crime of Sorcery. Proceedings of the Royal Anthropological
        Institute. pp. 15–23.
1971   Rainmaking Rites of Tswana Tribes. Cambridge and Leiden:
        African Social Research Documents 3.
n.d.   Unpublished Field Notes on Tswana Divination. (by permission
        of the author).

Schieffelin, E.
1985   Performance and the Cultural Construction of Reality. American
        Ethnologist 12:707–25.

Schoffeleers, J. M.
1979   Guardians of the Land. Gwelo, Zimbabwe: Mambo Press.

Schutz, Alfred
1945   The Homecomer. American Journal of Sociology 50:369–376.

Schwellnus, E.
1888   Unser Vorstoss zu dem Bakhalanga. Berlin Mission Berichte.
        506–12.

Searle, John
1969   Speech Acts. Cambridge: Cambridge University Press.

Sebina, A.M.
1947   Makalaka. African Studies 6:82–93.

Selous, F. C.
1896   Sunshine and Storm in Rhodesia. London: Rowland Ward and
        Company.

Sharron, A.
1981   Dimensions of Time. *In* Studies in Symbolic Interaction 4.
        Greenwich, Connecticut: JAI Press.

Shaw, R.
1981   Gender and Temne divination. Africa 55:286–303.
1985   Gender and the Structuring of Reality in Temne Divination: An
        Interactive Study. Africa 55:286–303.

Singer, M.
1980   Signs of the Self: An Exploration in Semiotic Anthropology.

Skinner, E.P.
    1963   Strangers in West African Societies. Africa 33: 307–320.
    1974   Theoretical Perspectives on the Stranger. *Paper presented at* The
            Conference on Strangers in Africa, *cited in* Niara Sudarkasa 1979.
            From Stranger to Alien: The Socio-Political History of the
            Nigerian Yoruba in Ghana, 1900-1970. *In* Strangers in African
            Societies. William A. Shack and E. P. Skinner, eds. Berkeley:
            University of California Press.
    1979   Conclusions. *In* Strangers in African Societies. William A. Shack
            and E. P. Skinner, eds. Berkeley: University of California Press.

Smith, Carol A., ed.
    1977   Regional Analysis 1. Economic Systems. New York: Academic
            Press.

Smith, P.
    1978   Aspects de l'Organisation des Rites. *In* La Fonction Symbolique.
            M. Izard and P. Smith, eds. Paris: Gallimard.

Sperber, D.
    1975   Rethinking Symbolism. Cambridge: Cambridge University Press.

Stanner, W.E.
    1959   On Aboriginal Religion I: The Lineaments of Sacrifice. Oceania
            30:108–27.

Stayt, H. A.
    1931   The Venda. Oxford: Oxford University Press for the
            International African Institute.

Strathern, Andrew
    1979   Gender, Ideology and Money in Mount Hagen. Man (N. S.)
            14:530–48.
    1981   "NOMAN": Representations of Identity in Mount Hagen. *In* The
            Structure of Folk Models. L. Holy and M. Stuchlik, eds.
            Association of Social Anthropologists Monograph 20. London:
            Academic Press.

Strathern, Marilyn
    1972   Women in Between. London: Seminar Press.
    1979   The Self in Self-Decoration. Oceania 49:240–256.
    1980   No Nature, No Culture: The Hagen Case. *In* Nature, Culture
            and Gender. C. MacCormack and M. Strathern, eds. Cambridge:
            Cambridge University Press.

Sudarkasa, N. From Stranger to Alien. *In* Strangers in African Societies.

Summers, R.
    1961   The Southern Rhodesian Iron Age. Journal of African History
            2:1–13.

Sundkler, Bengt
    1961   Bantu Prophets in South Africa. London: Oxford University Press.

Tambiah, S. J.
    1985   Culture, Thought and Social Action. Cambridge: Harvard University Press.

Thoden Van Velzen, Bonno
    1977   Bush Negro Ritual Cults: A Materialist Nation. *In* Regional Cults. R. P. Werbner, ed. London: Academic Press.

Tordoff, W.
    1965   Ashanti under the Prempehs. London: Oxford University Press.

Tredgold, Robert
    1956   The Matopos. Salisbury: Federal Government Printer.

Tuan, Yi-fu
    1977   Space and Place: The Perspective of Experience. London: Edward Arnold.

Turner, Victor
    1967   The Forest of Symbols: Aspects of Ndembu Ritual. Ithaca: Cornell University Press.
    1974   Dramas, Fields and Metaphors: Symbolic Action in Human Society. Ithaca: Cornell University Press.
    1975   Revelation and Divination in Ndembu Ritual. Ithaca: Cornell University Press.
    1982   From Ritual to Theatre: The Human Seriousness of Play. New York: Performing Arts Journal Publications.

Tuzin, Donald F.
    1976   The Ilahita Arapesh: Dimensions of Unity. Berkeley: University of California Press.

Van Gennep, Arnold
    1960   The Rites of Passage. Monika B. Vizedom and Gabriel L. Caffee, transl. London: Routledge and Kegan Paul.

Van Binsbergen, Wim M. J.
    1977   Regional and Non-Regional Cults of Affliction in Western Zambia. *In* Regional Cults. A.S.A. Monographs 16. R. P. Werbner, ed. London: Academic Press.
    1981   Religious Change in Zambia: Exploratory Studies. London: Kegan Paul International.

Van Binsbergen, Wim M. J., and Matthew Schoffeleers, eds.
    1985   Theoretical Explorations in African Religion. London: Kegan Paul International.

Van Warmelo, N. J., ed.
    1940   The Copper Miners and the Early History of the Zoutpansberg.

Ethnological Publication No. 8. Pretoria: Department of Native Affairs.

Von Sicard, Harald
  1952   Ngoma Lungundu. Uppsala: Studia Ethnographica Upsallensia V.

Wagner, R.
  1984   Ritual as Communication: Order, Meaning and Secrecy in Melanesian Initiation Rites. Annual Review of Anthropology 13:143-55.
  1986   Symbols that Stand for Themselves. Chicago: University of Chicago Press.

Walens, Stanley
  1981   Feasting with Cannibals: An Essay on the Kwakiutl Cosmology. Princeton: Princeton University Press.

Wallace, A. F. C.
  1956   Revitalization movements. American Anthropologist 58:264-81.

Ward, B. E.
  1956   Some Observations on Religious Cults in Ashanti. Africa 26:47-61.

Werbner, Pnina
  1979   Ritual and Social Networks: A Study of Pakistani Immigrants in Manchester. Ph.D. Thesis, Manchester University.
  1986   The Virgin and the Clown: Ritual Elaboration in Pakistani Migrants' Weddings. Man (N.S.) 21:227-50.

Werbner, Richard P.
  1964   Atonement Ritual and Guardian-Spirit Possession among Kalanga. Africa 34:206-23.
  1970   Guardian Spirits. Man, Myth and Magic 42:1183-87.
  1971a   Local Adaptation and the Transformation of an Imperial Concession in North-Eastern Botswana. Africa 41:32-41.
  1971b   Symbolic Dialogue and Personal Transactions among Kalanga and Ndembu. Ethnology 10:311-328.
  1972   Sin, Blame and Ritual Mediation. In The Allocation of Responsibility. Max Gluckman, ed. Manchester: Manchester University Press.
  1973   The Superabundance of Understanding: Kalanga Rhetoric and Domestic Divination. American Anthropologist 75:414-1440.
  1975   Land, movement and status among Kalanga of Botswana. In Essays in African Social Anthropology. Meyer Fortes and Sheila Patterson, eds. London: Academic Press.
  1977a   Continuity and Policy in Southern Africa's High God Cult. In Regional Cults. A.S.A. Monograph 16. R. P. Werbner, ed. London: Academic Press.
  1977b   Introduction. In Regional Cults. A.S.A. Monograph 16. R. P. Werbner, ed. London: Academic Press.
  1977c   Small Man Politics and the Rule of Law: Centre-Periphery

Relations in East-Central Botswana. Journal of African Law 21:24–39.

1977d   The Argument in and about Oratory. African Studies 36:1411–44.

1979   Totemism in History: The Ritual Passage of West African Strangers. Man (N.S.) 14:663–683.

1982a   The Quasi-Judicial and the Absurd: Remaking Land Law in North-Eastern Botswana. *In* Land Reform in the Making: Tradition, Public Policy and Ideology in Botswana. R. P. Werbner, ed. London: Rex Collings.

1982b   Production and Reproduction: The Dynamics of Botswana's North-Eastern Micro-Regions. *In* Proceedings of the Symposium on Settlement in Botswana—The Historical Development of a Human Landscape. R. Hitchcock and M. Smith, eds. Gaborone: Heinemann Educational Books Ltd.

1983   Central Africa's Territorial Cults: History and Systematics. Zimbabwean History 11:118–20.

1984   World Renewal: Masking in a New Guinea Festival. Man (N. S.) 19:267–90.

1985   *Review of* James W. Fernandez, *Bwiti*. Numen 32:15–17.

1986   The Political Economy of Bricolage. Journal of Southern African Studies 13:151–56.
On Dialectical Versions: The Cosmic Rebirth of West Sepik Regionalism. *In* Shooting at the Sun. Bernard Juillerat, ed. Forthcoming.

Westermark, E. A.
1968   Ritual and Belief in Morocco. Vol. 2. New Hyde Park: University Books (1st edition 1926).

Whitehead, Harriet
1986   The Varieties of Fertility Cultism in New Guinea: Part 1. American Ethnologist 13:80–89.

Wilks, I.
1975   Asante in the Nineteenth Century: the Structure and Evolution of a Political Order. Cambridge: Cambridge University Press.

Willoughby, W. C.
1928   The Soul of the Bantu. Westport: Negro University Press (reprinted 1970).

Wilson, B. R.
1967   The Migrating Sects. British Journal of Sociology 18:303–17.

Wilson, P.
1967   Status Ambiguity and Spirit Possession. Man (N. S.) 2:366–78.

Worsley, P.
1956   The Kinship System of the Tallensi: A Reevaluation. Journal of the Royal Anthropological Institute 86:37–75.

Wyllie, R.W.
  1973   Introspective Witchcraft among the Effutu of Southern Ghana.
          Man (N. S.) 8:74–79.

Yanagisako, S.
  1979   Family and Household: The Analysis of Domestic Groups.
          Annual Review of Anthropology 8:161–205.

Yeatman, A.
  1984   The Procreative Model: The Social Ontological Bases of the
          Gender-Kinship. Social Analysis 14:3–30.

ZAPU
  1962   Circular Number 2, 16 July 1962. Division of External Affairs.

Zuesse, E.
  1979   Ritual Cosmos: The Sanctification of Life in African Religions.
          Athens, Ohio: Ohio University Press.

INDEX